MEGAMAN
NT WARRIOR

Vol. 1

Story and Art by
Ryo Takamisaki

MEGAMAN™ NT WARRIOR

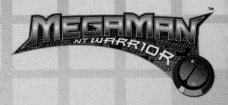

VIZ Kids Edition
Vol. 1

Story and Art by Ryo Takamisaki

English Adaptation/Gary Leach
Translation/Koji Goto
Touch-Up & Lettering/Gia Cam Luc
Graphics & Cover Design/Carolina Ugalde
Approvals Coordinator/Hiromi Kadowaki
Editor/Eric Searleman

Editor in Chief, Books/Alvin Lu
Editor in Chief, Magazines/Marc Weidenbaum
VP of Publishing Licensing/Rika Inouye
VP of Sales/Gonzalo Ferreyra
Sr. VP of Marketing/Liza Coppola
Publisher/Hyoe Narita

Printed in the U.S.A.

Published by VIZ Media, LLC
P.O. Box 77064
San Francisco, CA 94107

VIZ Kids Edition
10 9 8 7 6
First printing, April 2004
Sixth printing, May 2008

RATED A FOR ALL AGES

PARENTAL ADVISORY
MEGAMAN NT WARRIOR is rated A and is suitable for readers of all ages. This volume contains fantasy violence.

ratings.viz.com

store.viz.com

viz media

www.viz.com

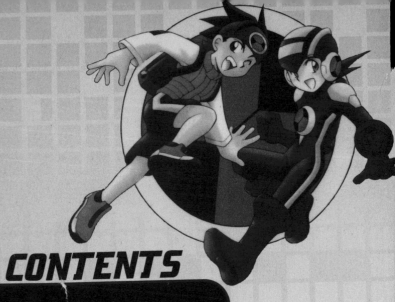

CONTENTS

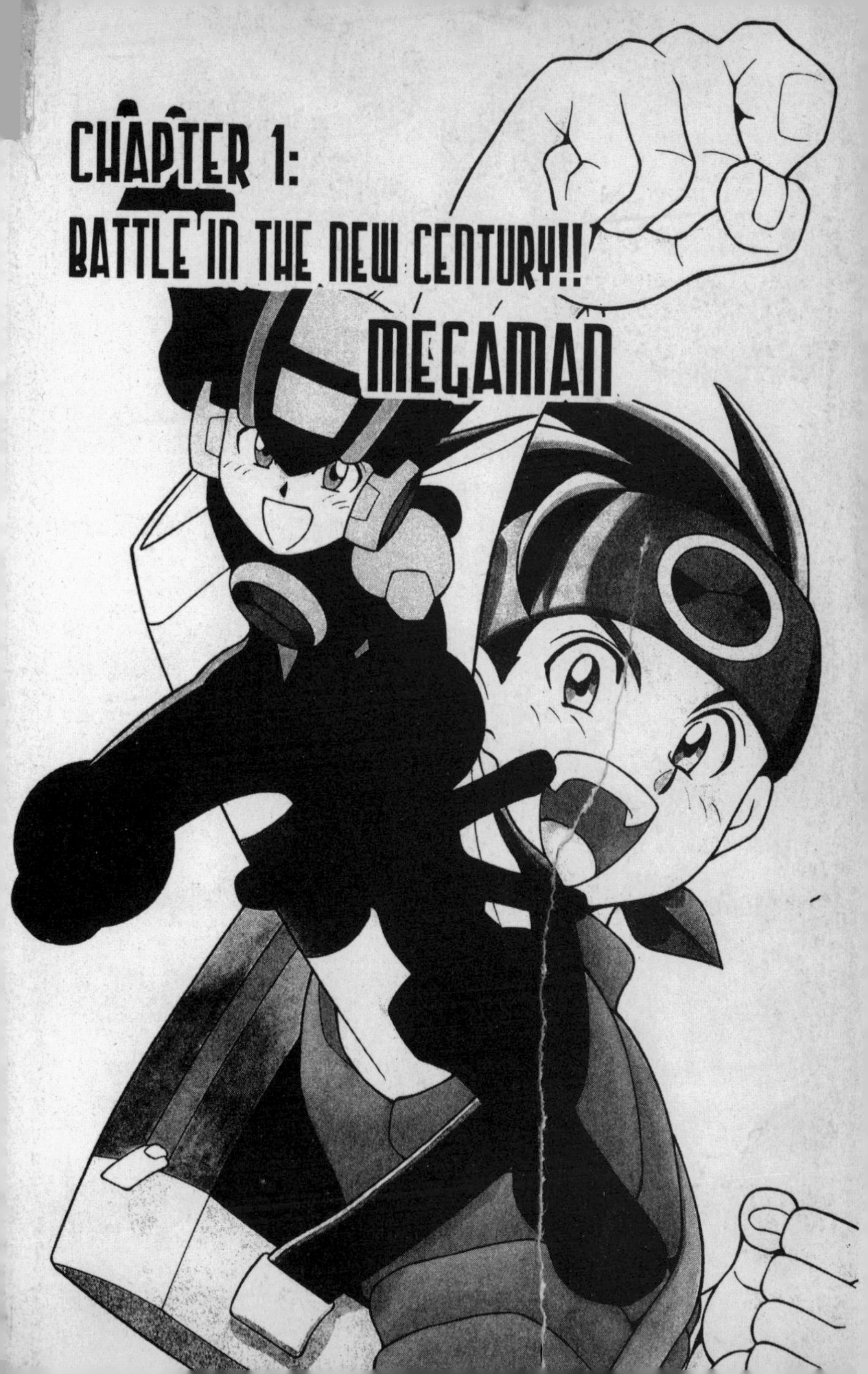
CHAPTER 1:
BATTLE IN THE NEW CENTURY!!
MEGAMAN

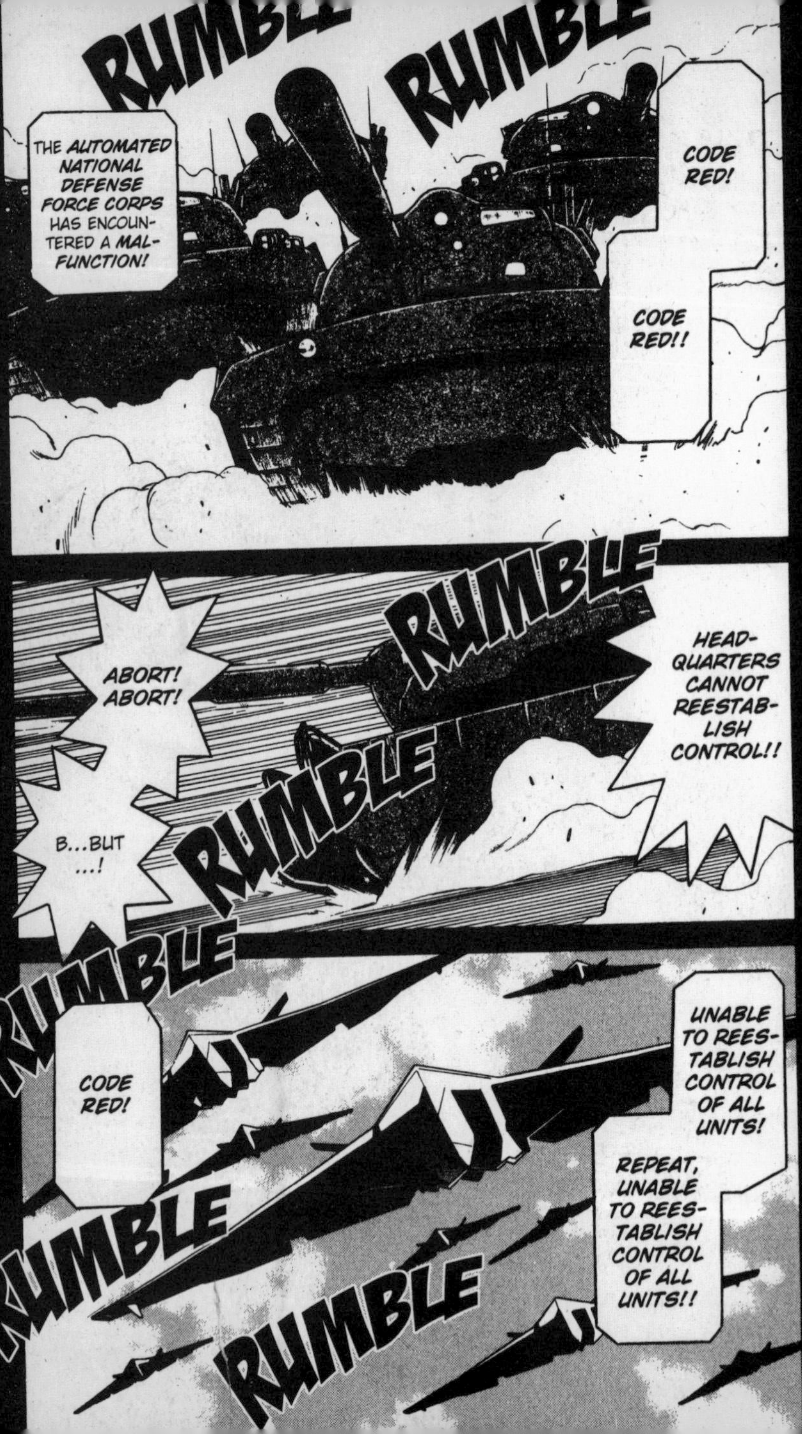
RUMBLE
RUMBLE
CODE RED!
THE AUTOMATED NATIONAL DEFENSE FORCE CORPS HAS ENCOUNTERED A MALFUNCTION!
CODE RED!!
RUMBLE
HEADQUARTERS CANNOT REESTABLISH CONTROL!!
ABORT! ABORT!
RUMBLE
B...BUT ...!
RUMBLE
RUMBLE
UNABLE TO REESTABLISH CONTROL OF ALL UNITS!
CODE RED!
REPEAT, UNABLE TO REESTABLISH CONTROL OF ALL UNITS!!
RUMBLE
RUMBLE

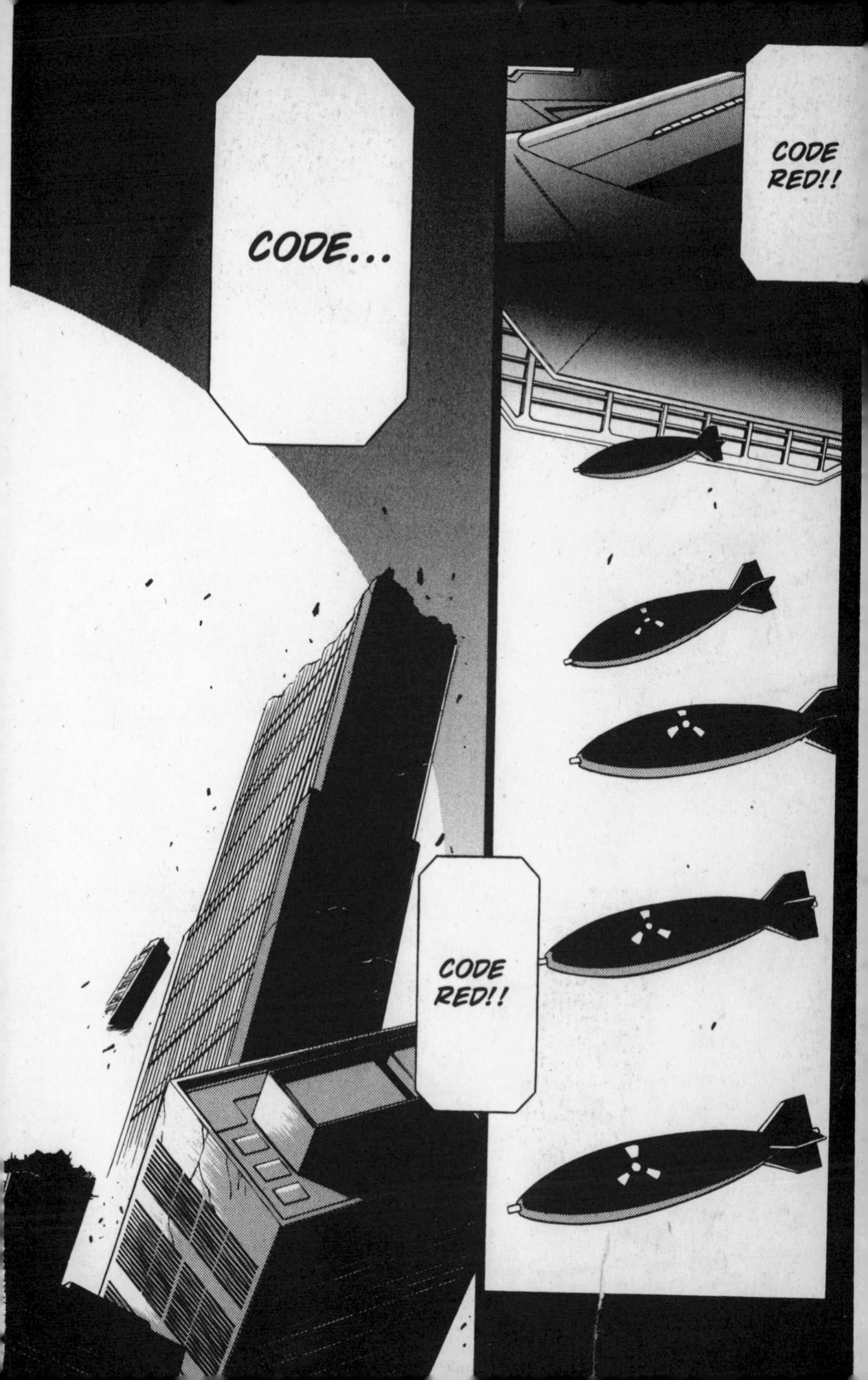
CODE RED!!
CODE...
CODE RED!!

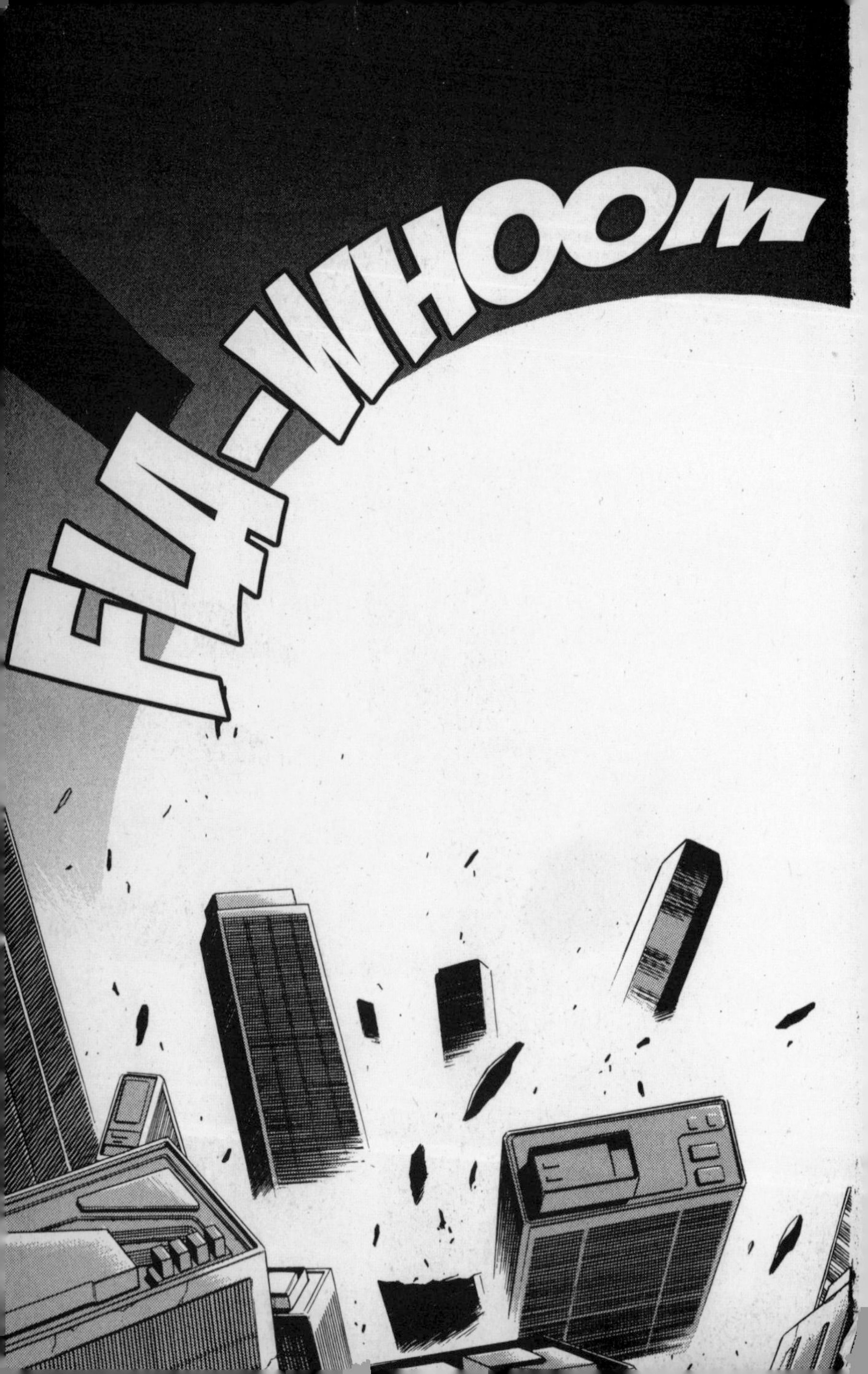
FWA-WHOOM

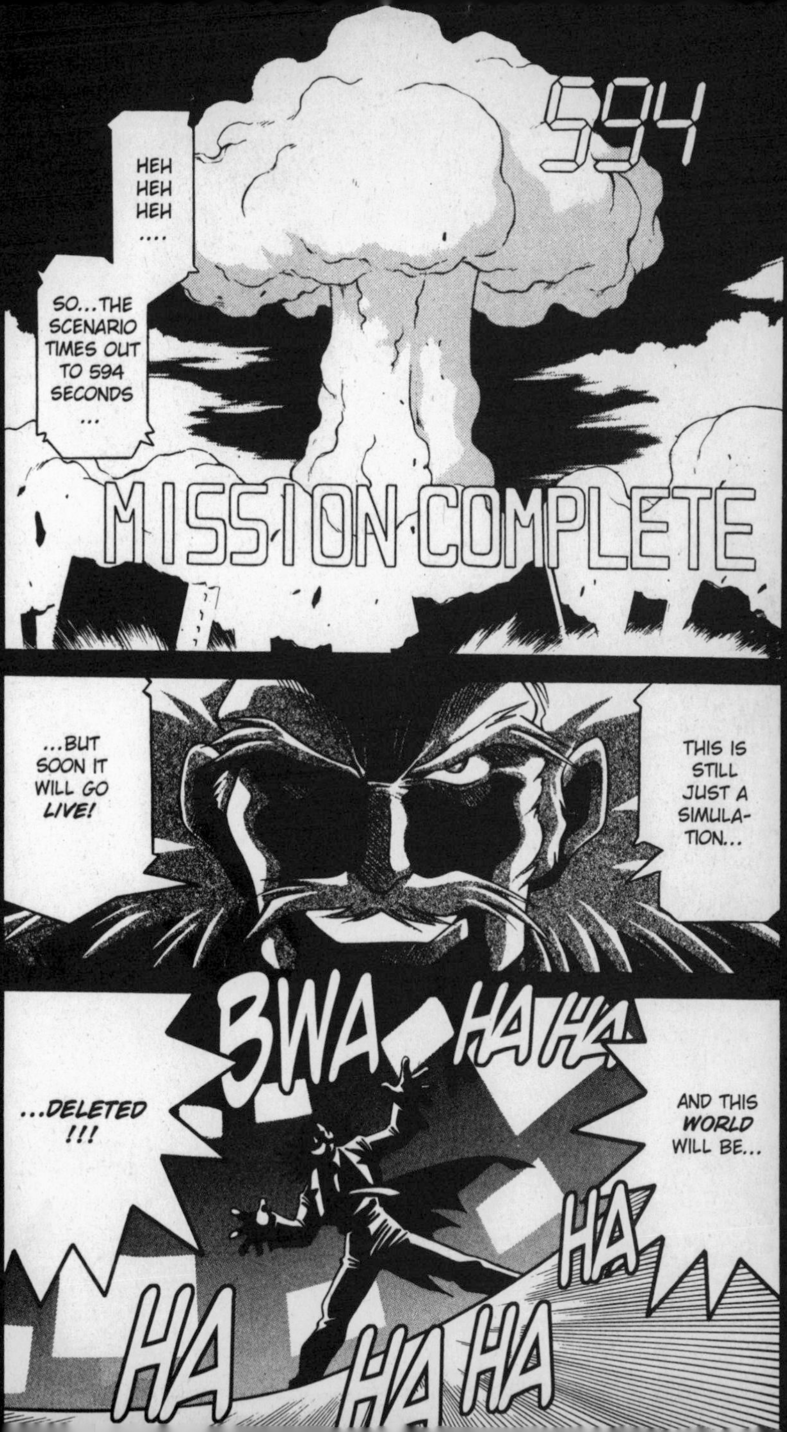
594
HEH HEH HEH ....
SO... THE SCENARIO TIMES OUT TO 594 SECONDS ...
MISSION COMPLETE
THIS IS STILL JUST A SIMULATION...
...BUT SOON IT WILL GO *LIVE!*
AND THIS *WORLD* WILL BE...
...DELETED !!!
BWA HA HA
HA
HA
HA HA HA

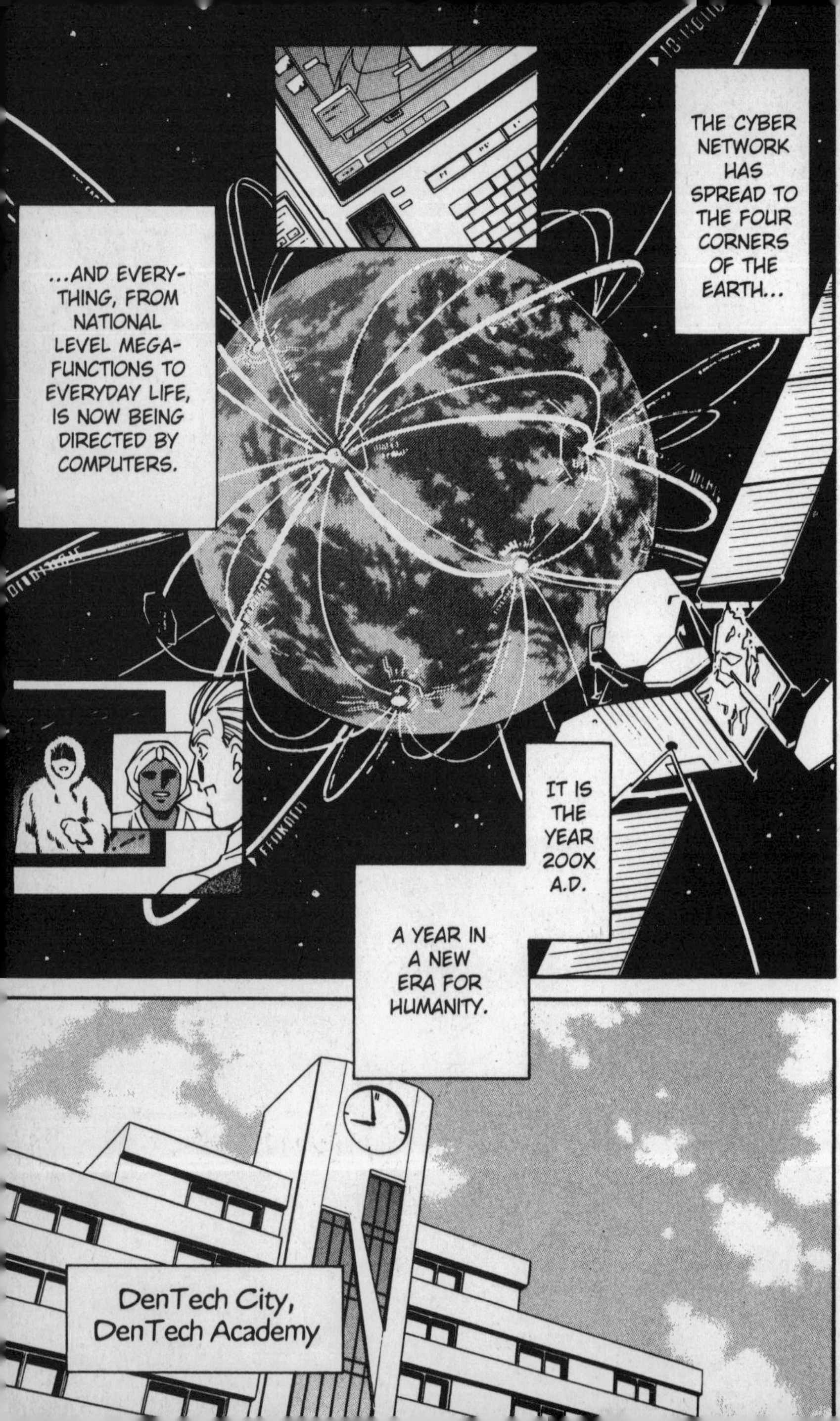
THE CYBER NETWORK HAS SPREAD TO THE FOUR CORNERS OF THE EARTH...
...AND EVERYTHING, FROM NATIONAL LEVEL MEGA-FUNCTIONS TO EVERYDAY LIFE, IS NOW BEING DIRECTED BY COMPUTERS.
IT IS THE YEAR 200X A.D.
A YEAR IN A NEW ERA FOR HUMANITY.
DenTech City, DenTech Academy

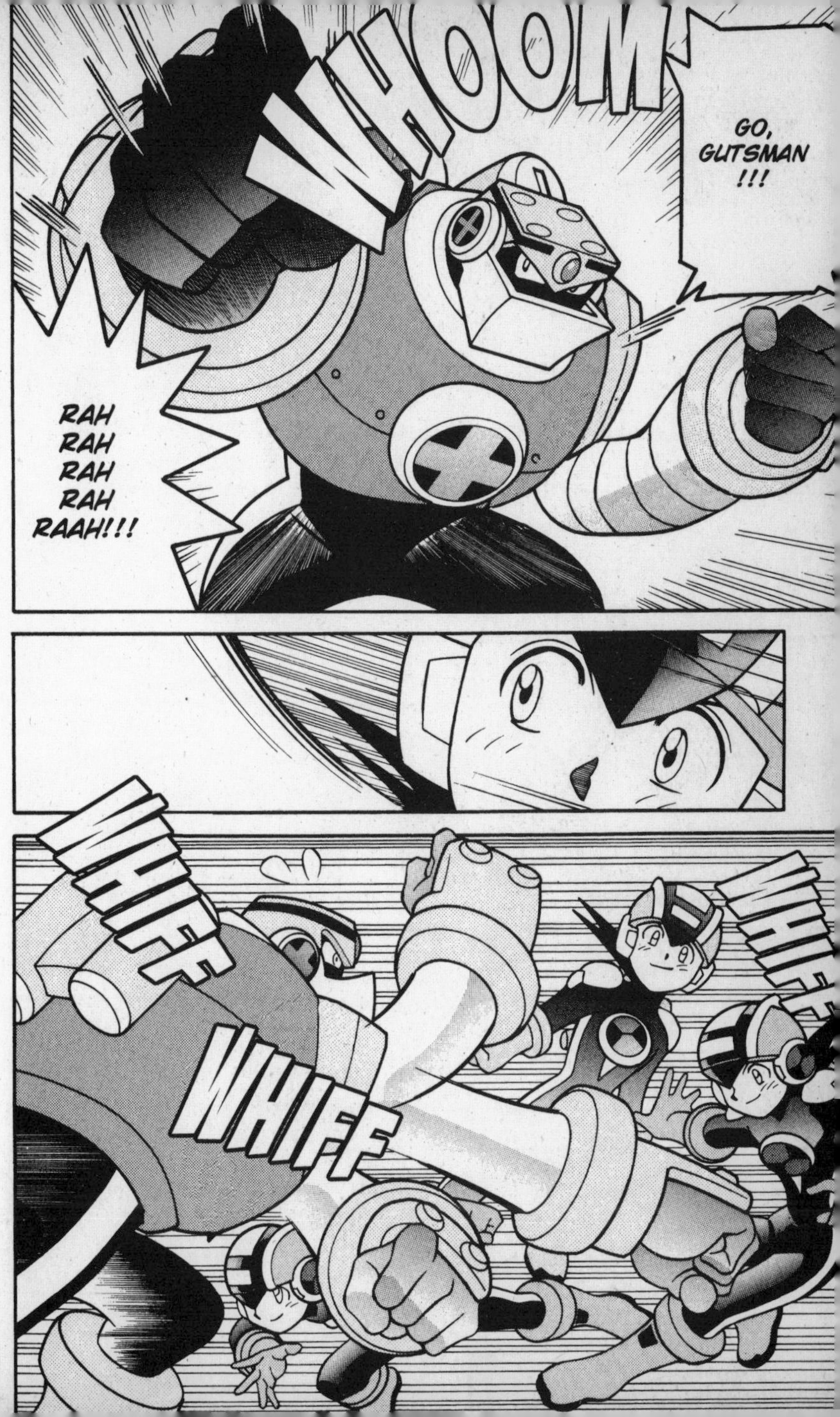
GO, GUTSMAN !!!
WHOOM
RAH RAH RAH RAH RAAH!!!
WHIFF
WHIFF
WHIFF

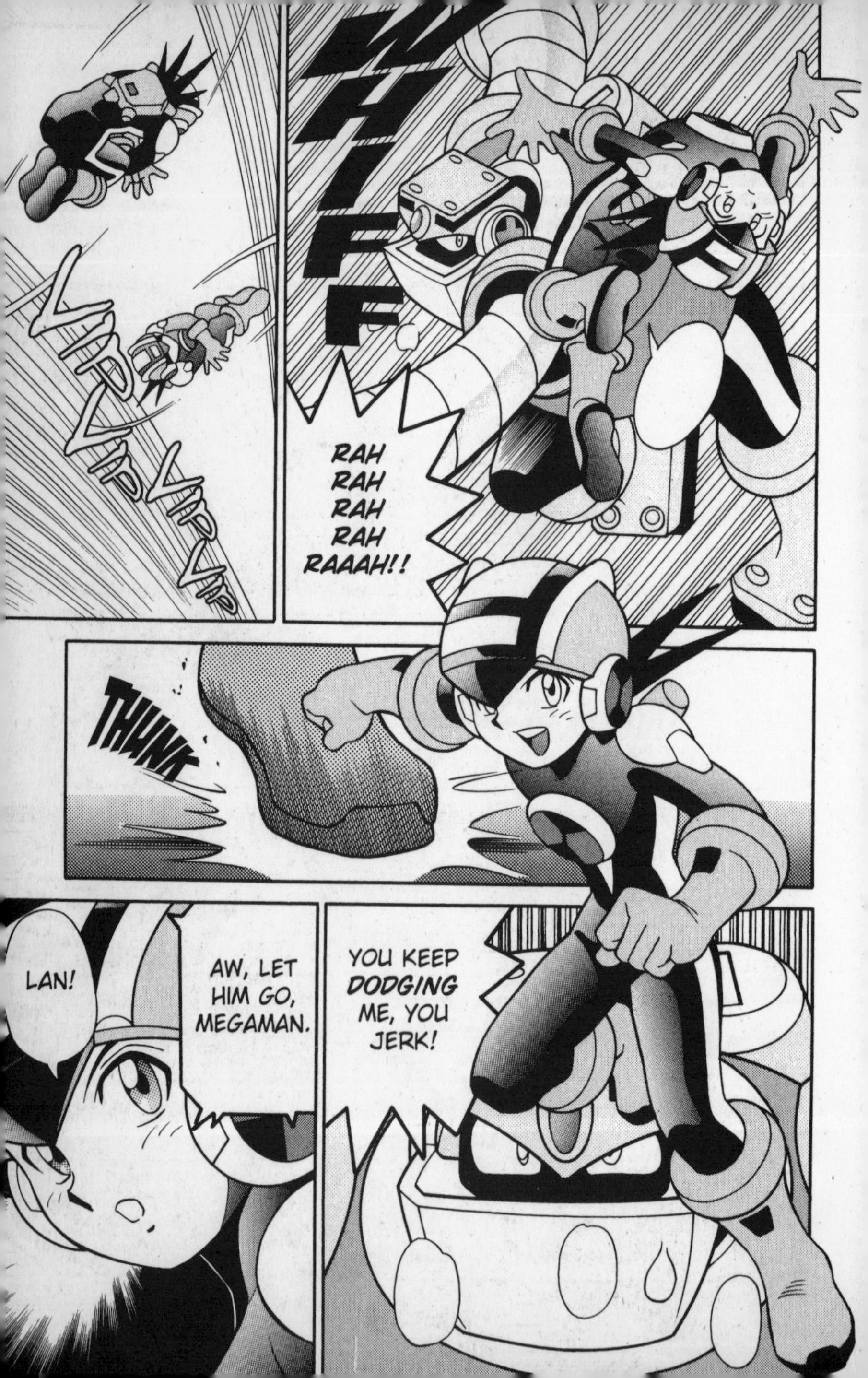
WHIFF
RAH RAH RAH RAH RAAAH!!
VIPVIPVIPVIP
THUNK
YOU KEEP DODGING ME, YOU JERK!
AW, LET HIM GO, MEGAMAN.
LAN!

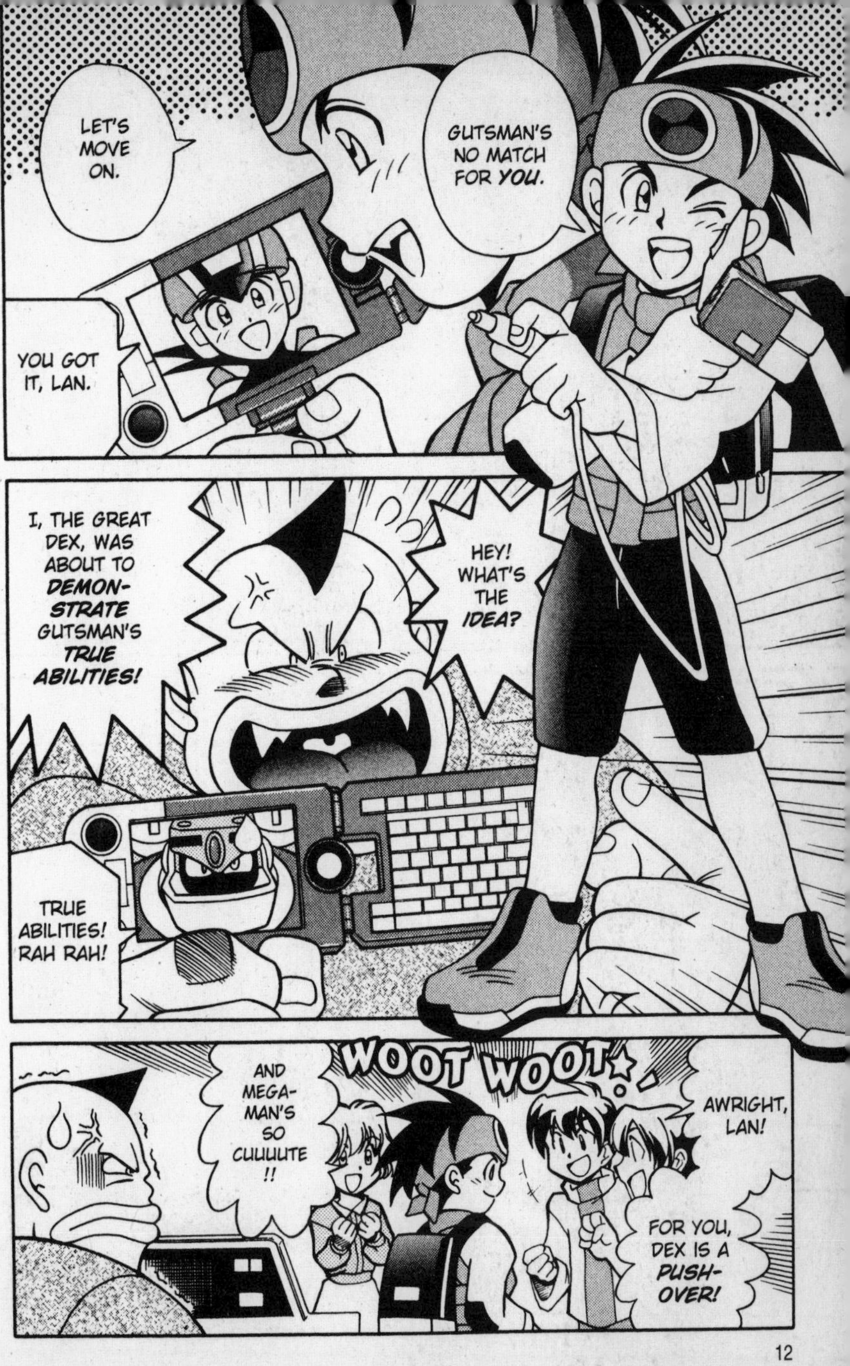
GUTSMAN'S NO MATCH FOR YOU.
LET'S MOVE ON.
YOU GOT IT, LAN.
HEY! WHAT'S THE IDEA?
I, THE GREAT DEX, WAS ABOUT TO DEMON-STRATE GUTSMAN'S TRUE ABILITIES!
TRUE ABILITIES! RAH RAH!
WOOT WOOT
AWRIGHT, LAN!
FOR YOU, DEX IS A PUSH-OVER!
AND MEGA-MAN'S SO CUUUUTE!!

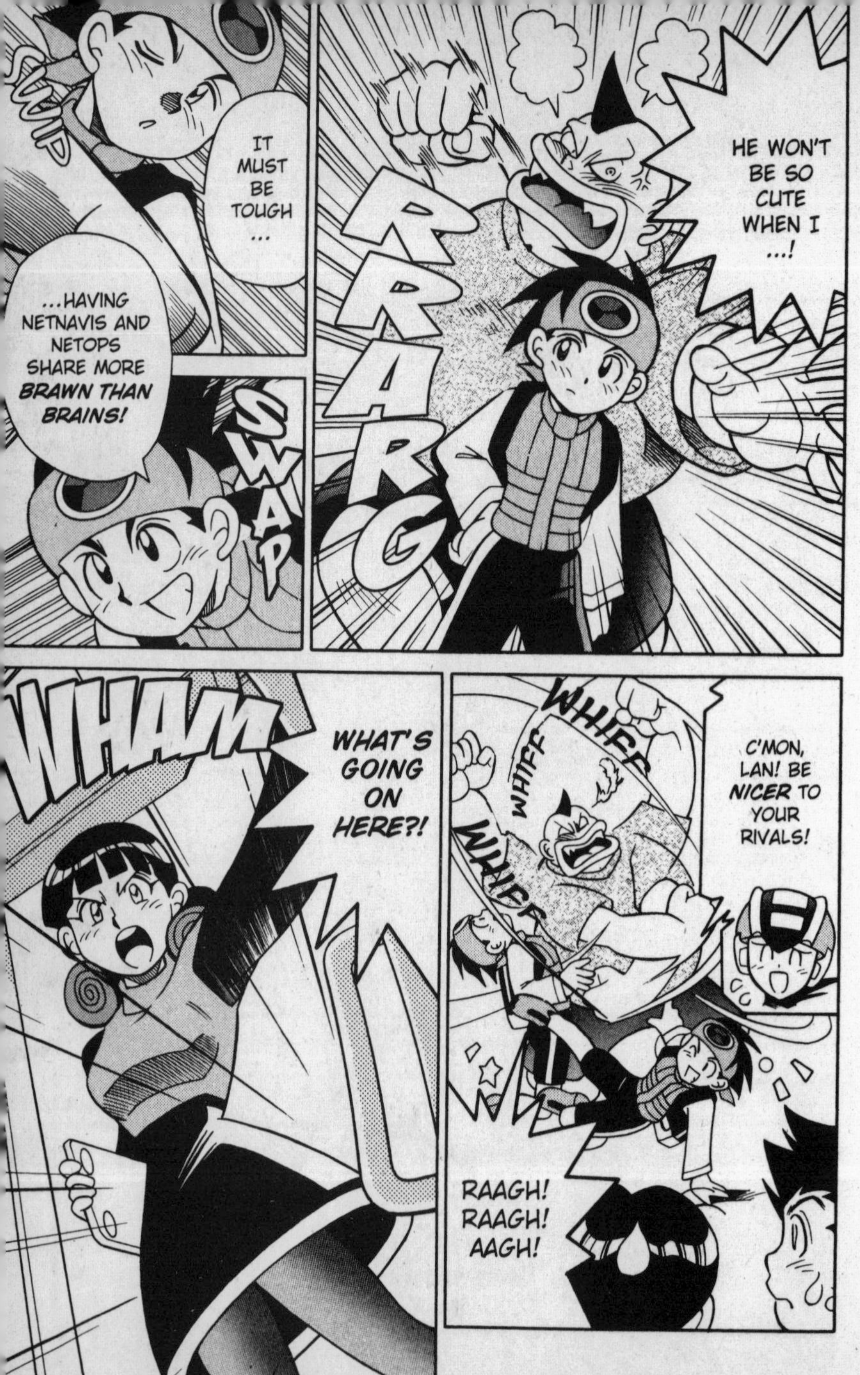
HE WON'T BE SO CUTE WHEN I ...!
RRARG
SWIP
IT MUST BE TOUGH ...
...HAVING NETNAVIS AND NETOPS SHARE MORE ***BRAWN THAN BRAINS!***
SWAP
C'MON, LAN! BE ***NICER*** TO YOUR RIVALS!
WHIFF
WHIFF
WHIFF
WHIFF
RAAGH! RAAGH! AAGH!
WHAM
WHAT'S GOING ON HERE?!

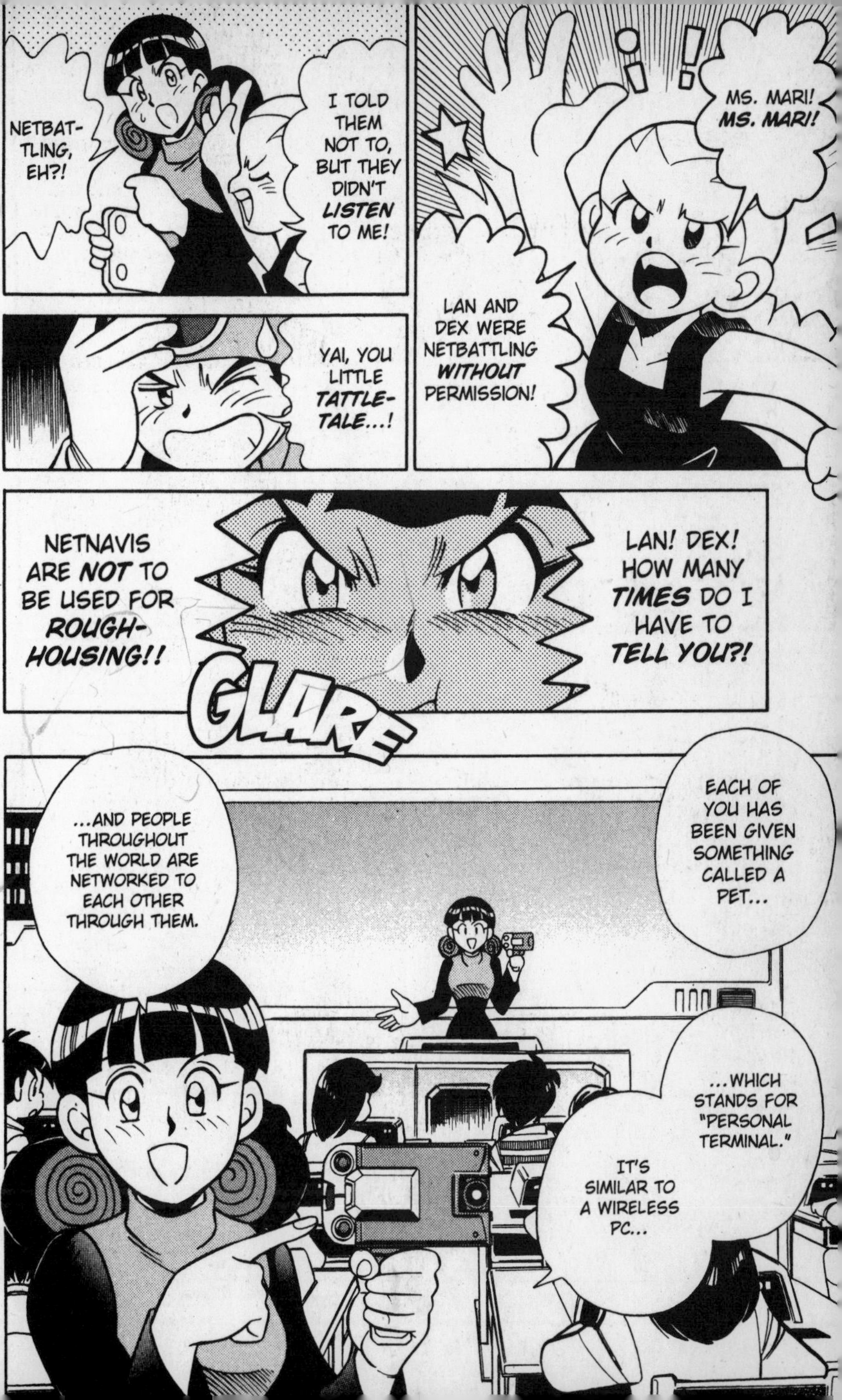
MS. MARI! MS. MARI!
LAN AND DEX WERE NETBATTLING WITHOUT PERMISSION!
I TOLD THEM NOT TO, BUT THEY DIDN'T LISTEN TO ME!
NETBATTLING, EH?!
YAI, YOU LITTLE TATTLE-TALE...!
LAN! DEX! HOW MANY TIMES DO I HAVE TO TELL YOU?!
NETNAVIS ARE NOT TO BE USED FOR ROUGH-HOUSING!!
GLARE
EACH OF YOU HAS BEEN GIVEN SOMETHING CALLED A PET...
...WHICH STANDS FOR "PERSONAL TERMINAL."
IT'S SIMILAR TO A WIRELESS PC...
...AND PEOPLE THROUGHOUT THE WORLD ARE NETWORKED TO EACH OTHER THROUGH THEM.

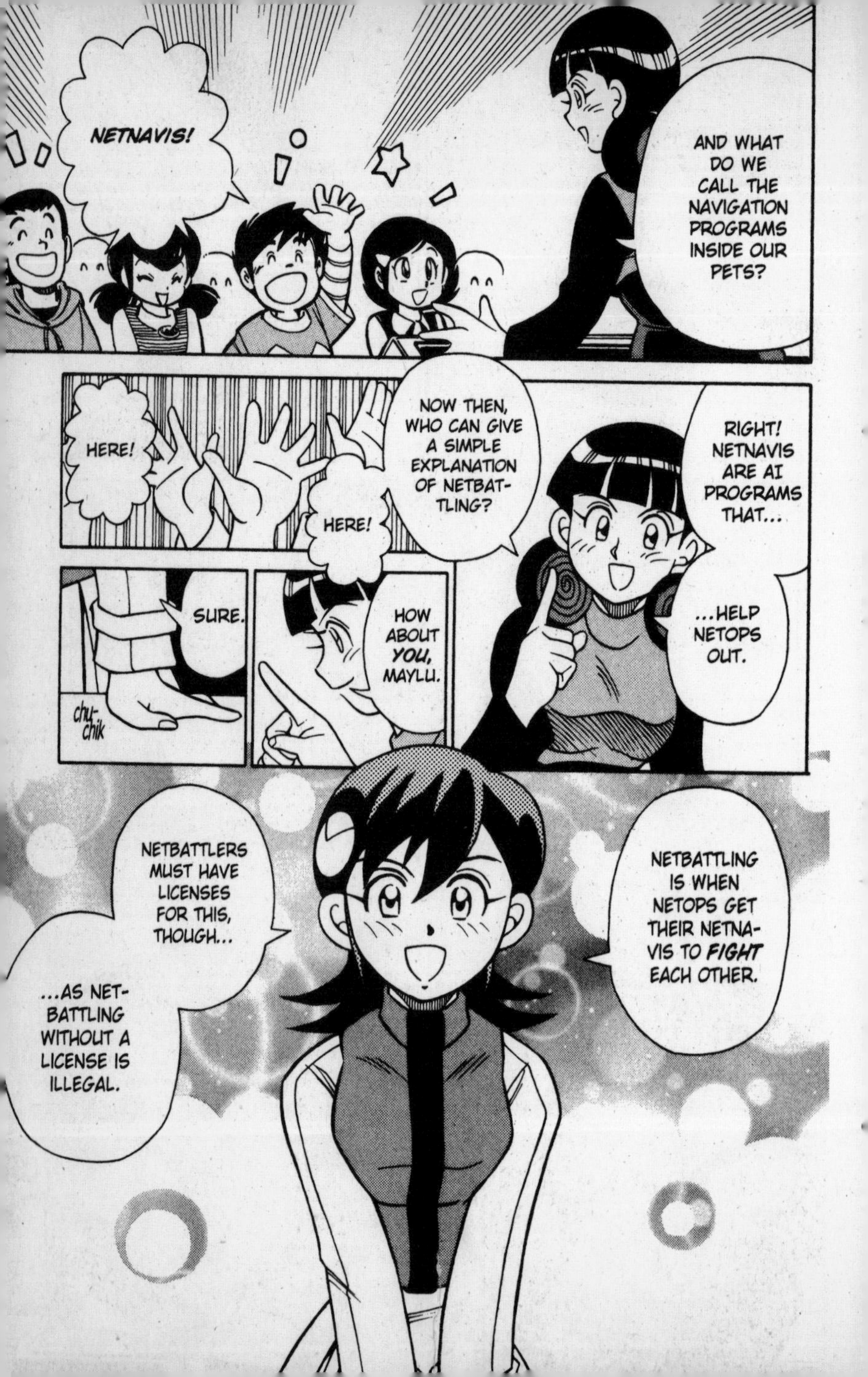
AND WHAT DO WE CALL THE NAVIGATION PROGRAMS INSIDE OUR PETS?
NETNAVIS!
RIGHT! NETNAVIS ARE AI PROGRAMS THAT...
...HELP NETOPS OUT.
NOW THEN, WHO CAN GIVE A SIMPLE EXPLANATION OF NETBAT-TLING?
HERE!
HERE!
HOW ABOUT *YOU*, MAYLU.
SURE.
chu-chik
NETBATTLING IS WHEN NETOPS GET THEIR NETNA-VIS TO *FIGHT* EACH OTHER.
NETBATTLERS MUST HAVE LICENSES FOR THIS, THOUGH...
...AS NET-BATTLING WITHOUT A LICENSE IS ILLEGAL.

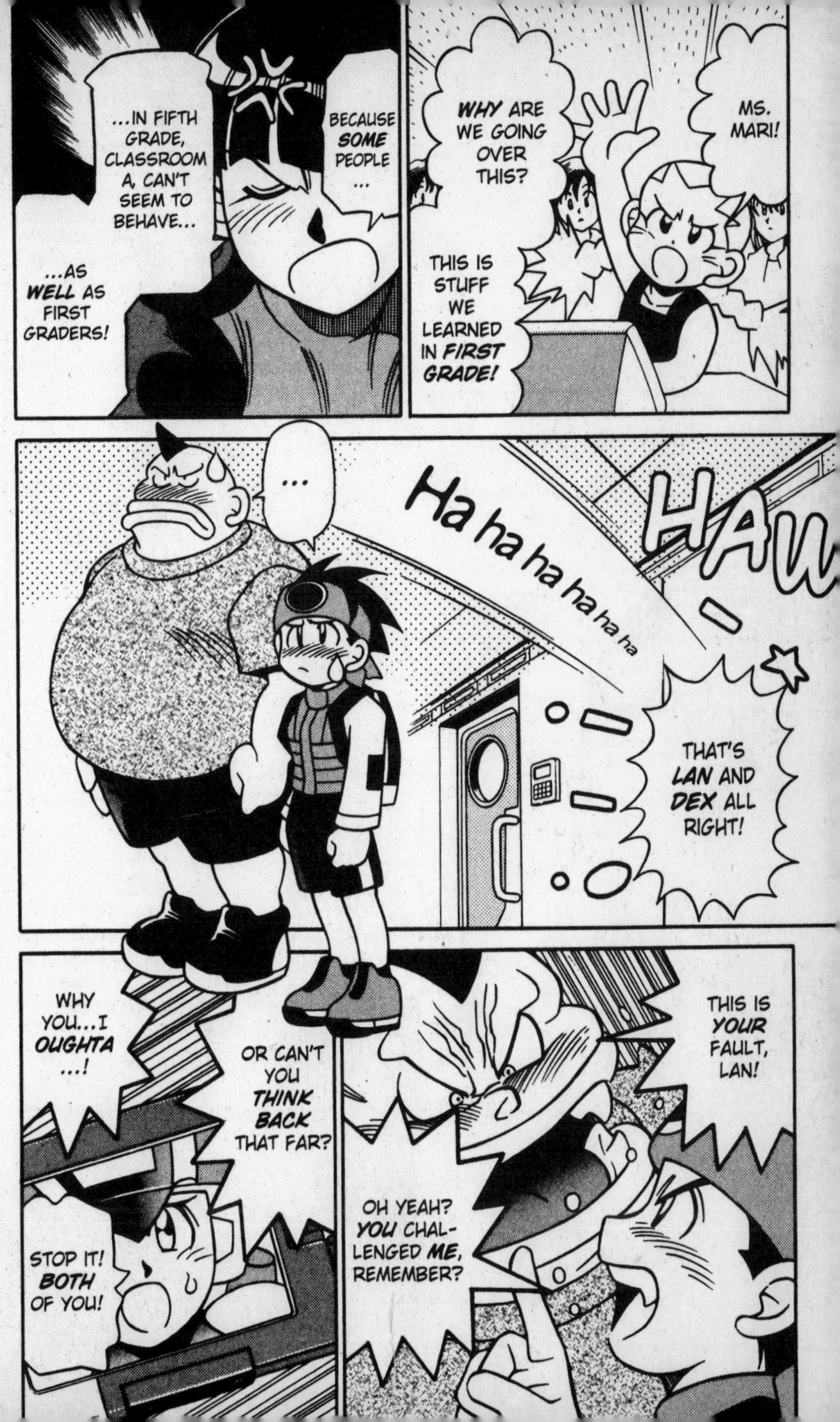
MS. MARI!
WHY ARE WE GOING OVER THIS?
THIS IS STUFF WE LEARNED IN FIRST GRADE!
BECAUSE SOME PEOPLE ...
...IN FIFTH GRADE, CLASSROOM A, CAN'T SEEM TO BEHAVE...
...AS WELL AS FIRST GRADERS!
HAU
Ha ha ha ha ha ha ha
THAT'S LAN AND DEX ALL RIGHT!
...
THIS IS YOUR FAULT, LAN!
OH YEAH? YOU CHALLENGED ME, REMEMBER?
OR CAN'T YOU THINK BACK THAT FAR?
WHY YOU...I OUGHTA ...!
STOP IT! BOTH OF YOU!

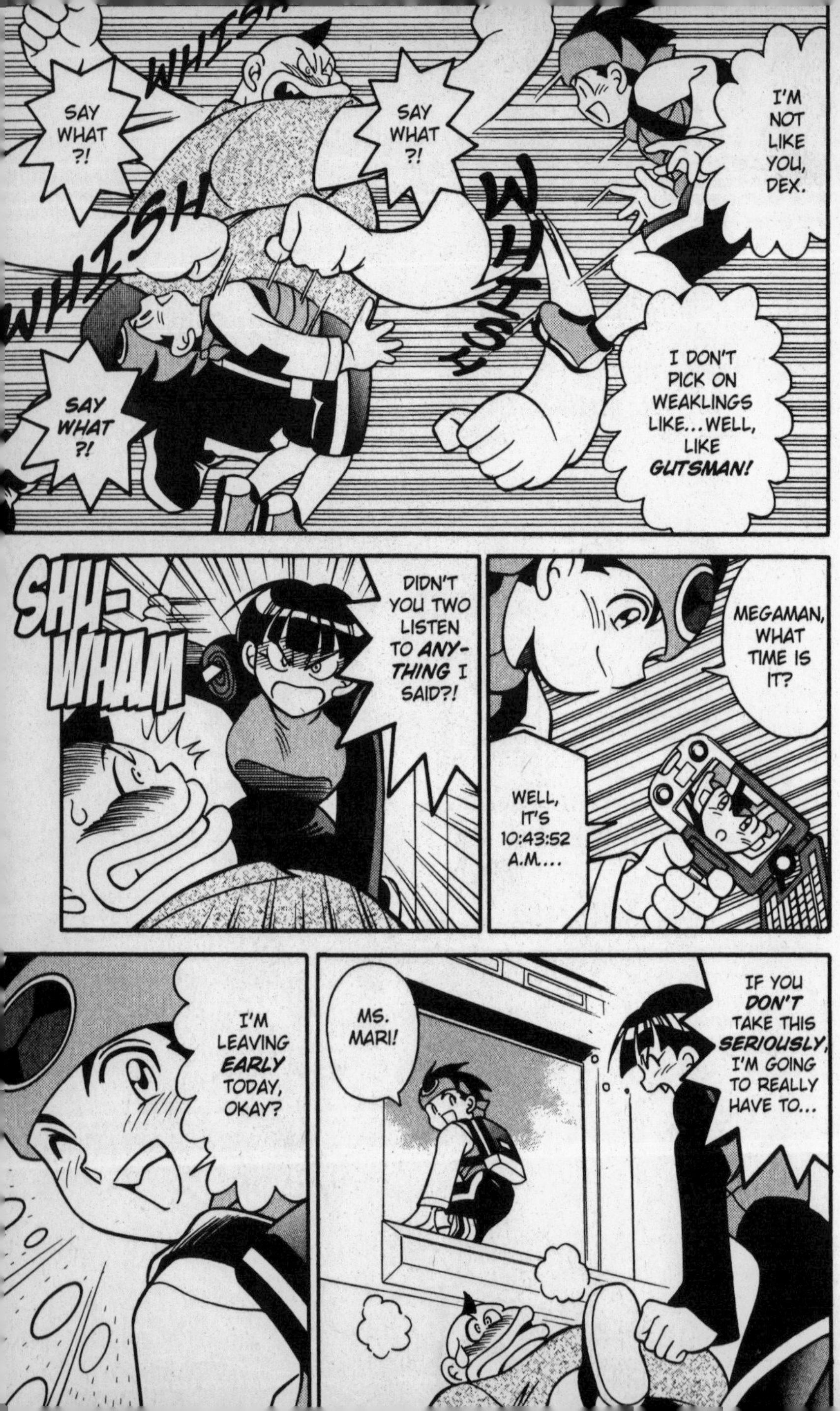
I'M NOT LIKE YOU, DEX.
I DON'T PICK ON WEAKLINGS LIKE...WELL, LIKE GUTSMAN!
SAY WHAT ?!
WHIZSH
SAY WHAT ?!
WHIZSH
WHIZSH
SAY WHAT ?!
MEGAMAN, WHAT TIME IS IT?
WELL, IT'S 10:43:52 A.M...
DIDN'T YOU TWO LISTEN TO ANYTHING I SAID?!
SHU-WHAM
IF YOU DON'T TAKE THIS SERIOUSLY, I'M GOING TO REALLY HAVE TO...
MS. MARI!
I'M LEAVING EARLY TODAY, OKAY?

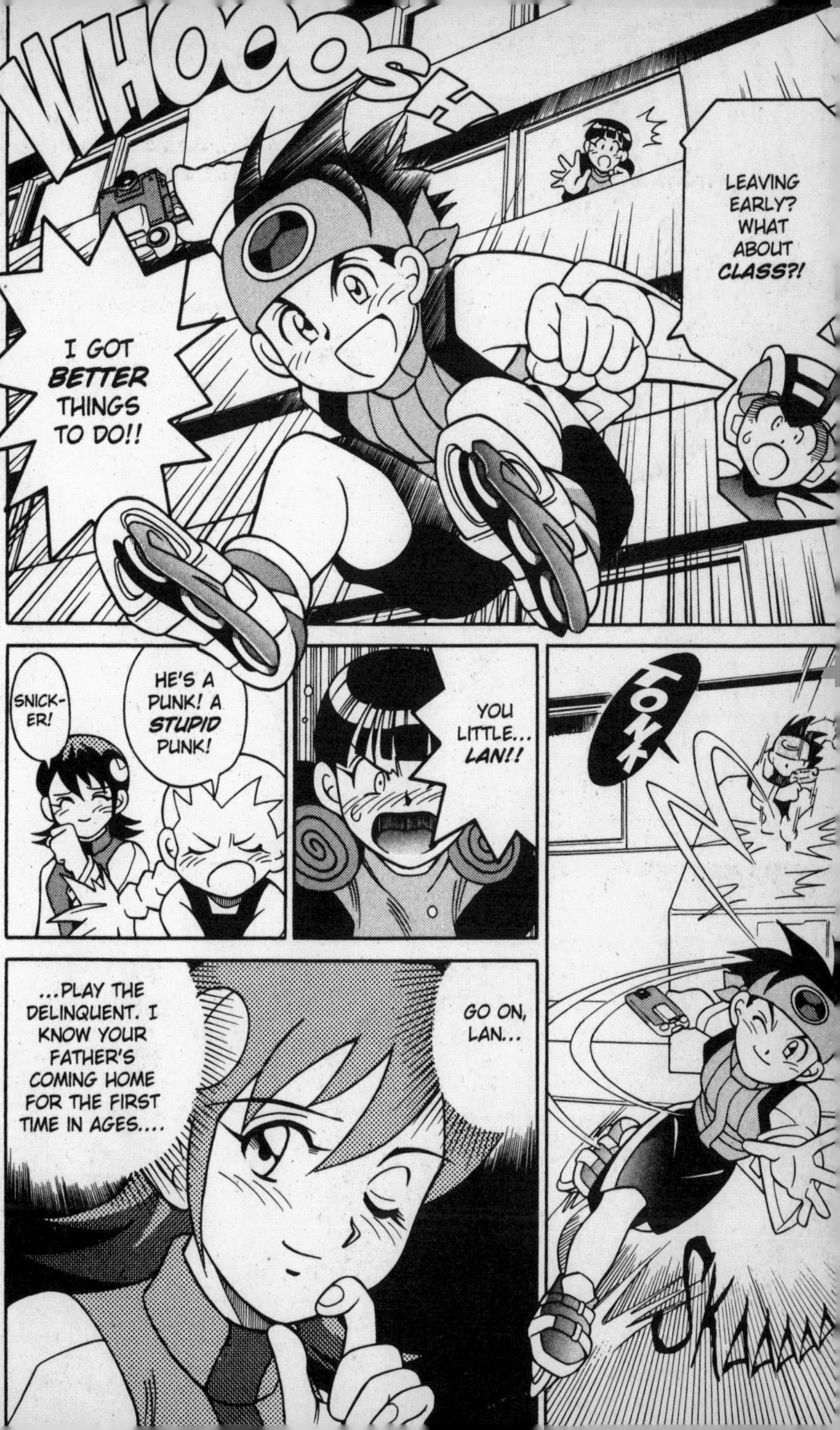
LEAVING EARLY? WHAT ABOUT CLASS?!
WHOOOSH
I GOT BETTER THINGS TO DO!!
TONK
SKAAAA
YOU LITTLE... LAN!!
HE'S A PUNK! A STUPID PUNK!
SNICKER!
GO ON, LAN...
...PLAY THE DELINQUENT. I KNOW YOUR FATHER'S COMING HOME FOR THE FIRST TIME IN AGES....

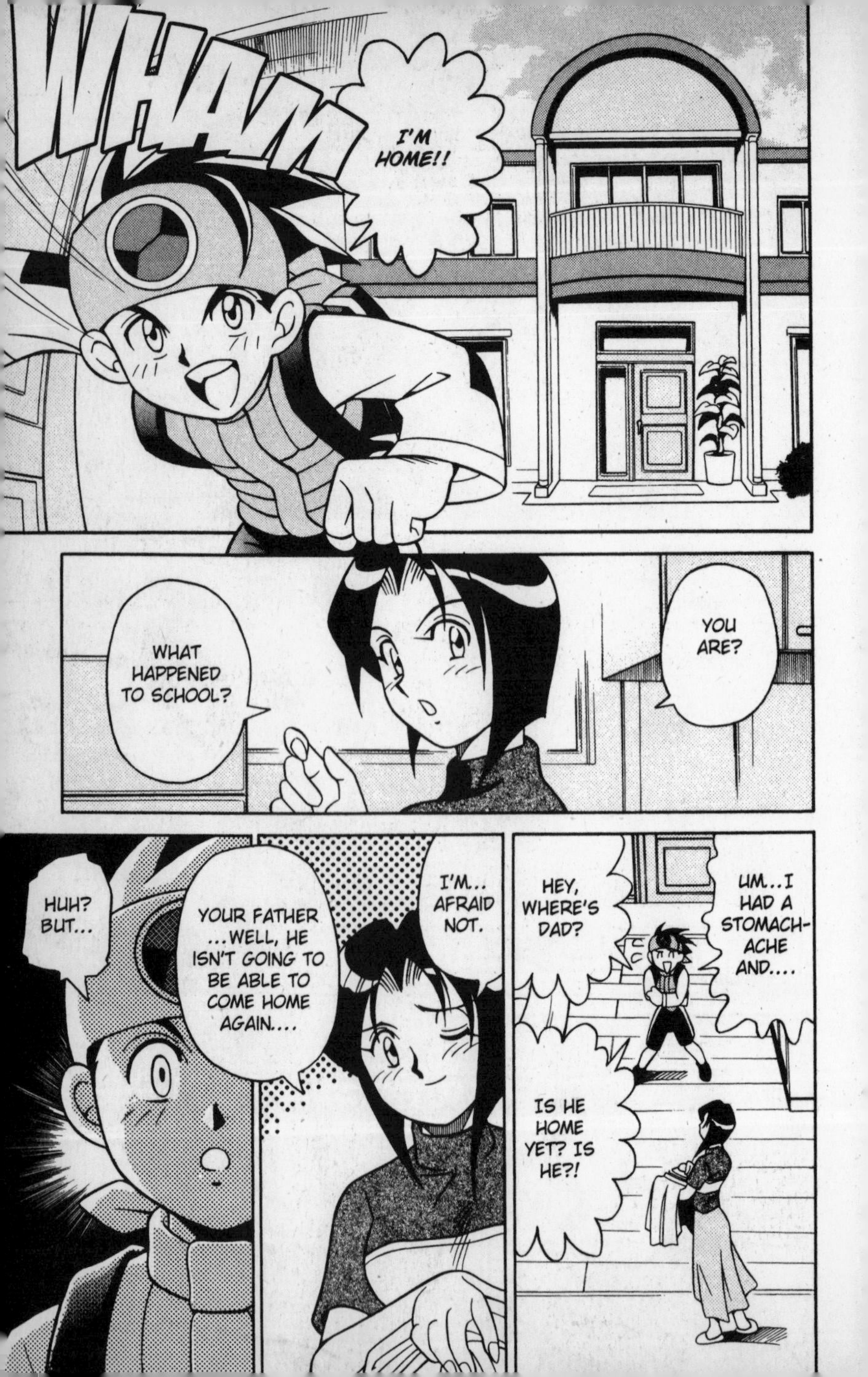
WHAM
I'M HOME!!
YOU ARE?
WHAT HAPPENED TO SCHOOL?
UM...I HAD A STOMACH-ACHE AND....
HEY, WHERE'S DAD?
IS HE HOME YET? IS HE?!
I'M... AFRAID NOT.
YOUR FATHER ...WELL, HE ISN'T GOING TO BE ABLE TO COME HOME AGAIN....
HUH? BUT...

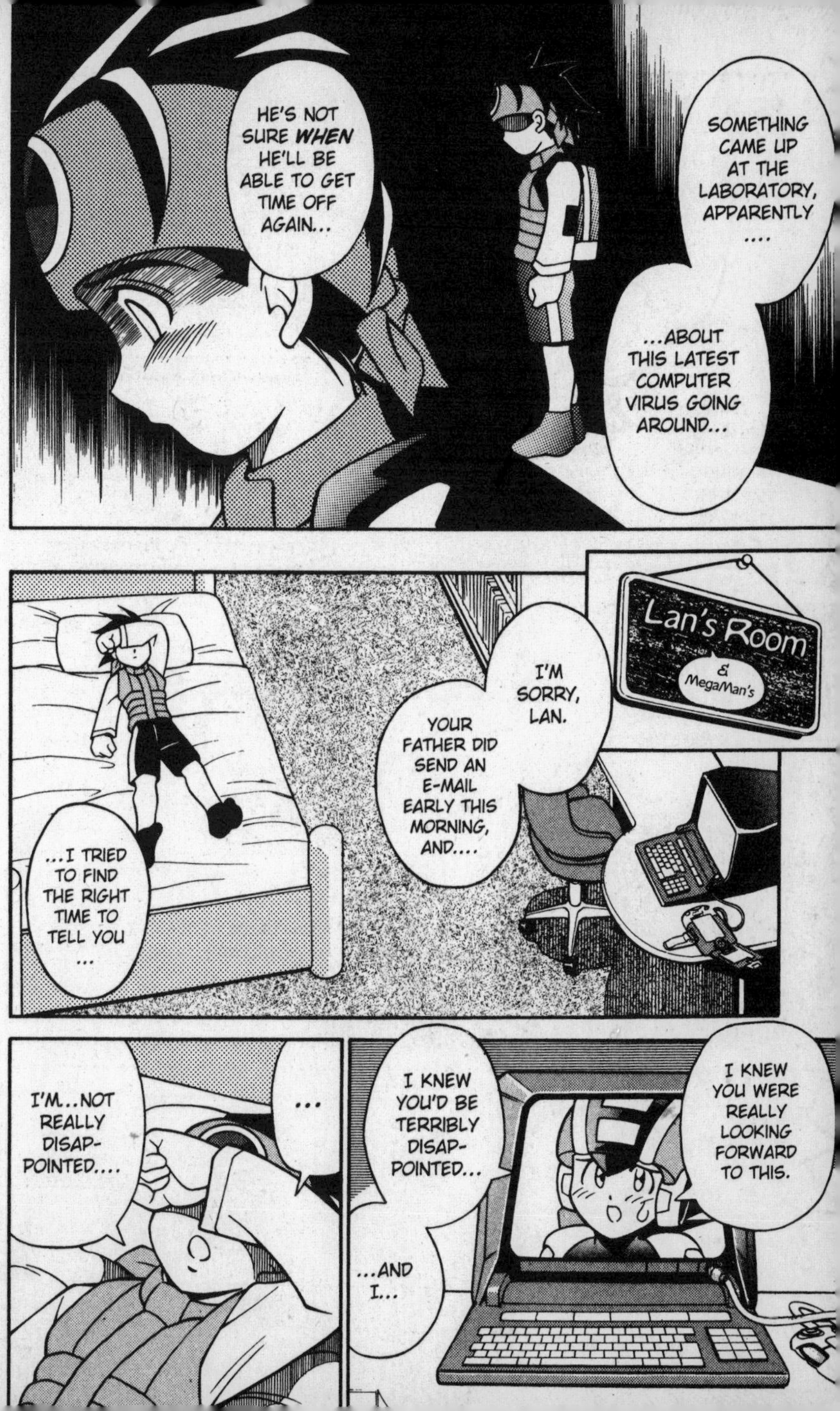
SOMETHING CAME UP AT THE LABORATORY, APPARENTLY ....
...ABOUT THIS LATEST COMPUTER VIRUS GOING AROUND...
HE'S NOT SURE *WHEN* HE'LL BE ABLE TO GET TIME OFF AGAIN...
Lan's Room
& MegaMan's
I'M SORRY, LAN.
YOUR FATHER DID SEND AN E-MAIL EARLY THIS MORNING, AND....
...I TRIED TO FIND THE RIGHT TIME TO TELL YOU ...
I KNEW YOU WERE REALLY LOOKING FORWARD TO THIS.
I KNEW YOU'D BE TERRIBLY DISAP-POINTED...
...AND I...
...
I'M...NOT REALLY DISAP-POINTED....

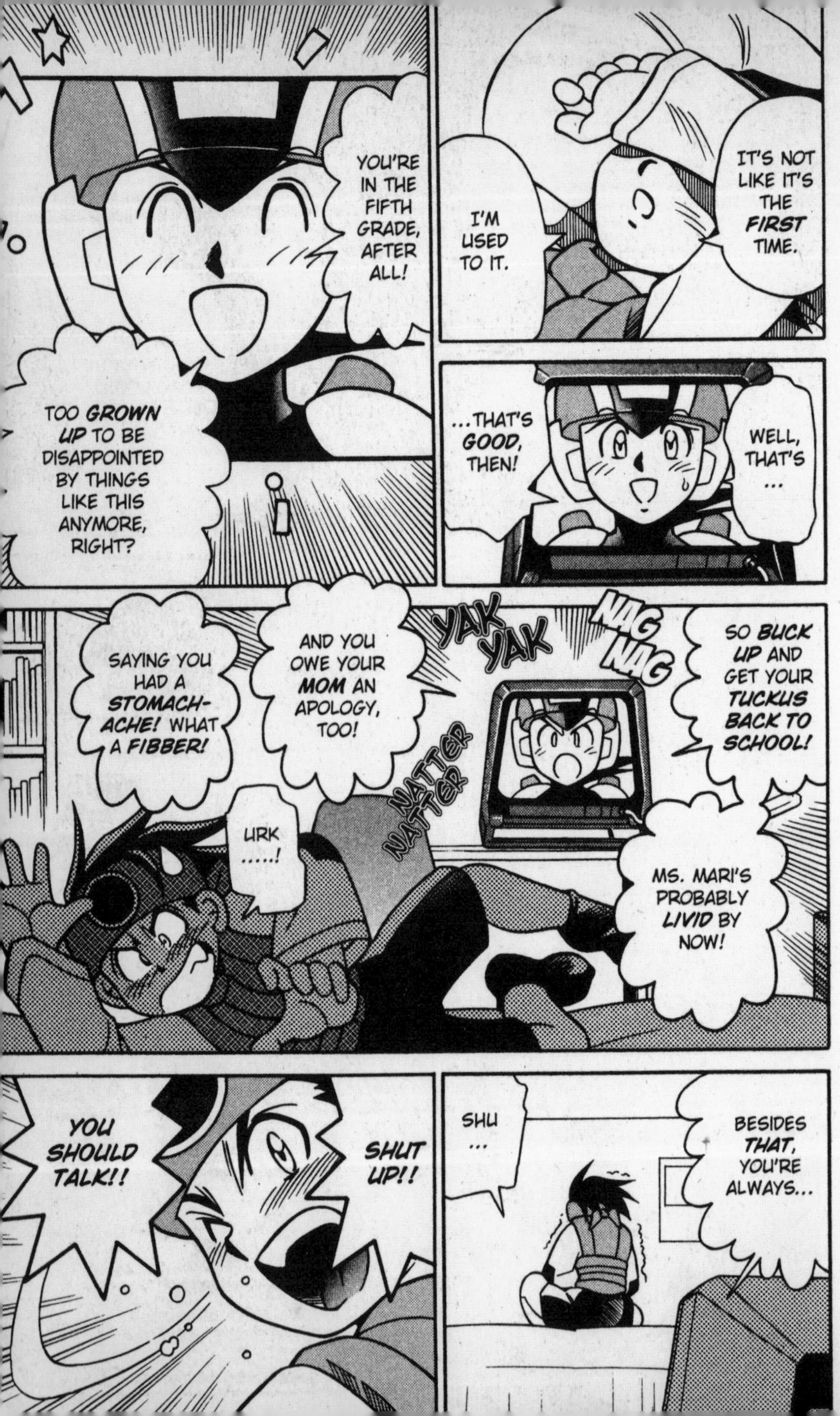
IT'S NOT LIKE IT'S THE FIRST TIME.
I'M USED TO IT.
WELL, THAT'S ...
...THAT'S GOOD, THEN!
YOU'RE IN THE FIFTH GRADE, AFTER ALL!
TOO GROWN UP TO BE DISAPPOINTED BY THINGS LIKE THIS ANYMORE, RIGHT?
SO BUCK UP AND GET YOUR TUCKUS BACK TO SCHOOL!
NAG NAG
YAK YAK
AND YOU OWE YOUR MOM AN APOLOGY, TOO!
SAYING YOU HAD A STOMACH-ACHE! WHAT A FIBBER!
MS. MARI'S PROBABLY LIVID BY NOW!
NATTER NATTER
URK .....!
BESIDES THAT, YOU'RE ALWAYS...
SHU ...
SHUT UP!!
YOU SHOULD TALK!!

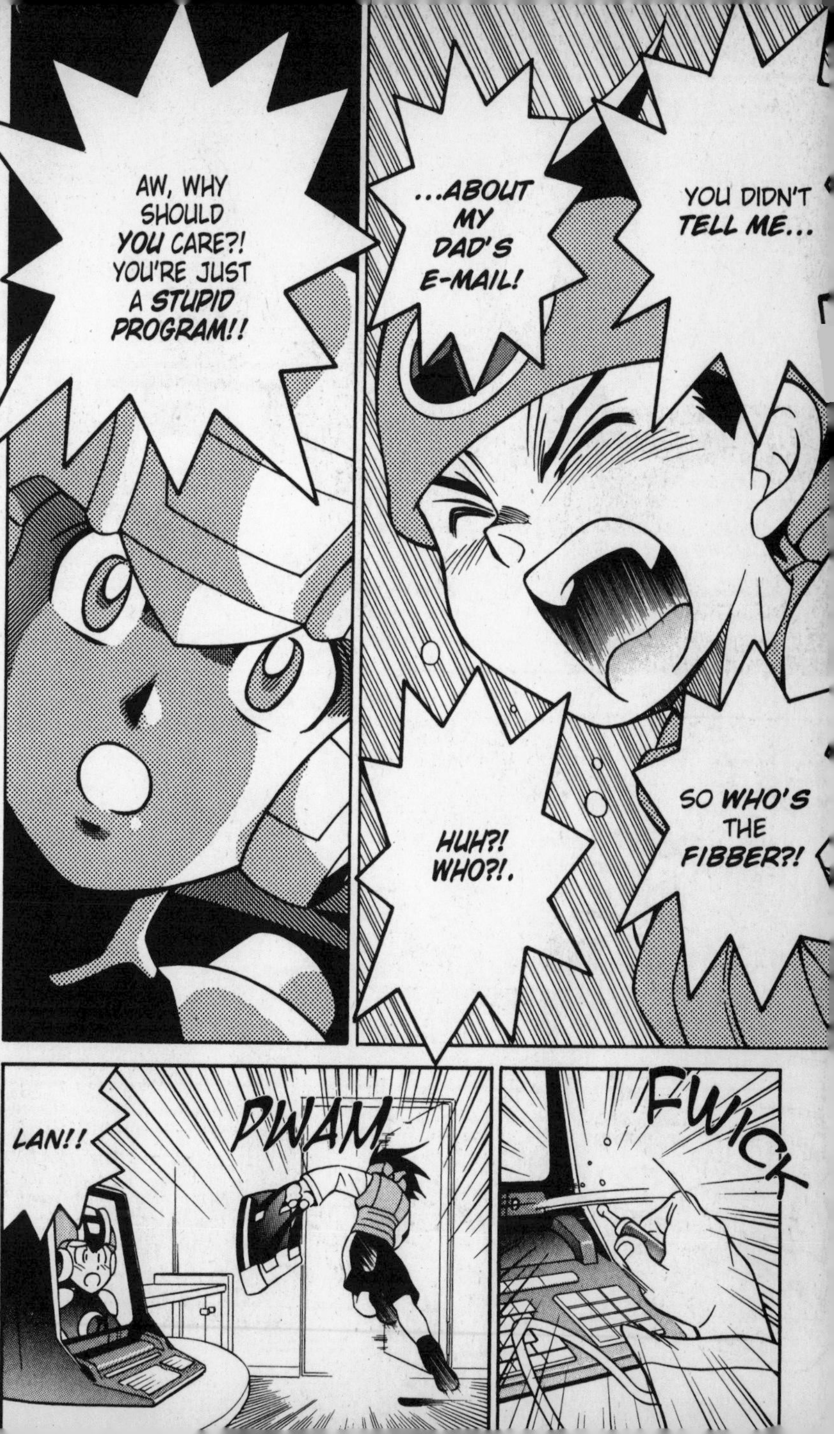
YOU DIDN'T TELL ME...
...ABOUT MY DAD'S E-MAIL!
SO WHO'S THE FIBBER?!
HUH?! WHO?!.
AW, WHY SHOULD YOU CARE?! YOU'RE JUST A STUPID PROGRAM!!
FWICK
DWAM
LAN!!

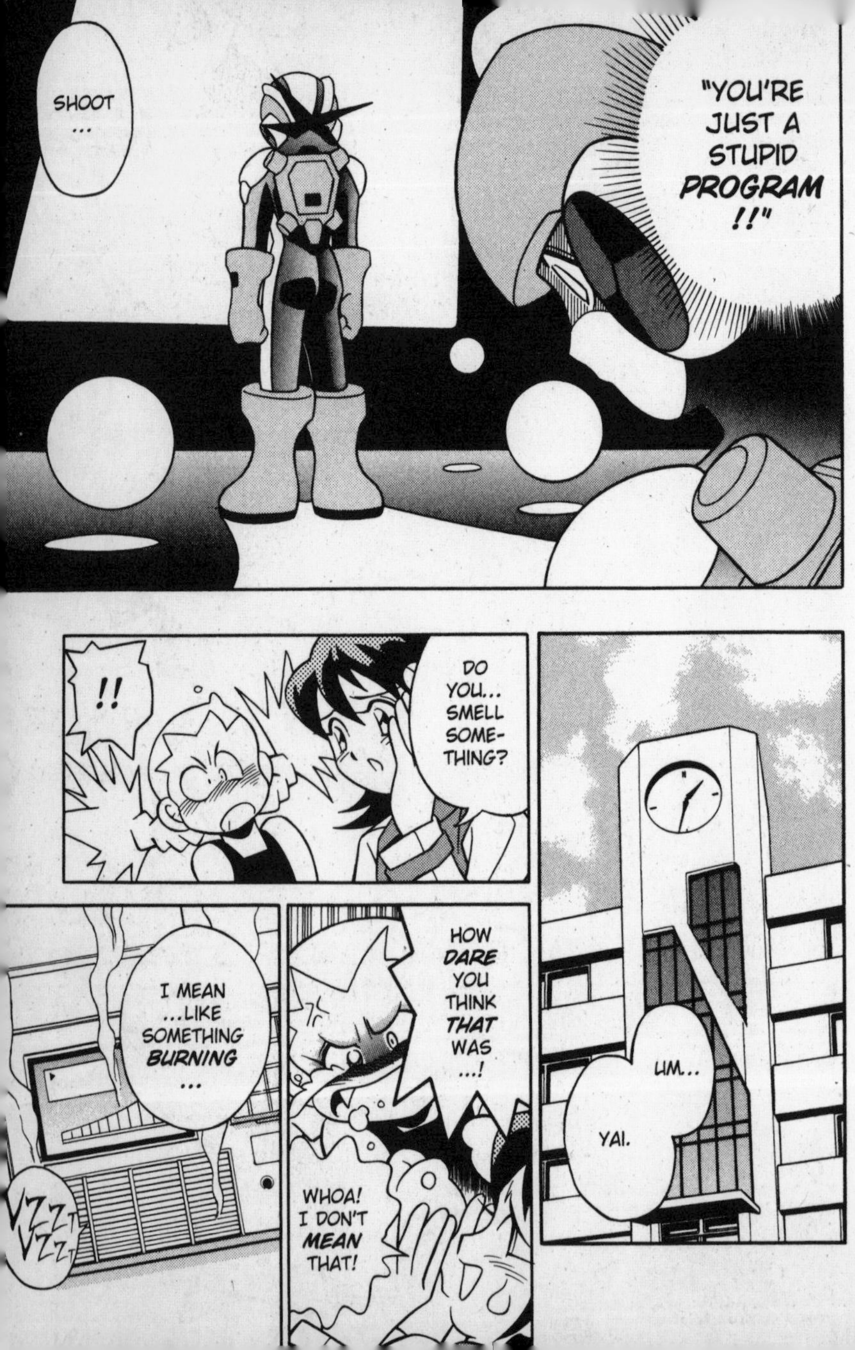
"YOU'RE JUST A STUPID PROGRAM!!"
SHOOT...
UM...
YAI.
DO YOU... SMELL SOMETHING?
!!
HOW DARE YOU THINK THAT WAS...!
WHOA! I DON'T MEAN THAT!
I MEAN ...LIKE SOMETHING BURNING ...
ZZZT ZZZT

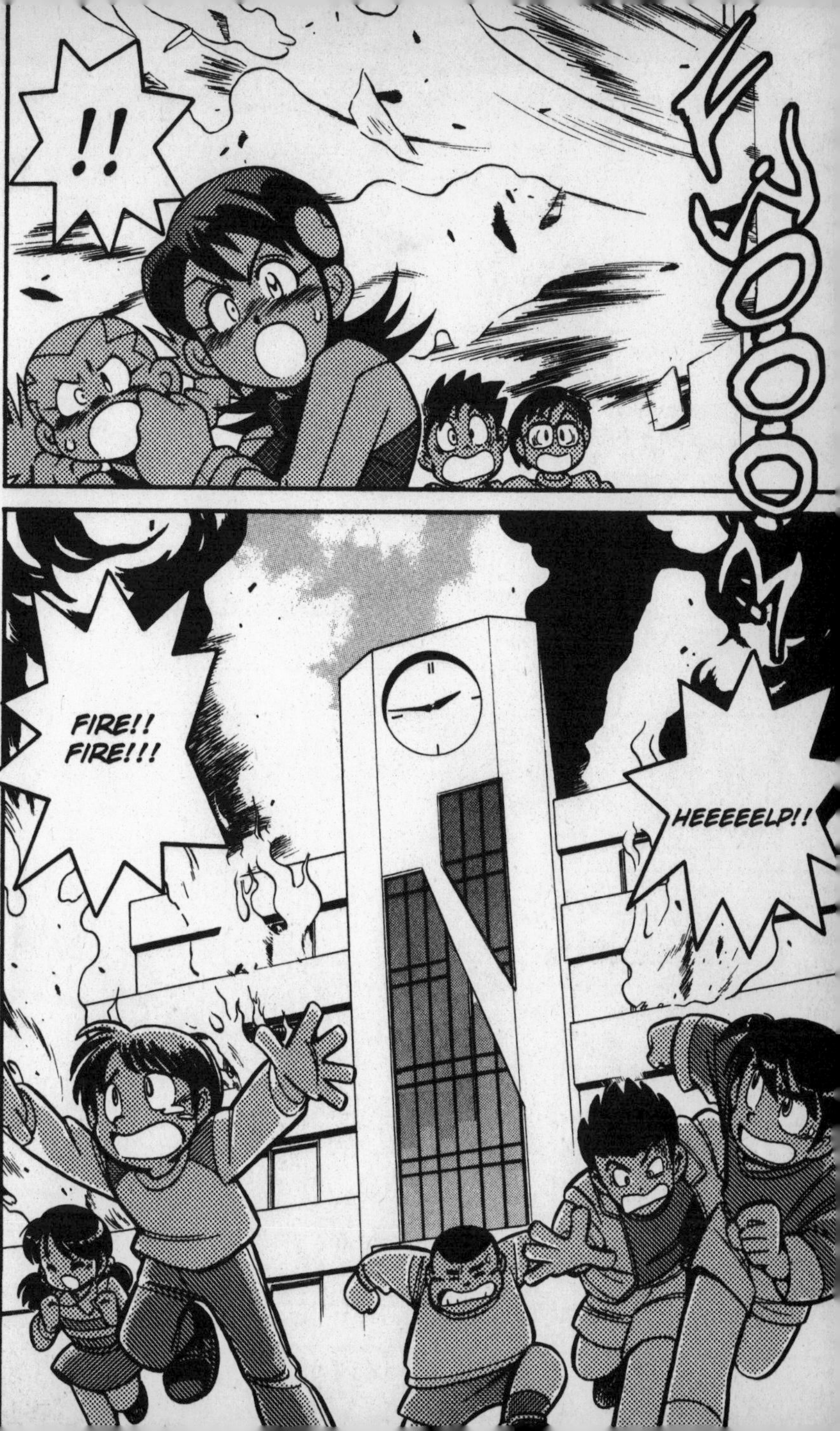
!!
HEEEEELP!!
FIRE!!
FIRE!!!

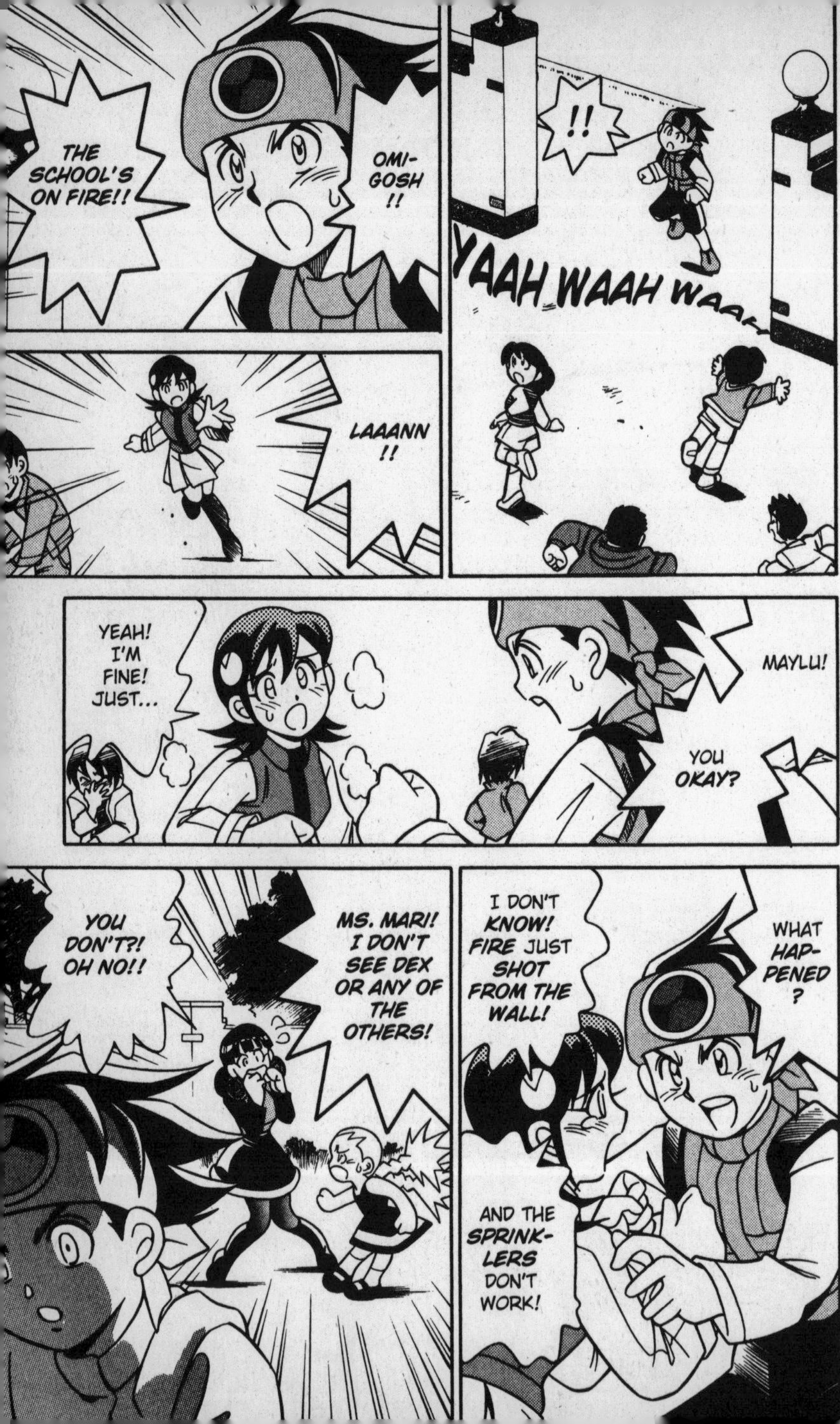
!!
YAAH WAAH WAA
OMI-GOSH !!
THE SCHOOL'S ON FIRE!!
LAAANN !!
MAYLU!
YOU OKAY?
YEAH! I'M FINE! JUST...
WHAT HAP-PENED ?
I DON'T KNOW! FIRE JUST SHOT FROM THE WALL!
AND THE SPRINK-LERS DON'T WORK!
MS. MARI! I DON'T SEE DEX OR ANY OF THE OTHERS!
YOU DON'T?! OH NO!!

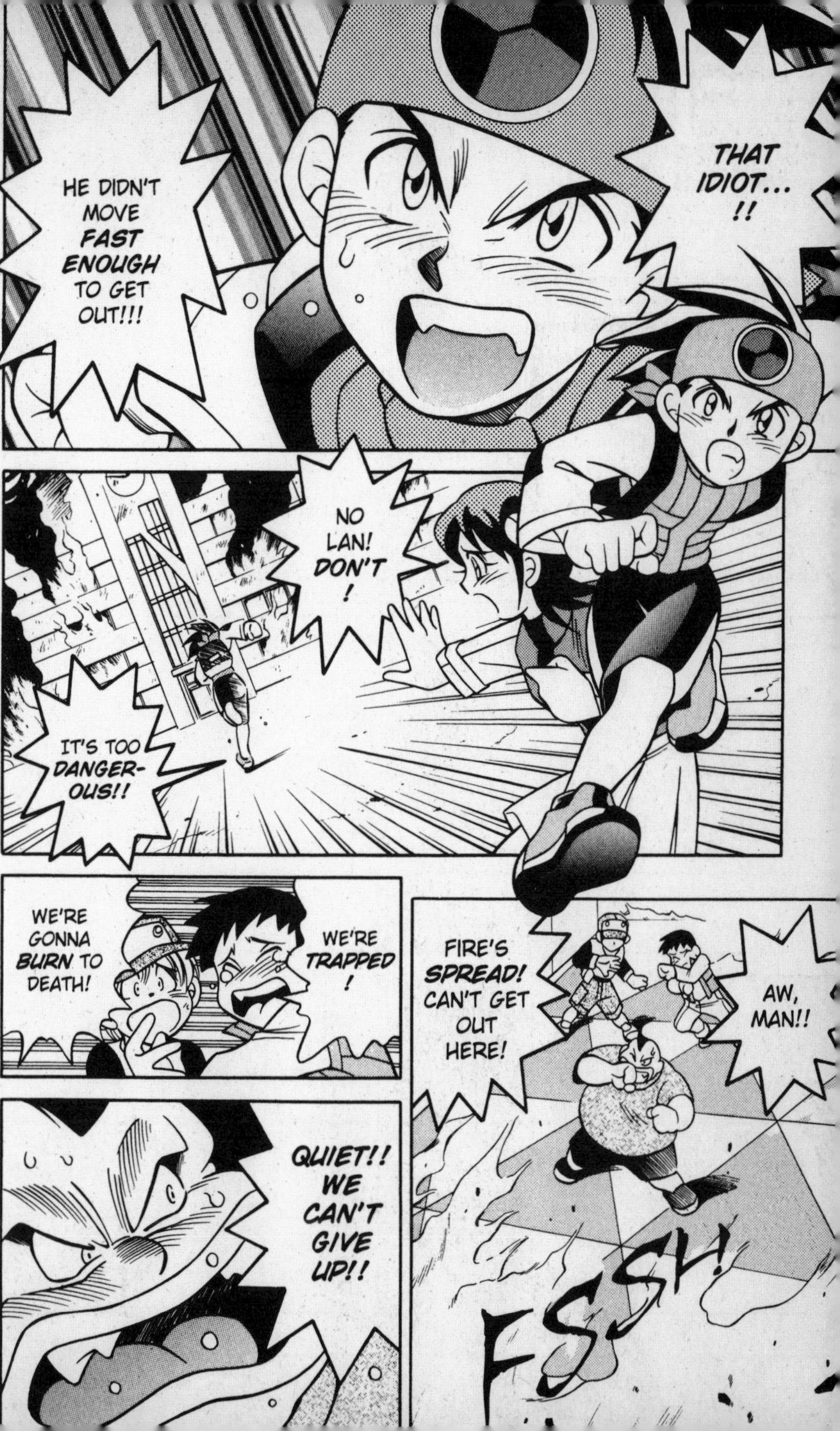
THAT IDIOT... !!
HE DIDN'T MOVE FAST ENOUGH TO GET OUT!!!
NO LAN! DON'T !
IT'S TOO DANGER-OUS!!
AW, MAN!!
FIRE'S SPREAD! CAN'T GET OUT HERE!
FSSH!
WE'RE TRAPPED !
WE'RE GONNA BURN TO DEATH!
QUIET!! WE CAN'T GIVE UP!!

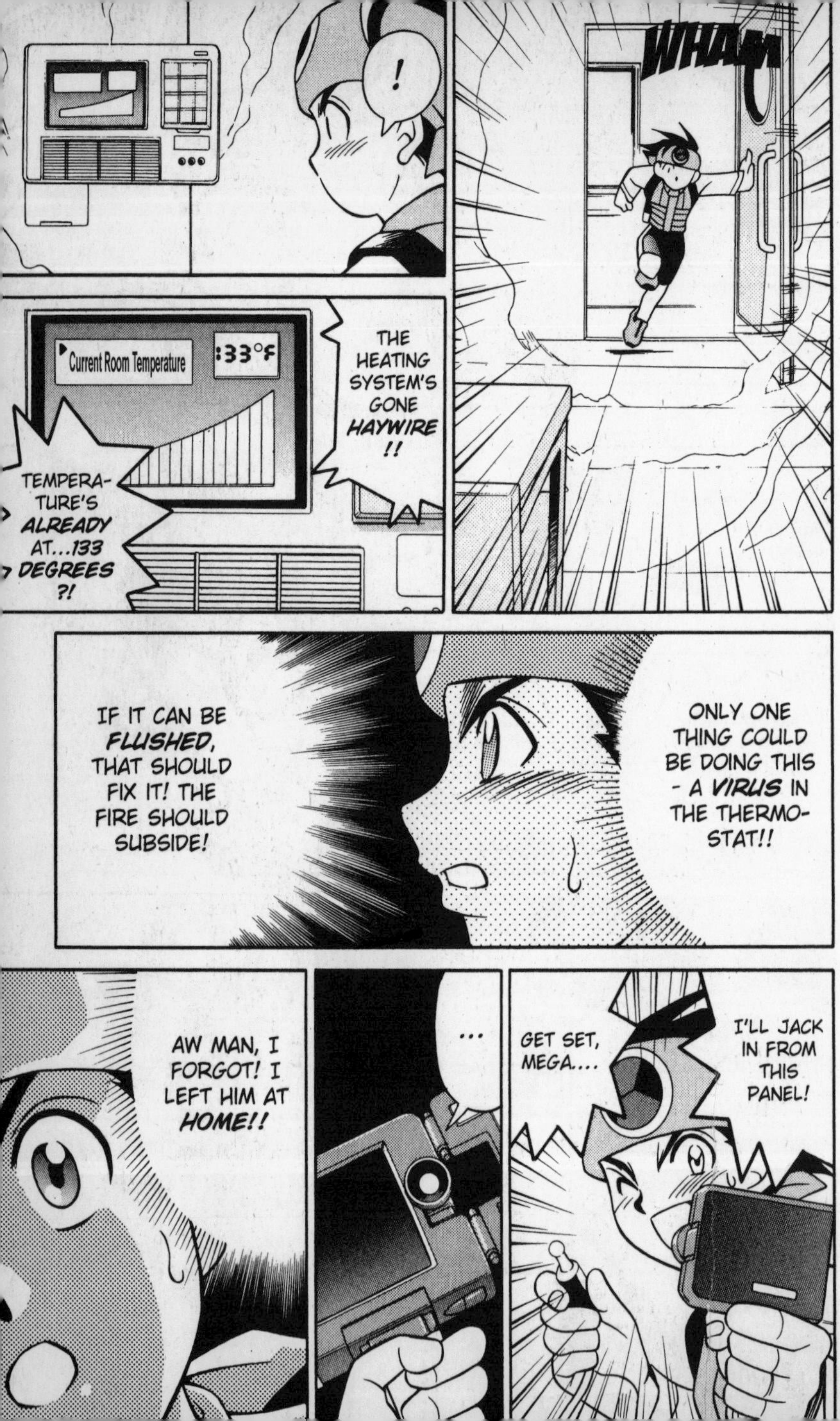
WHAM
!
THE HEATING SYSTEM'S GONE HAYWIRE!!
Current Room Temperature
:33°F
TEMPERA-TURE'S ALREADY AT...133 DEGREES?!
ONLY ONE THING COULD BE DOING THIS - A VIRUS IN THE THERMO-STAT!!
IF IT CAN BE FLUSHED, THAT SHOULD FIX IT! THE FIRE SHOULD SUBSIDE!
I'LL JACK IN FROM THIS PANEL!
GET SET, MEGA....
...
AW MAN, I FORGOT! I LEFT HIM AT HOME!!

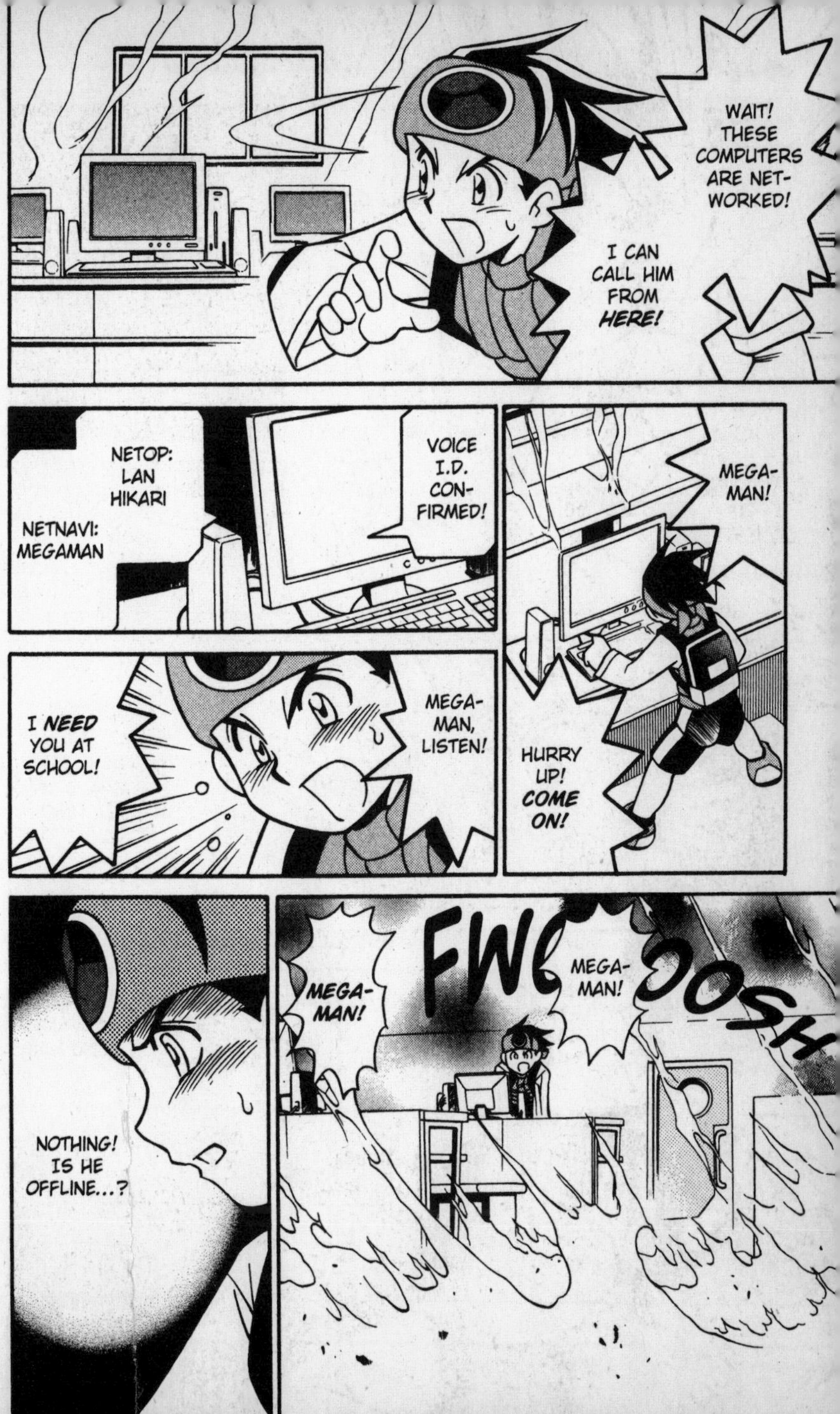
WAIT! THESE COMPUTERS ARE NET-WORKED!
I CAN CALL HIM FROM *HERE!*
MEGA-MAN!
HURRY UP! *COME ON!*
VOICE I.D. CON-FIRMED!
NETOP: LAN HIKARI
NETNAVI: MEGAMAN
MEGA-MAN, LISTEN!
I *NEED* YOU AT SCHOOL!
FWOOOSH
MEGA-MAN!
MEGA-MAN!
NOTHING! IS HE OFFLINE...?

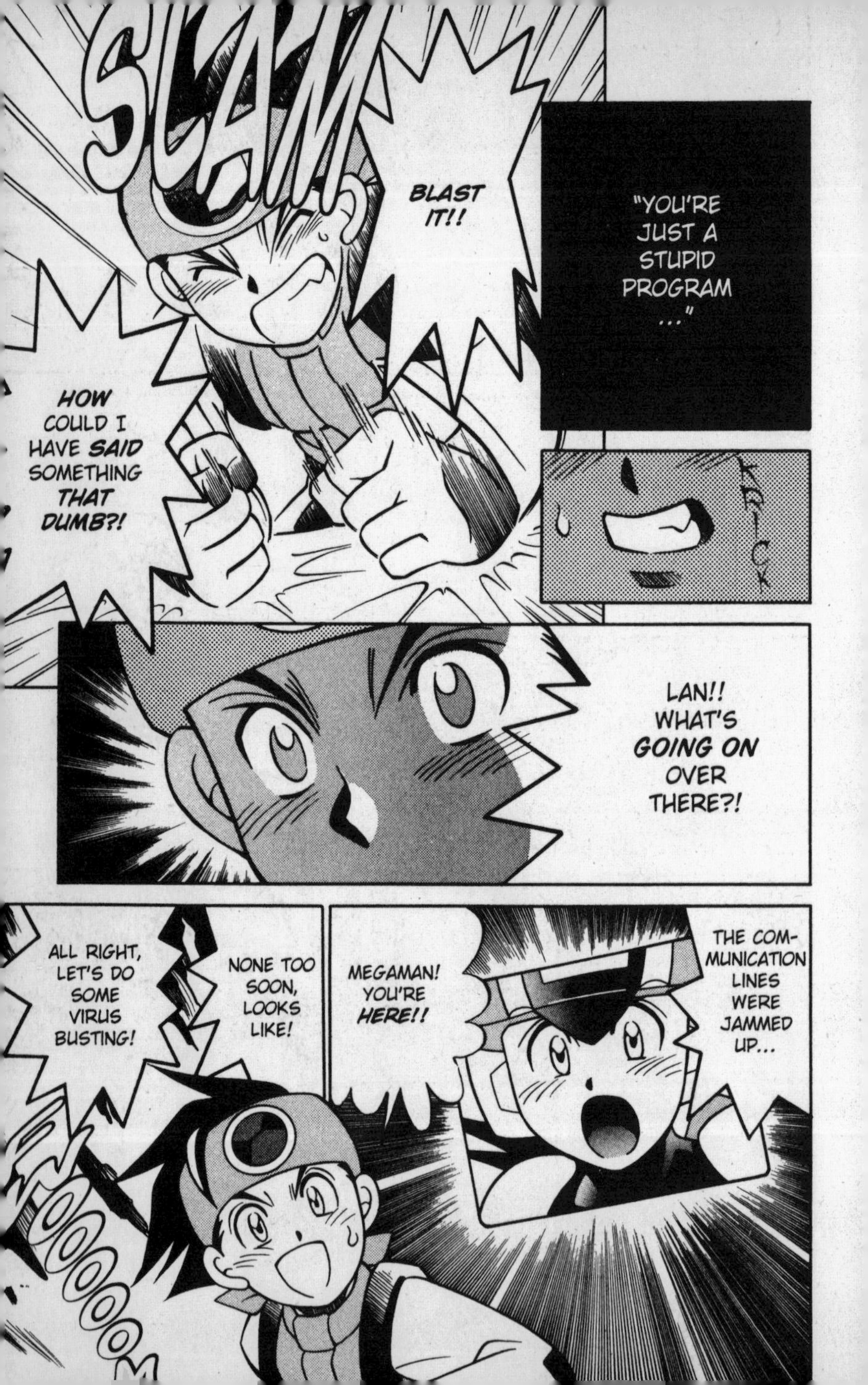
"YOU'RE JUST A STUPID PROGRAM ..."
SLAM
BLAST IT!!
HOW COULD I HAVE SAID SOMETHING THAT DUMB?!
LAN!! WHAT'S GOING ON OVER THERE?!
THE COM-MUNICATION LINES WERE JAMMED UP...
MEGAMAN! YOU'RE HERE!!
NONE TOO SOON, LOOKS LIKE!
ALL RIGHT, LET'S DO SOME VIRUS BUSTING!

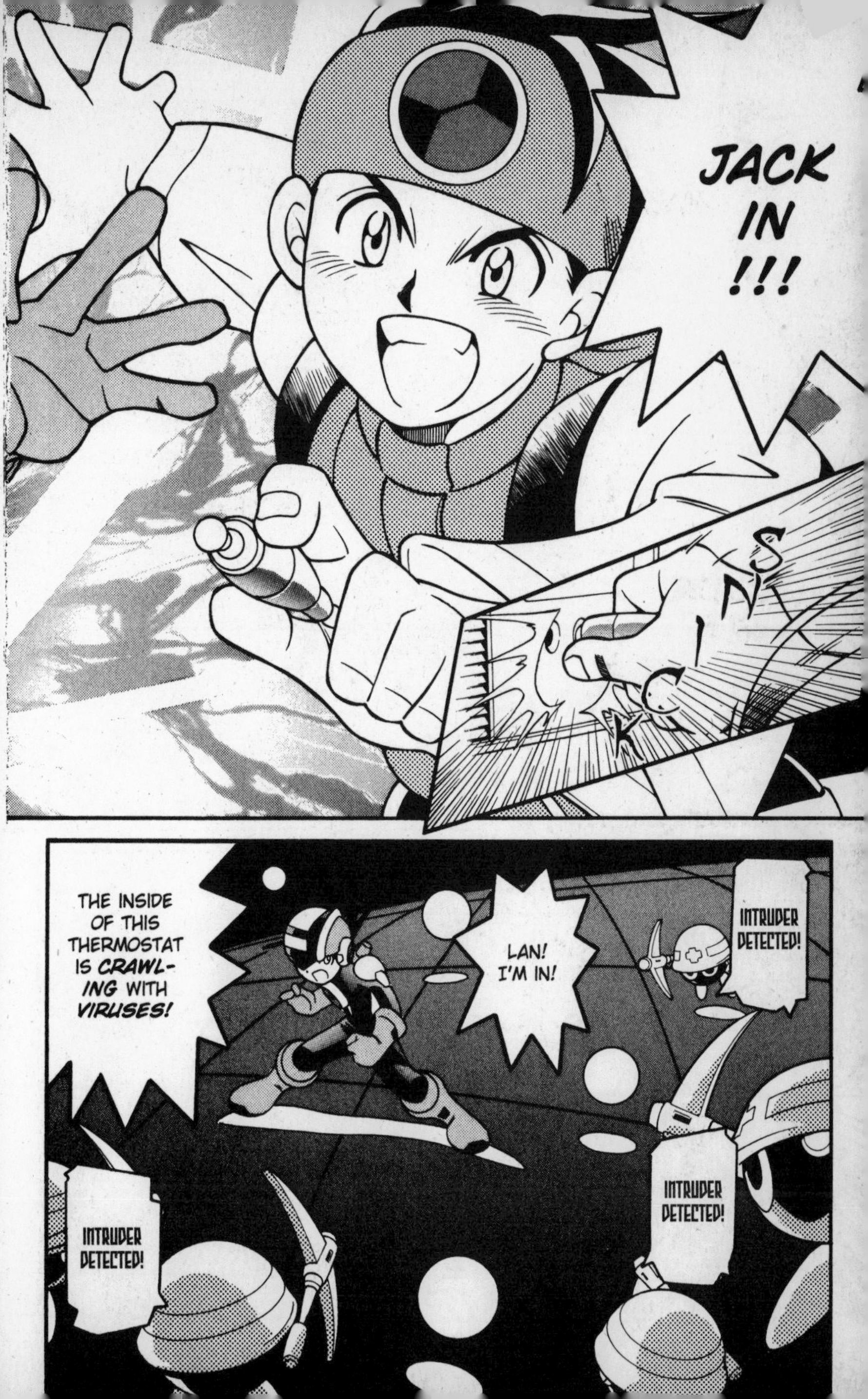
JACK IN !!!
INTRUDER DETECTED!
LAN! I'M IN!
THE INSIDE OF THIS THERMOSTAT IS CRAWL-ING WITH VIRUSES!
INTRUDER DETECTED!
INTRUDER DETECTED!

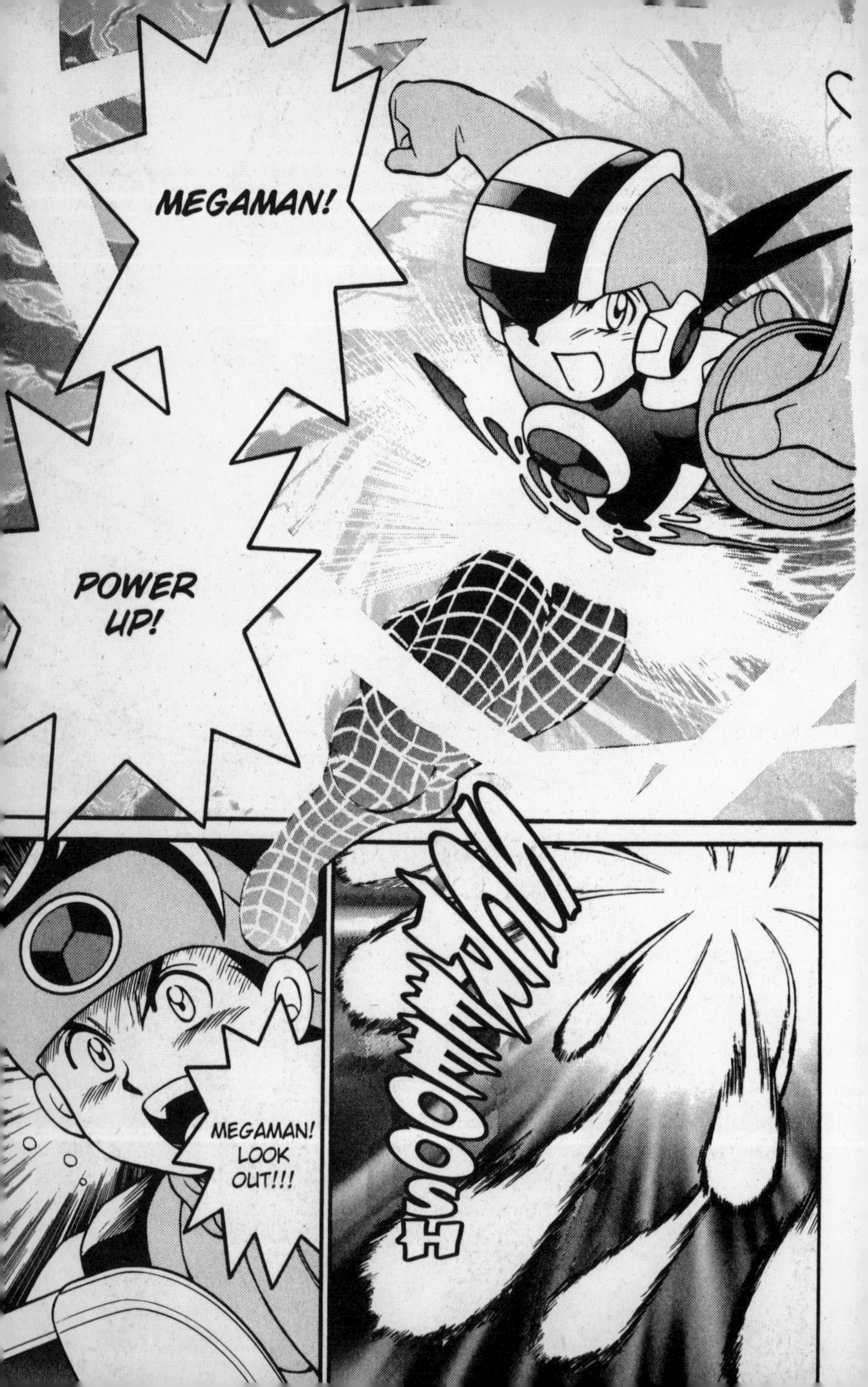
MEGAMAN!
POWER UP!
WHOOSH
MEGAMAN! LOOK OUT!!!

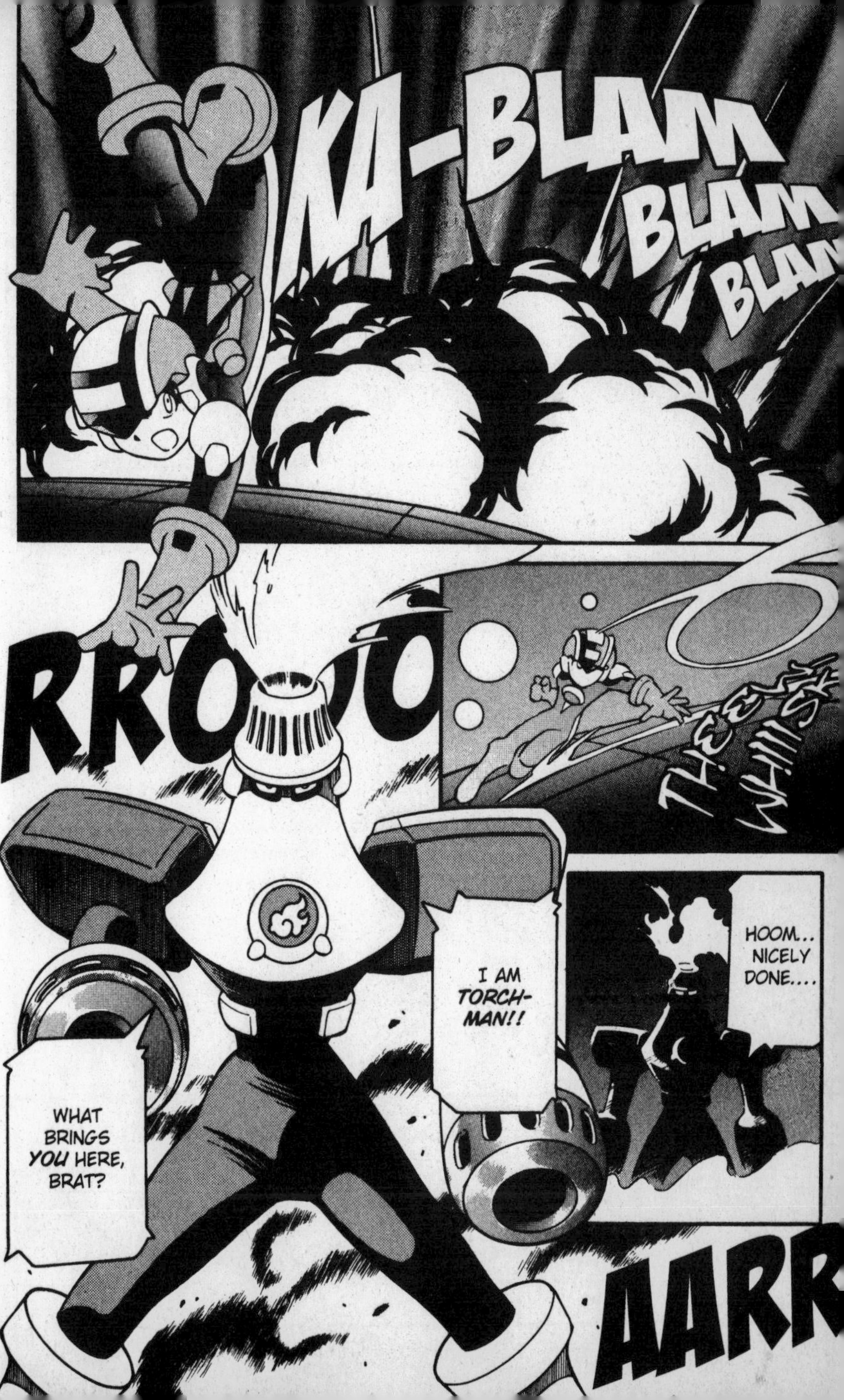
KA-BLAM
BLAM
BLAM
RROOO
HOOM... NICELY DONE....
I AM TORCH-MAN!!
WHAT BRINGS YOU HERE, BRAT?
AARR

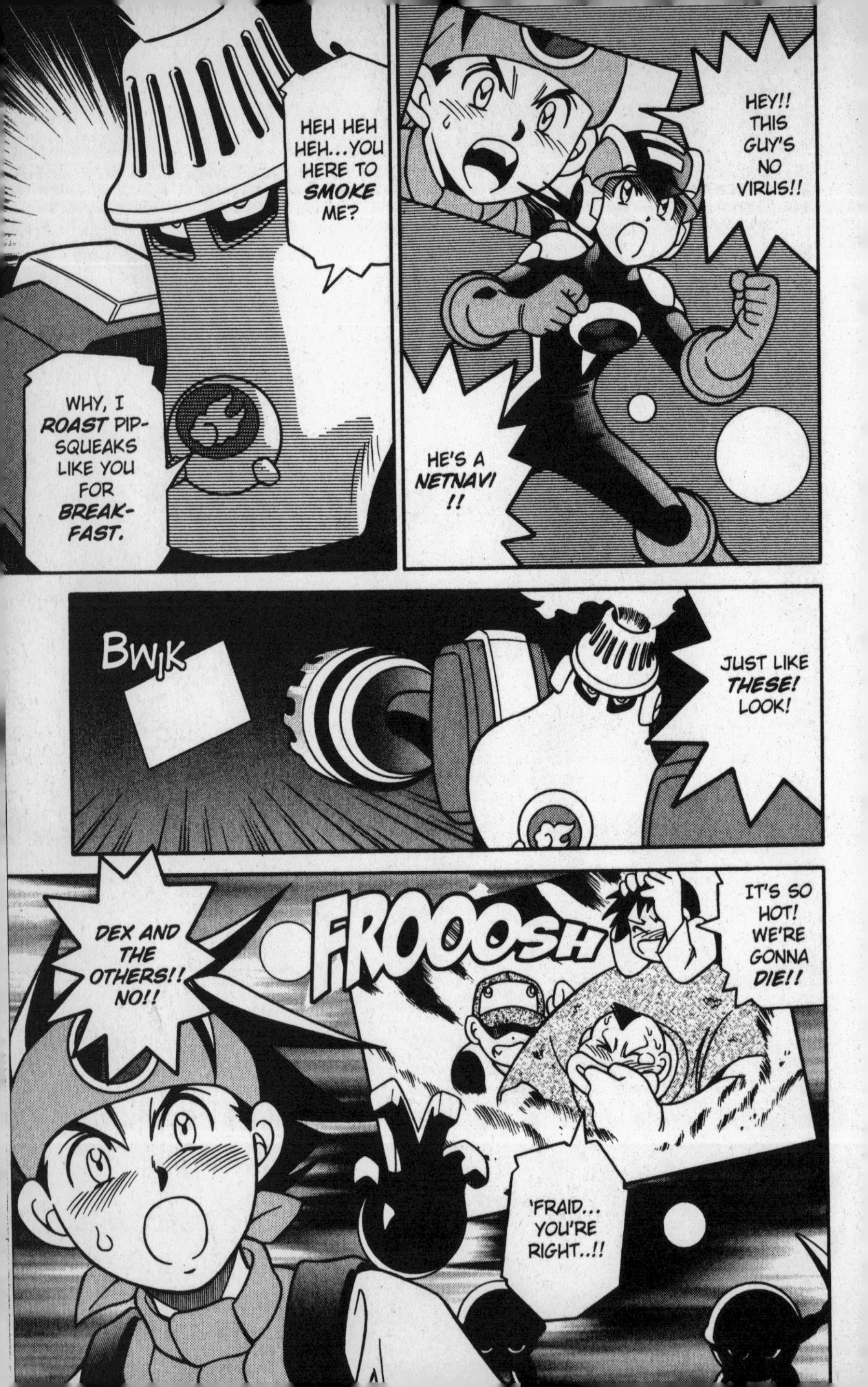
HEY!! THIS GUY'S NO VIRUS!!
HE'S A NETNAVI !!
HEH HEH HEH...YOU HERE TO SMOKE ME?
WHY, I ROAST PIP-SQUEAKS LIKE YOU FOR BREAK-FAST.
JUST LIKE THESE! LOOK!
BWIK
IT'S SO HOT! WE'RE GONNA DIE!!
FROOOSH
DEX AND THE OTHERS!! NO!!
'FRAID... YOU'RE RIGHT..!!

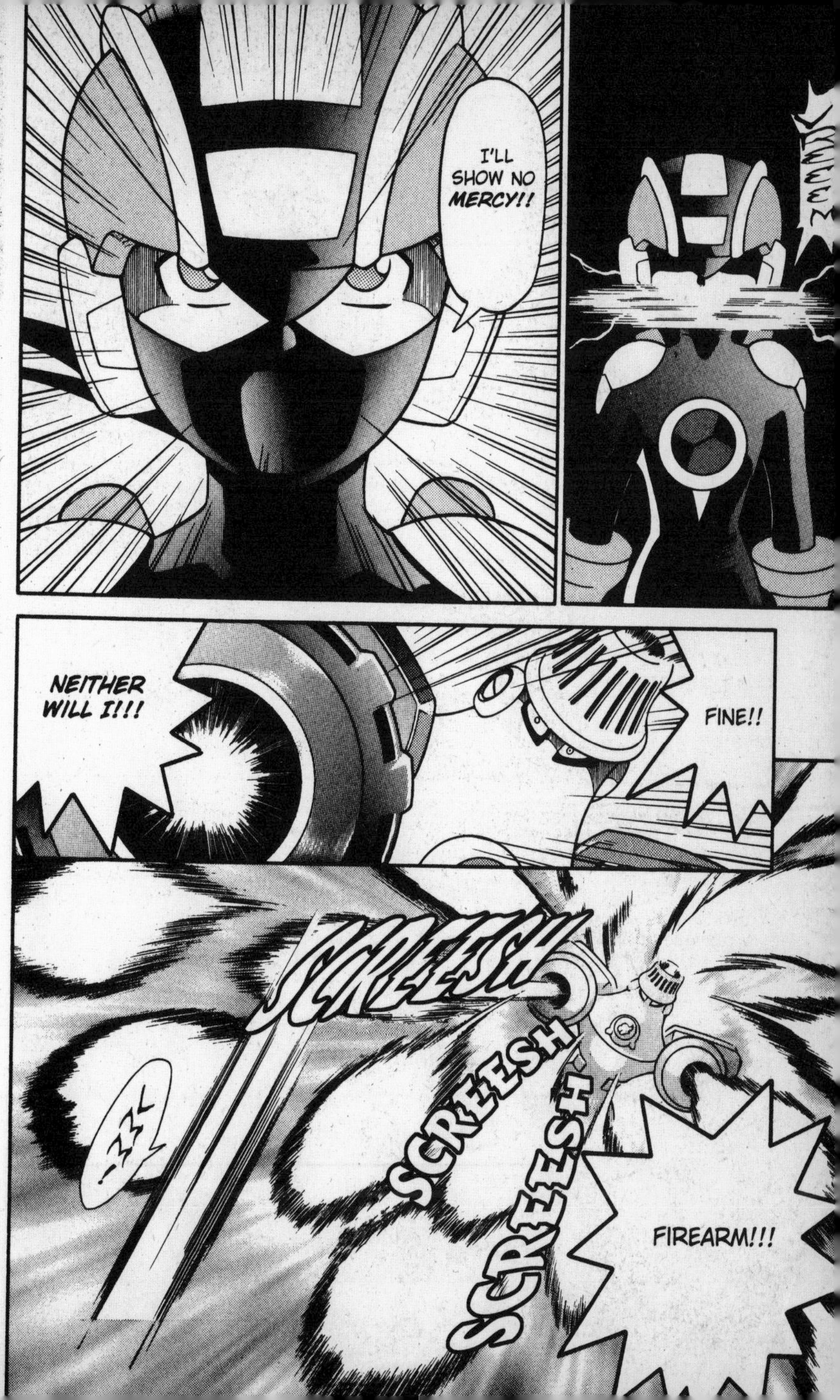
I'LL SHOW NO MERCY!!
FINE!!
NEITHER WILL I!!!
FIREARM!!!
SCREESH
SCREESH
SCREESH

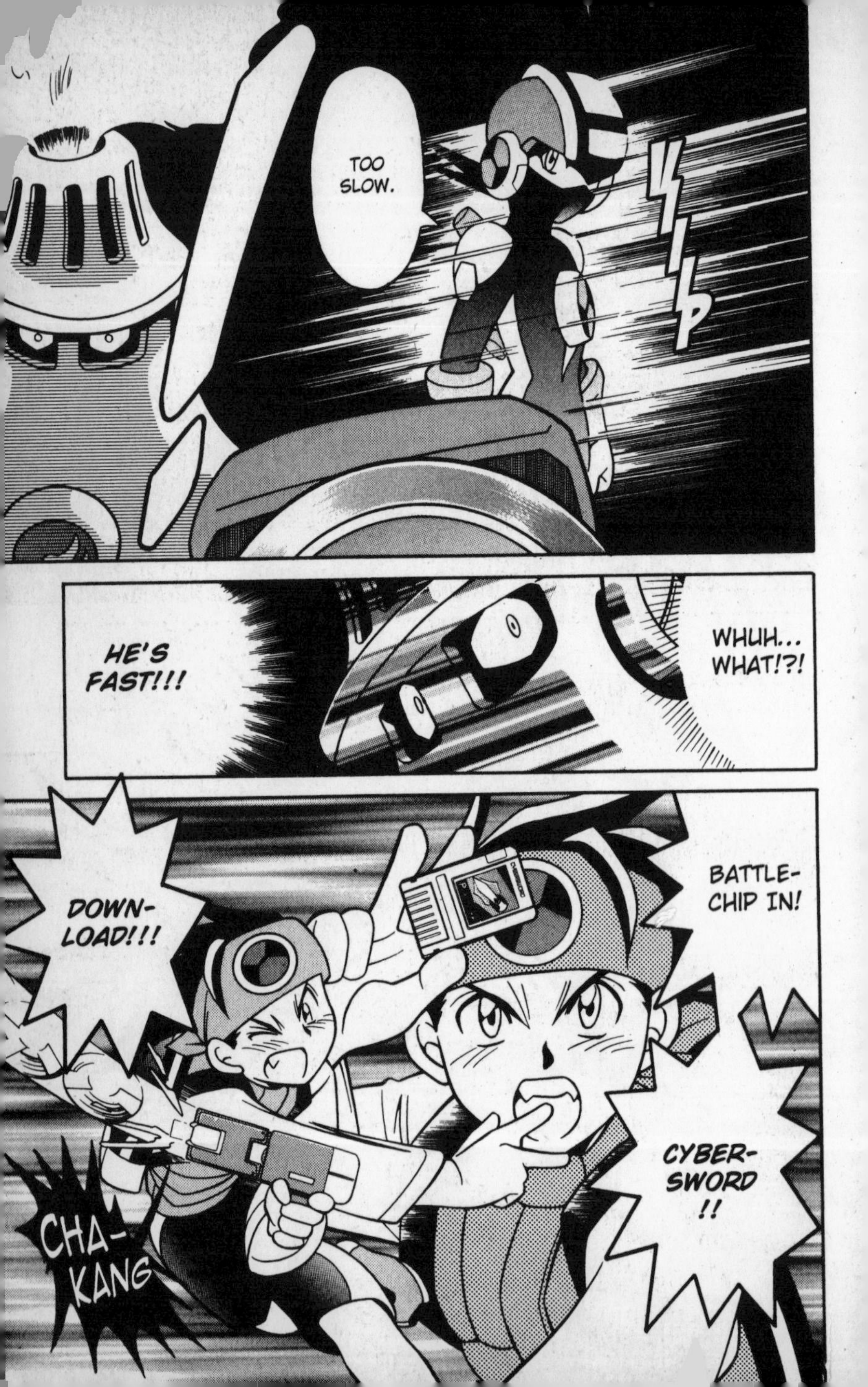
TOO SLOW.
WHUH... WHAT!?!
HE'S FAST!!!
BATTLE-CHIP IN!
DOWN-LOAD!!!
CYBER-SWORD !!
CHA-KANG

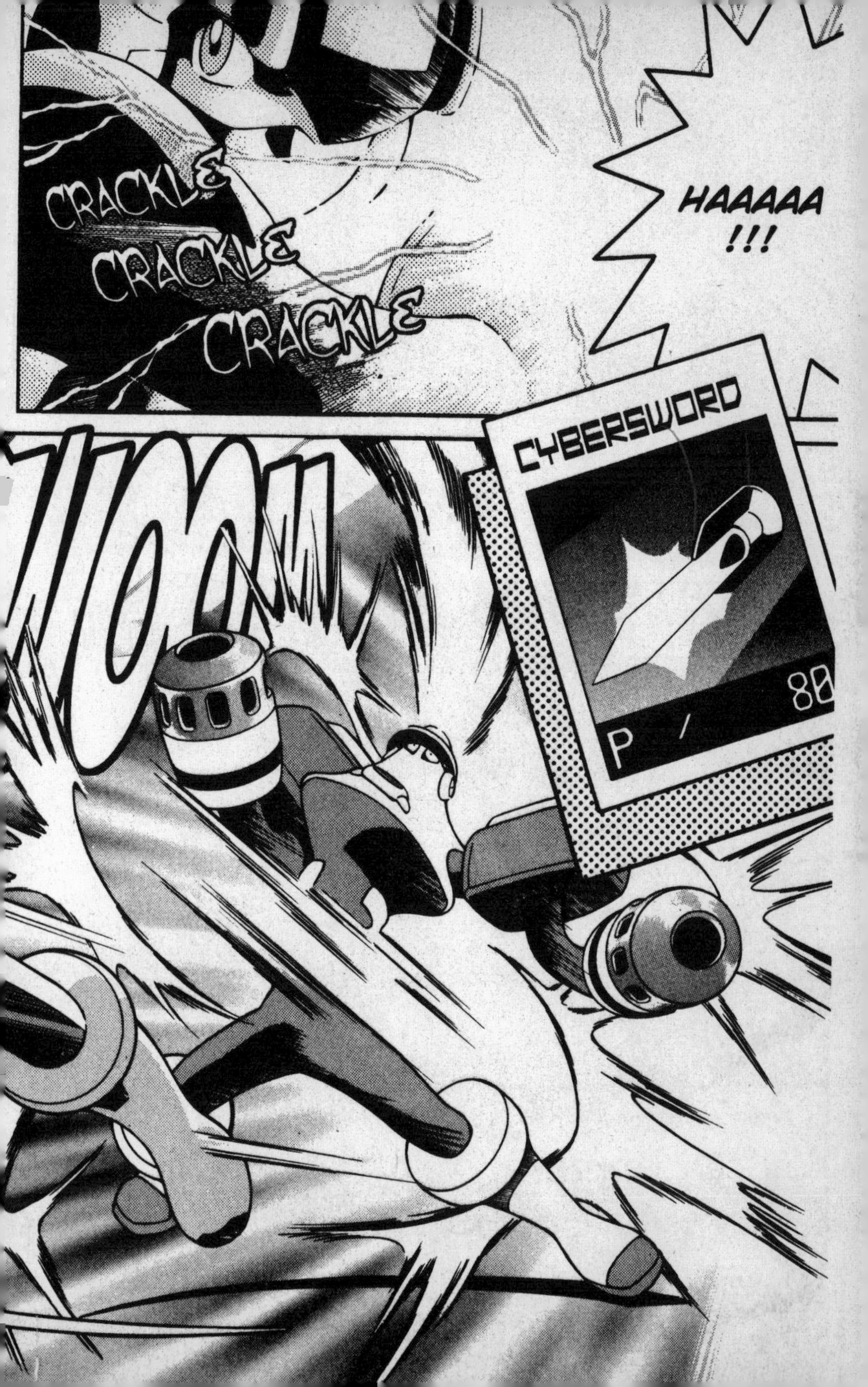
HAAAAA !!!
CRACKLE
CRACKLE
CRACKLE
CYBERSWORD
80
P

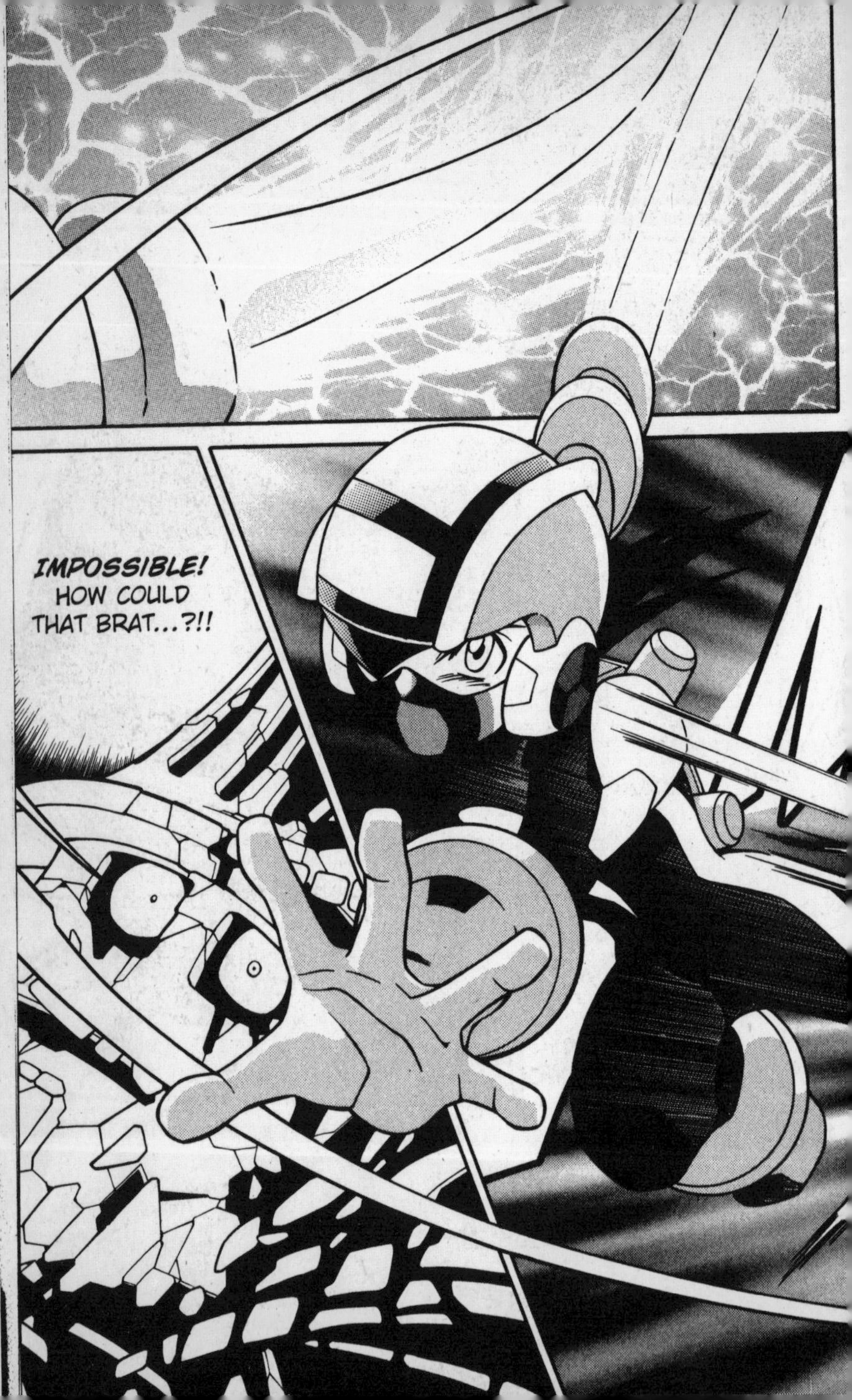
IMPOSSIBLE! HOW COULD THAT BRAT...?!!

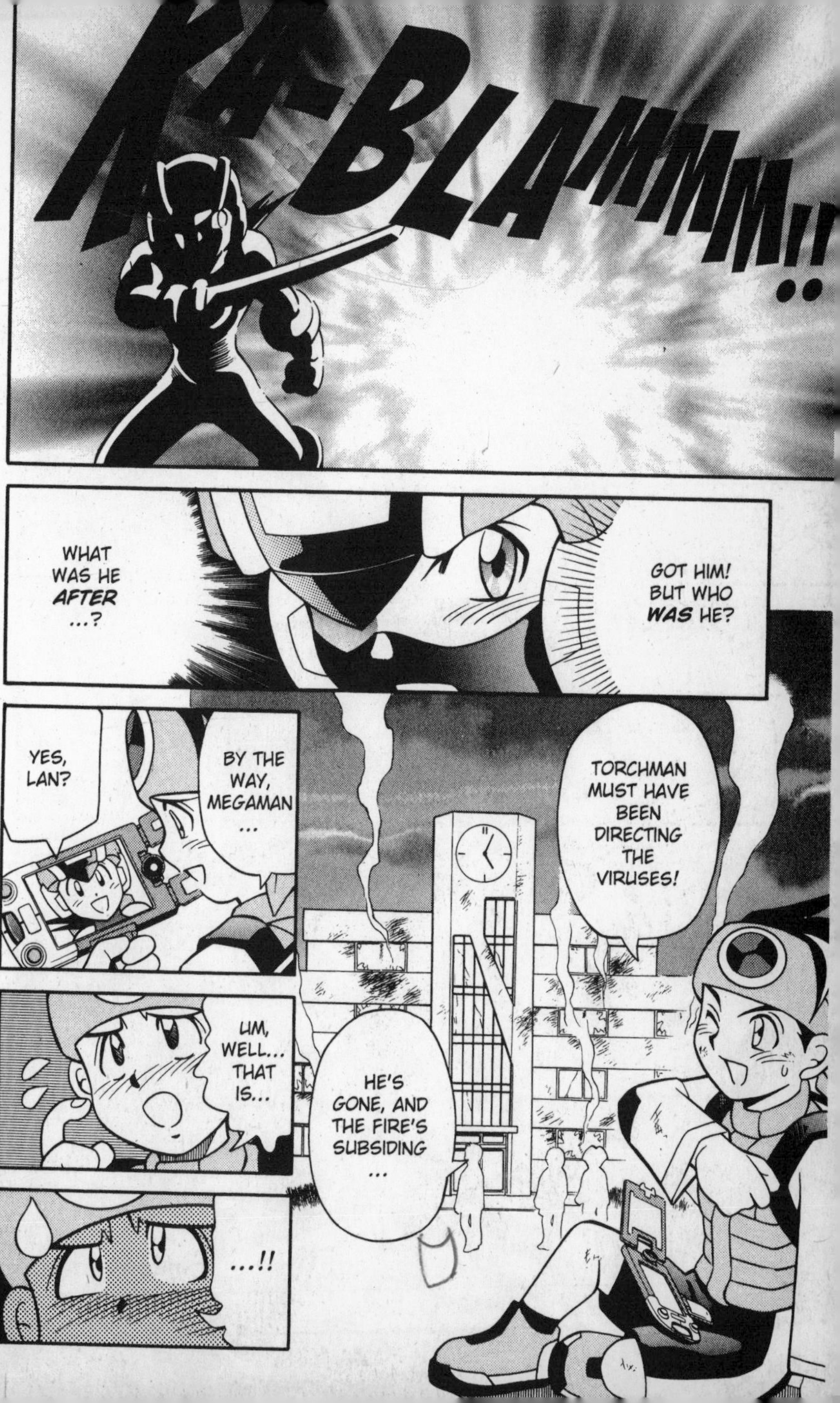
KA-BLAMMM!!
GOT HIM! BUT WHO WAS HE?
WHAT WAS HE AFTER ...?
TORCHMAN MUST HAVE BEEN DIRECTING THE VIRUSES!
HE'S GONE, AND THE FIRE'S SUBSIDING ...
BY THE WAY, MEGAMAN ...
YES, LAN?
UM, WELL... THAT IS...
...!!

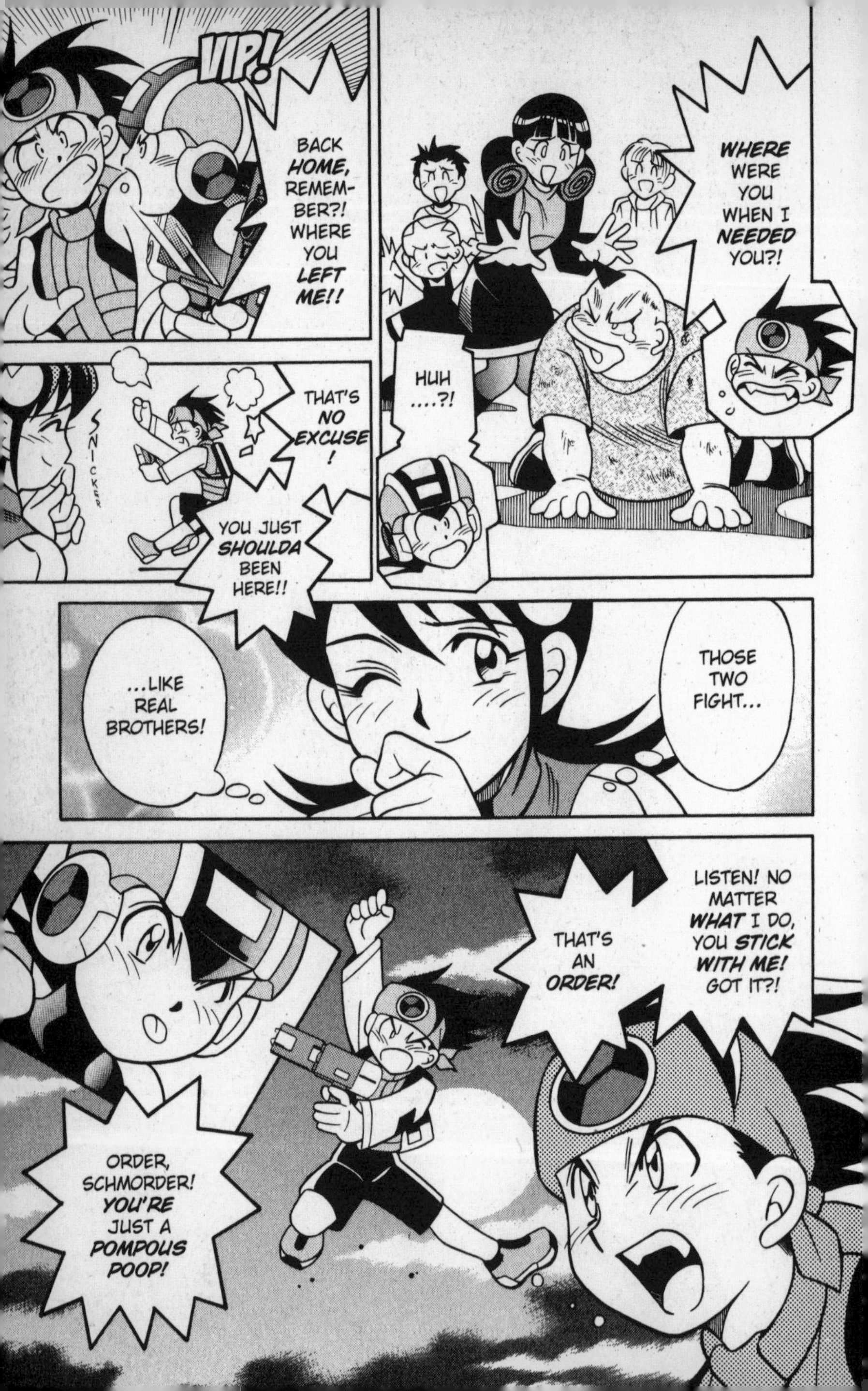

WHERE WERE YOU WHEN I NEEDED YOU?!
HUH ....?!
VIP!
BACK HOME, REMEMBER?! WHERE YOU LEFT ME!!
THAT'S NO EXCUSE!
YOU JUST SHOULDA BEEN HERE!!
SNICKER
THOSE TWO FIGHT...
...LIKE REAL BROTHERS!
LISTEN! NO MATTER WHAT I DO, YOU STICK WITH ME! GOT IT?!
THAT'S AN ORDER!
ORDER, SCHMORDER! YOU'RE JUST A POMPOUS POOP!

CHAPTER 2: TARGET MEGAMAN!!

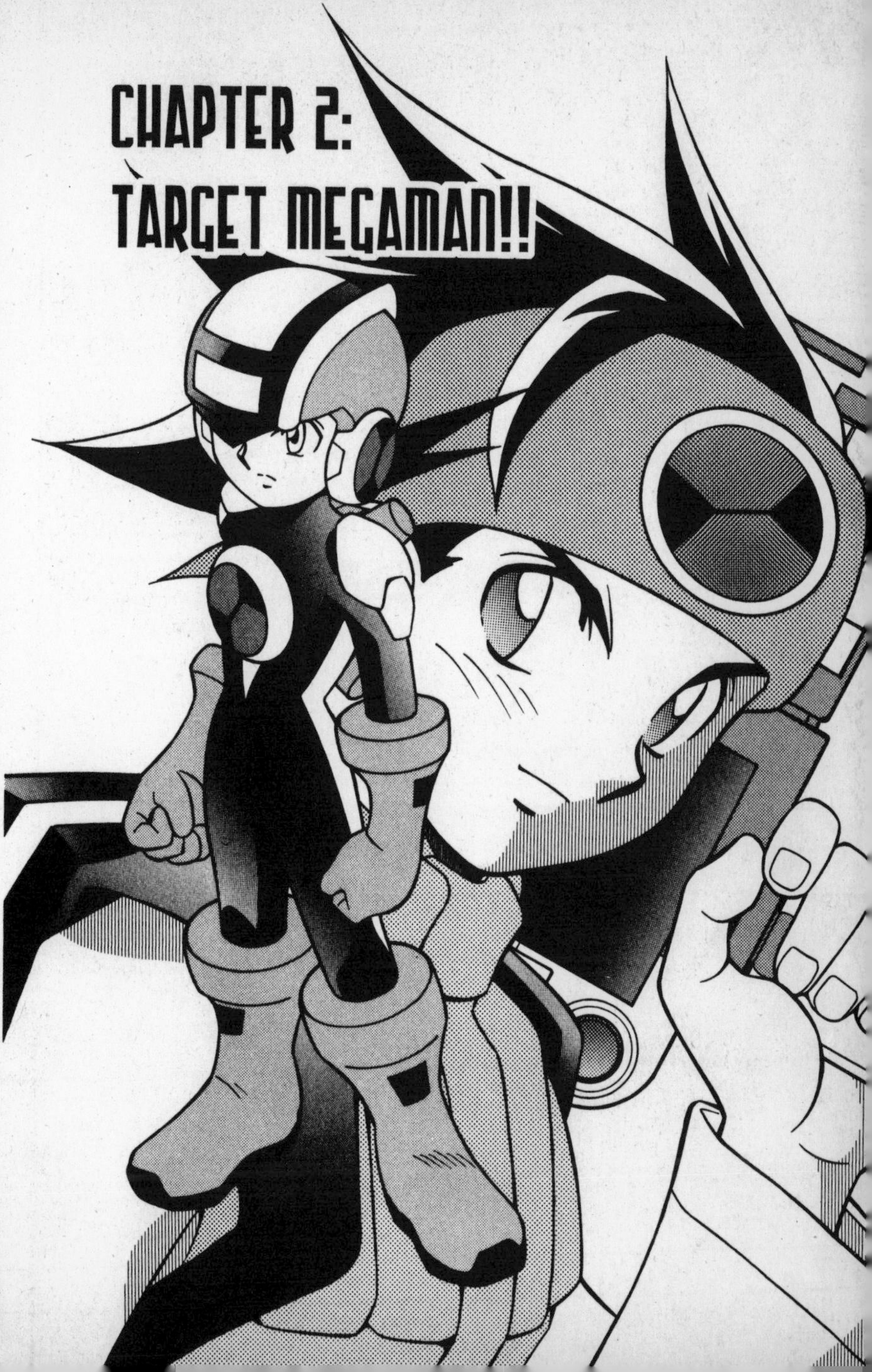

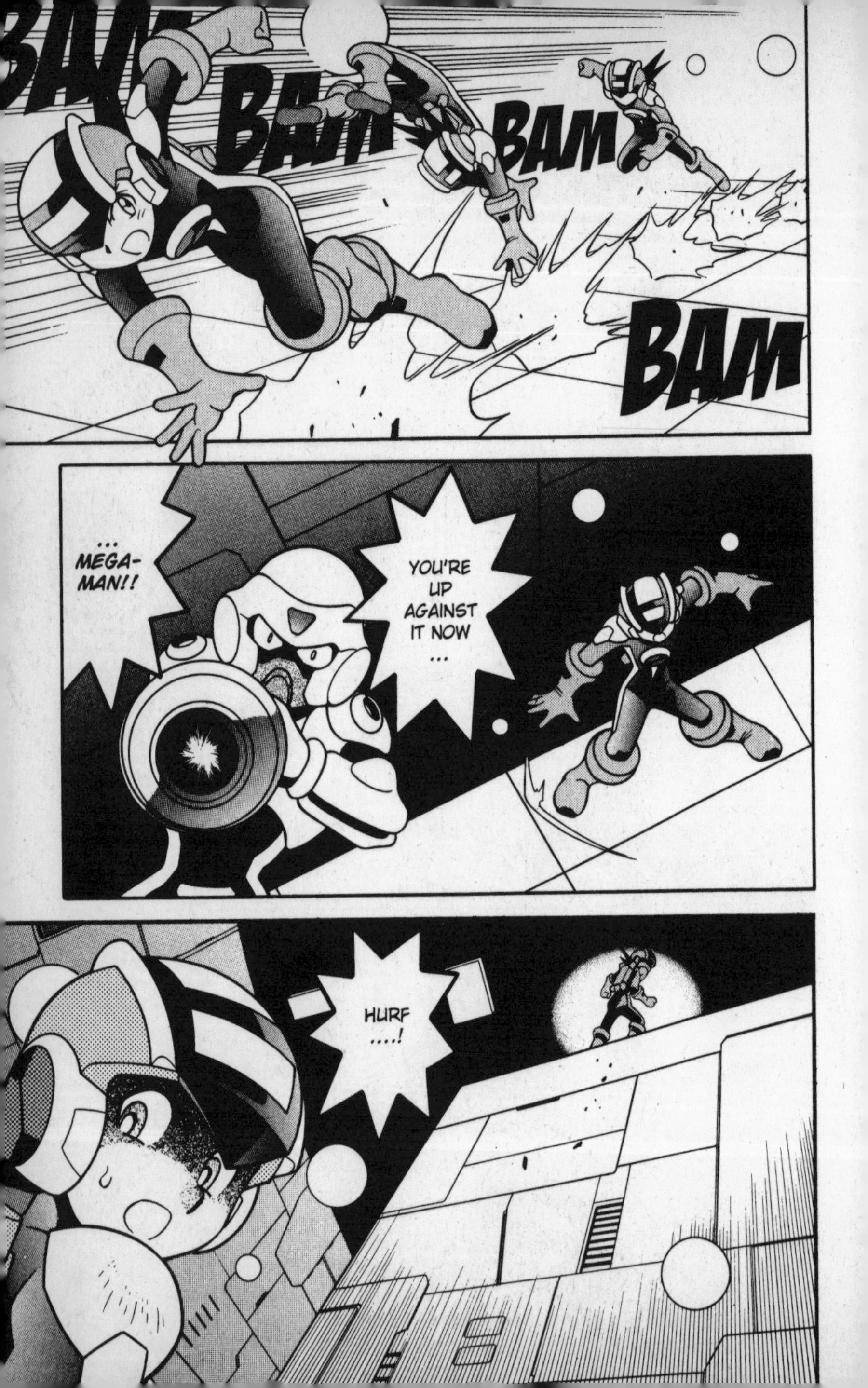
BAM
BAM
BAM
BAM
YOU'RE UP AGAINST IT NOW ...
... MEGA-MAN!!
HURF ....!

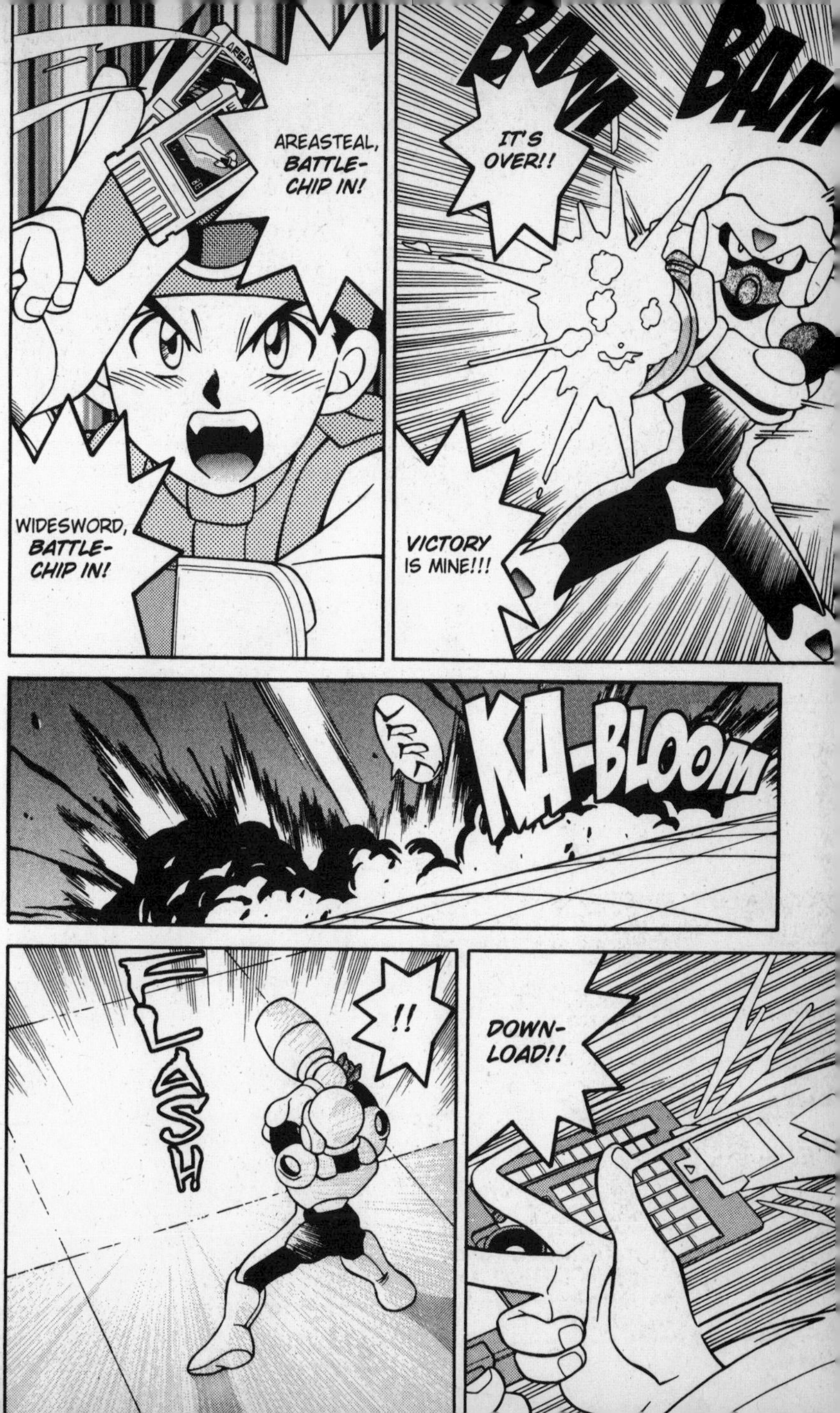
BAM
BAM
IT'S OVER!!
VICTORY IS MINE!!!
AREASTEAL, BATTLE-CHIP IN!
WIDESWORD, BATTLE-CHIP IN!
KA-BLOOM
DOWN-LOAD!!
!!
FLASH

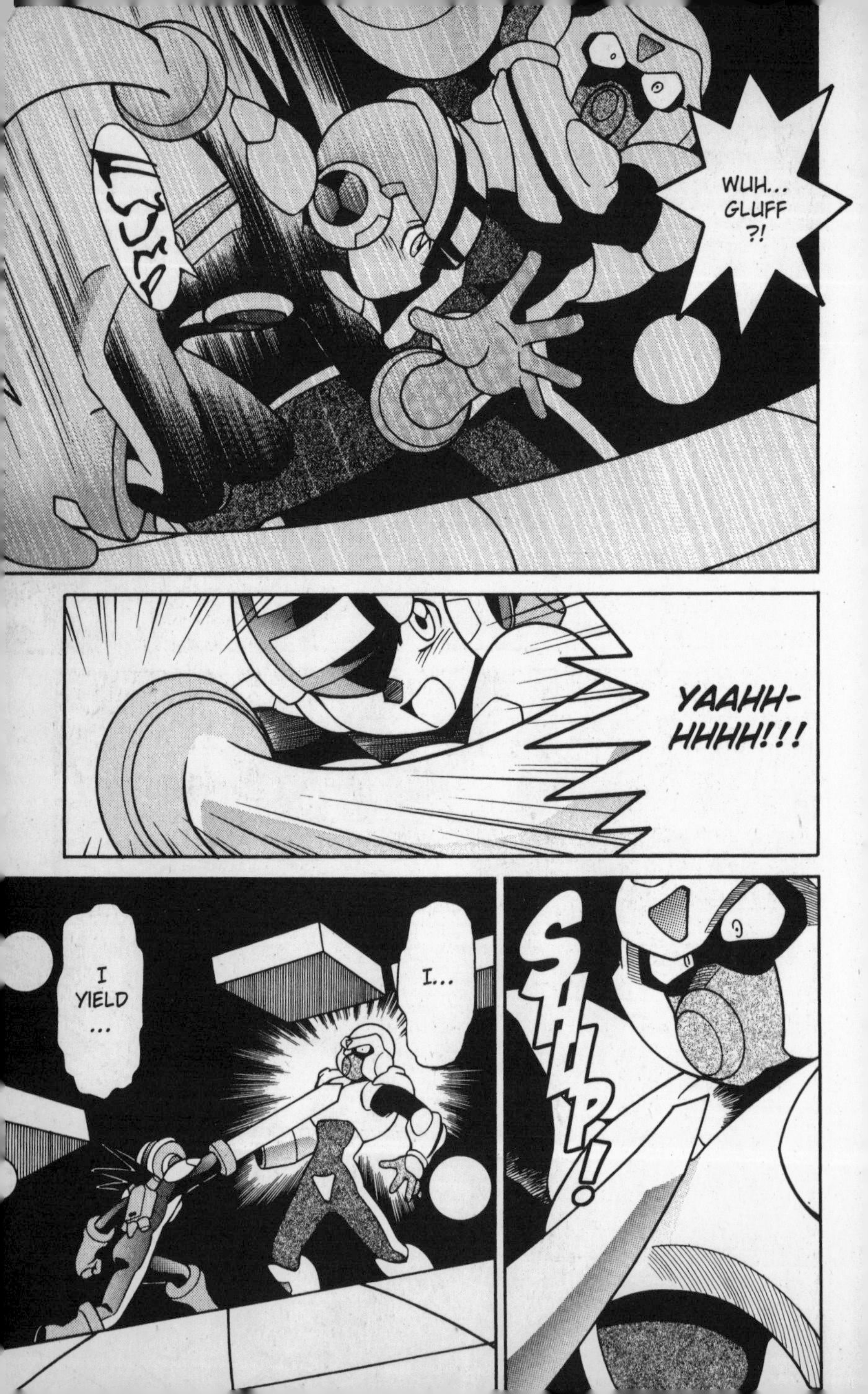
WUH... GLUFF ?!
YAAHH-HHHH!!!
SHUP!
I...
I YIELD ...

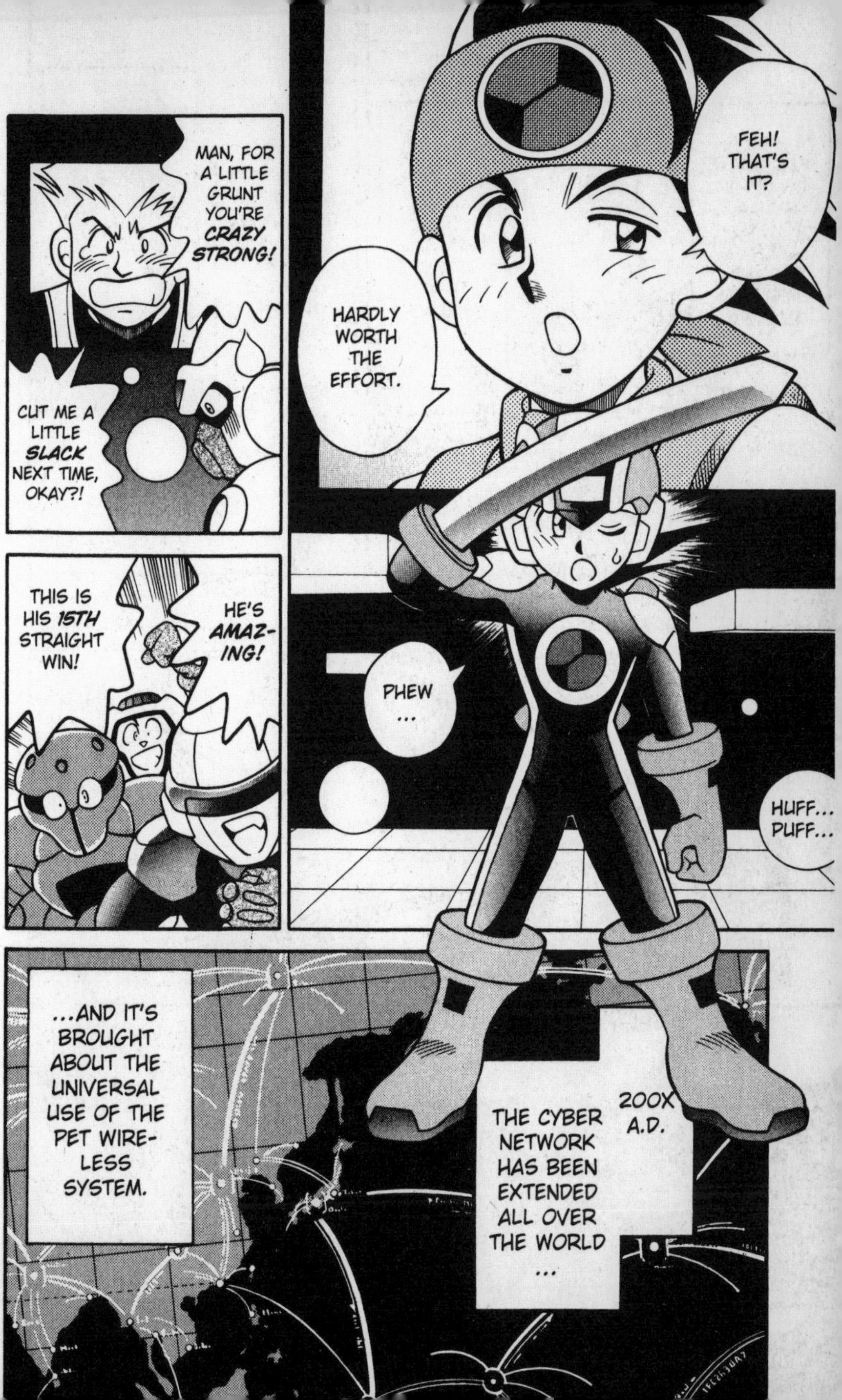
FEH! THAT'S IT?
HARDLY WORTH THE EFFORT.
PHEW ...
HUFF... PUFF...
MAN, FOR A LITTLE GRUNT YOU'RE CRAZY STRONG!
CUT ME A LITTLE SLACK NEXT TIME, OKAY?!
HE'S AMAZ-ING!
THIS IS HIS 15TH STRAIGHT WIN!
200X A.D.
THE CYBER NETWORK HAS BEEN EXTENDED ALL OVER THE WORLD ...
...AND IT'S BROUGHT ABOUT THE UNIVERSAL USE OF THE PET WIRE-LESS SYSTEM.

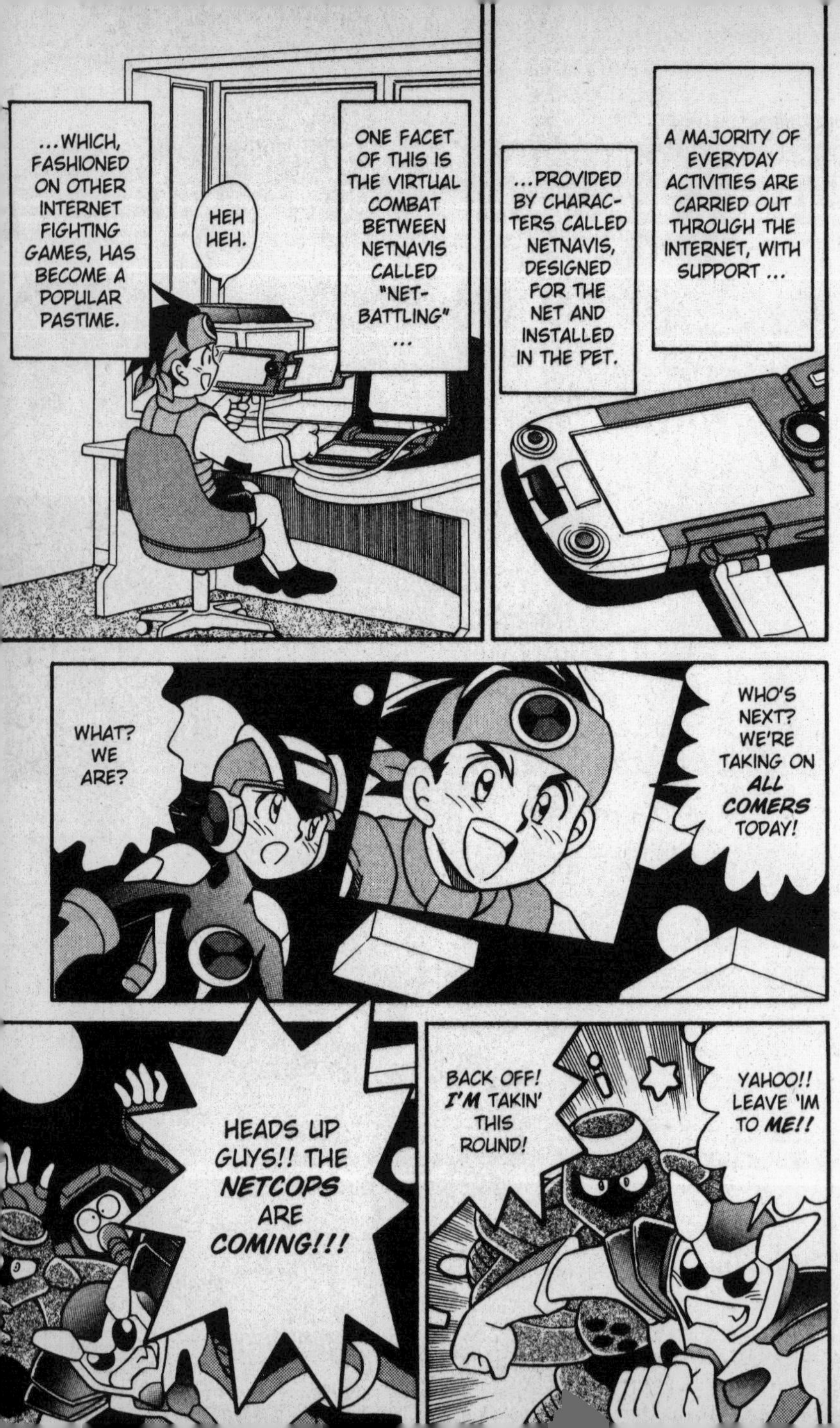
A MAJORITY OF EVERYDAY ACTIVITIES ARE CARRIED OUT THROUGH THE INTERNET, WITH SUPPORT ...
...PROVIDED BY CHARAC-TERS CALLED NETNAVIS, DESIGNED FOR THE NET AND INSTALLED IN THE PET.
ONE FACET OF THIS IS THE VIRTUAL COMBAT BETWEEN NETNAVIS CALLED "NET-BATTLING" ...
HEH HEH.
...WHICH, FASHIONED ON OTHER INTERNET FIGHTING GAMES, HAS BECOME A POPULAR PASTIME.
WHO'S NEXT? WE'RE TAKING ON ALL COMERS TODAY!
WHAT? WE ARE?
YAHOO!! LEAVE 'IM TO ME!!
BACK OFF! I'M TAKIN' THIS ROUND!
HEADS UP GUYS!! THE NETCOPS ARE COMING!!!

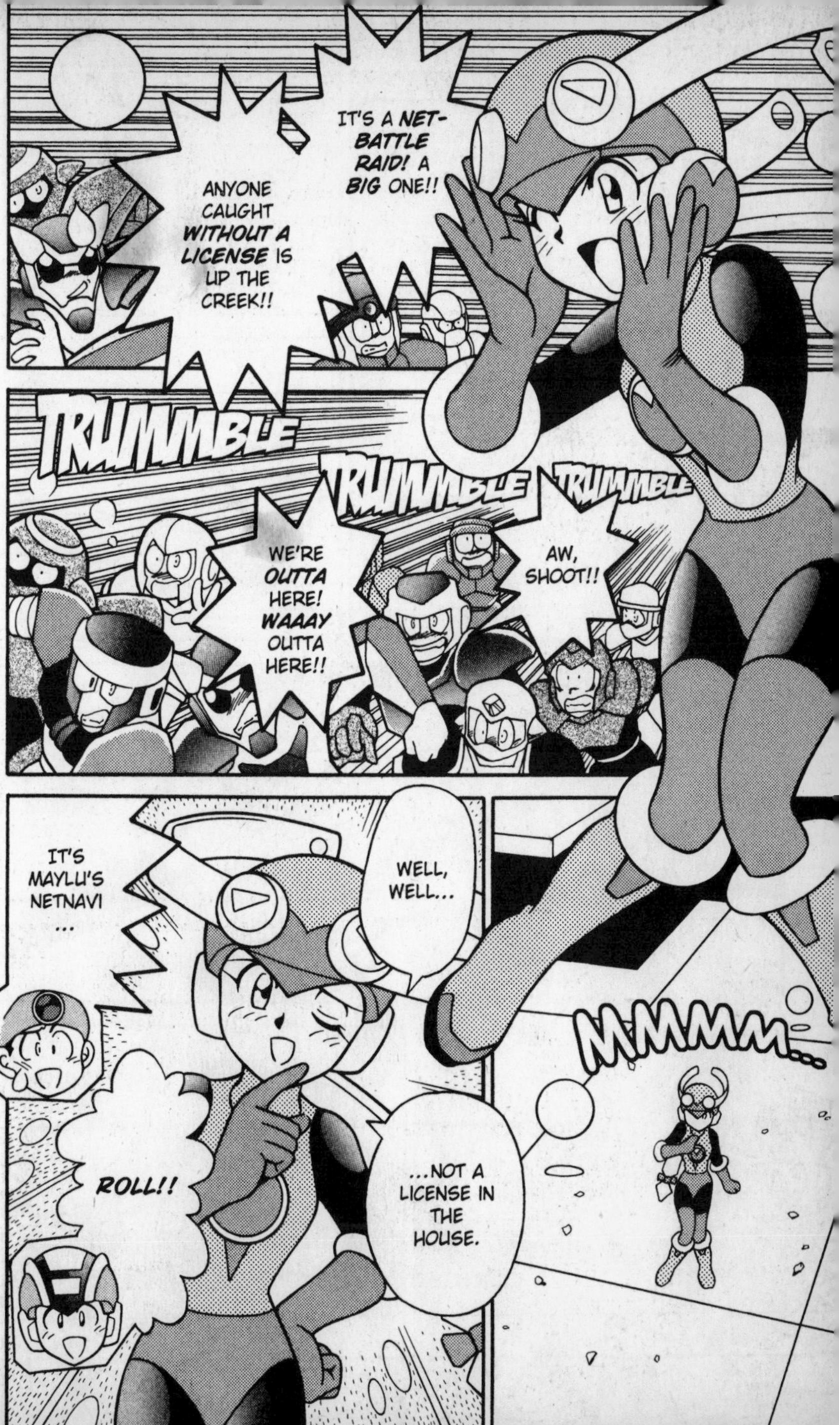

IT'S A NET-BATTLE RAID! A BIG ONE!!
ANYONE CAUGHT WITHOUT A LICENSE IS UP THE CREEK!!
TRUMMBLE
TRUMMBLE
TRUMMBLE
AW, SHOOT!!
WE'RE OUTTA HERE! WAAAY OUTTA HERE!!
MMMMM...
WELL, WELL...
IT'S MAYLU'S NETNAVI...
...NOT A LICENSE IN THE HOUSE.
ROLL!!

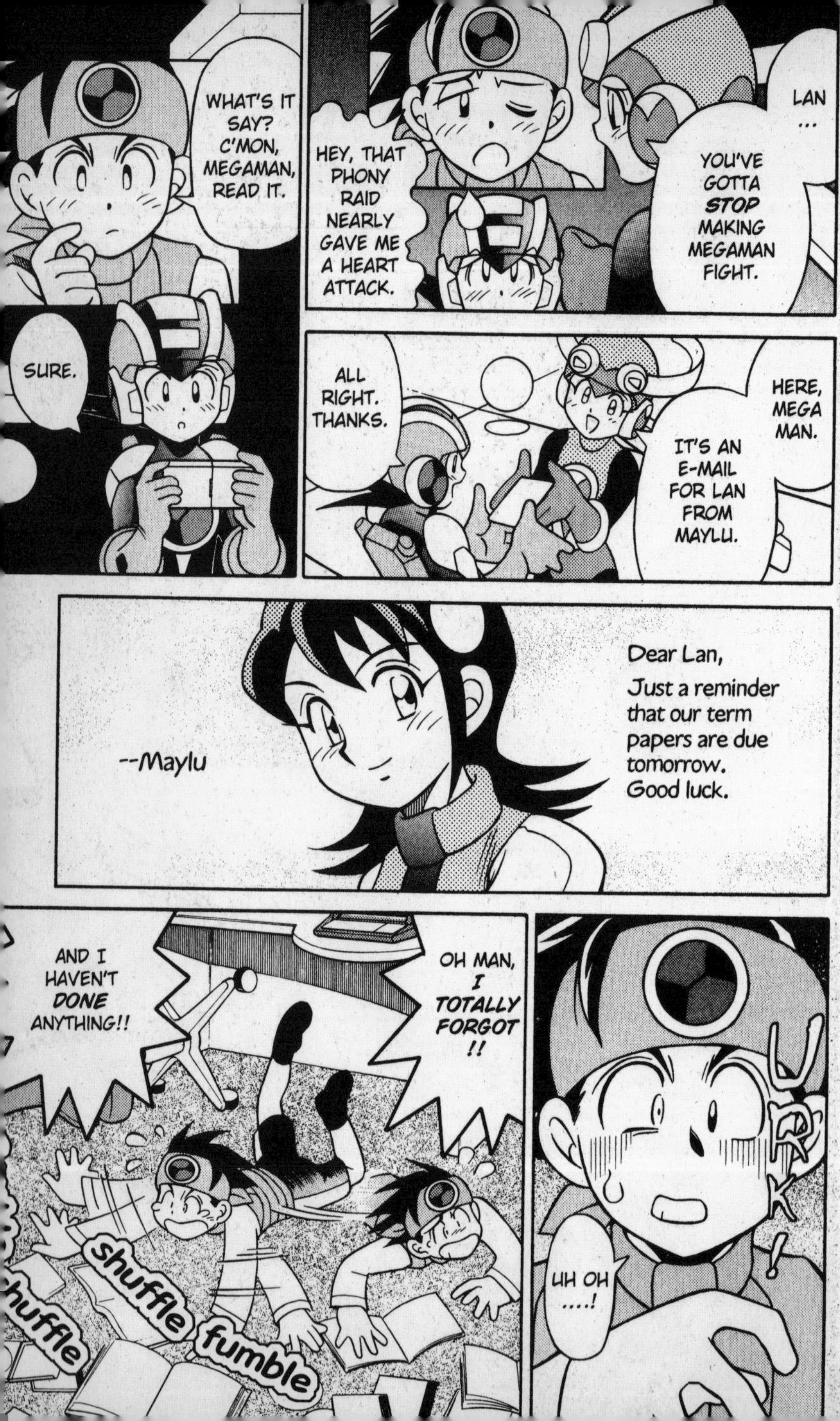

LAN ...
YOU'VE GOTTA *STOP* MAKING MEGAMAN FIGHT.
HEY, THAT PHONY RAID NEARLY GAVE ME A HEART ATTACK.
WHAT'S IT SAY? C'MON, MEGAMAN, READ IT.
HERE, MEGA MAN.
IT'S AN E-MAIL FOR LAN FROM MAYLU.
ALL RIGHT. THANKS.
SURE.
Dear Lan,
Just a reminder that our term papers are due tomorrow. Good luck.
--Maylu
UH OH ....!
OH MAN, *I TOTALLY FORGOT* !!
AND I HAVEN'T *DONE* ANYTHING!!
fumble
shuffle
shuffle

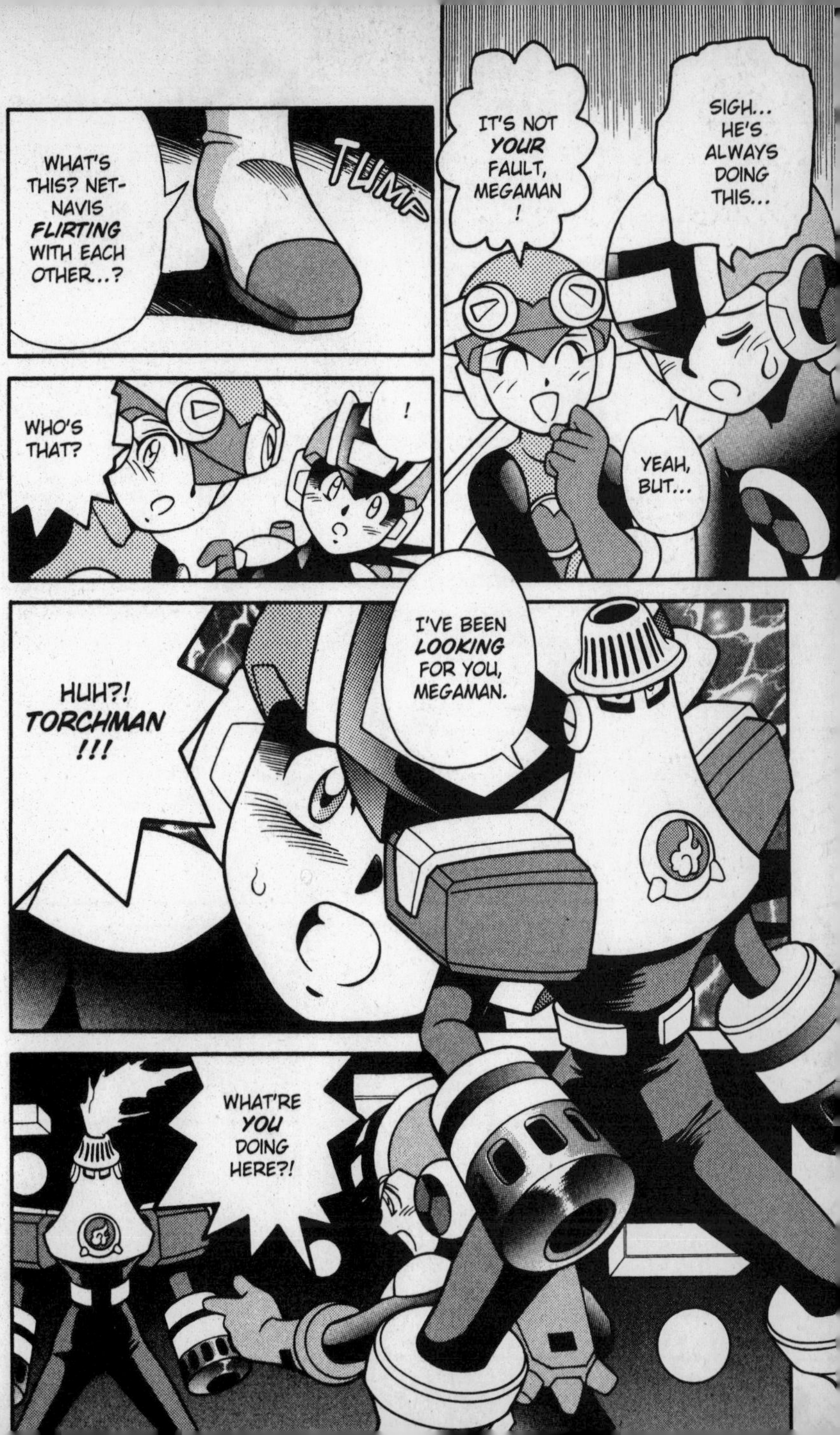
SIGH... HE'S ALWAYS DOING THIS...
IT'S NOT YOUR FAULT, MEGAMAN!
YEAH, BUT...
TUMP
WHAT'S THIS? NET-NAVIS FLIRTING WITH EACH OTHER...?
!
WHO'S THAT?
I'VE BEEN LOOKING FOR YOU, MEGAMAN.
HUH?! TORCHMAN!!!
WHAT'RE YOU DOING HERE?!

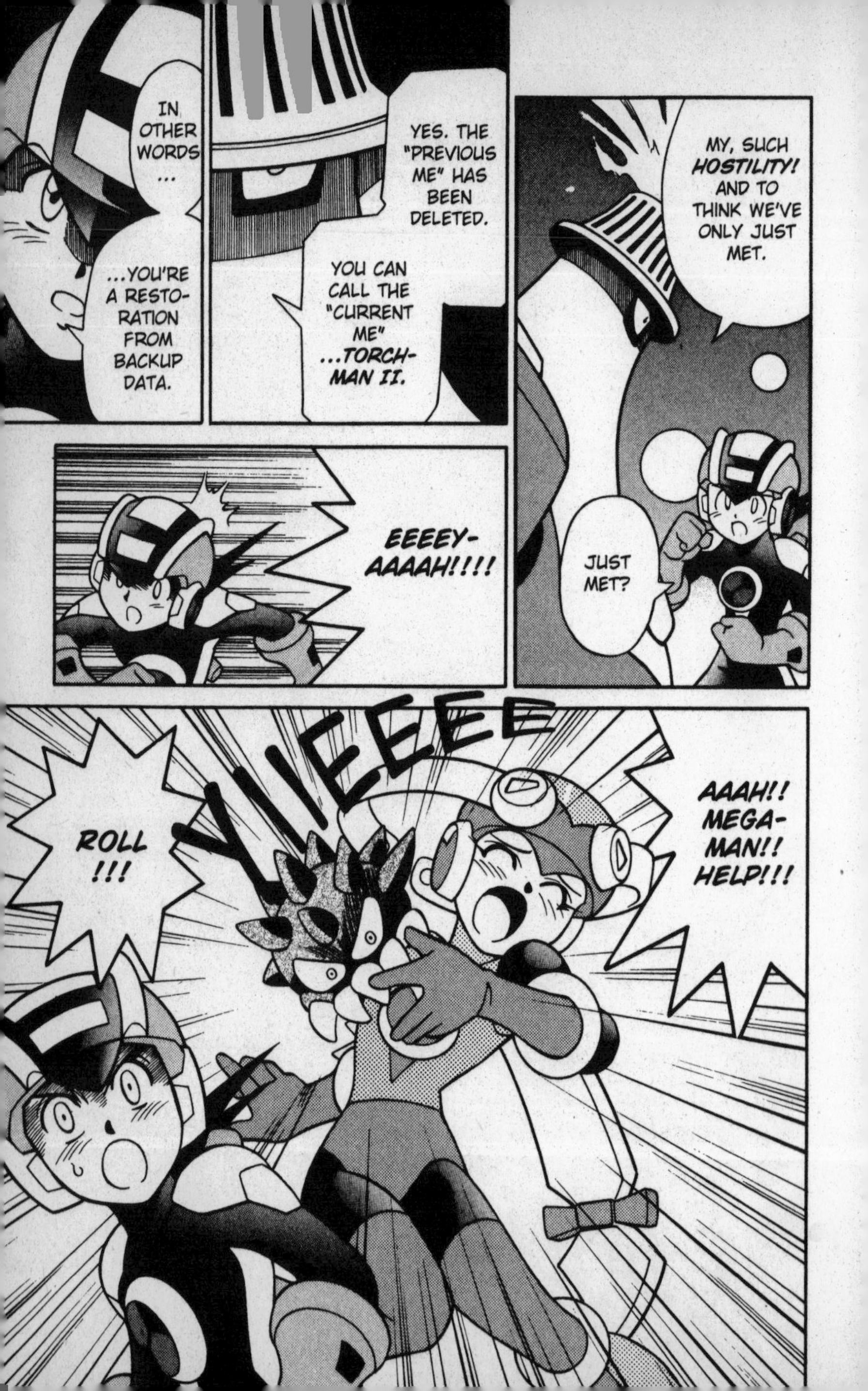
IN OTHER WORDS ...
...YOU'RE A RESTO-RATION FROM BACKUP DATA.
YES. THE "PREVIOUS ME" HAS BEEN DELETED.
YOU CAN CALL THE "CURRENT ME" ...TORCH-MAN II.
MY, SUCH HOSTILITY! AND TO THINK WE'VE ONLY JUST MET.
JUST MET?
EEEEY-AAAAH!!!!
ROLL !!!
YIIEEEEE
AAAH!! SUCH MEGA-MAN!! HELP!!!

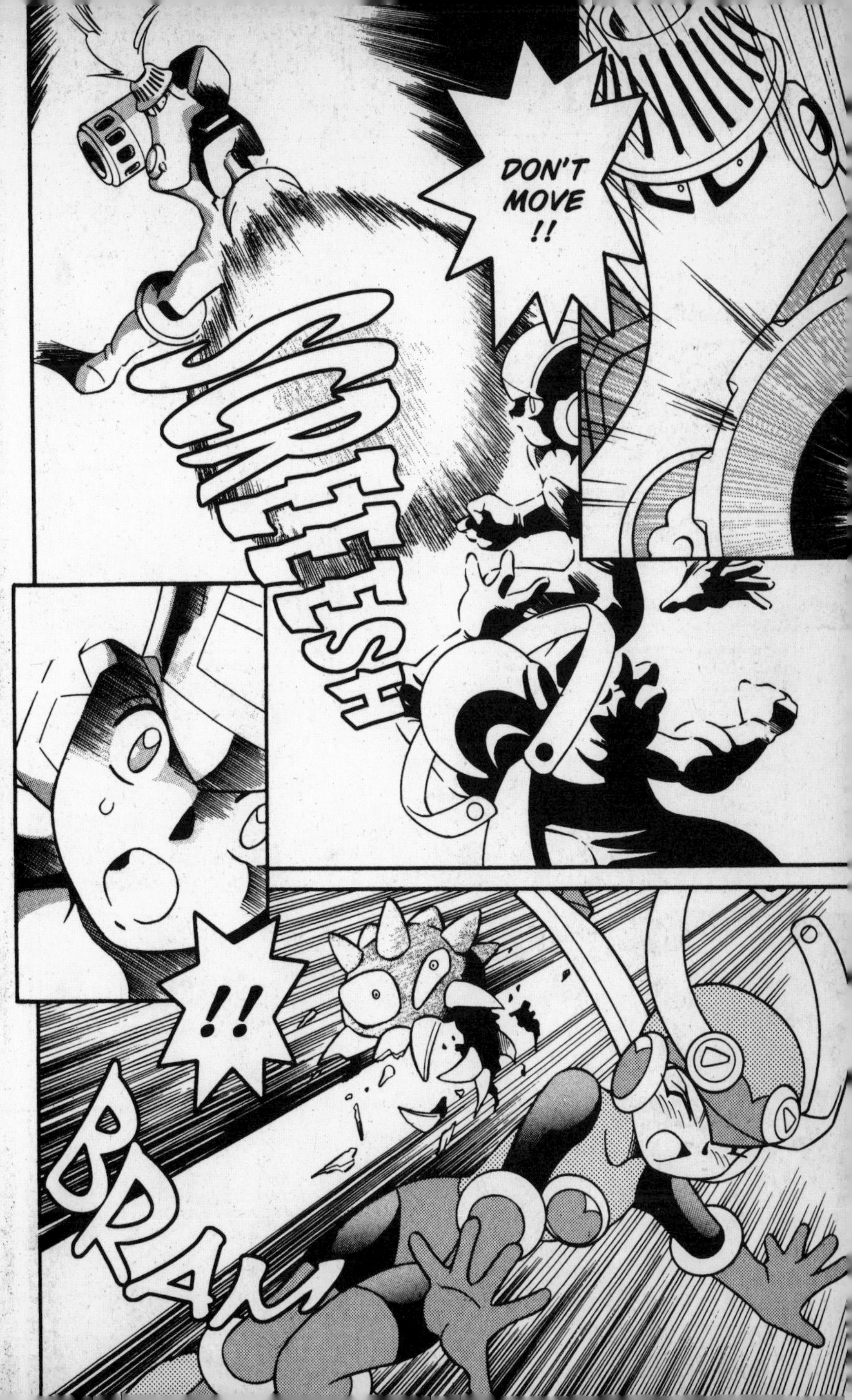
DON'T MOVE !!
SCREEEESH
!!
BRAM

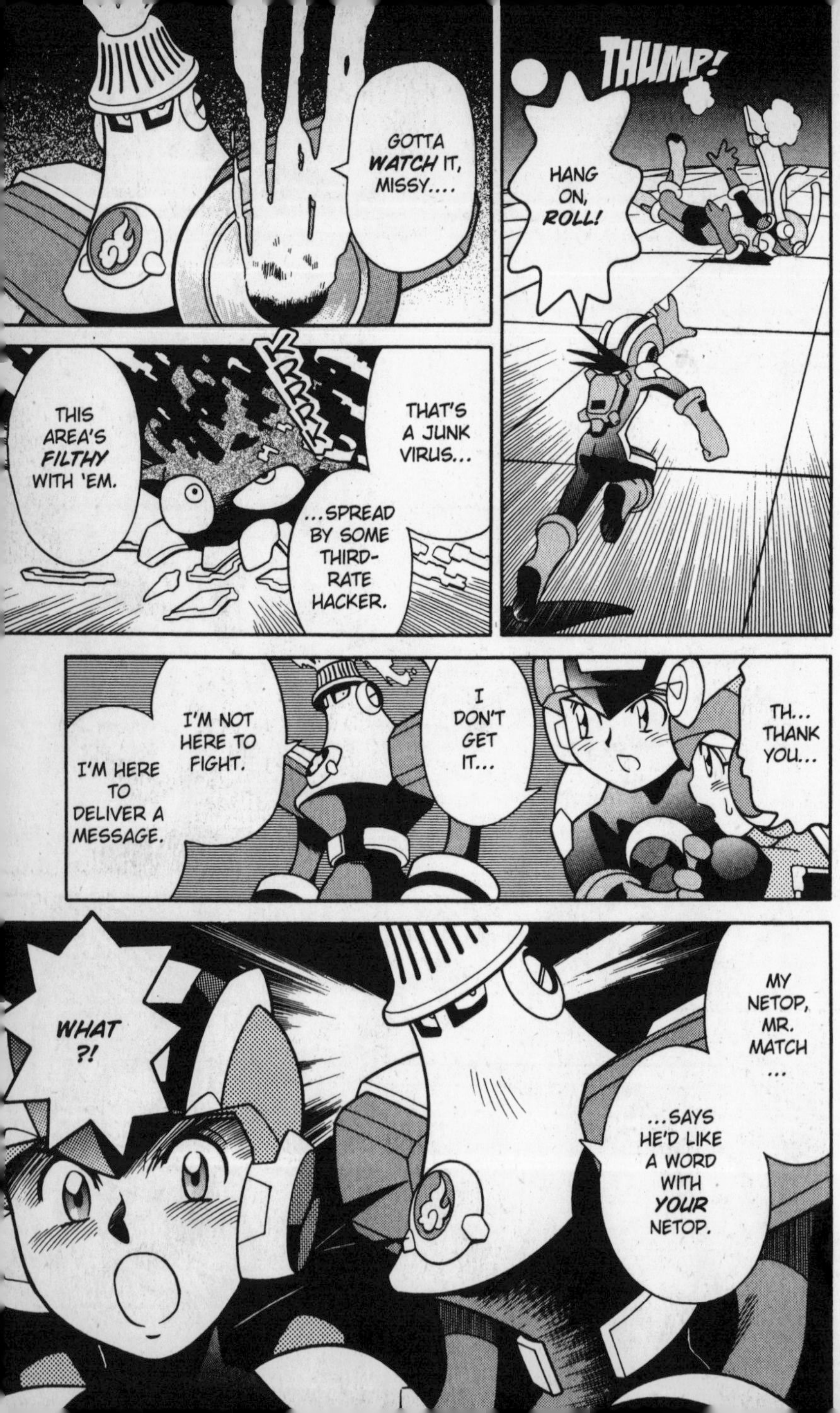
THUMP!
HANG ON, ROLL!
GOTTA WATCH IT, MISSY....
THAT'S A JUNK VIRUS...
...SPREAD BY SOME THIRD-RATE HACKER.
THIS AREA'S FILTHY WITH 'EM.
TH... THANK YOU...
I DON'T GET IT...
I'M NOT HERE TO FIGHT.
I'M HERE TO DELIVER A MESSAGE.
MY NETOP, MR. MATCH ...
...SAYS HE'D LIKE A WORD WITH YOUR NETOP.
WHAT?!

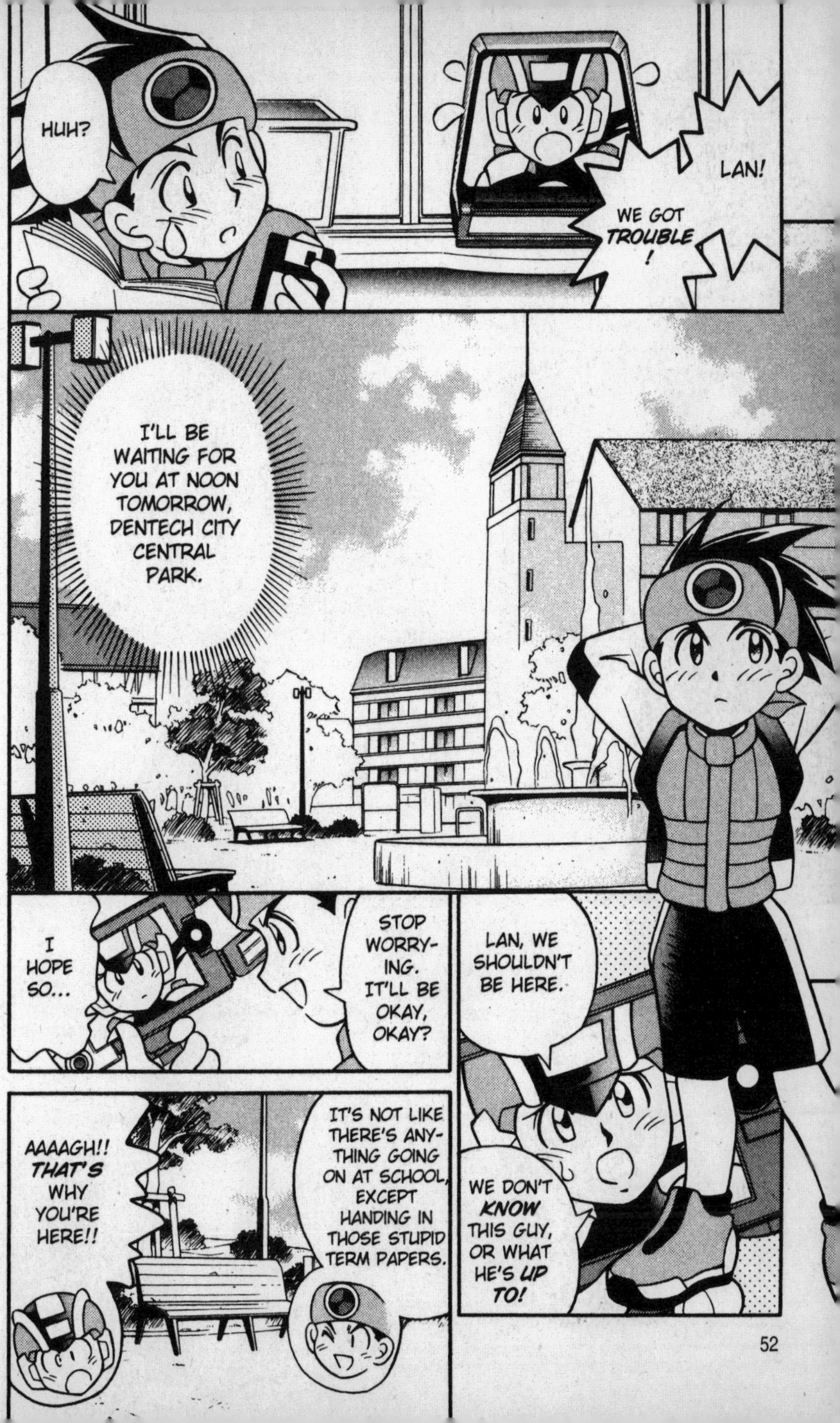
LAN!
WE GOT TROUBLE!
HUH?
I'LL BE WAITING FOR YOU AT NOON TOMORROW, DENTECH CITY CENTRAL PARK.
LAN, WE SHOULDN'T BE HERE.
WE DON'T KNOW THIS GUY, OR WHAT HE'S UP TO!
STOP WORRYING. IT'LL BE OKAY, OKAY?
I HOPE SO...
IT'S NOT LIKE THERE'S ANYTHING GOING ON AT SCHOOL, EXCEPT HANDING IN THOSE STUPID TERM PAPERS.
AAAAGH!! THAT'S WHY YOU'RE HERE!!

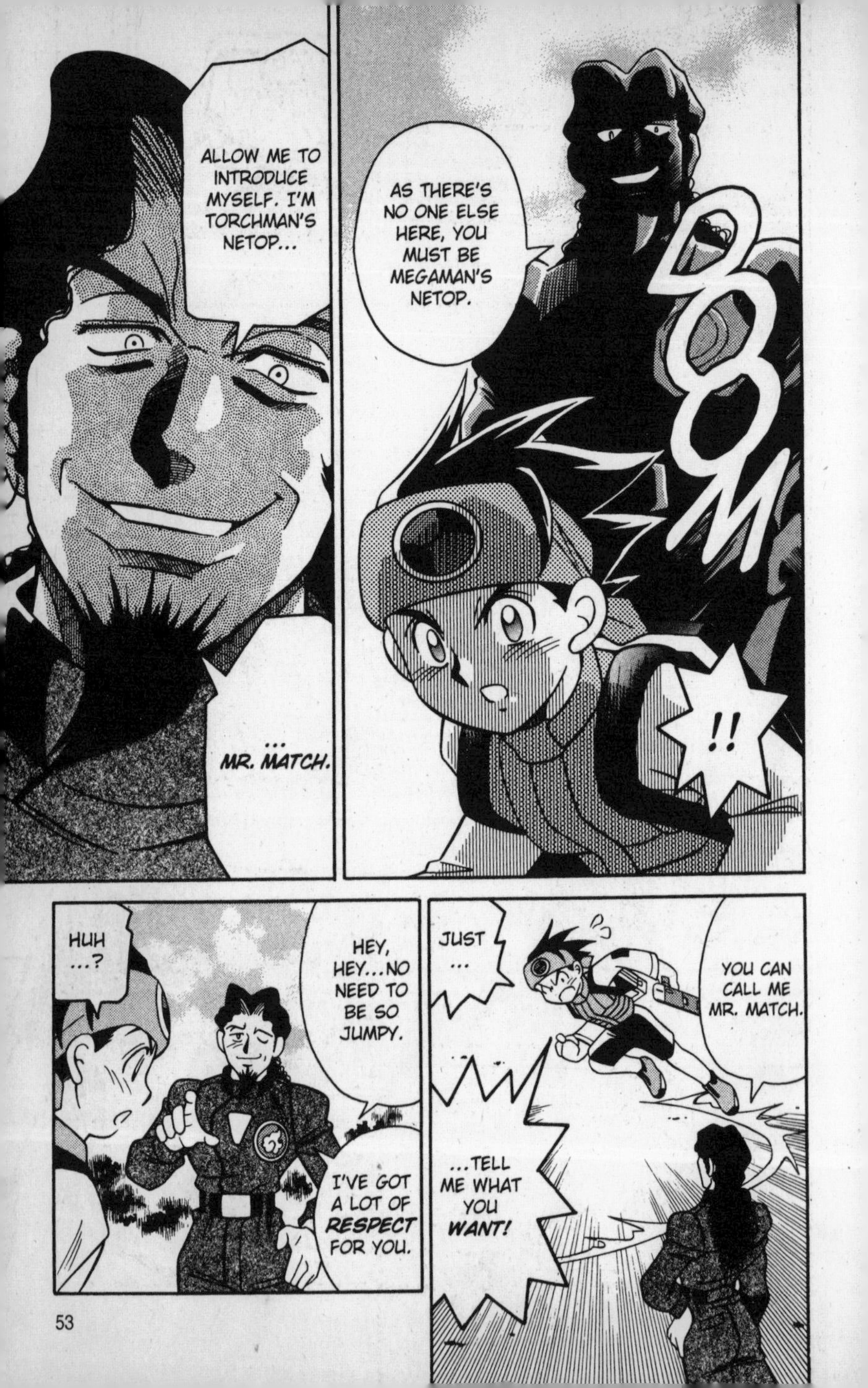
AS THERE'S NO ONE ELSE HERE, YOU MUST BE MEGAMAN'S NETOP.
DOOM
!!
ALLOW ME TO INTRODUCE MYSELF. I'M TORCHMAN'S NETOP...
...MR. MATCH.
YOU CAN CALL ME MR. MATCH.
JUST...
...TELL ME WHAT YOU WANT!
HEY, HEY...NO NEED TO BE SO JUMPY.
HUH...?
I'VE GOT A LOT OF RESPECT FOR YOU.

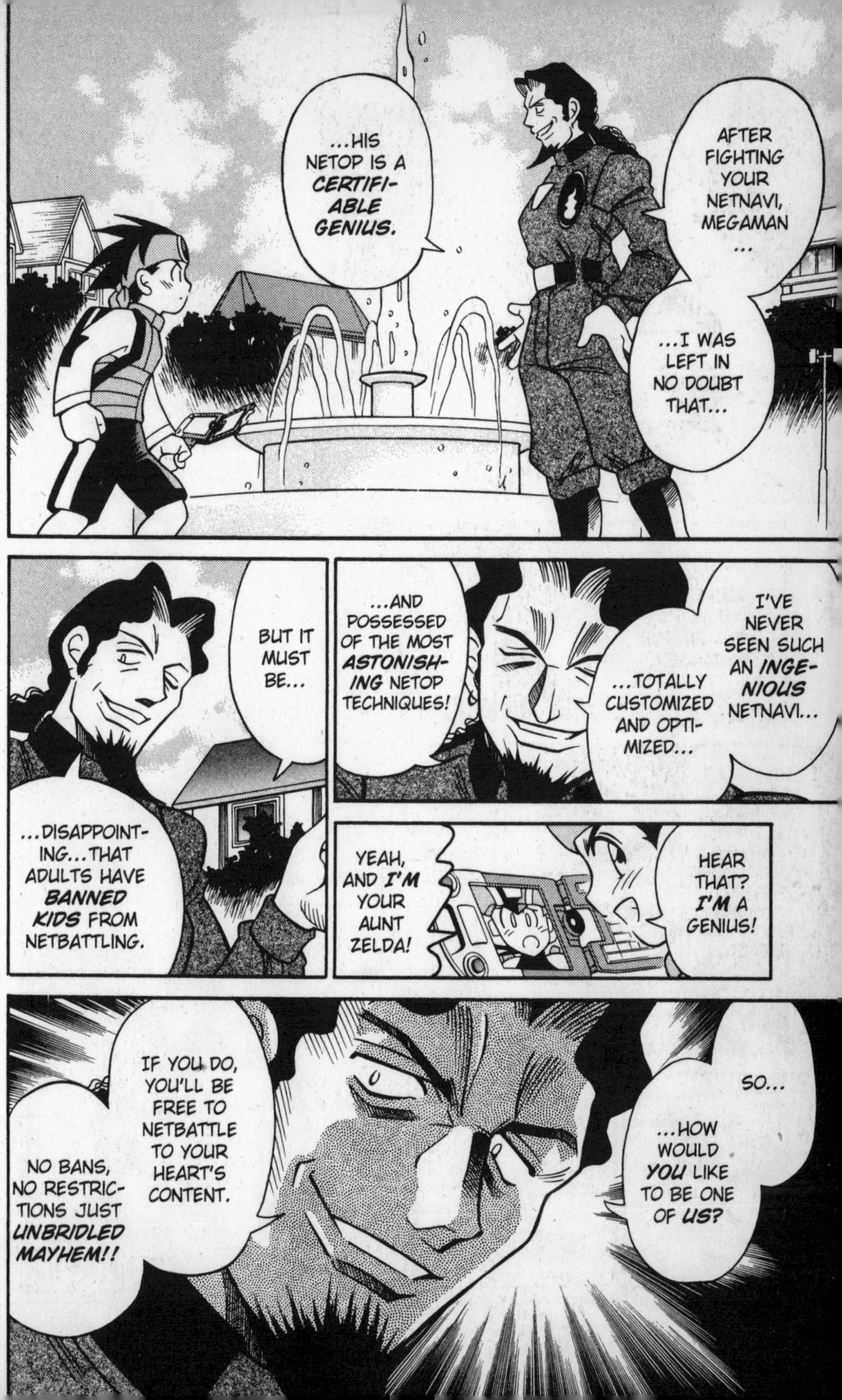
AFTER FIGHTING YOUR NETNAVI, MEGAMAN ...
...I WAS LEFT IN NO DOUBT THAT...
...HIS NETOP IS A *CERTIFIABLE GENIUS.*
I'VE NEVER SEEN SUCH AN *INGENIOUS* NETNAVI...
...TOTALLY CUSTOMIZED AND OPTIMIZED...
...AND POSSESSED OF THE MOST *ASTONISHING* NETOP TECHNIQUES!
HEAR THAT? *I'M* A GENIUS!
YEAH, AND *I'M* YOUR AUNT ZELDA!
BUT IT MUST BE...
...DISAPPOINTING...THAT ADULTS HAVE *BANNED KIDS* FROM NETBATTLING.
SO...
...HOW WOULD *YOU* LIKE TO BE ONE OF *US?*
IF YOU DO, YOU'LL BE FREE TO NETBATTLE TO YOUR HEART'S CONTENT.
NO BANS, NO RESTRICTIONS JUST *UNBRIDLED MAYHEM!!*

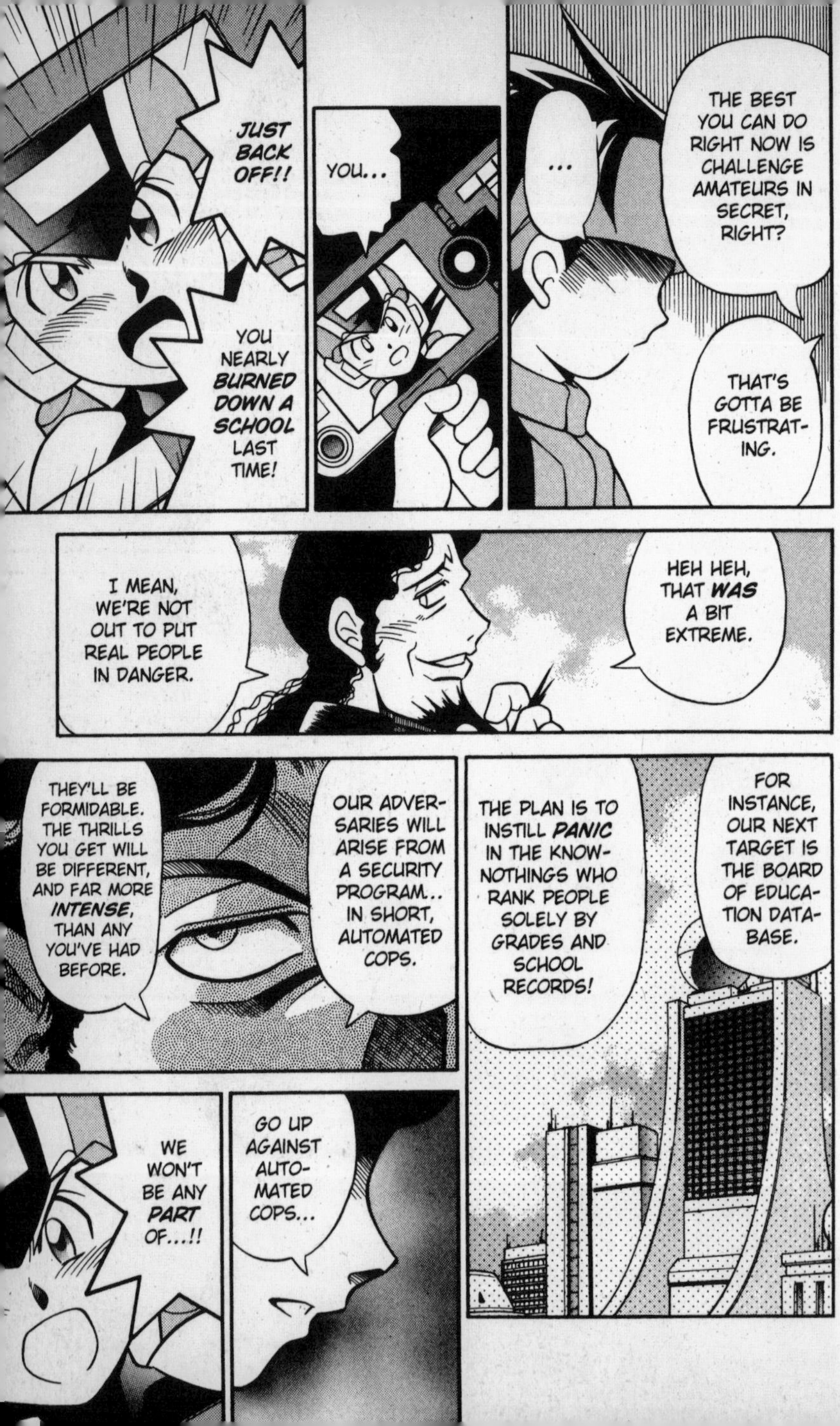
...
THE BEST YOU CAN DO RIGHT NOW IS CHALLENGE AMATEURS IN SECRET, RIGHT?
THAT'S GOTTA BE FRUSTRAT-ING.
YOU...
JUST BACK OFF!!
YOU NEARLY BURNED DOWN A SCHOOL LAST TIME!
HEH HEH, THAT WAS A BIT EXTREME.
I MEAN, WE'RE NOT OUT TO PUT REAL PEOPLE IN DANGER.
FOR INSTANCE, OUR NEXT TARGET IS THE BOARD OF EDUCA-TION DATA-BASE.
THE PLAN IS TO INSTILL PANIC IN THE KNOW-NOTHINGS WHO RANK PEOPLE SOLELY BY GRADES AND SCHOOL RECORDS!
OUR ADVER-SARIES WILL ARISE FROM A SECURITY PROGRAM... IN SHORT, AUTOMATED COPS.
THEY'LL BE FORMIDABLE. THE THRILLS YOU GET WILL BE DIFFERENT, AND FAR MORE INTENSE, THAN ANY YOU'VE HAD BEFORE.
GO UP AGAINST AUTO-MATED COPS...
WE WON'T BE ANY PART OF...!!

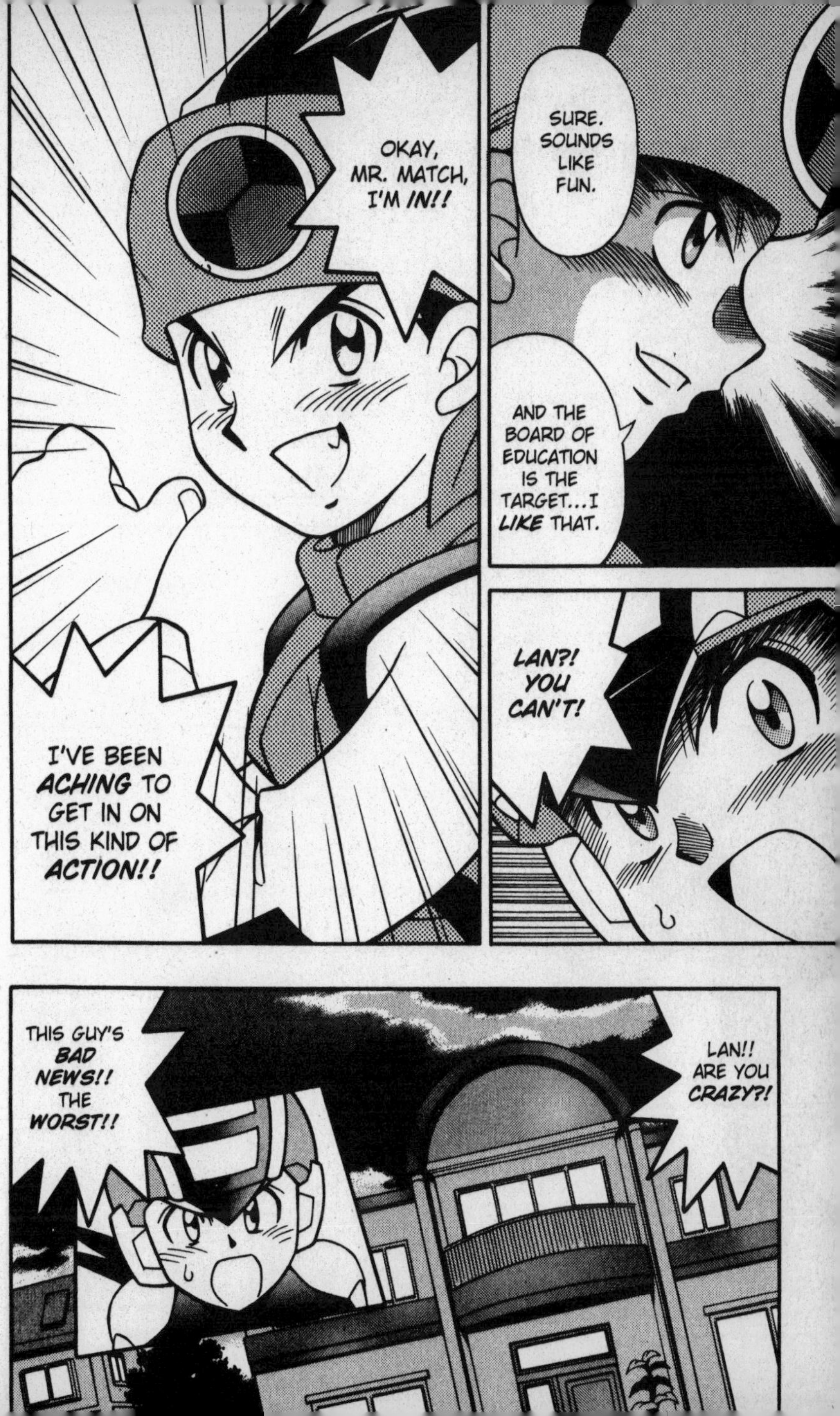
SURE. SOUNDS LIKE FUN.
AND THE BOARD OF EDUCATION IS THE TARGET...I *LIKE* THAT.
LAN?! YOU CAN'T!
OKAY, MR. MATCH, I'M *IN!!*
I'VE BEEN *ACHING* TO GET IN ON THIS KIND OF *ACTION!!*
LAN!! ARE YOU *CRAZY?!*
THIS GUY'S *BAD NEWS!!* THE *WORST!!*

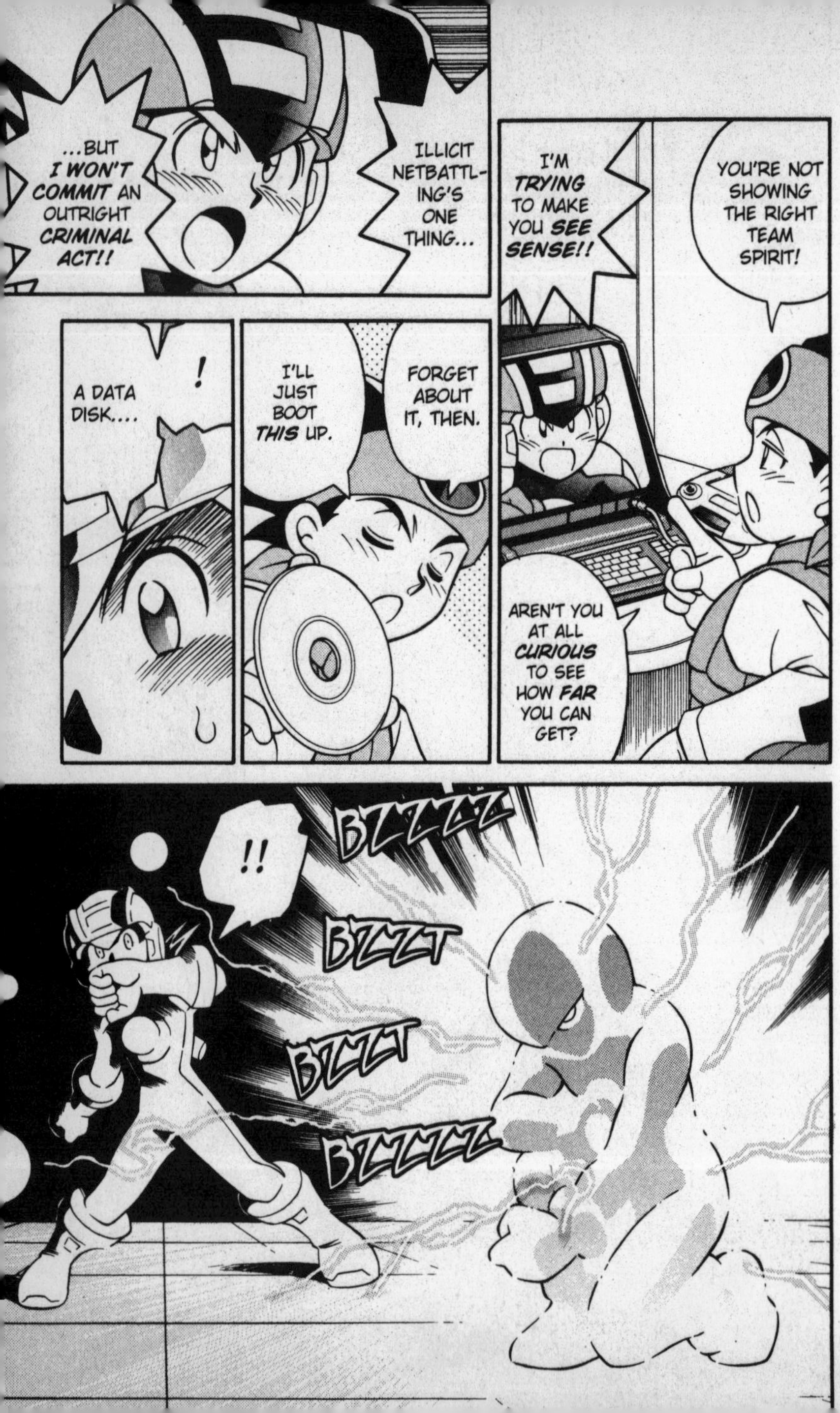
ILLICIT NETBATTLING'S ONE THING...
...BUT I WON'T COMMIT AN OUTRIGHT CRIMINAL ACT!!
YOU'RE NOT SHOWING THE RIGHT TEAM SPIRIT!
I'M TRYING TO MAKE YOU SEE SENSE!!
AREN'T YOU AT ALL CURIOUS TO SEE HOW FAR YOU CAN GET?
FORGET ABOUT IT, THEN.
I'LL JUST BOOT THIS UP.
!
A DATA DISK....
BZZZZZ
!!
BZZZT
BZZZT
BZZZZZZ

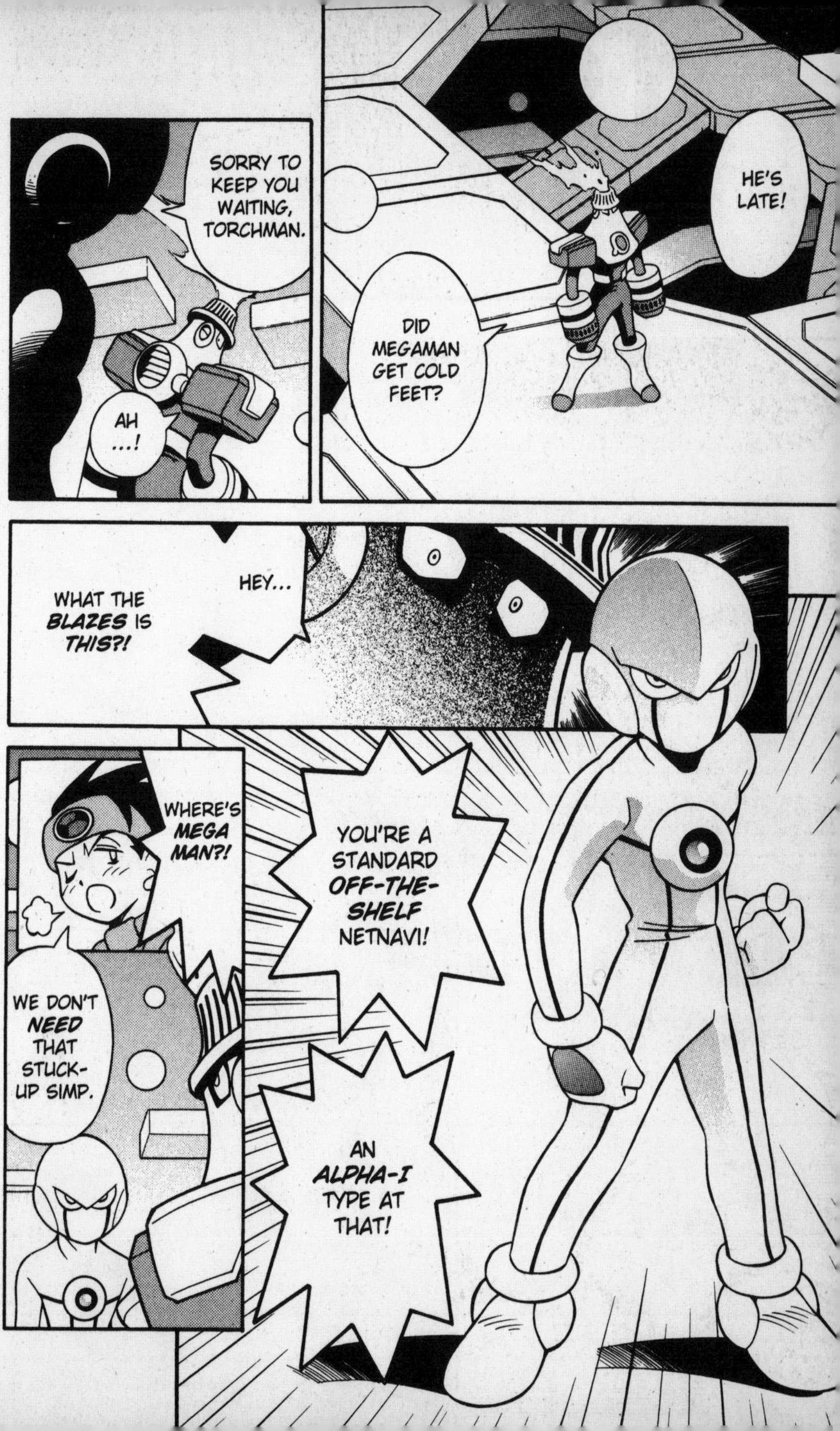
HE'S LATE!
DID MEGAMAN GET COLD FEET?
SORRY TO KEEP YOU WAITING, TORCHMAN.
AH ....!
HEY...
WHAT THE *BLAZES* IS *THIS?!*
YOU'RE A STANDARD *OFF-THE-SHELF* NETNAVI!
AN *ALPHA-I* TYPE AT THAT!
WHERE'S *MEGA MAN?!*
WE DON'T *NEED* THAT STUCK-UP SIMP.

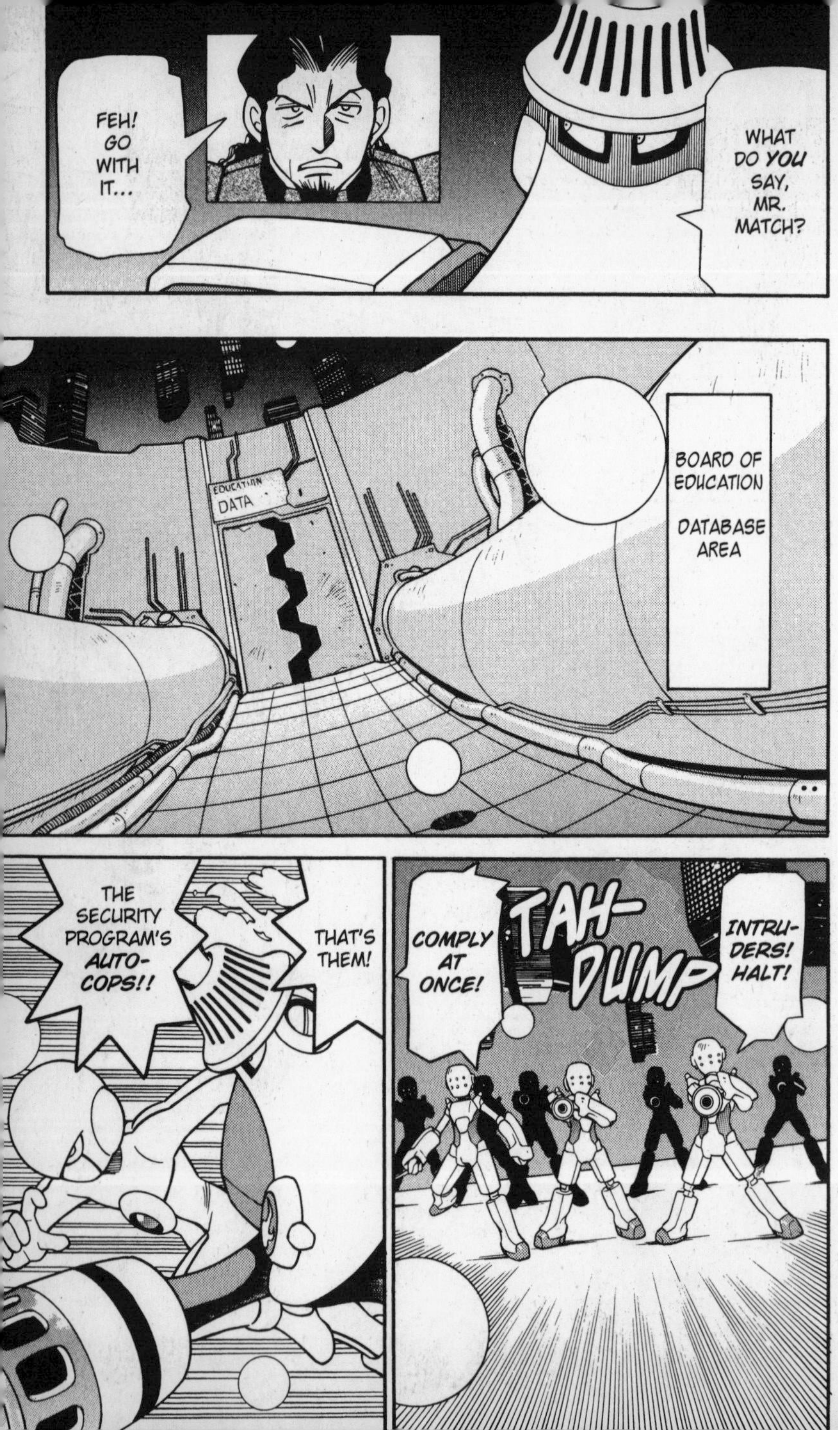
WHAT DO *YOU* SAY, MR. MATCH?
FEH! GO WITH IT...
EDUCATION DATA
BOARD OF EDUCATION DATABASE AREA
INTRU-DERS! HALT!
TAH-DUMP
COMPLY AT ONCE!
THAT'S THEM!
THE SECURITY PROGRAM'S AUTO-COPS!!

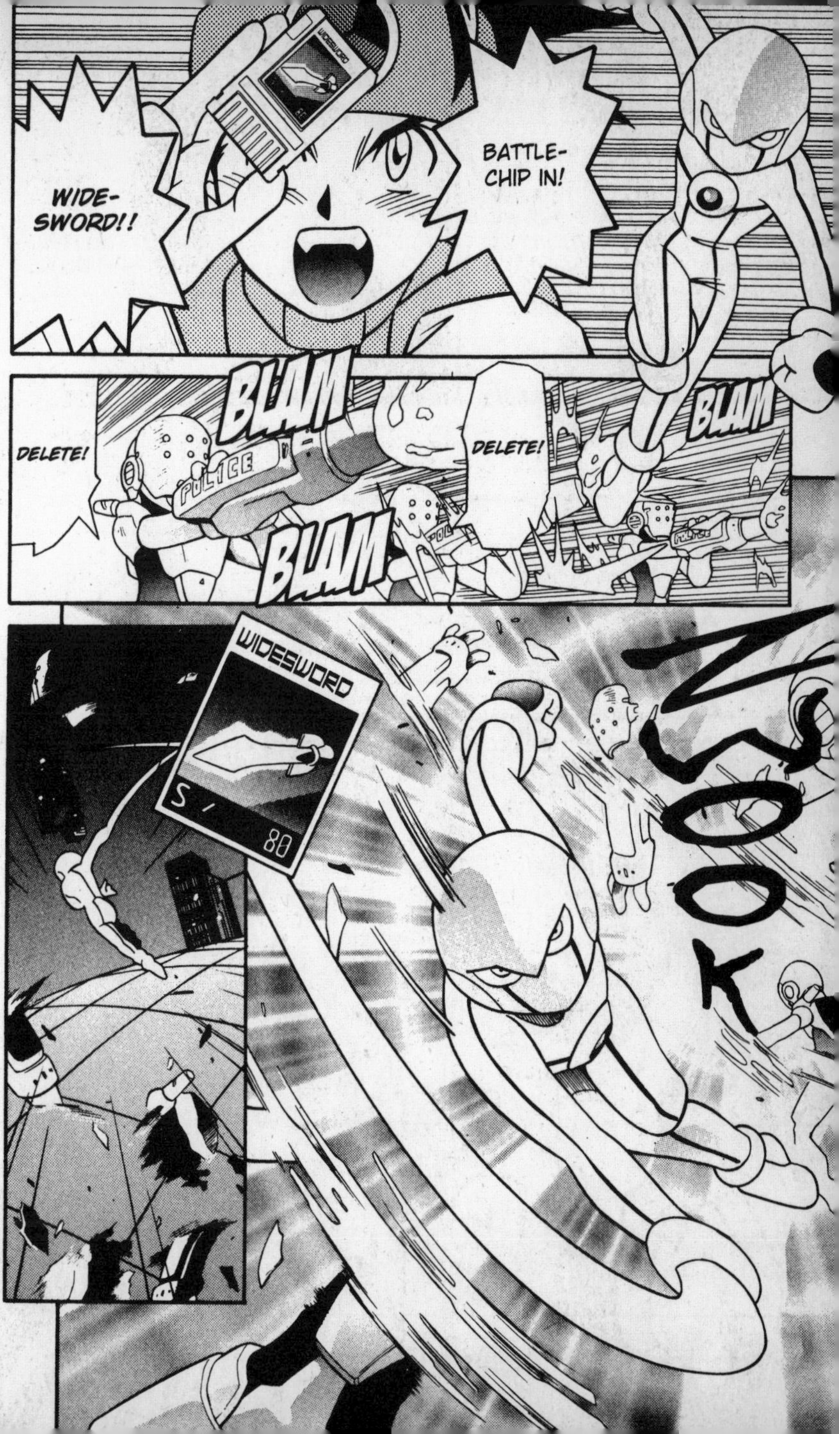
BATTLE-CHIP IN!
WIDE-SWORD!!
BLAM
DELETE!
BLAM
DELETE!
BLAM
SWOOSH
WIDESWORD
S
80

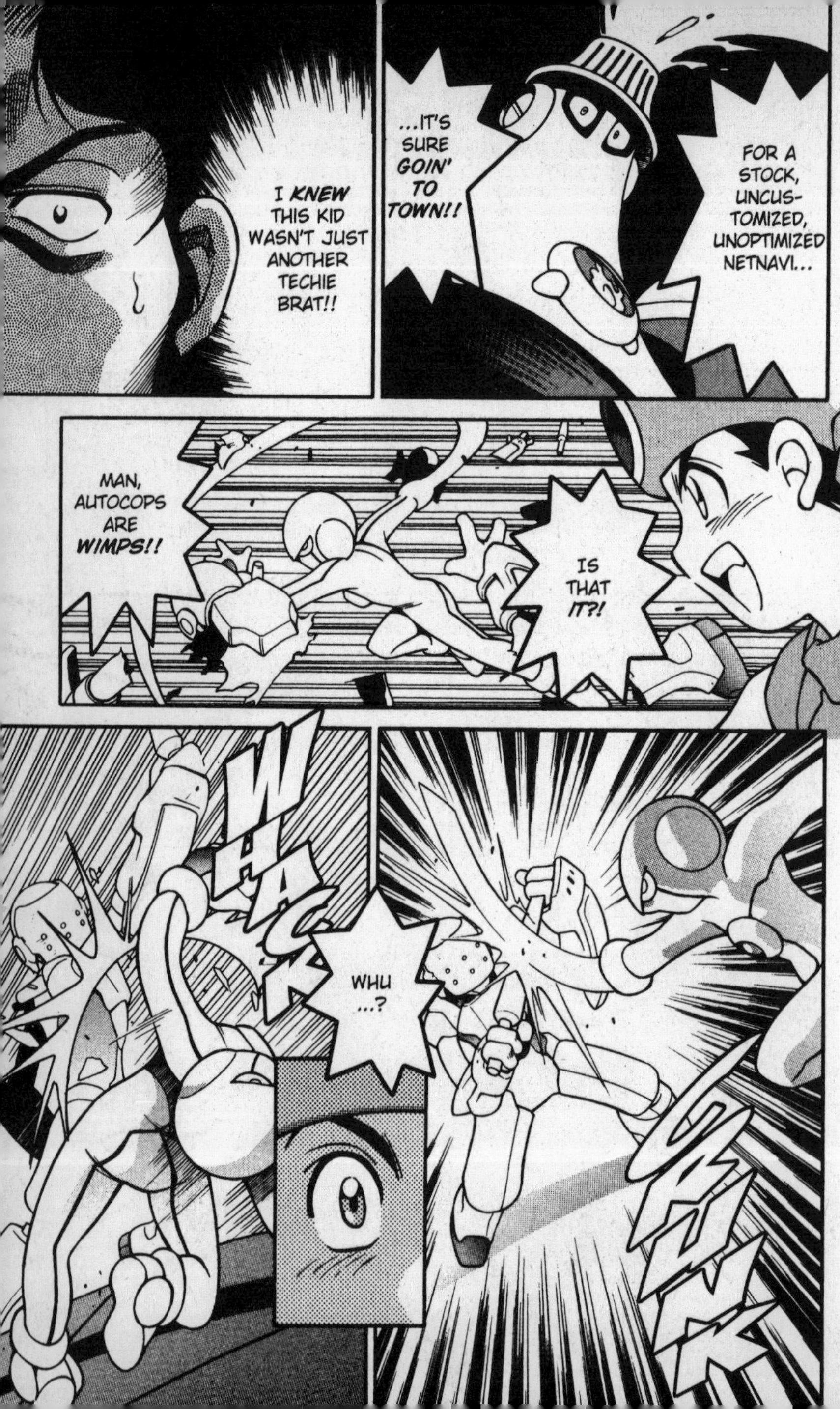
FOR A STOCK, UNCUSTOMIZED, UNOPTIMIZED NETNAVI...
...IT'S SURE *GOIN' TO TOWN!!*
I *KNEW* THIS KID WASN'T JUST ANOTHER TECHIE BRAT!!
IS THAT *IT?!*
MAN, AUTOCOPS ARE *WIMPS!!*
WHU ...?
WHACK

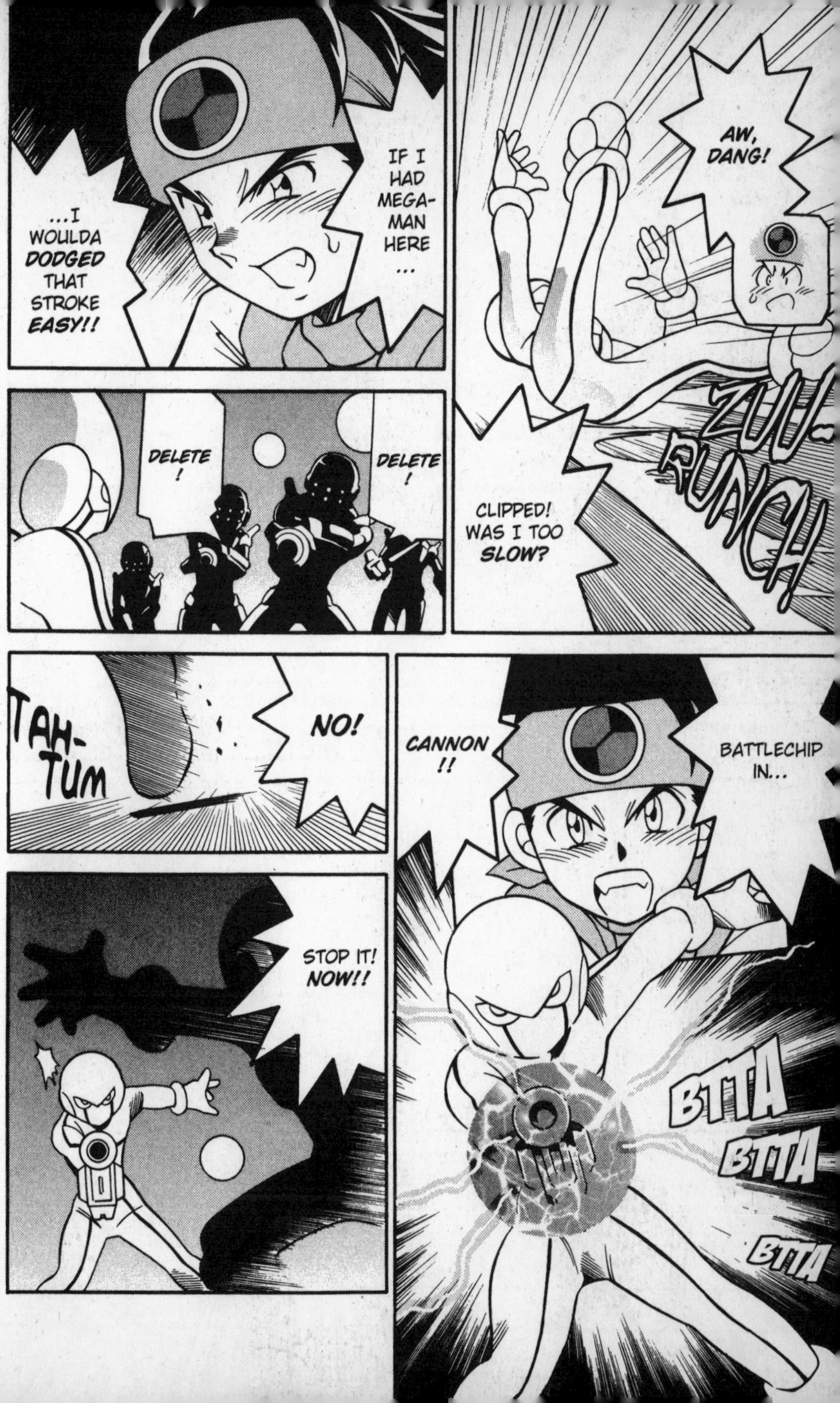
AW, DANG!
ZUU-RUNCH
CLIPPED! WAS I TOO SLOW?
IF I HAD MEGA-MAN HERE ...
...I WOULDA DODGED THAT STROKE EASY!!
DELETE!
DELETE!
BATTLECHIP IN...
CANNON!!
BTTA
BTTA
BTTA
NO!
TAH-TUM
STOP IT! NOW!!

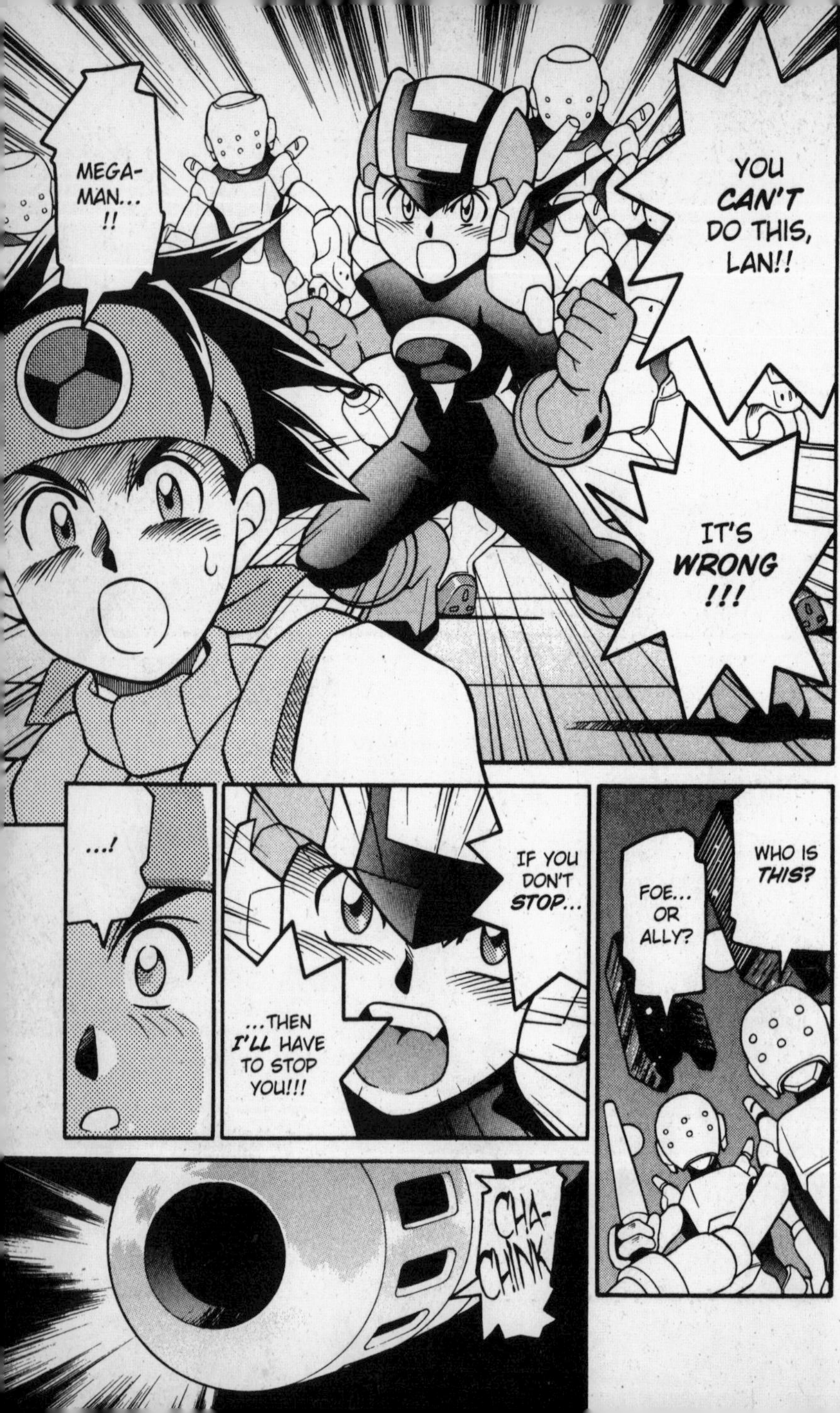
YOU CAN'T DO THIS, LAN!!
IT'S WRONG!!!
MEGA-MAN...!!
WHO IS THIS?
FOE... OR ALLY?
IF YOU DON'T STOP...
...THEN I'LL HAVE TO STOP YOU!!!
...!
CHA-CHINK

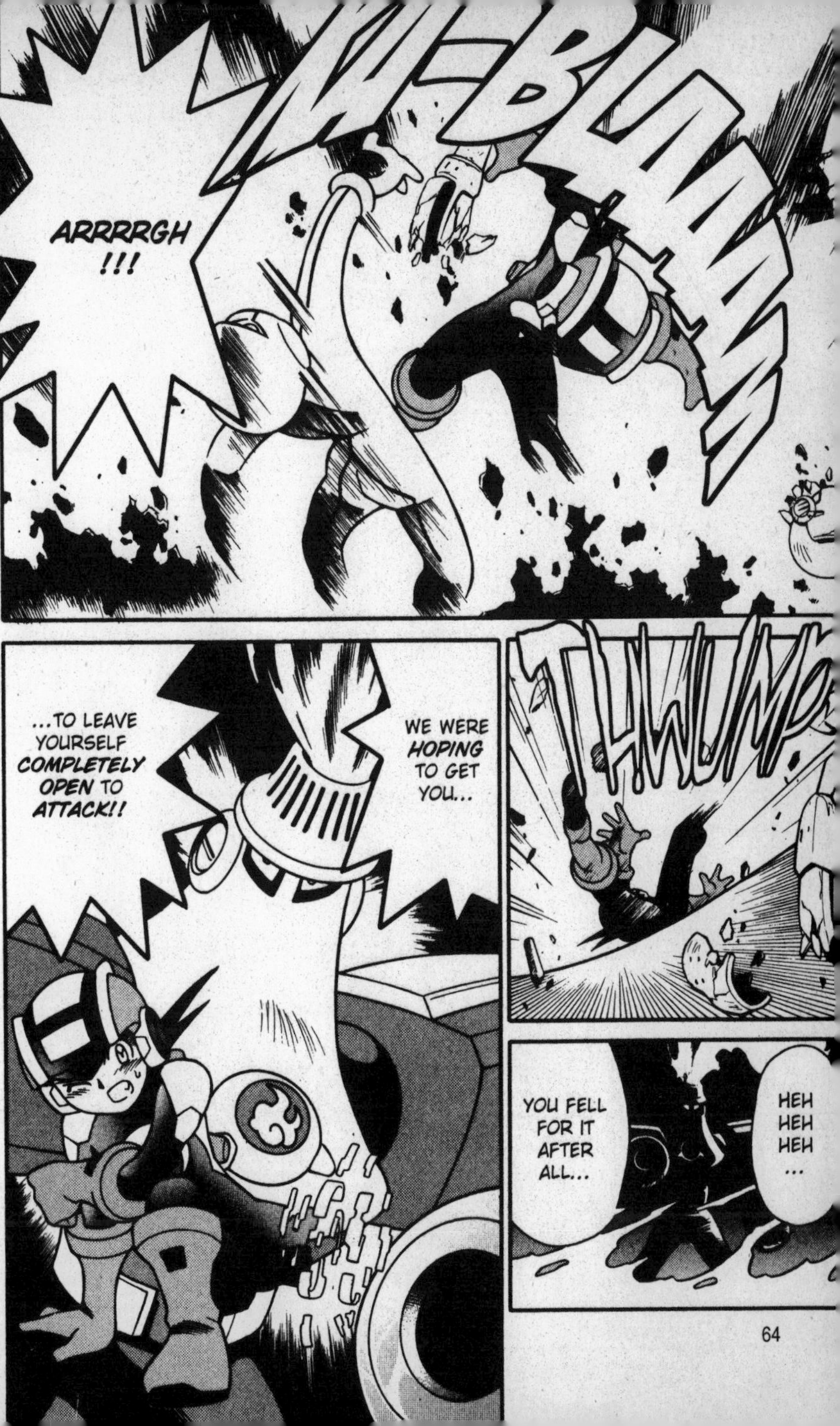
ARRRRGH !!!
THWUMP
HEH HEH HEH...
YOU FELL FOR IT AFTER ALL...
WE WERE HOPING TO GET YOU...
...TO LEAVE YOURSELF COMPLETELY OPEN TO ATTACK!!

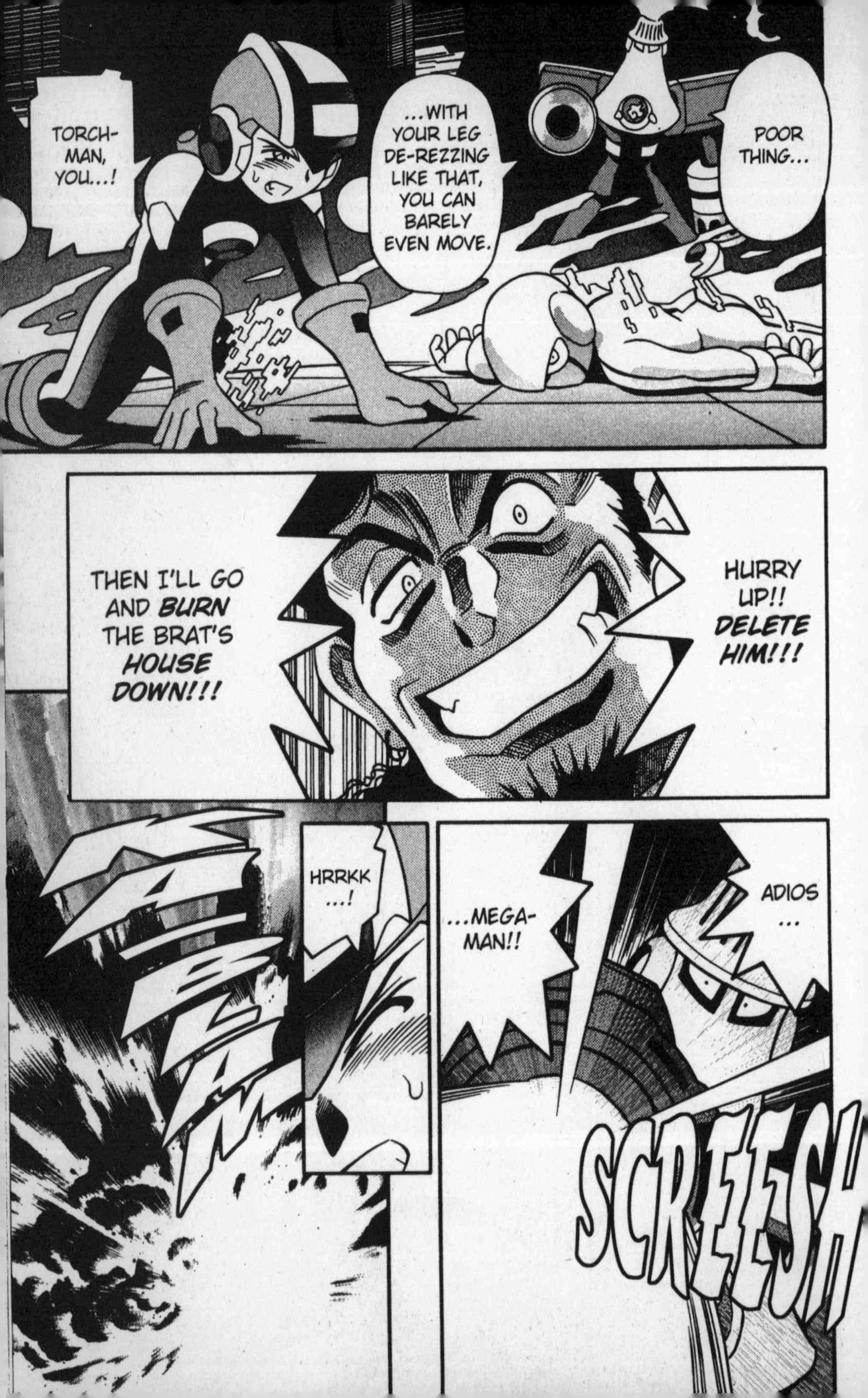
POOR THING...
...WITH YOUR LEG DE-REZZING LIKE THAT, YOU CAN BARELY EVEN MOVE.
TORCH-MAN, YOU...!
HURRY UP!! DELETE HIM!!!
THEN I'LL GO AND BURN THE BRAT'S HOUSE DOWN!!!
ADIOS ...
...MEGA-MAN!!
SCREESH
HRRKK ...!

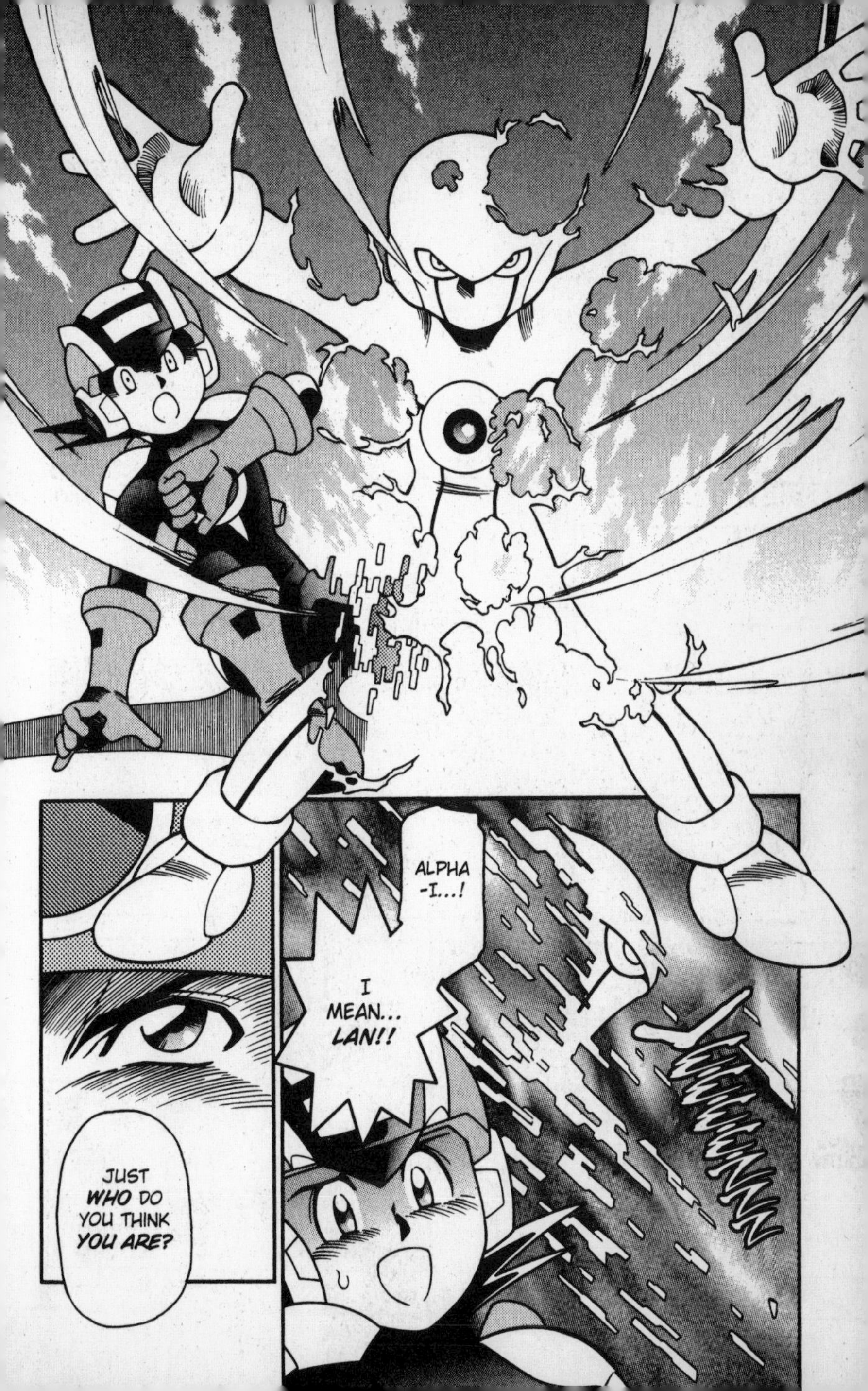
ALPHA
-I...!
I
MEAN...
LAN!!
JUST
WHO DO
YOU THINK
YOU ARE?

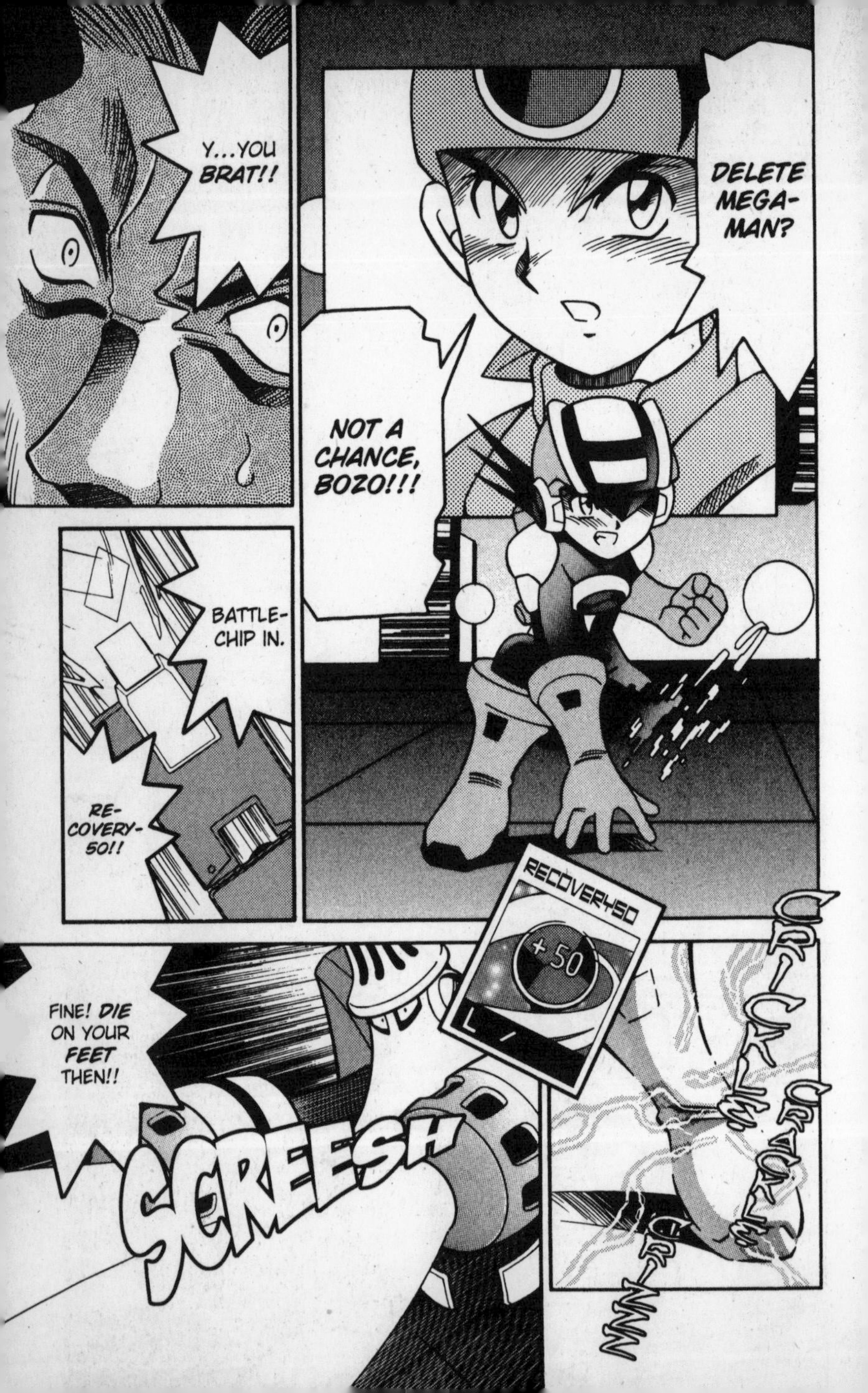
DELETE MEGA-MAN?
NOT A CHANCE, BOZO!!!
Y...YOU BRAT!!
BATTLE-CHIP IN.
RE-COVERY-50!!
RECOVERY50
+50
FINE! DIE ON YOUR FEET THEN!!
SCREESH

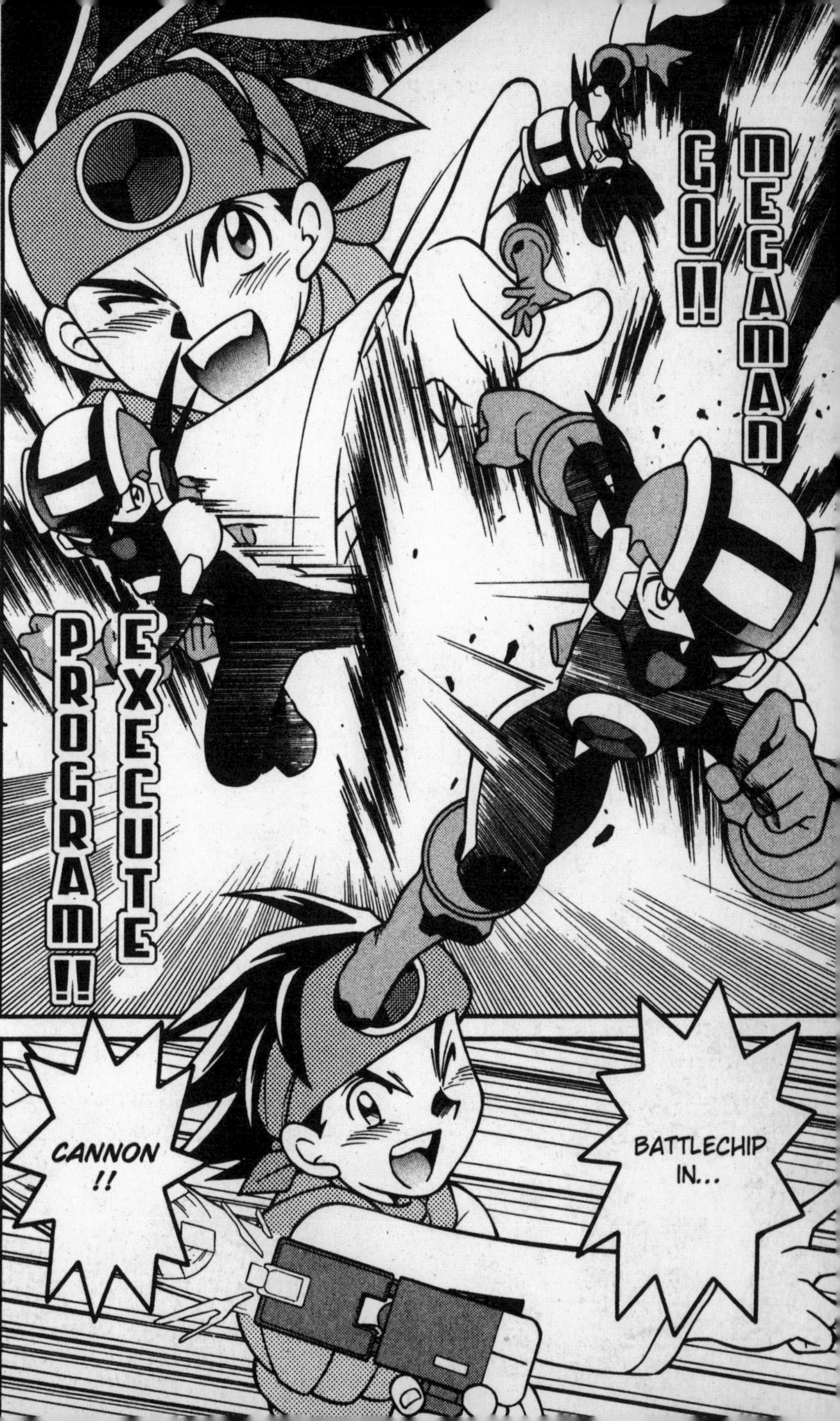
MEGAMAN
GO!!
EXECUTE
PROGRAM!!
BATTLECHIP IN...
CANNON !!

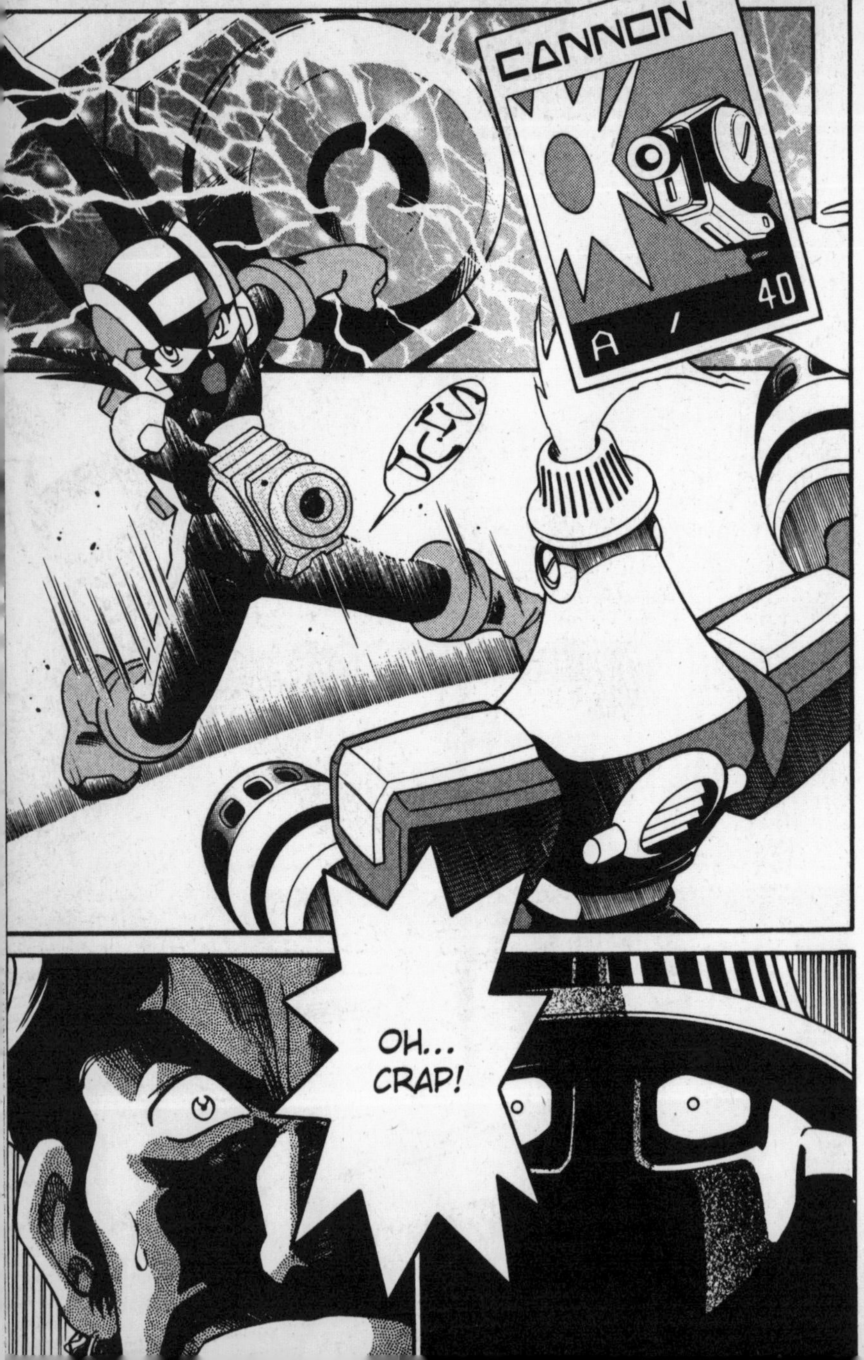
CANNON
A /
40
OH... CRAP!

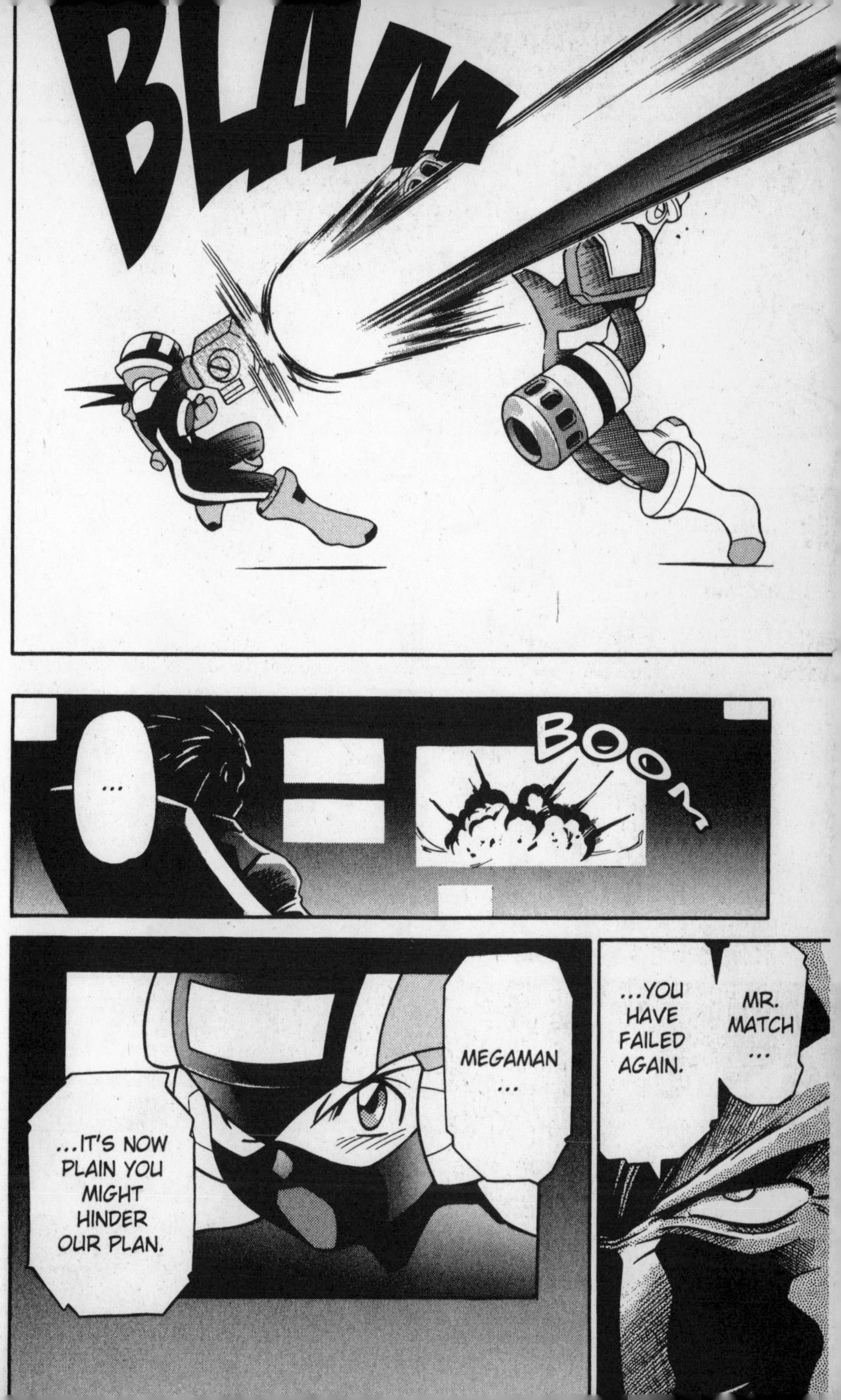
BLAM
BOOM
...
MR. MATCH ...
...YOU HAVE FAILED AGAIN.
MEGAMAN ...
...IT'S NOW PLAIN YOU MIGHT HINDER OUR PLAN.

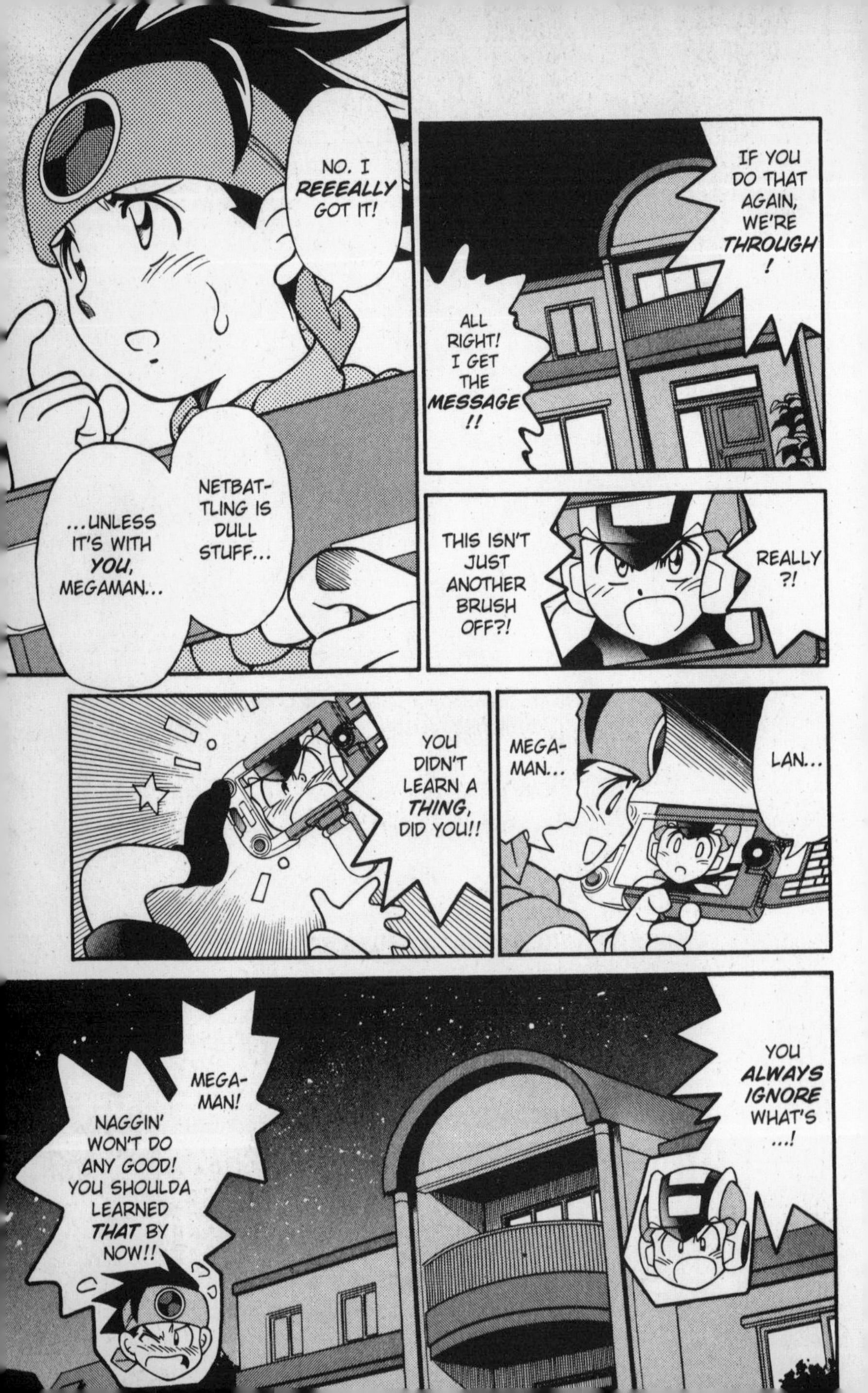
IF YOU DO THAT AGAIN, WE'RE THROUGH!
ALL RIGHT! I GET THE MESSAGE!!
REALLY?!
THIS ISN'T JUST ANOTHER BRUSH OFF?!
NO. I REEEALLY GOT IT!
NETBAT-TLING IS DULL STUFF...
...UNLESS IT'S WITH YOU, MEGAMAN...
LAN...
MEGA-MAN...
YOU DIDN'T LEARN A THING, DID YOU!!
YOU ALWAYS IGNORE WHAT'S ...!
MEGA-MAN!
NAGGIN' WON'T DO ANY GOOD! YOU SHOULDA LEARNED THAT BY NOW!!

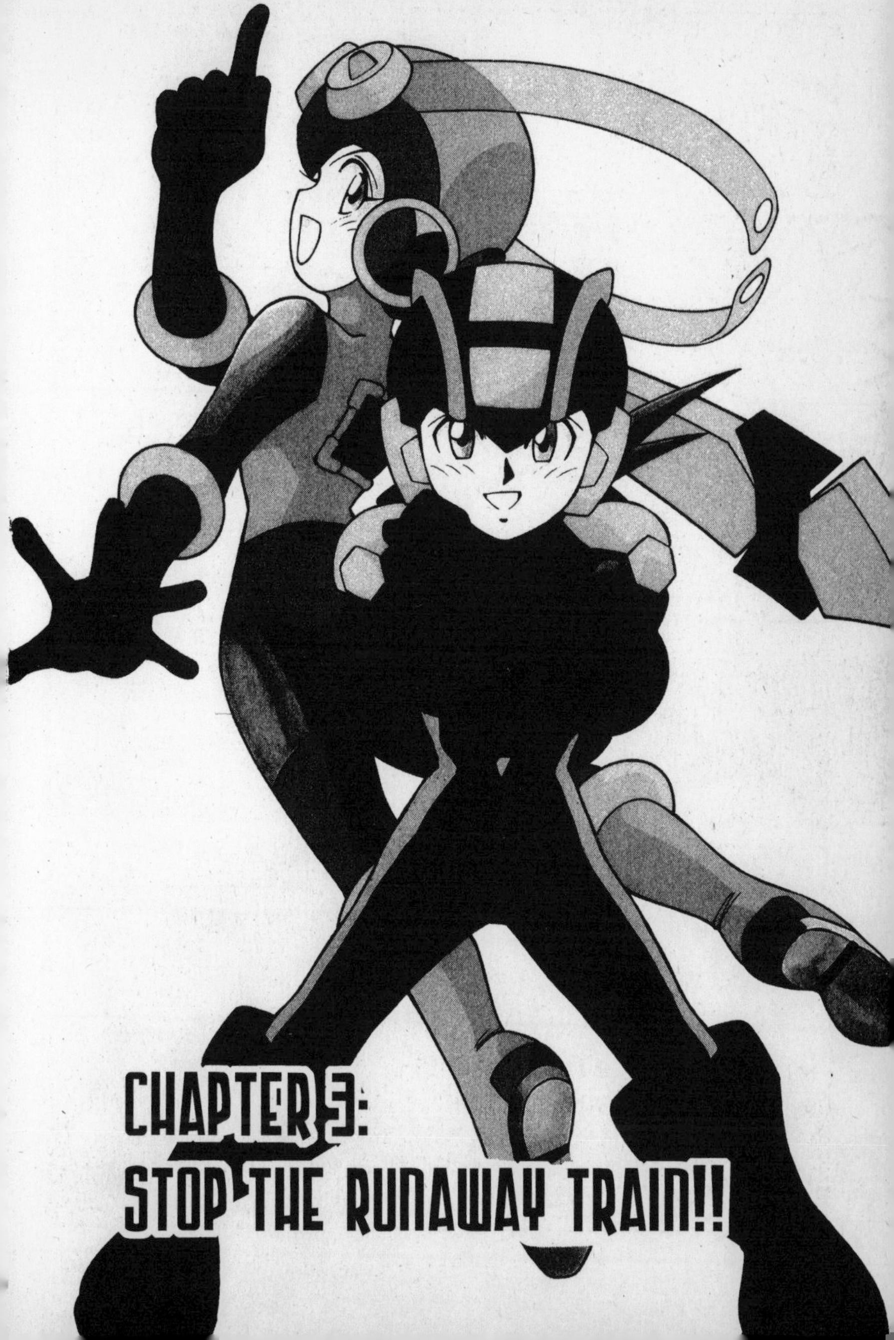

CHAPTER 3: STOP THE RUNAWAY TRAIN!!

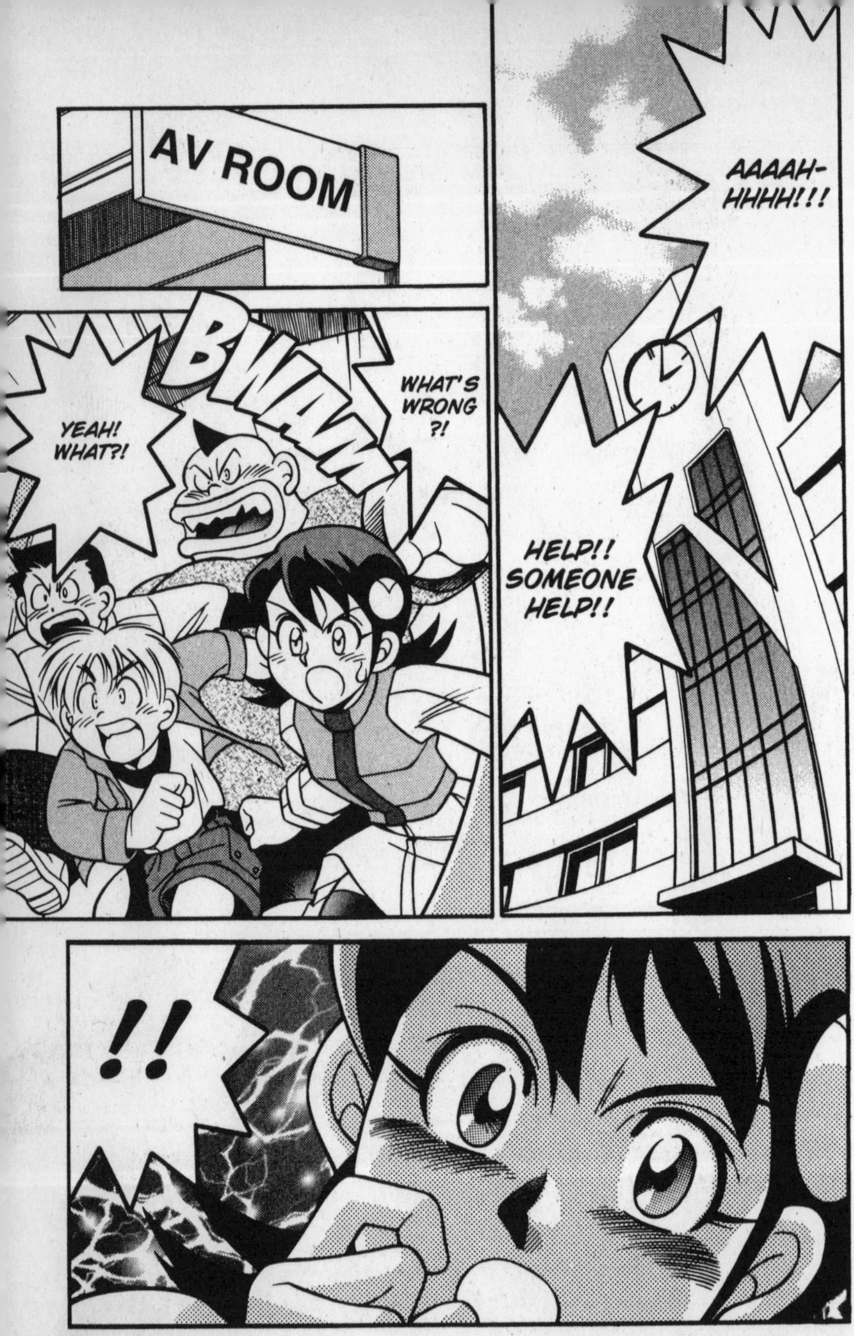
AAAAH-HHHH!!!
HELP!! SOMEONE HELP!!
AV ROOM
BWAM
WHAT'S WRONG ?!
YEAH! WHAT?!
!!

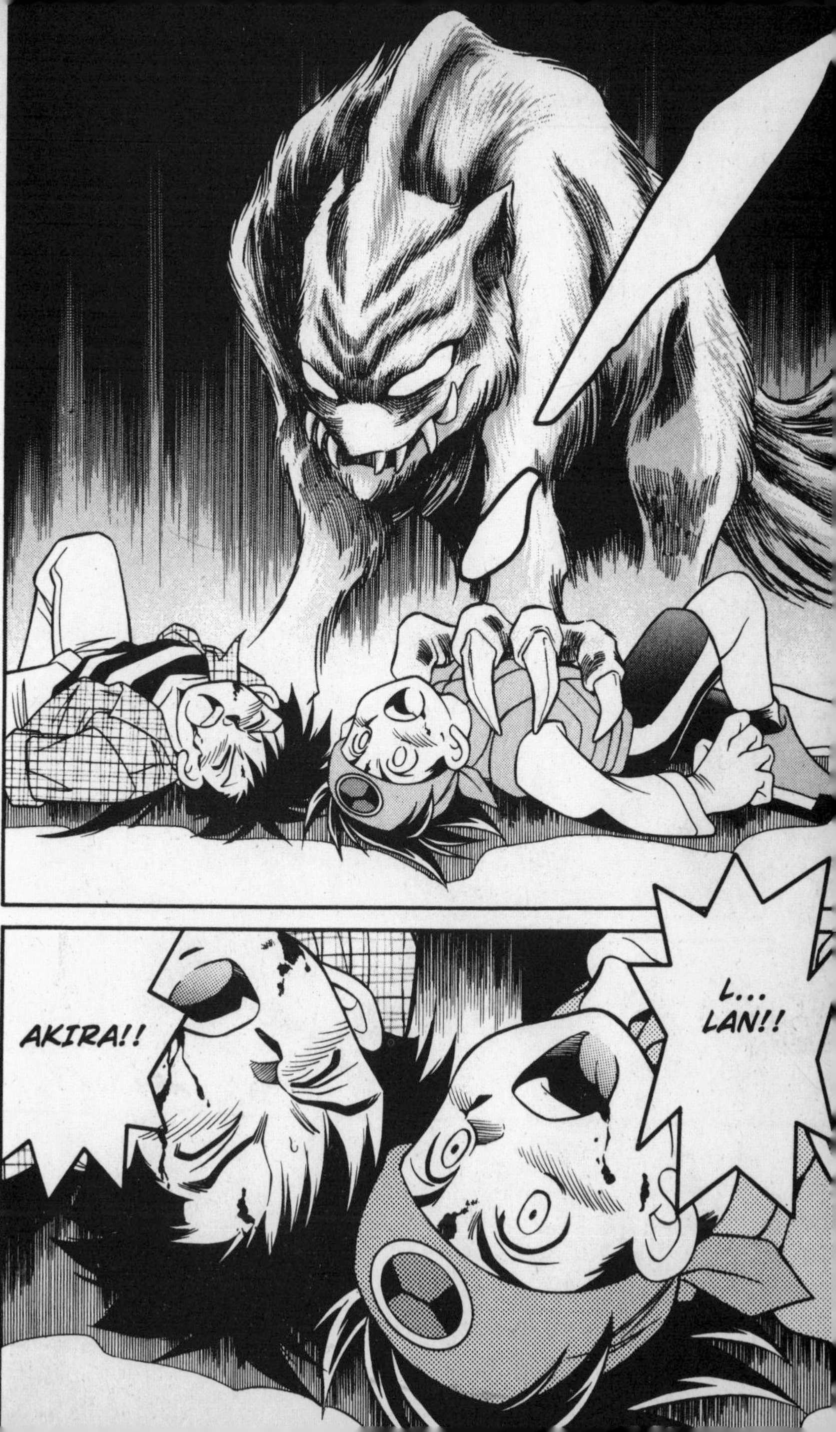

L... LAN!!
AKIRA!!

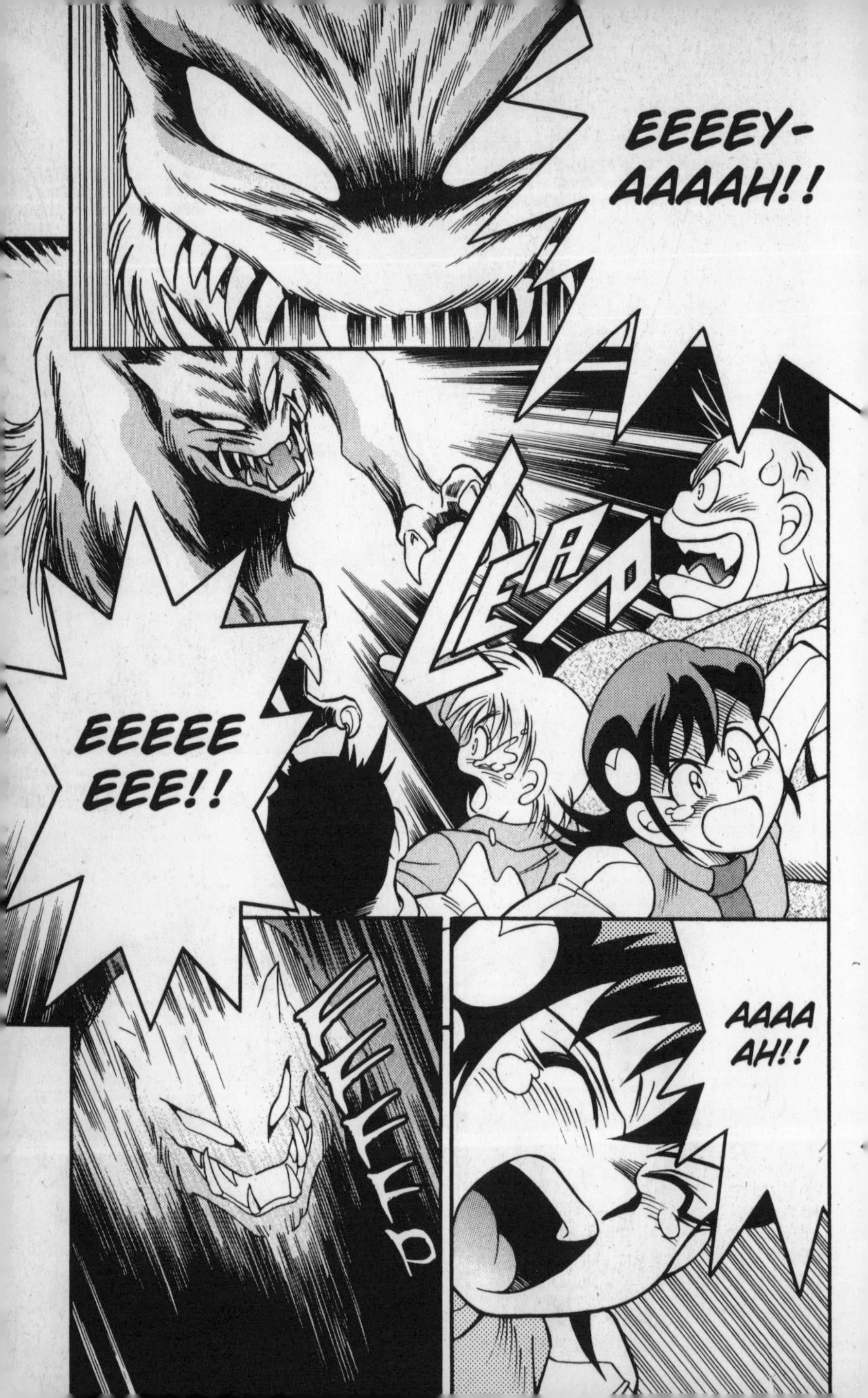
EEEEY-AAAAH!!
LEAP
EEEEE EEE!!
AAAA AH!!

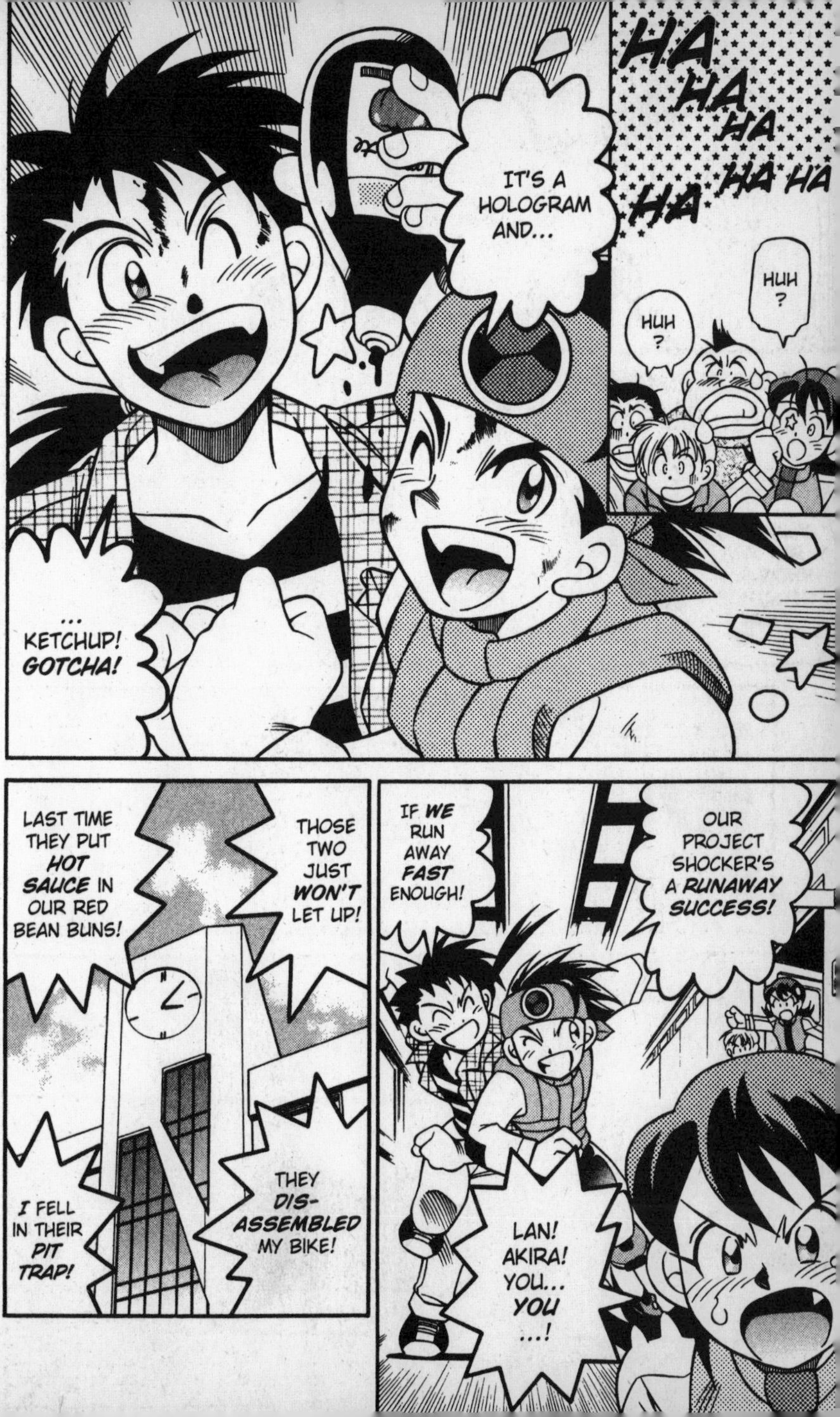
HA HA HA HA HA HA
HUH ?
HUH ?
IT'S A HOLOGRAM AND...
... KETCHUP! GOTCHA!
OUR PROJECT SHOCKER'S A RUNAWAY SUCCESS!
IF WE RUN AWAY FAST ENOUGH!
LAN! AKIRA! YOU... YOU ...!
THOSE TWO JUST WON'T LET UP!
LAST TIME THEY PUT HOT SAUCE IN OUR RED BEAN BUNS!
THEY DIS-ASSEMBLED MY BIKE!
I FELL IN THEIR PIT TRAP!

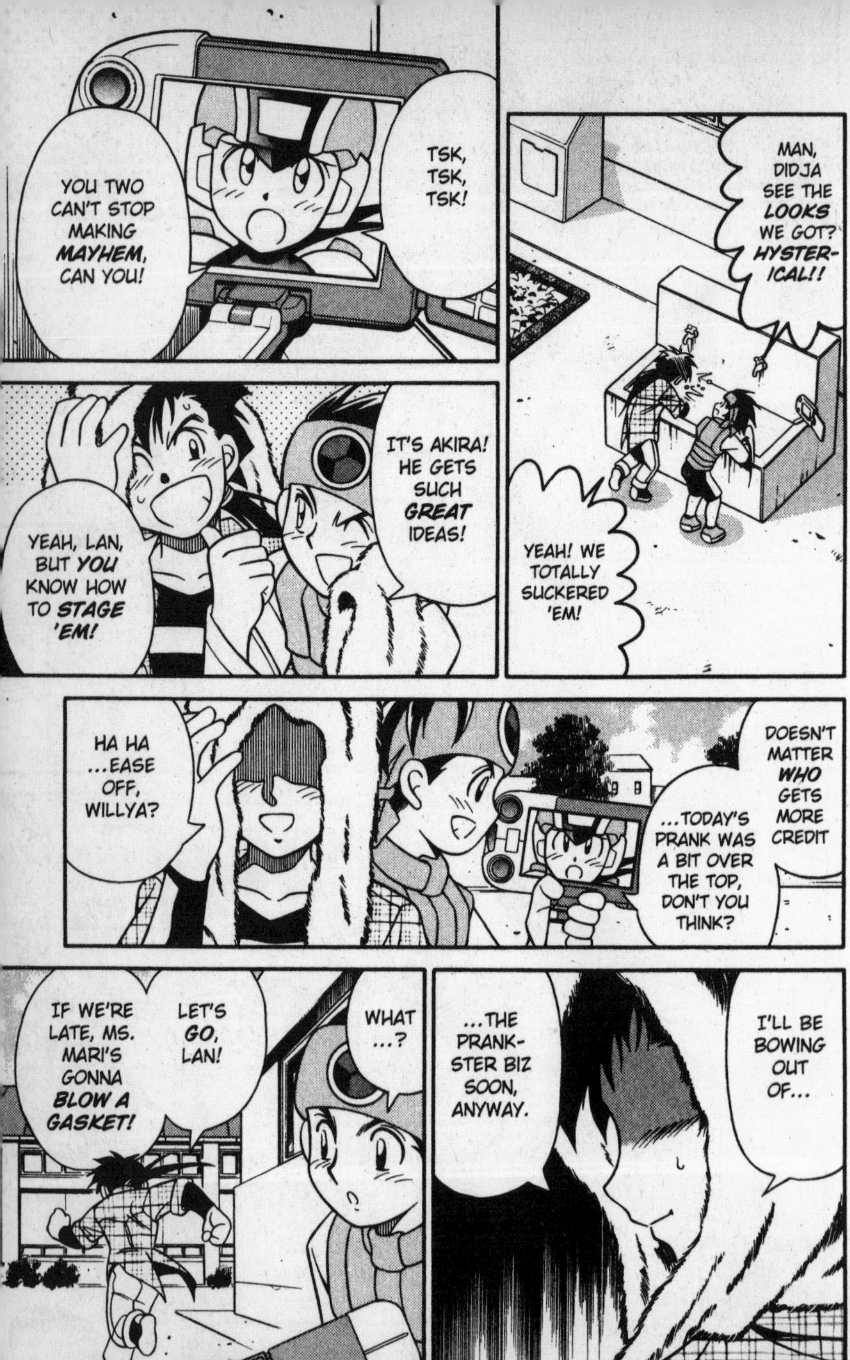
MAN, DIDJA SEE THE LOOKS WE GOT? HYSTER-ICAL!!
YEAH! WE TOTALLY SUCKERED 'EM!
TSK, TSK, TSK!
YOU TWO CAN'T STOP MAKING MAYHEM, CAN YOU!
IT'S AKIRA! HE GETS SUCH GREAT IDEAS!
YEAH, LAN, BUT YOU KNOW HOW TO STAGE 'EM!
DOESN'T MATTER WHO GETS MORE CREDIT
...TODAY'S PRANK WAS A BIT OVER THE TOP, DON'T YOU THINK?
HA HA ...EASE OFF, WILLYA?
I'LL BE BOWING OUT OF...
...THE PRANK-STER BIZ SOON, ANYWAY.
WHAT ...?
LET'S GO, LAN!
IF WE'RE LATE, MS. MARI'S GONNA BLOW A GASKET!

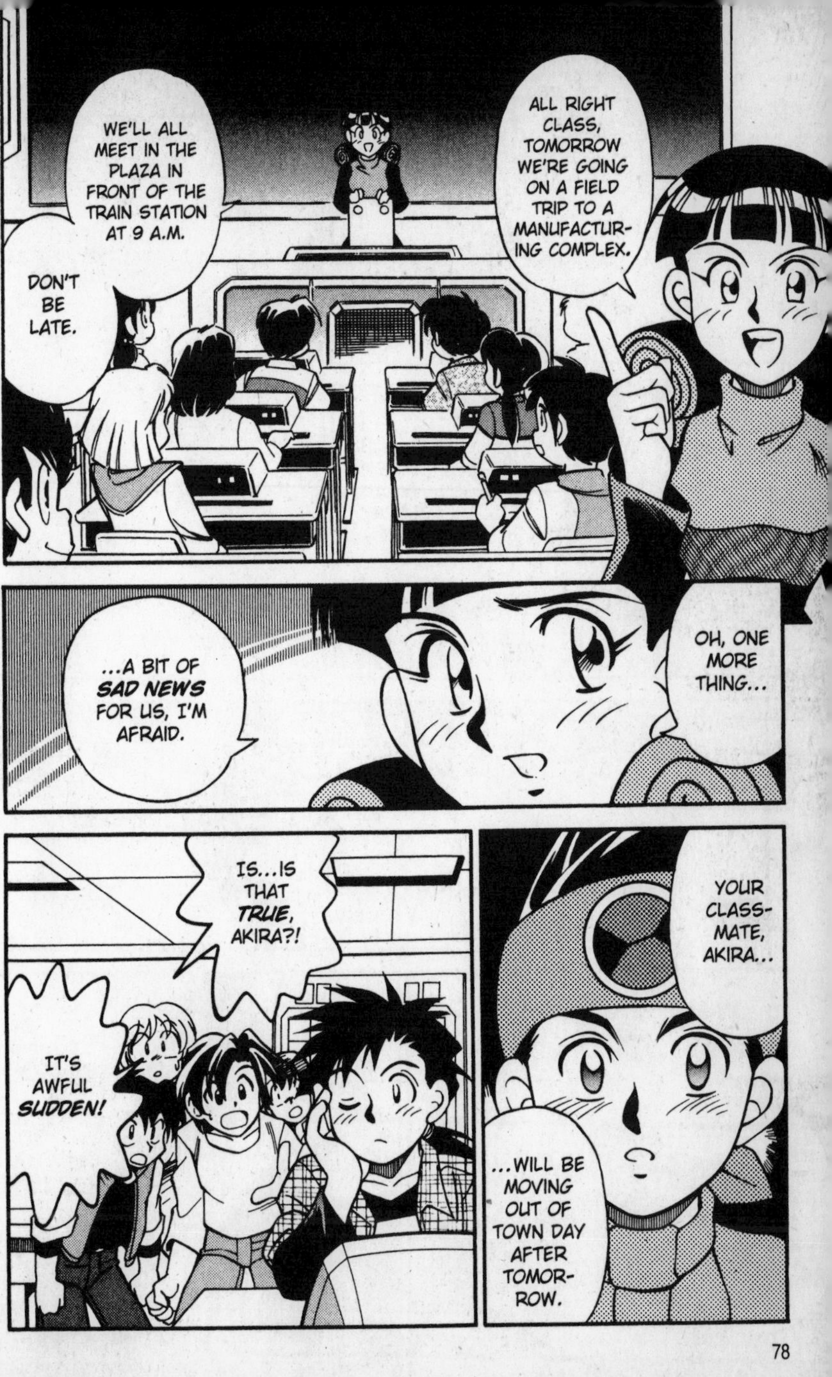
ALL RIGHT CLASS, TOMORROW WE'RE GOING ON A FIELD TRIP TO A MANUFACTURING COMPLEX.
WE'LL ALL MEET IN THE PLAZA IN FRONT OF THE TRAIN STATION AT 9 A.M.
DON'T BE LATE.
OH, ONE MORE THING...
...A BIT OF ***SAD NEWS*** FOR US, I'M AFRAID.
YOUR CLASSMATE, AKIRA...
...WILL BE MOVING OUT OF TOWN DAY AFTER TOMORROW.
IS...IS THAT ***TRUE***, AKIRA?!
IT'S AWFUL ***SUDDEN!***

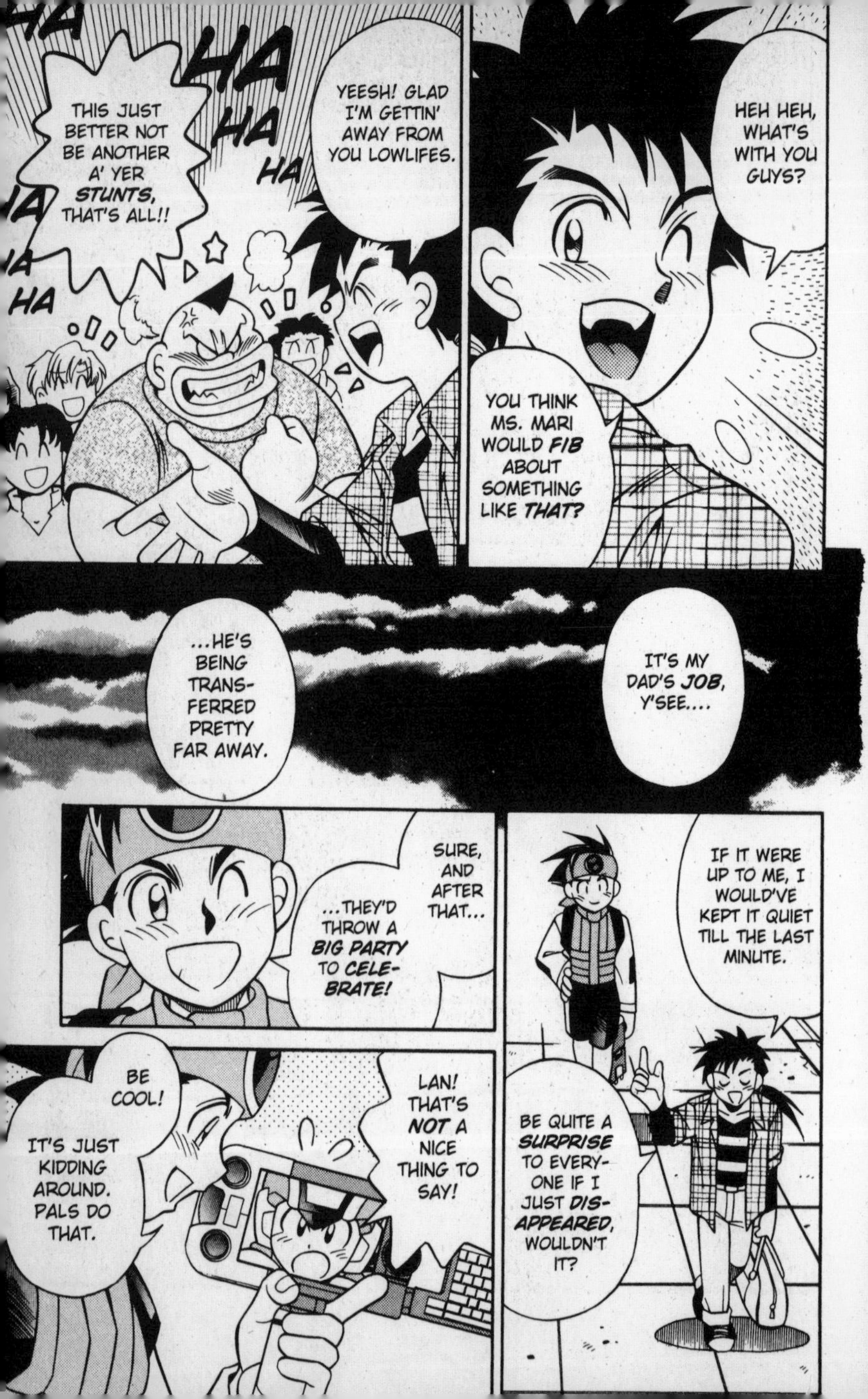
HEH HEH, WHAT'S WITH YOU GUYS?
YOU THINK MS. MARI WOULD *FIB* ABOUT SOMETHING LIKE *THAT?*
YEESH! GLAD I'M GETTIN' AWAY FROM YOU LOWLIFES.
HA HA HA
THIS JUST BETTER NOT BE ANOTHER A' YER *STUNTS,* THAT'S ALL!!
HA HA HA HA
IT'S MY DAD'S *JOB,* Y'SEE....
...HE'S BEING TRANS-FERRED PRETTY FAR AWAY.
IF IT WERE UP TO ME, I WOULD'VE KEPT IT QUIET TILL THE LAST MINUTE.
BE QUITE A *SURPRISE* TO EVERY-ONE IF I JUST *DIS-APPEARED,* WOULDN'T IT?
SURE, AND AFTER THAT...
...THEY'D THROW A *BIG PARTY* TO *CELE-BRATE!*
LAN! THAT'S *NOT* A NICE THING TO SAY!
BE COOL!
IT'S JUST KIDDING AROUND. PALS DO THAT.

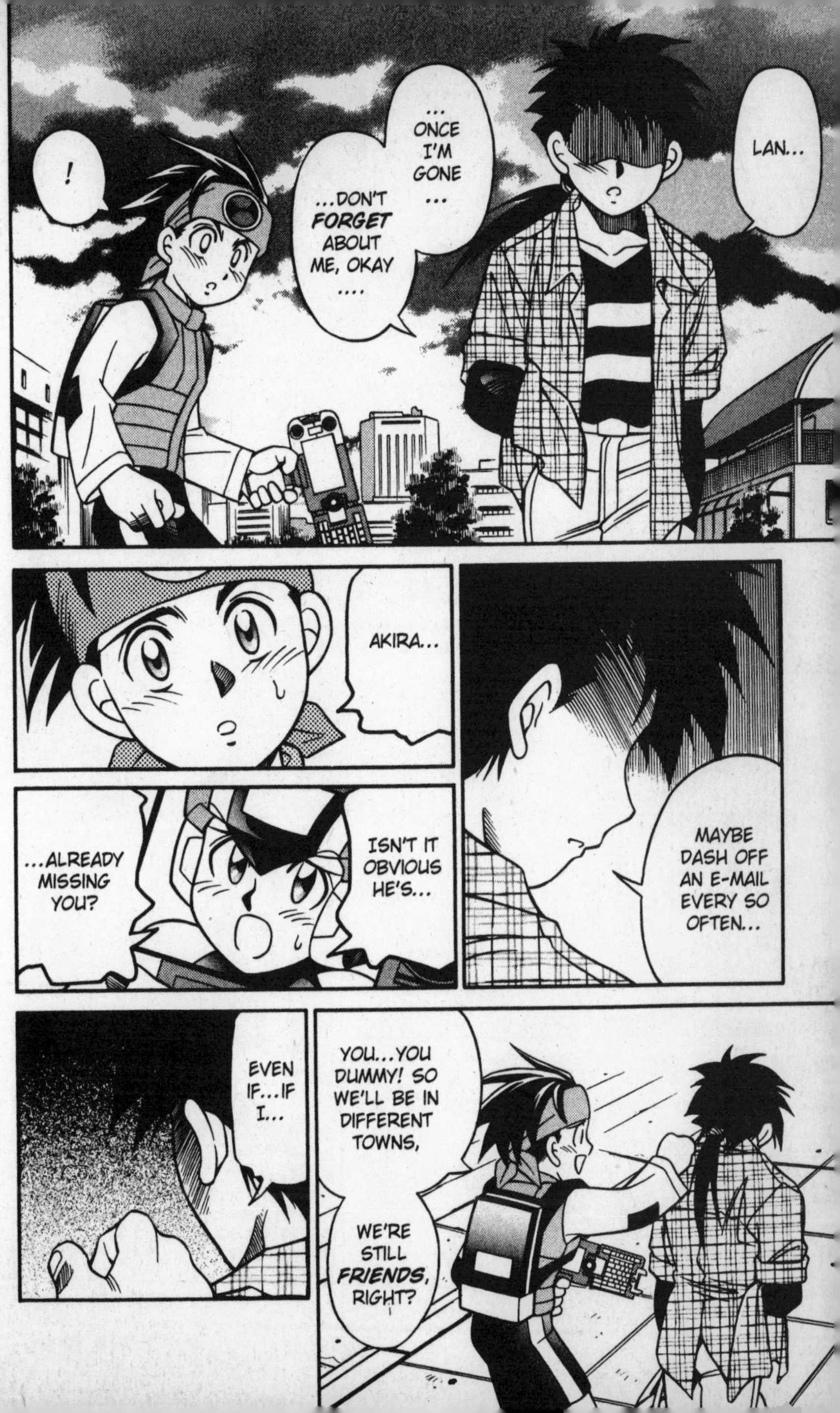
LAN...
...ONCE I'M GONE ...
...DON'T FORGET ABOUT ME, OKAY ....
!
MAYBE DASH OFF AN E-MAIL EVERY SO OFTEN...
AKIRA...
ISN'T IT OBVIOUS HE'S...
...ALREADY MISSING YOU?
YOU...YOU DUMMY! SO WE'LL BE IN DIFFERENT TOWNS,
WE'RE STILL FRIENDS, RIGHT?
EVEN IF...IF I...

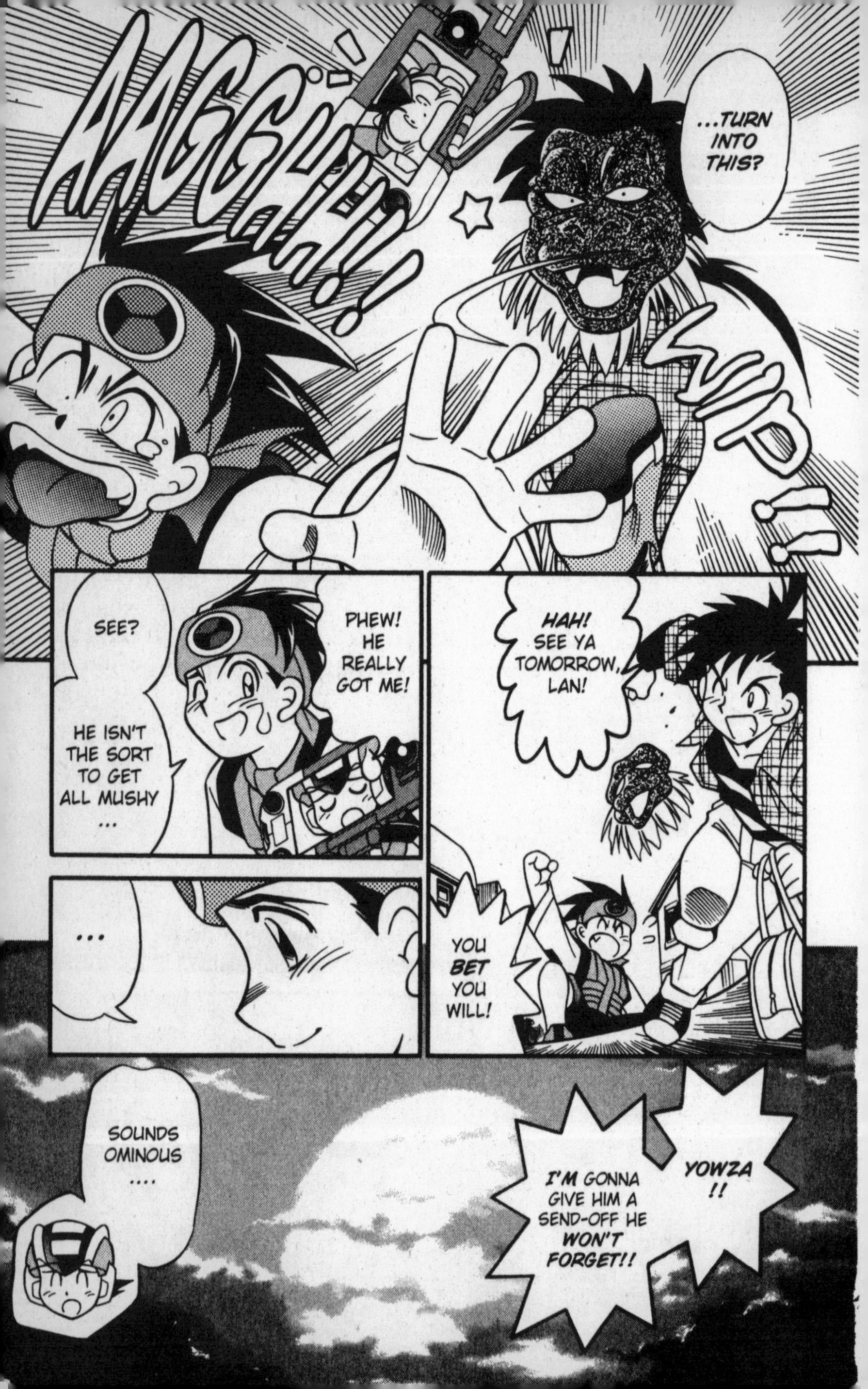
...TURN INTO THIS?
WHIP!!
HAH! SEE YA TOMORROW, LAN!
YOU BET YOU WILL!
PHEW! HE REALLY GOT ME!
SEE?
HE ISN'T THE SORT TO GET ALL MUSHY ...
...
YOWZA !!
I'M GONNA GIVE HIM A SEND-OFF HE WON'T FORGET!!
SOUNDS OMINOUS ....

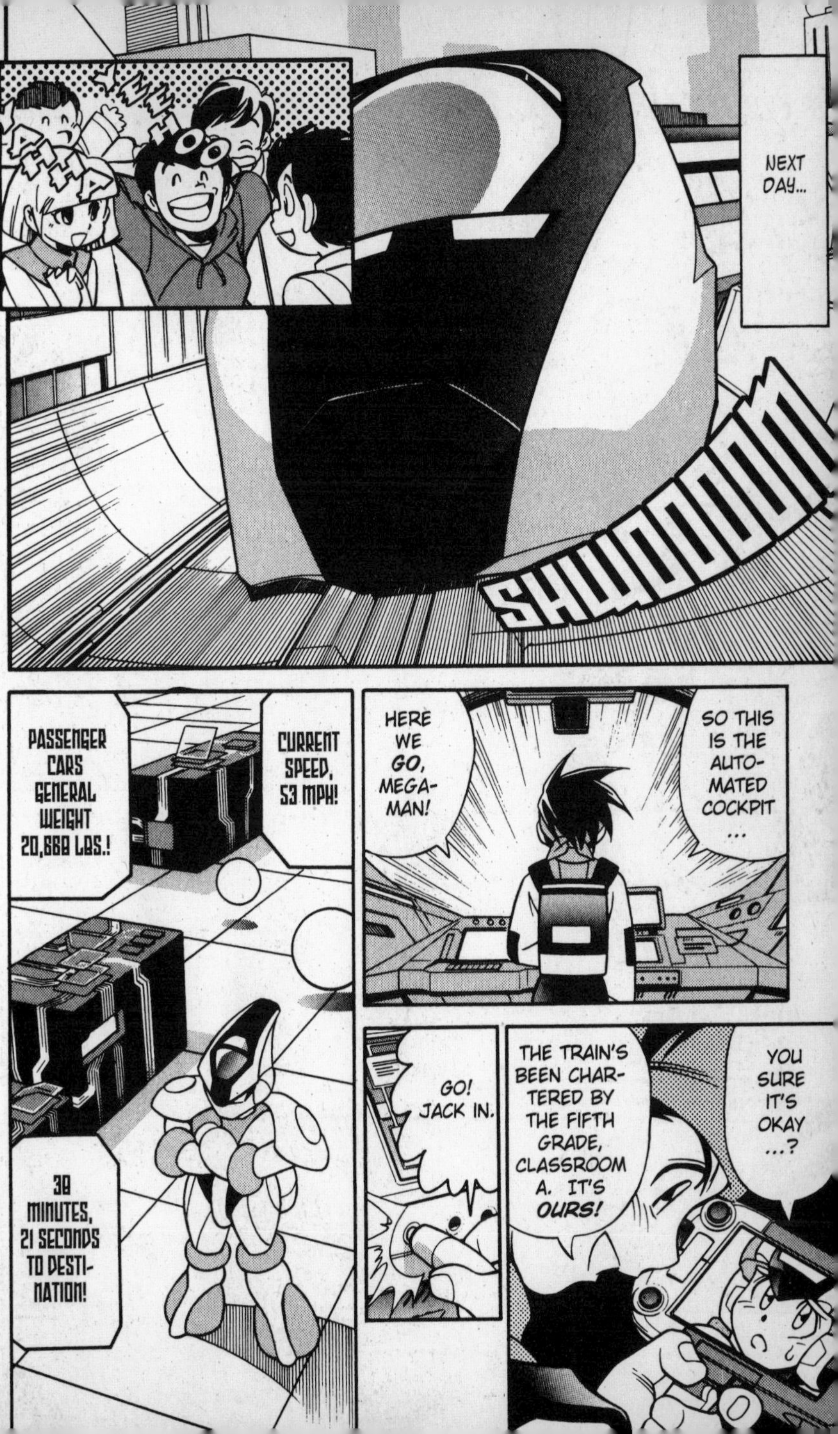
NEXT DAY...
SHWOOOM
YAHHA
YEEHOO
SO THIS IS THE AUTOMATED COCKPIT...
HERE WE GO, MEGAMAN!
YOU SURE IT'S OKAY...?
THE TRAIN'S BEEN CHARTERED BY THE FIFTH GRADE, CLASSROOM A. IT'S OURS!
GO! JACK IN.
CURRENT SPEED, 53 MPH!
PASSENGER CARS GENERAL WEIGHT 20,668 LBS.!
38 MINUTES, 21 SECONDS TO DESTINATION!

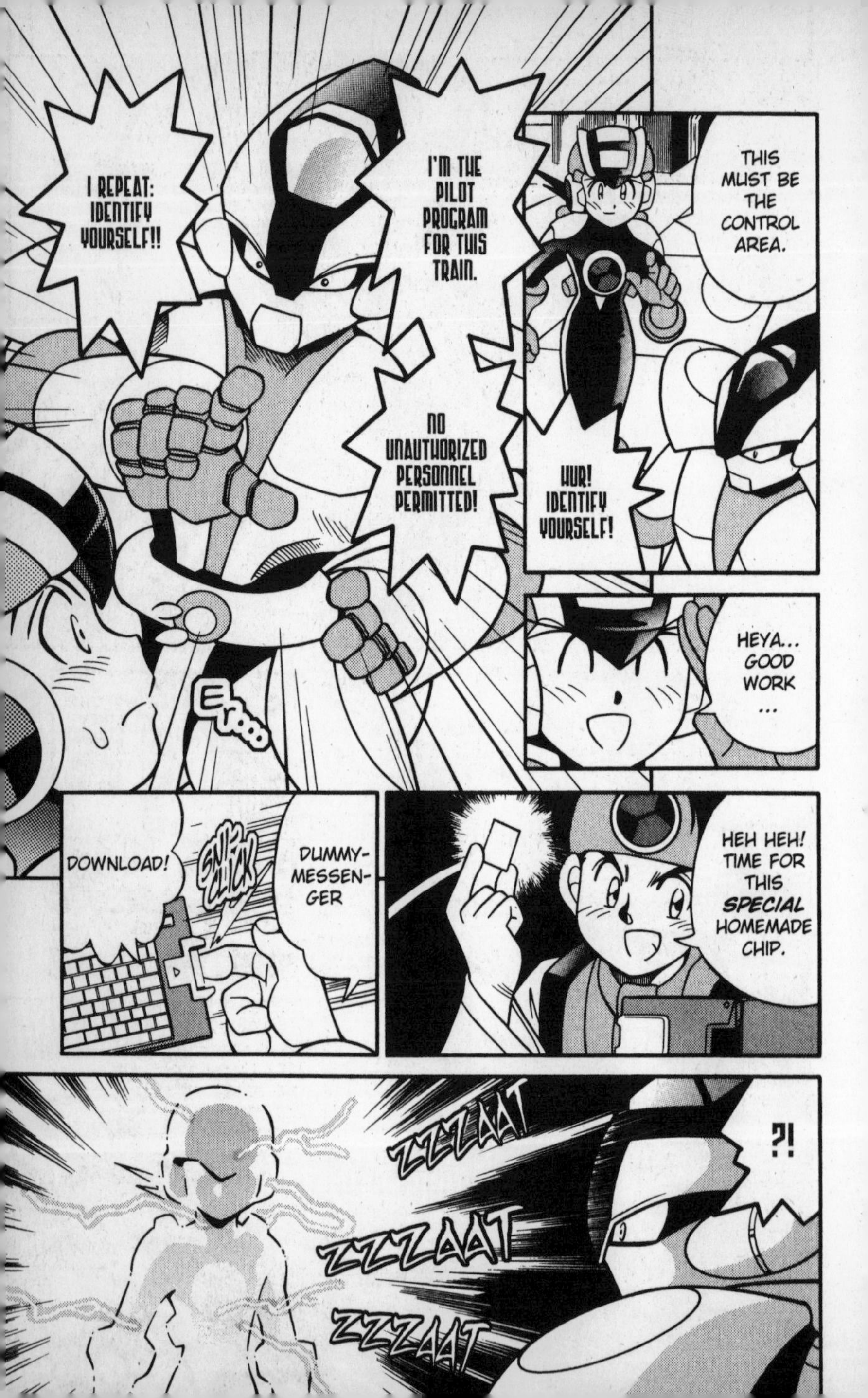
THIS MUST BE THE CONTROL AREA.
HUR! IDENTIFY YOURSELF!
HEYA... GOOD WORK ...
I'M THE PILOT PROGRAM FOR THIS TRAIN.
I REPEAT: IDENTIFY YOURSELF!!
NO UNAUTHORIZED PERSONNEL PERMITTED!
Er...
HEH HEH! TIME FOR THIS *SPECIAL* HOMEMADE CHIP.
DUMMY-MESSENGER
SNICK CLICK
DOWNLOAD!
?!
ZZZZAAT
ZZZZAAT
ZZZAAT

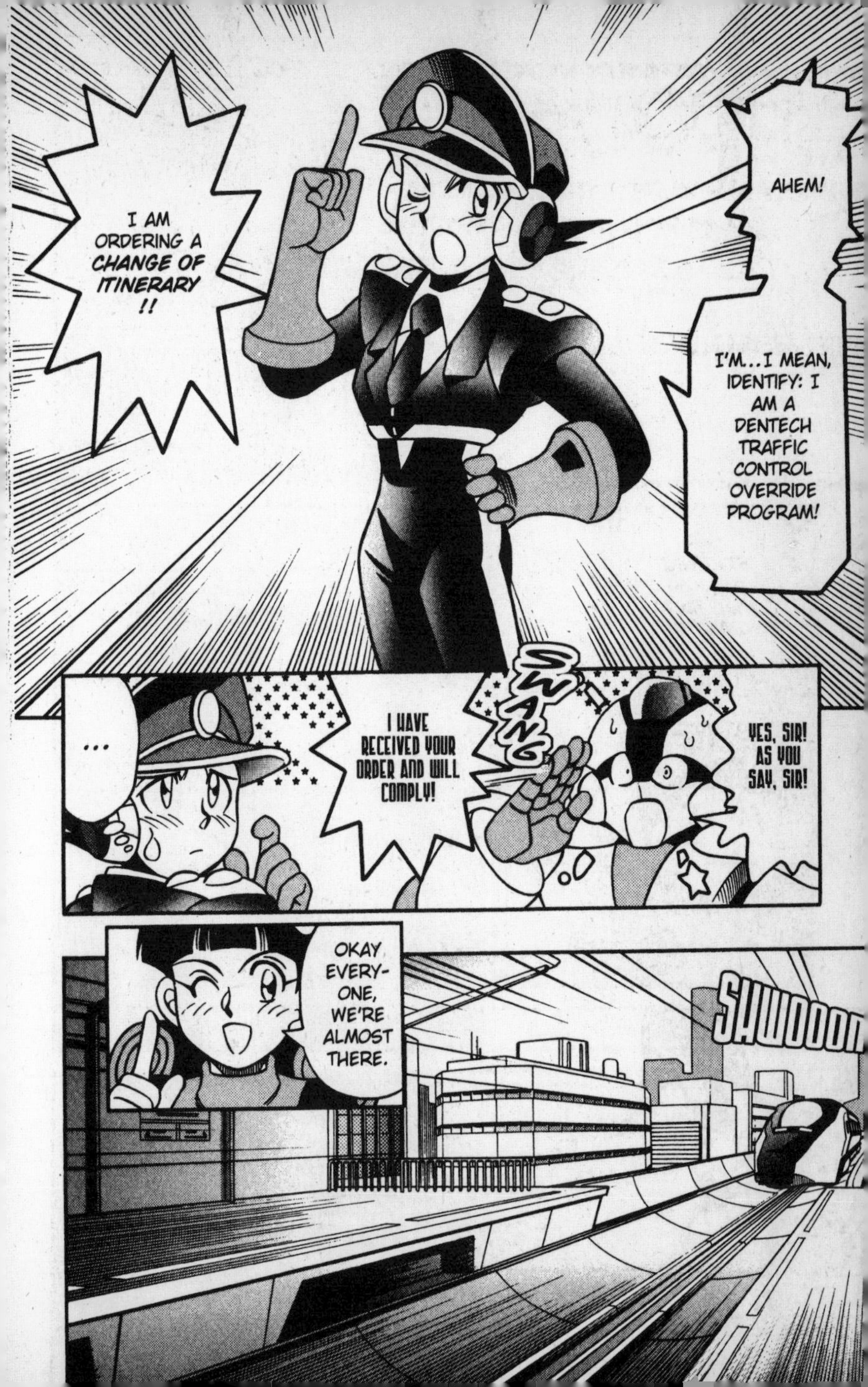
AHEM!
I'M...I MEAN, IDENTIFY: I AM A DENTECH TRAFFIC CONTROL OVERRIDE PROGRAM!
I AM ORDERING A CHANGE OF ITINERARY !!
YES, SIR! AS YOU SAY, SIR!
SWANG
I HAVE RECEIVED YOUR ORDER AND WILL COMPLY!
...
SHWOOO
OKAY EVERY-ONE, WE'RE ALMOST THERE.

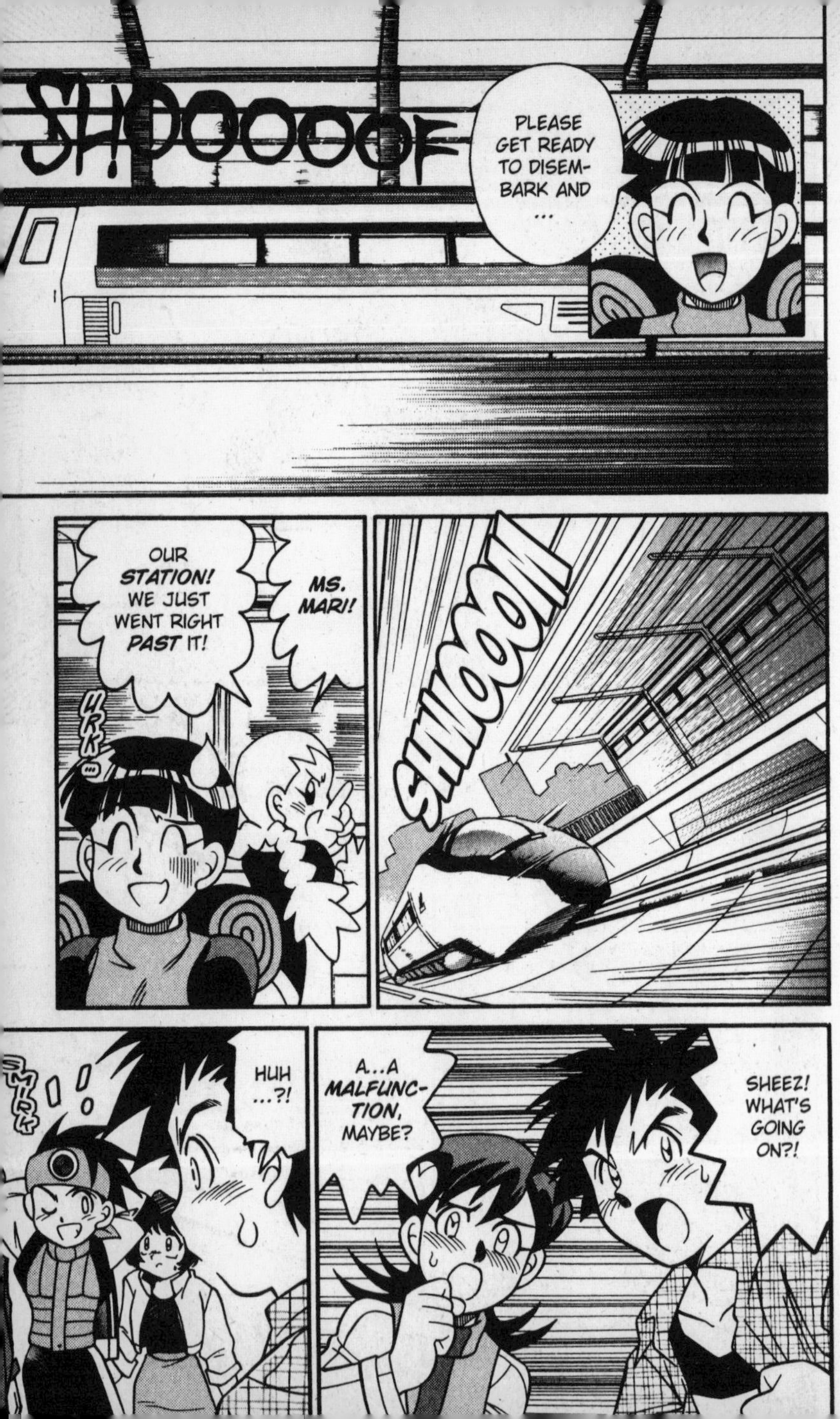
PLEASE GET READY TO DISEMBARK AND ...
SHOOOOOF
SHWOOOM
OUR STATION! WE JUST WENT RIGHT PAST IT!
MS. MARI!
URK...
SHEEZ! WHAT'S GOING ON?!
A...A MALFUNCTION, MAYBE?
HUH ...?!
SMIRK

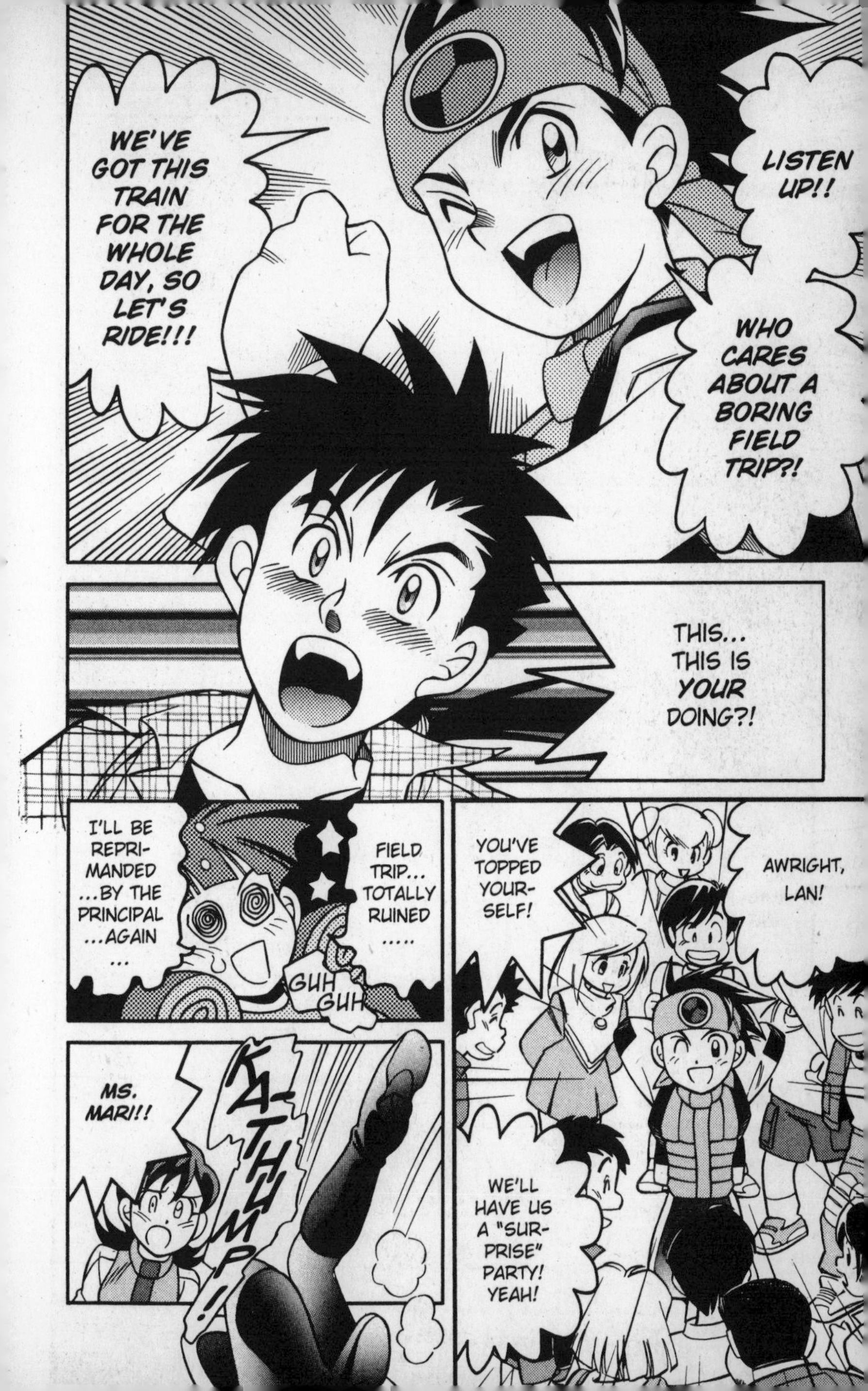
LISTEN UP!!
WHO CARES ABOUT A BORING FIELD TRIP?!
WE'VE GOT THIS TRAIN FOR THE WHOLE DAY, SO LET'S RIDE!!!
THIS... THIS IS YOUR DOING?!
AWRIGHT, LAN!
YOU'VE TOPPED YOUR-SELF!
WE'LL HAVE US A "SUR-PRISE" PARTY! YEAH!
FIELD TRIP... TOTALLY RUINED .....
I'LL BE REPRI-MANDED ...BY THE PRINCIPAL ...AGAIN ...
GUH GUH
KA-THUMP!
MS. MARI!!

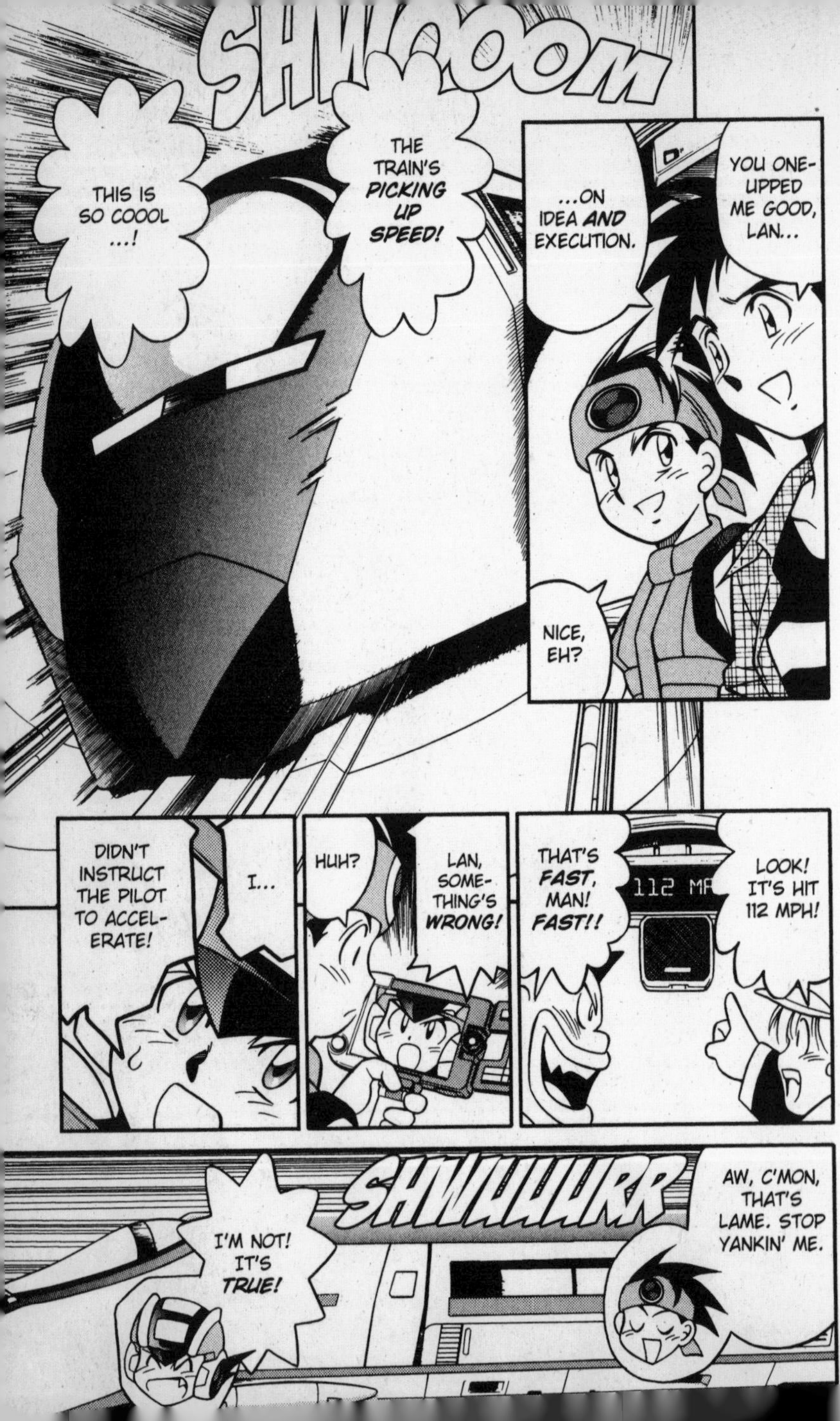
YOU ONE-UPPED ME GOOD, LAN...
...ON IDEA AND EXECUTION.
NICE, EH?
SHWOOOM
THE TRAIN'S PICKING UP SPEED!
THIS IS SO COOOL ...!
LOOK! IT'S HIT 112 MPH!
112 MP
THAT'S FAST, MAN! FAST!!
LAN, SOME-THING'S WRONG!
HUH?
I...
DIDN'T INSTRUCT THE PILOT TO ACCEL-ERATE!
AW, C'MON, THAT'S LAME. STOP YANKIN' ME.
SHWUUUURR
I'M NOT! IT'S TRUE!

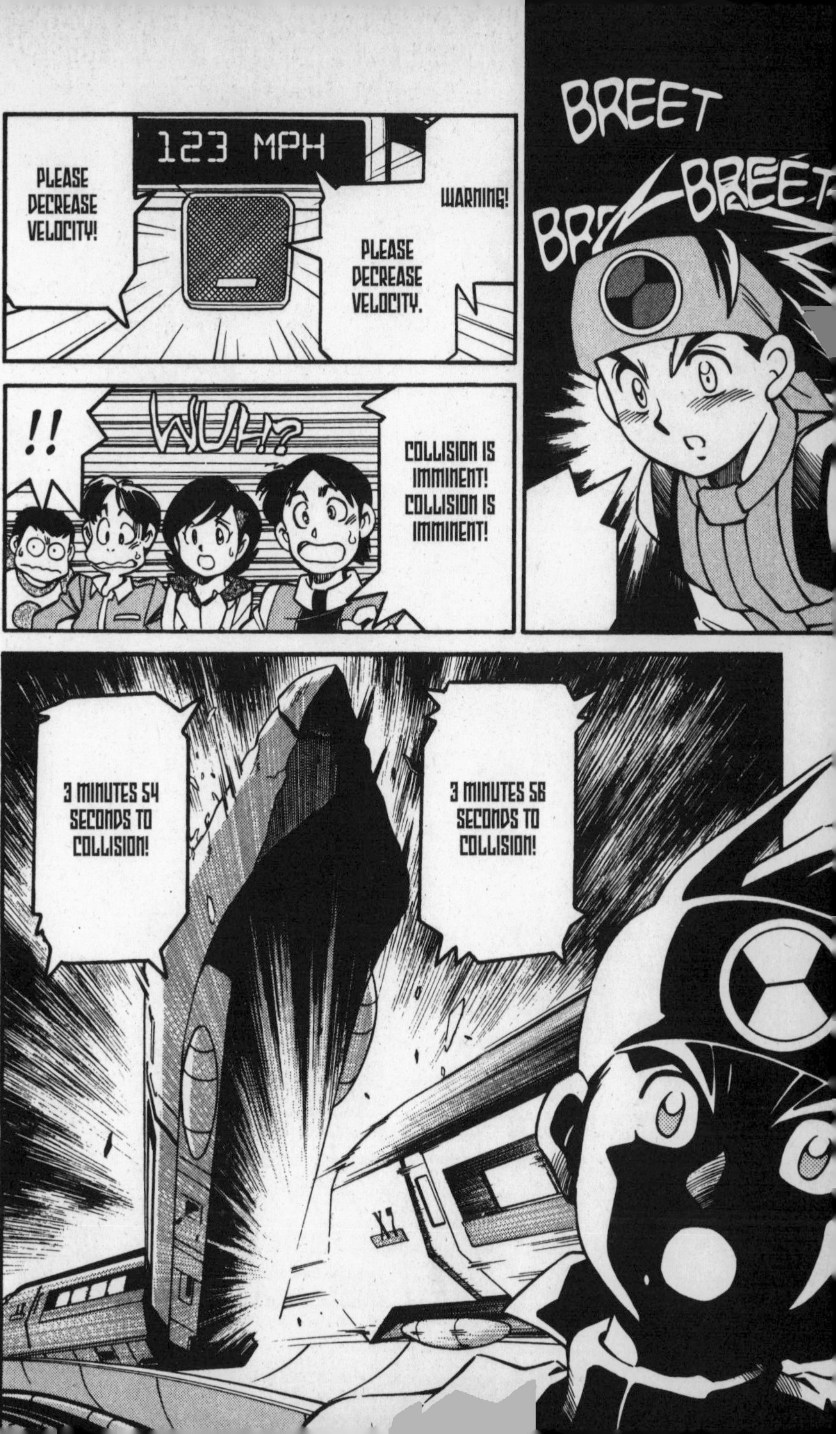

BREET
BREET
123 MPH
WARNING!
PLEASE DECREASE VELOCITY.
PLEASE DECREASE VELOCITY!
COLLISION IS IMMINENT! COLLISION IS IMMINENT!
WUH!?
!!
3 MINUTES 56 SECONDS TO COLLISION!
3 MINUTES 54 SECONDS TO COLLISION!

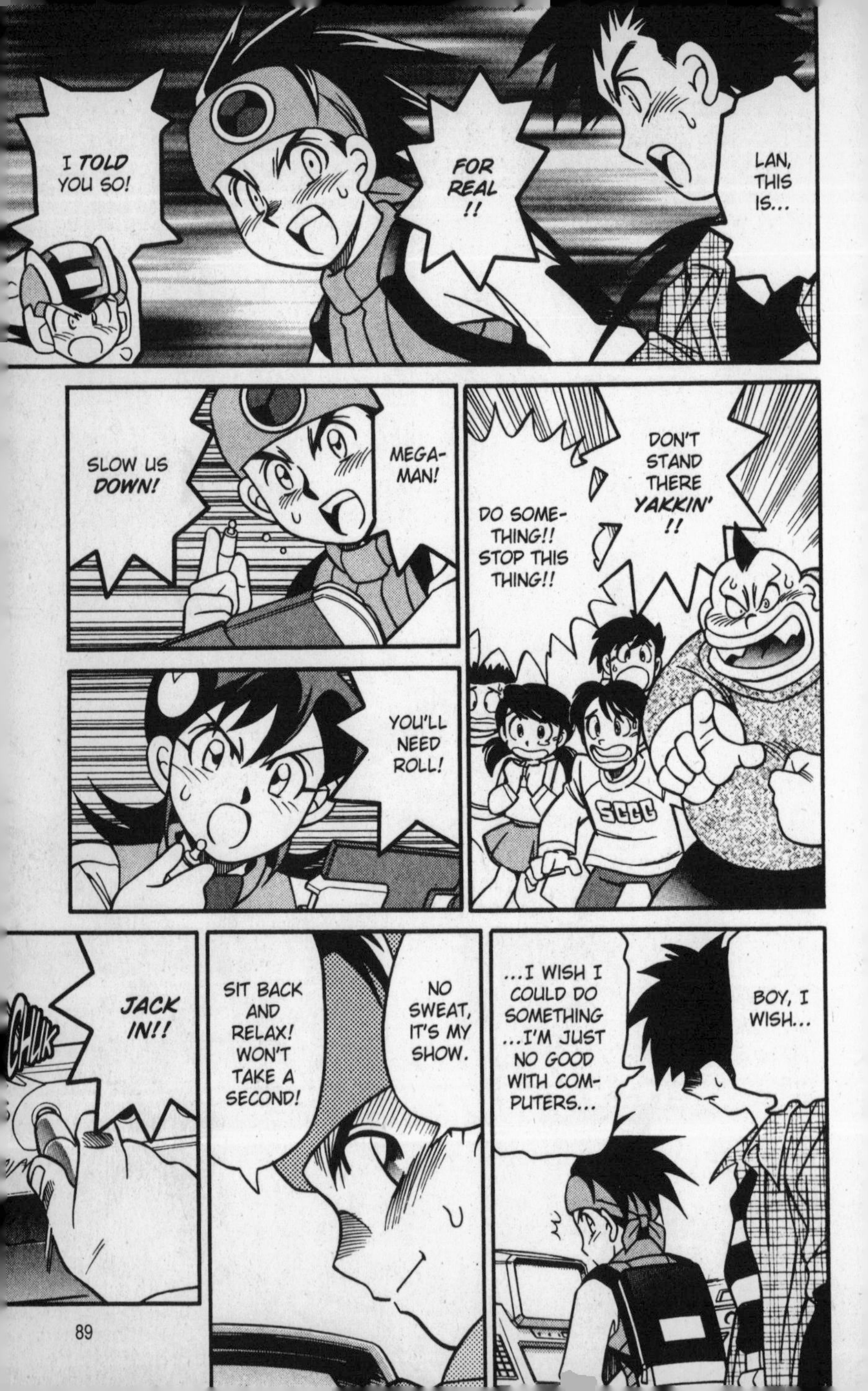
LAN, THIS IS...
FOR REAL!!
I TOLD YOU SO!
DON'T STAND THERE YAKKIN'!!
DO SOME-THING!! STOP THIS THING!!
MEGA-MAN!
SLOW US DOWN!
YOU'LL NEED ROLL!
BOY, I WISH...
...I WISH I COULD DO SOMETHING ...I'M JUST NO GOOD WITH COM-PUTERS...
NO SWEAT, IT'S MY SHOW.
SIT BACK AND RELAX! WON'T TAKE A SECOND!
JACK IN!!
CHUK

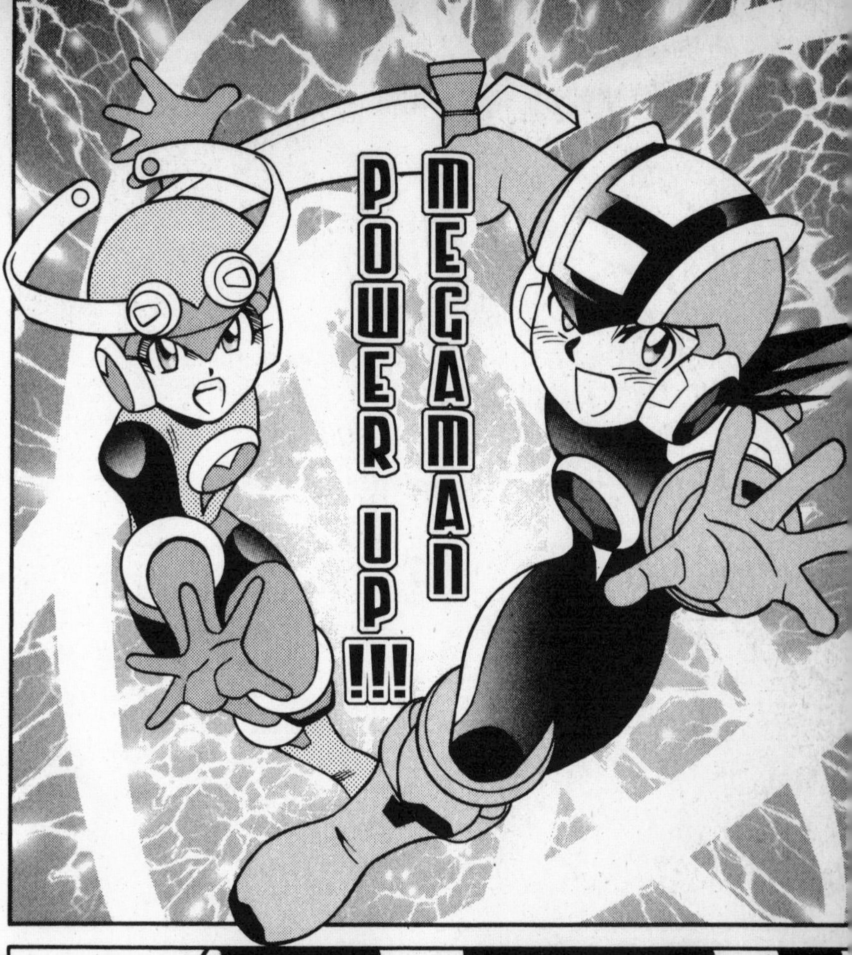
MEGAMAN
POWER UP!!!
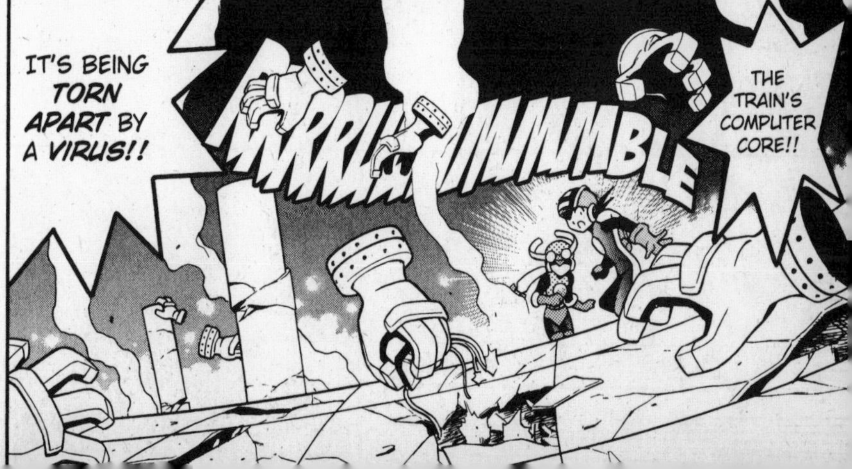
THE TRAIN'S COMPUTER CORE!!
IT'S BEING *TORN APART* BY A *VIRUS!!*

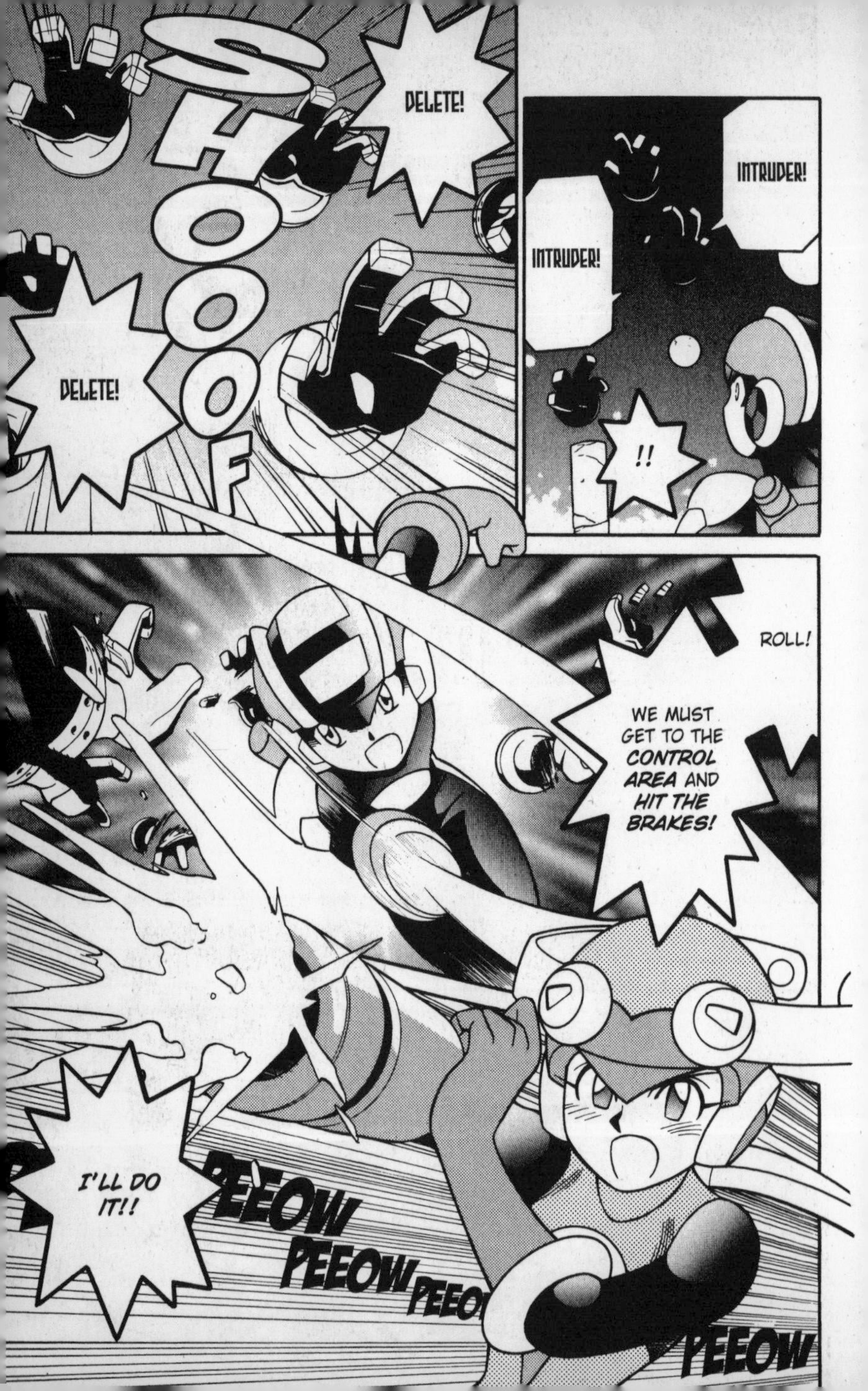
INTRUDER!
INTRUDER!
!!
SHOOOOF
DELETE!
DELETE!
ROLL!
WE MUST GET TO THE CONTROL AREA AND HIT THE BRAKES!
I'LL DO IT!!
PEEOW
PEEOW
PEEOW
PEEOW

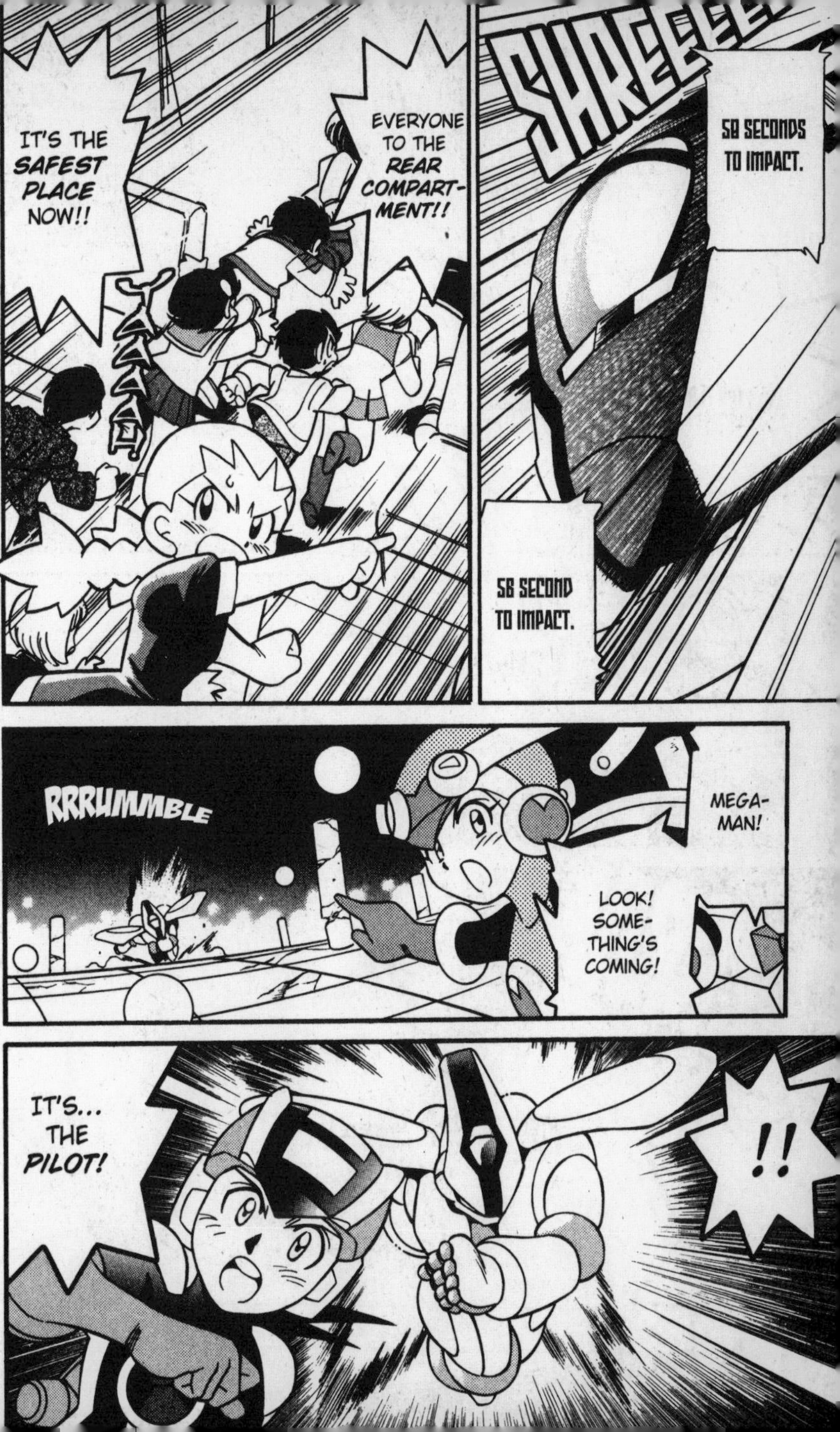
SHREEEE
58 SECONDS TO IMPACT.
56 SECOND TO IMPACT.
EVERYONE TO THE REAR COMPART- MENT!!
IT'S THE SAFEST PLACE NOW!!
MEGA- MAN!
LOOK! SOME- THING'S COMING!
RRRUMMBLE
!!
IT'S... THE PILOT!

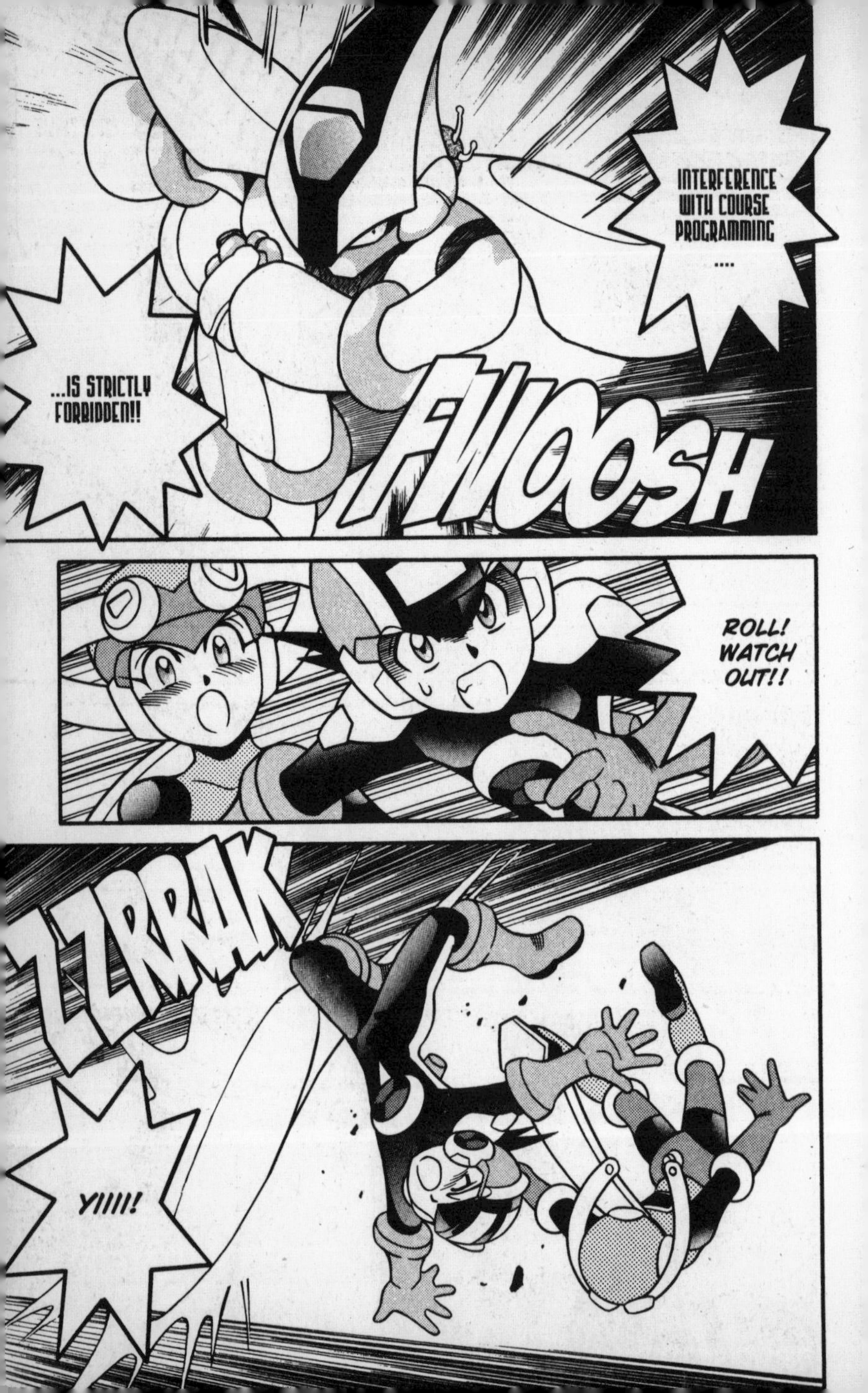
INTERFERENCE WITH COURSE PROGRAMMING ....
...IS STRICTLY FORBIDDEN!!
FWOOSH
ROLL! WATCH OUT!!
ZZRRAK
YIIII!

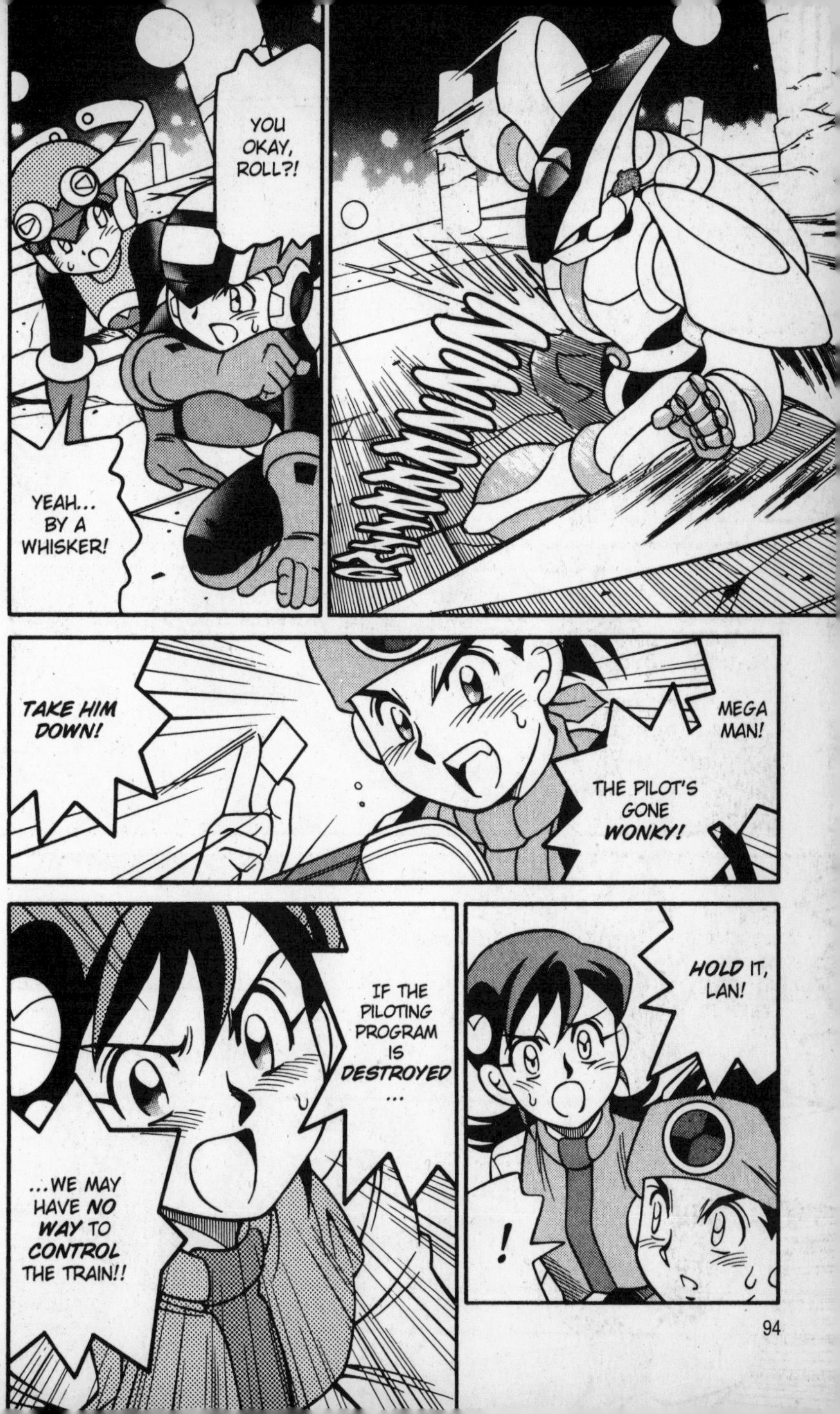
YOU OKAY, ROLL?!
YEAH... BY A WHISKER!
MEGA MAN!
THE PILOT'S GONE **WONKY!**
TAKE HIM DOWN!
HOLD IT, LAN!
!
IF THE PILOTING PROGRAM IS **DESTROYED** ...
...WE MAY HAVE **NO WAY** TO **CONTROL** THE TRAIN!!

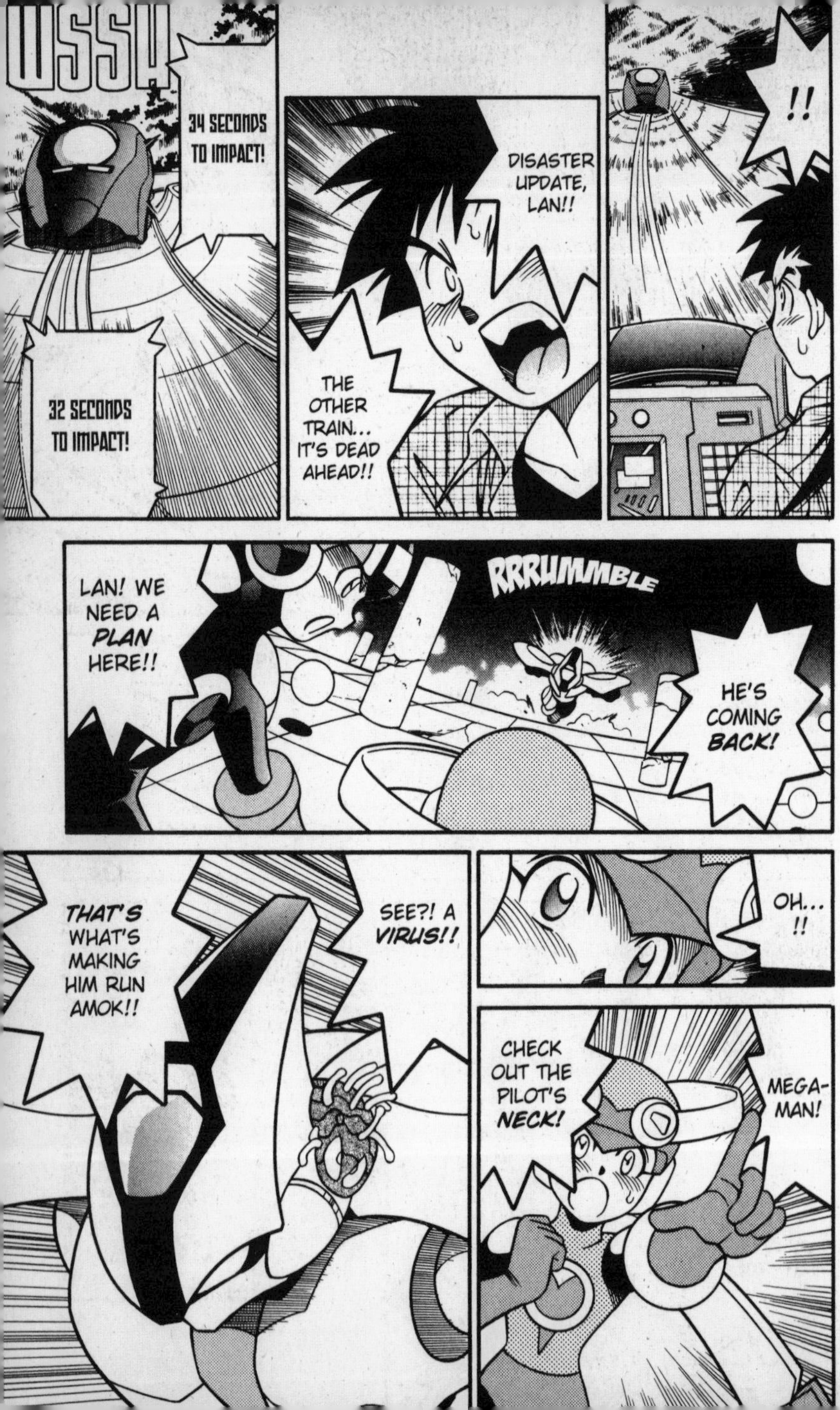
!!
DISASTER UPDATE, LAN!!
THE OTHER TRAIN... IT'S DEAD AHEAD!!
WSSH
34 SECONDS TO IMPACT!
32 SECONDS TO IMPACT!
RRRUMMBLE
HE'S COMING BACK!
LAN! WE NEED A PLAN HERE!!
OH... !!
MEGA-MAN!
CHECK OUT THE PILOT'S NECK!
SEE?! A VIRUS!!
THAT'S WHAT'S MAKING HIM RUN AMOK!!

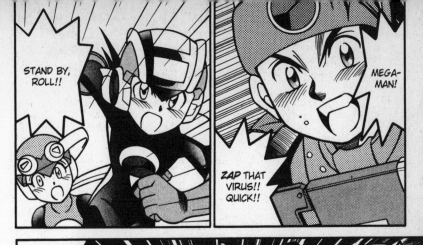

STAND BY, ROLL!!

MEGA-MAN!

ZAP THAT VIRUS!! QUICK!!

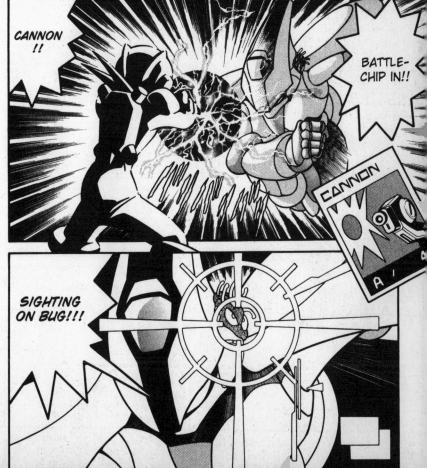

CANNON!!

BATTLE-CHIP IN!!

CANNON

SIGHTING ON BUG!!!

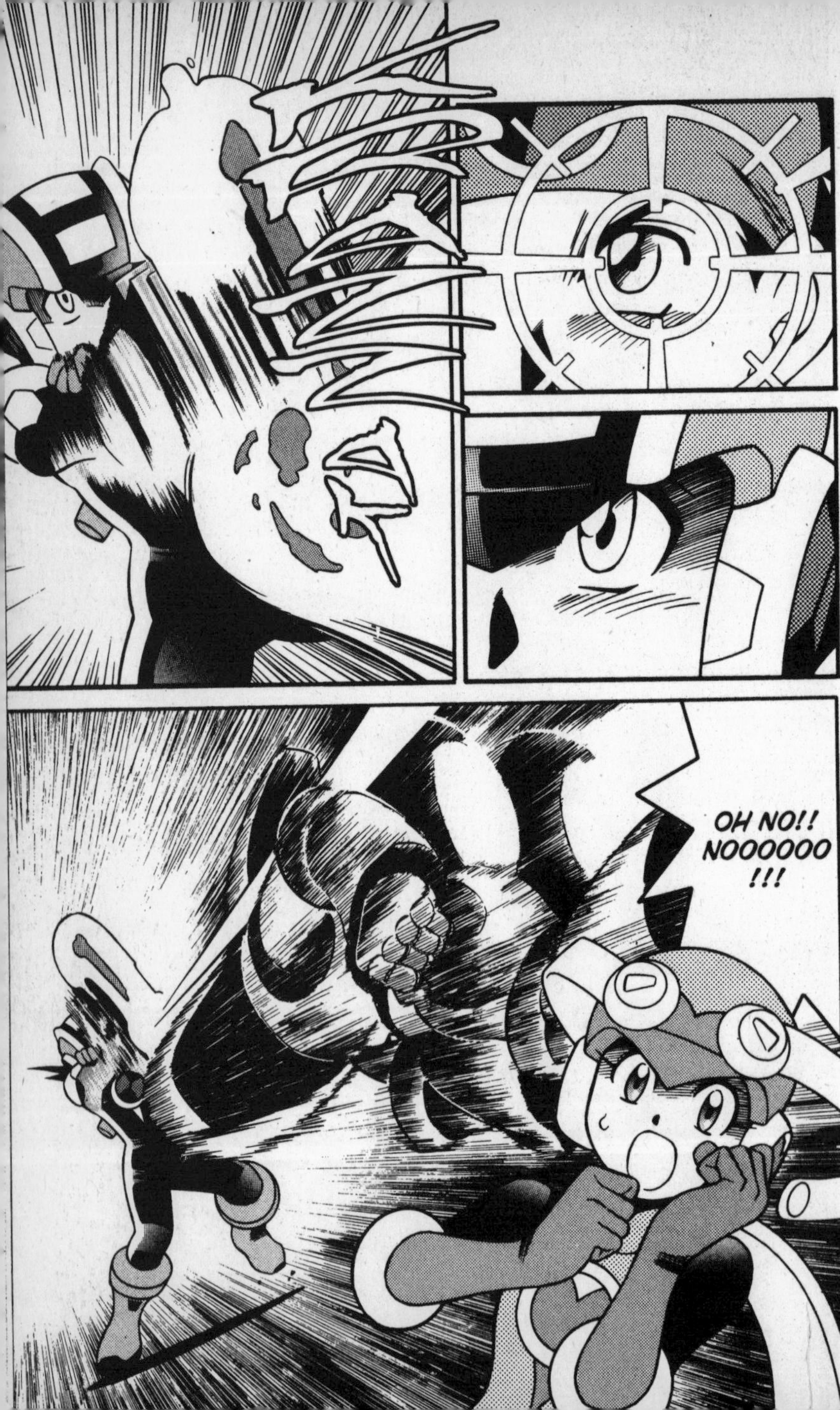
OH NO!! NOOOOOO !!!

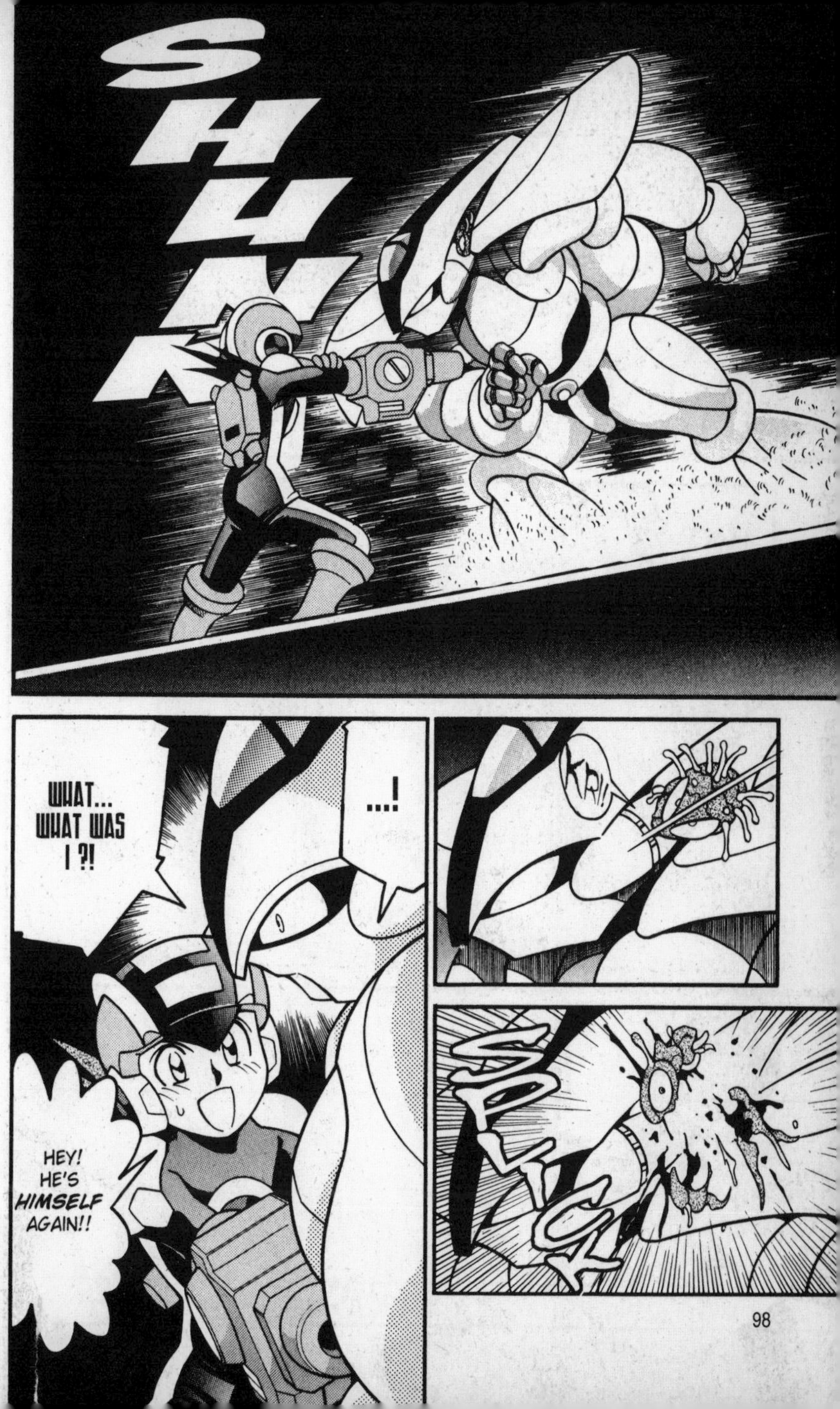
SHUNK
KRI!!
...!
WHAT... WHAT WAS I ?!
HEY! HE'S *HIMSELF* AGAIN!!

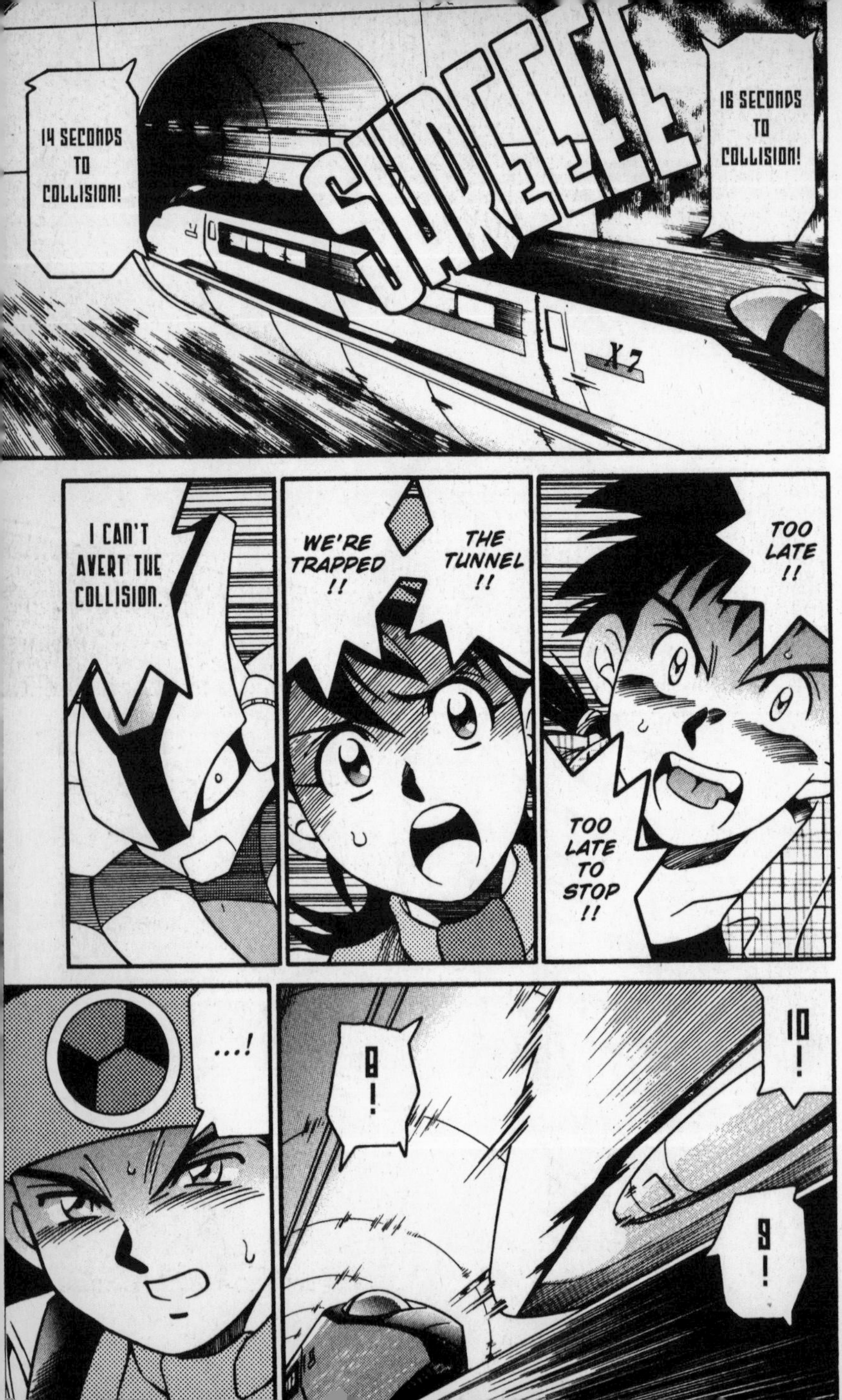
16 SECONDS TO COLLISION!
SWREEEE
14 SECONDS TO COLLISION!
TOO LATE!!
TOO LATE TO STOP!!
THE TUNNEL!!
WE'RE TRAPPED!!
I CAN'T AVERT THE COLLISION.
10!
9!
8!
...!

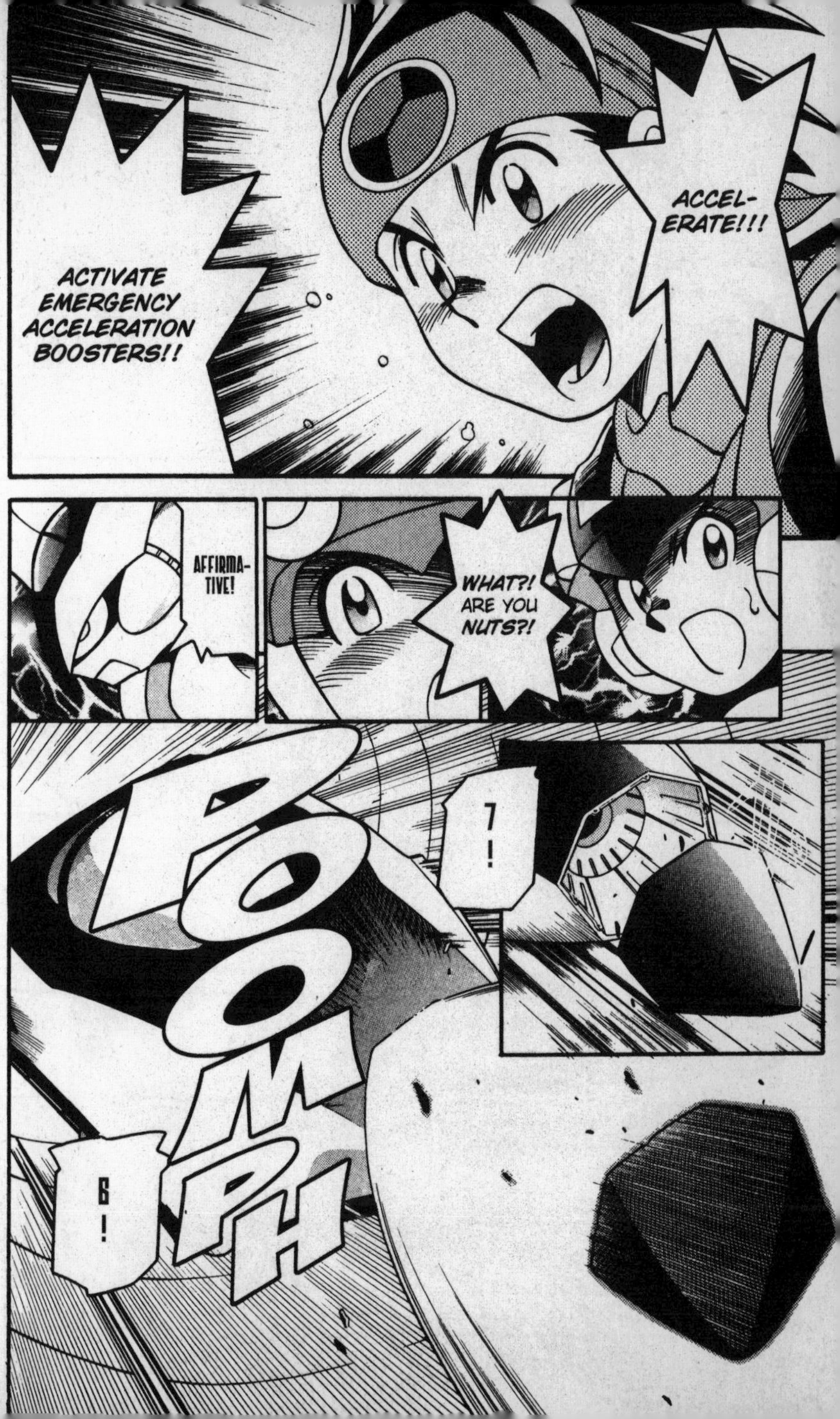
ACCEL-ERATE!!!
ACTIVATE EMERGENCY ACCELERATION BOOSTERS!!
WHAT?! ARE YOU NUTS?!
AFFIRMA-TIVE!
7 !
BOOMPH
6 !

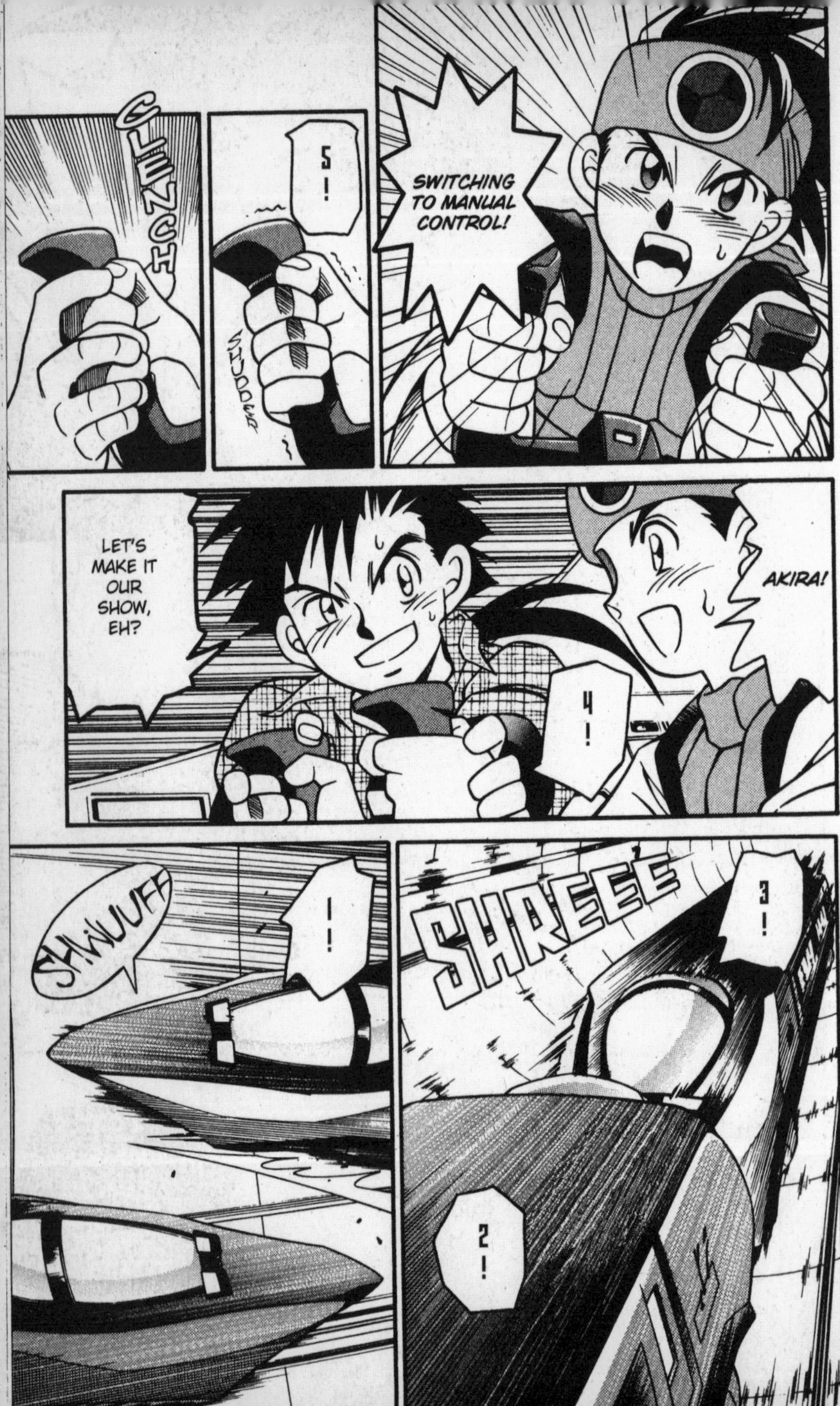
SWITCHING TO MANUAL CONTROL!
5!
SHUDDER
CLENCH
AKIRA!
LET'S MAKE IT OUR SHOW, EH?
4!
3!
SHREEE
2!
1!
SHWUUFF

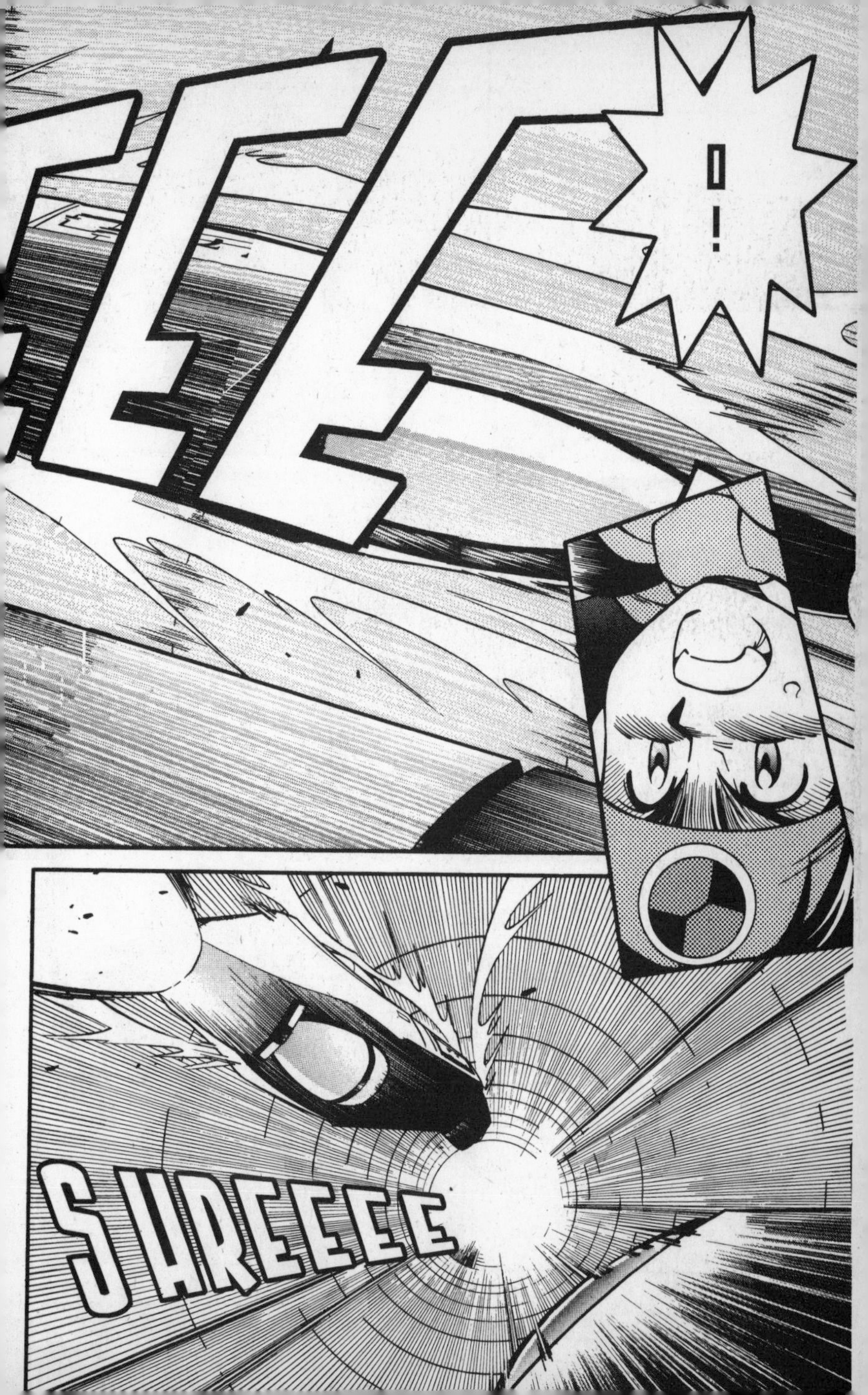
EEE
!!
SHREEEE

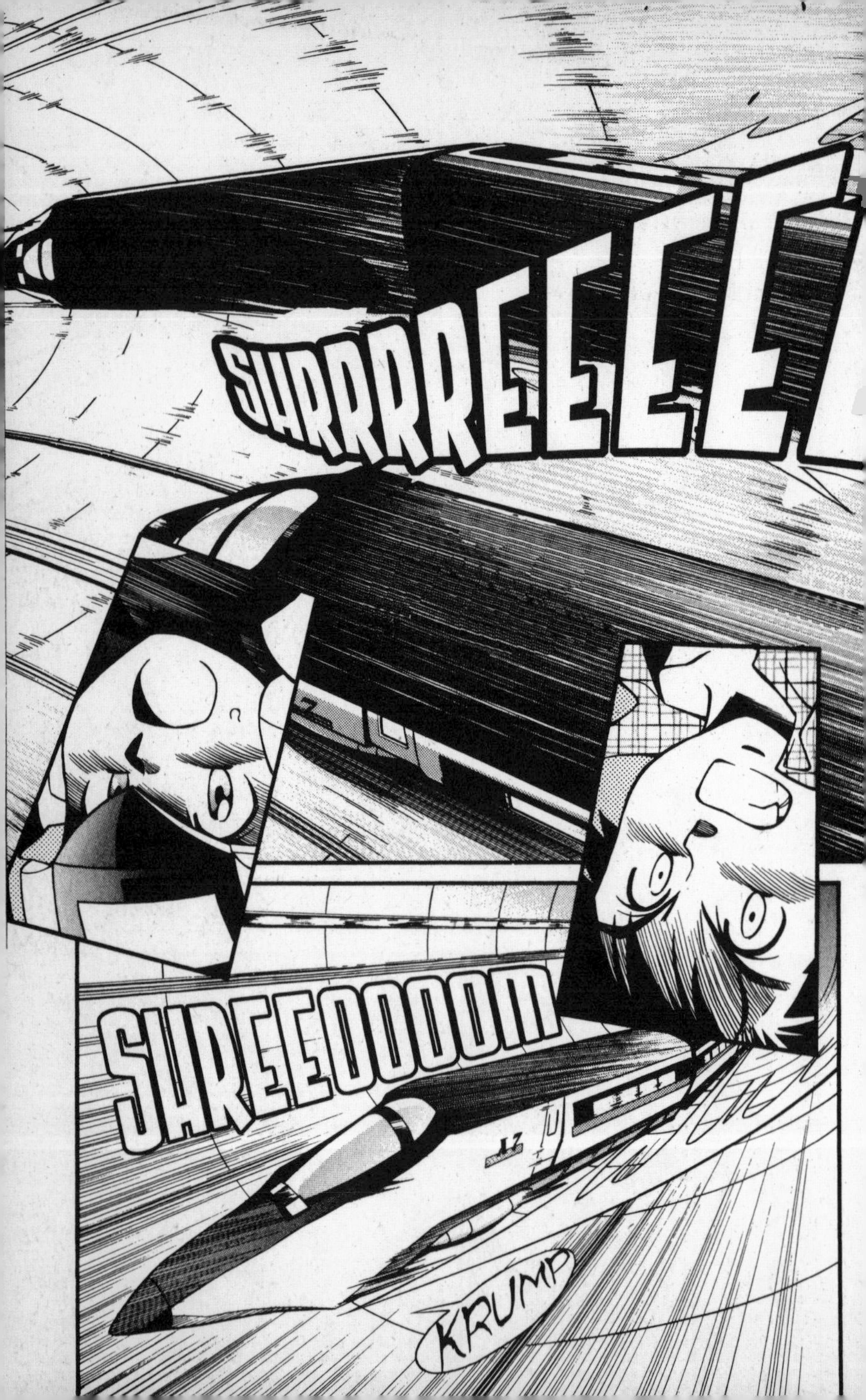
SURRRREEEE
SHREEOOOOM
KRUMP

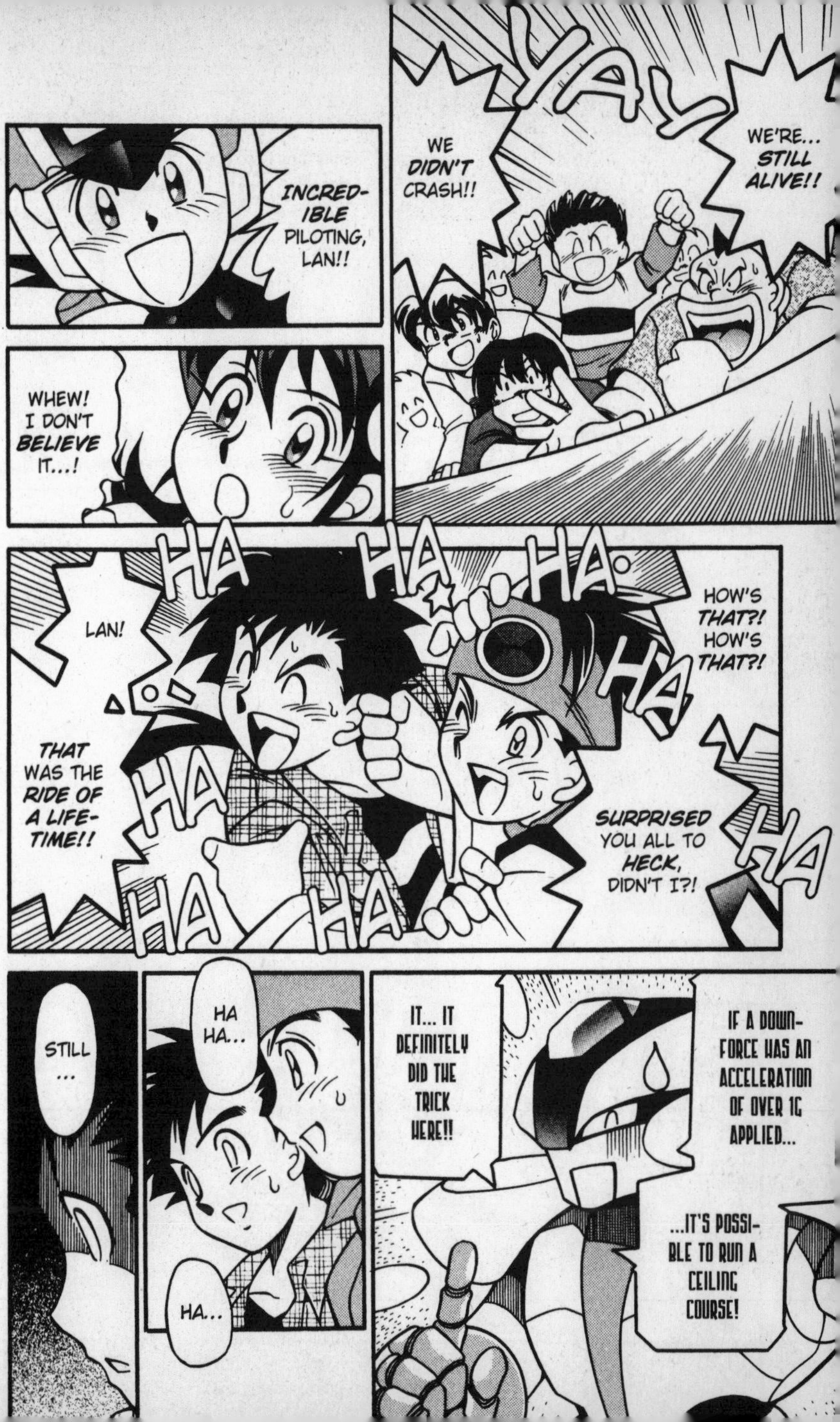
YAY
WE'RE... STILL ALIVE!!
WE DIDN'T CRASH!!
INCREDIBLE PILOTING, LAN!!
WHEW! I DON'T BELIEVE IT...!
HA HA HA HA HA
HOW'S THAT?! HOW'S THAT?!
SURPRISED YOU ALL TO HECK, DIDN'T I?!
LAN!
THAT WAS THE RIDE OF A LIFETIME!!
HA HA HA
IF A DOWNFORCE HAS AN ACCELERATION OF OVER 1G APPLIED...
IT... IT DEFINITELY DID THE TRICK HERE!!
...IT'S POSSIBLE TO RUN A CEILING COURSE!
HA HA...
HA...
STILL ...

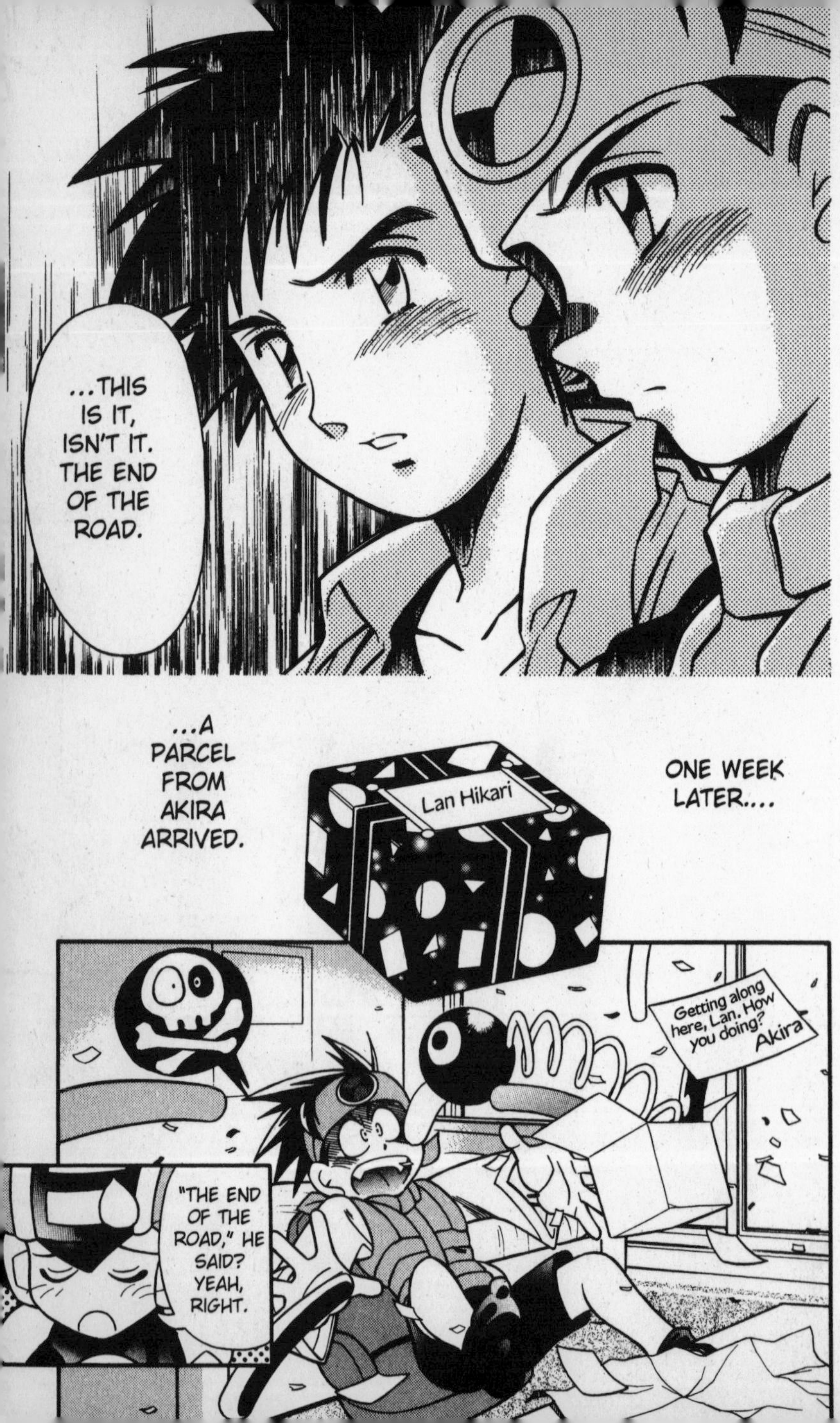
...THIS IS IT, ISN'T IT. THE END OF THE ROAD.
ONE WEEK LATER....
Lan Hikari
...A PARCEL FROM AKIRA ARRIVED.
Getting along here, Lan. How you doing? Akira
"THE END OF THE ROAD," HE SAID? YEAH, RIGHT.

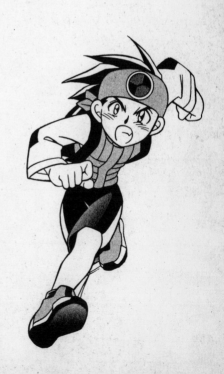

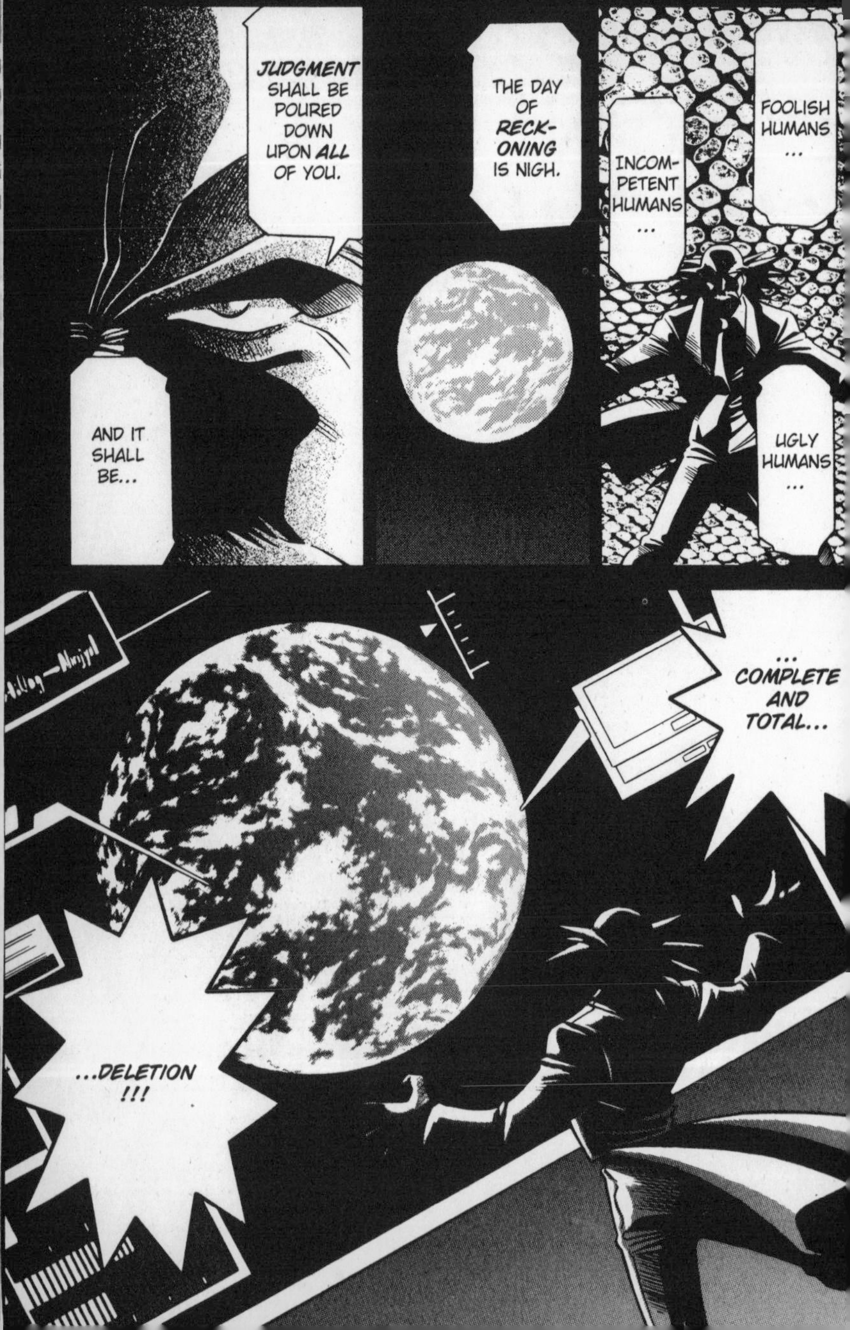
FOOLISH HUMANS ...
INCOM-PETENT HUMANS ...
UGLY HUMANS ...
THE DAY OF RECK-ONING IS NIGH.
JUDGMENT SHALL BE POURED DOWN UPON ALL OF YOU.
AND IT SHALL BE...
... COMPLETE AND TOTAL...
...DELETION !!!

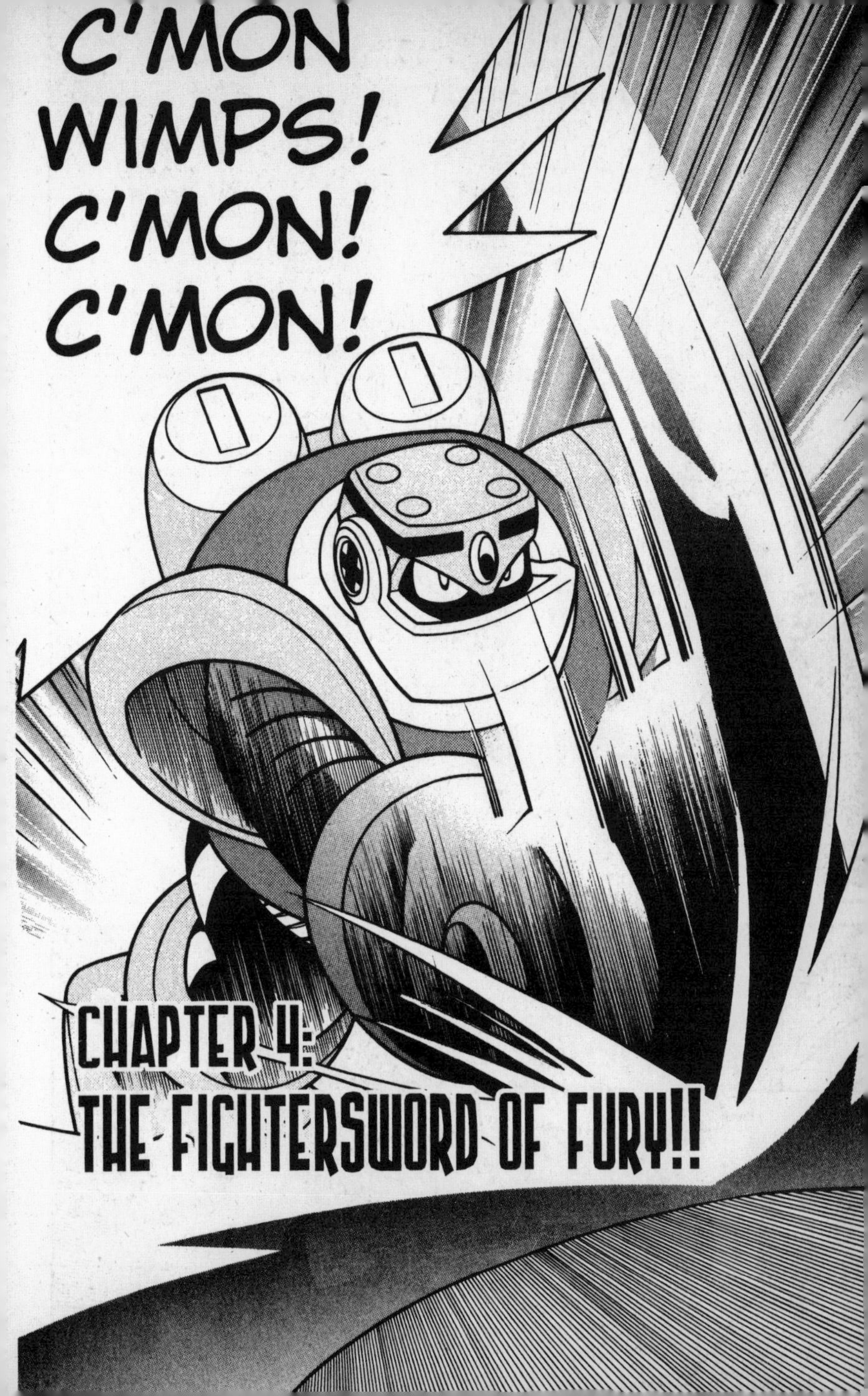
C'MON WIMPS! C'MON! C'MON!
CHAPTER 4:
THE FIGHTERSWORD OF FURY!!

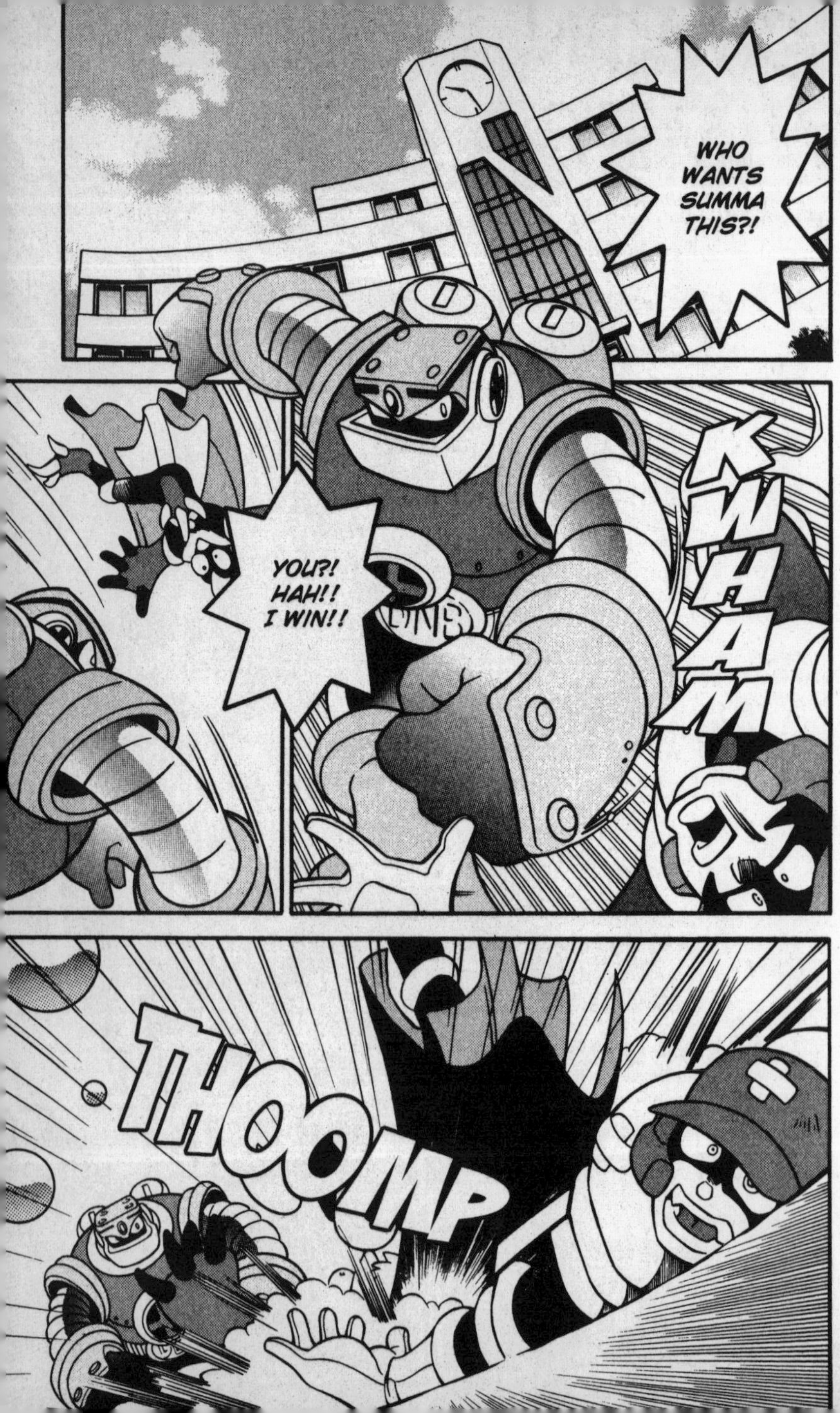
WHO WANTS SUMMA THIS?!
KWHAM
YOU?! HAH!! I WIN!!
THOOMP

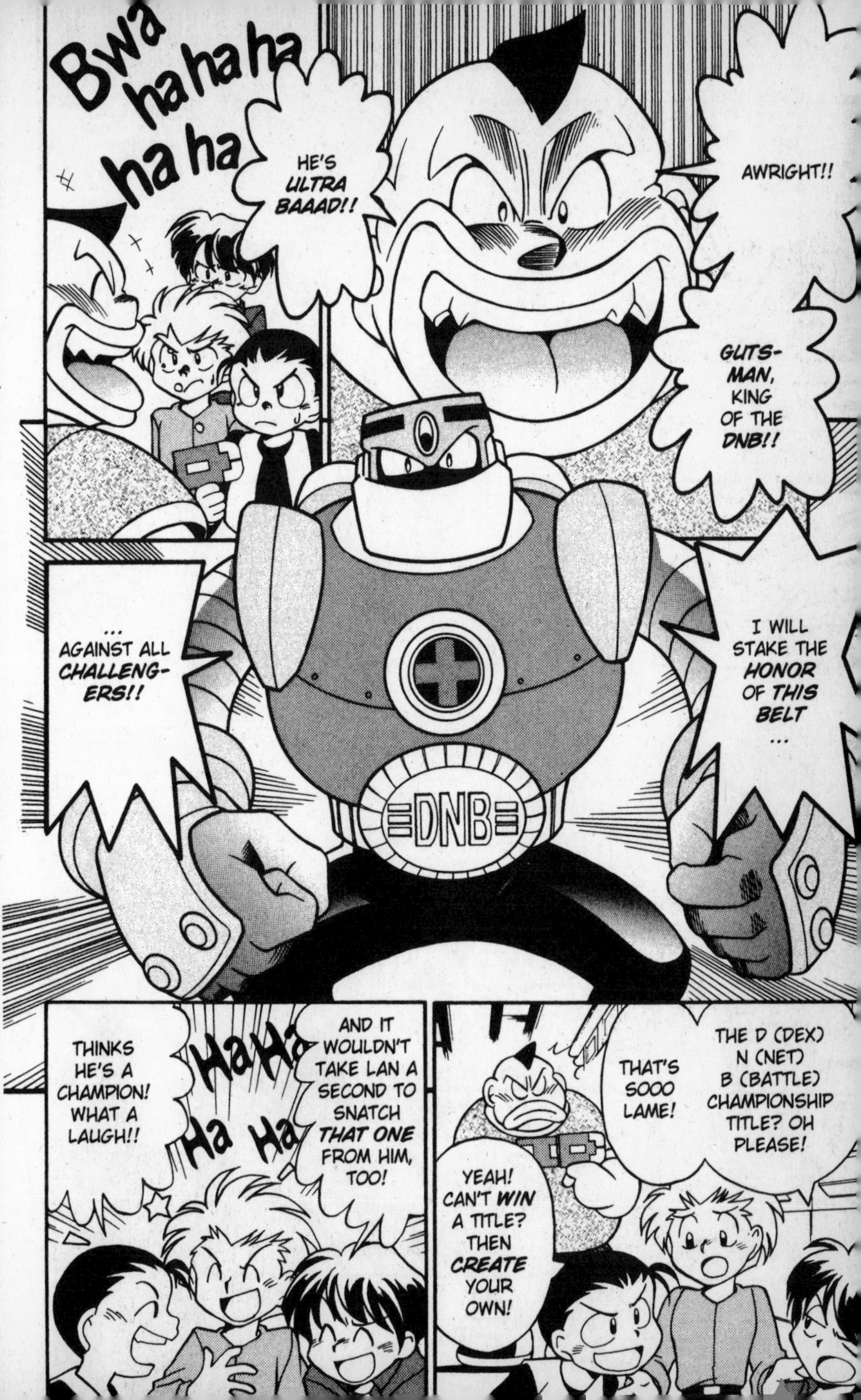
AWRIGHT!!
GUTS-MAN, KING OF THE DNB!!
HE'S ULTRA BAAAD!!
Bwa ha ha ha ha ha ha
I WILL STAKE THE HONOR OF THIS BELT ...
... AGAINST ALL CHALLENGERS!!
THE D (DEX) N (NET) B (BATTLE) CHAMPIONSHIP TITLE? OH PLEASE!
THAT'S SOOO LAME!
YEAH! CAN'T WIN A TITLE? THEN CREATE YOUR OWN!
AND IT WOULDN'T TAKE LAN A SECOND TO SNATCH THAT ONE FROM HIM, TOO!
Ha Ha Ha Ha
THINKS HE'S A CHAMPION! WHAT A LAUGH!!

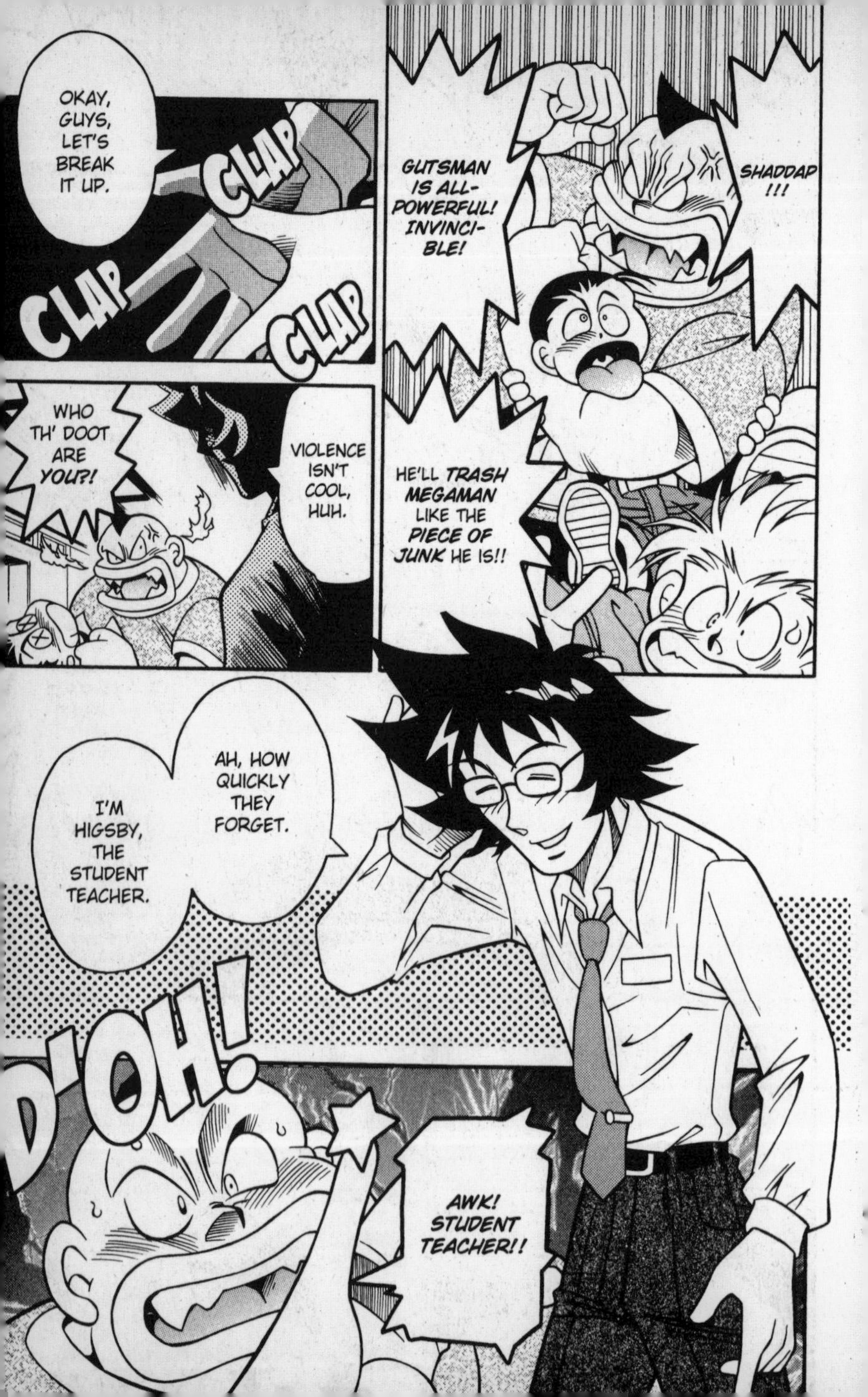
SHADDAP!!!
GUTSMAN IS ALL-POWERFUL! INVINCIBLE!
HE'LL TRASH MEGAMAN LIKE THE PIECE OF JUNK HE IS!!
OKAY, GUYS, LET'S BREAK IT UP.
CLAP
CLAP
CLAP
CLAP
VIOLENCE ISN'T COOL, HUH.
WHO TH' DOOT ARE YOU?!
AH, HOW QUICKLY THEY FORGET.
I'M HIGSBY, THE STUDENT TEACHER.
D'OH!
AWK! STUDENT TEACHER!!

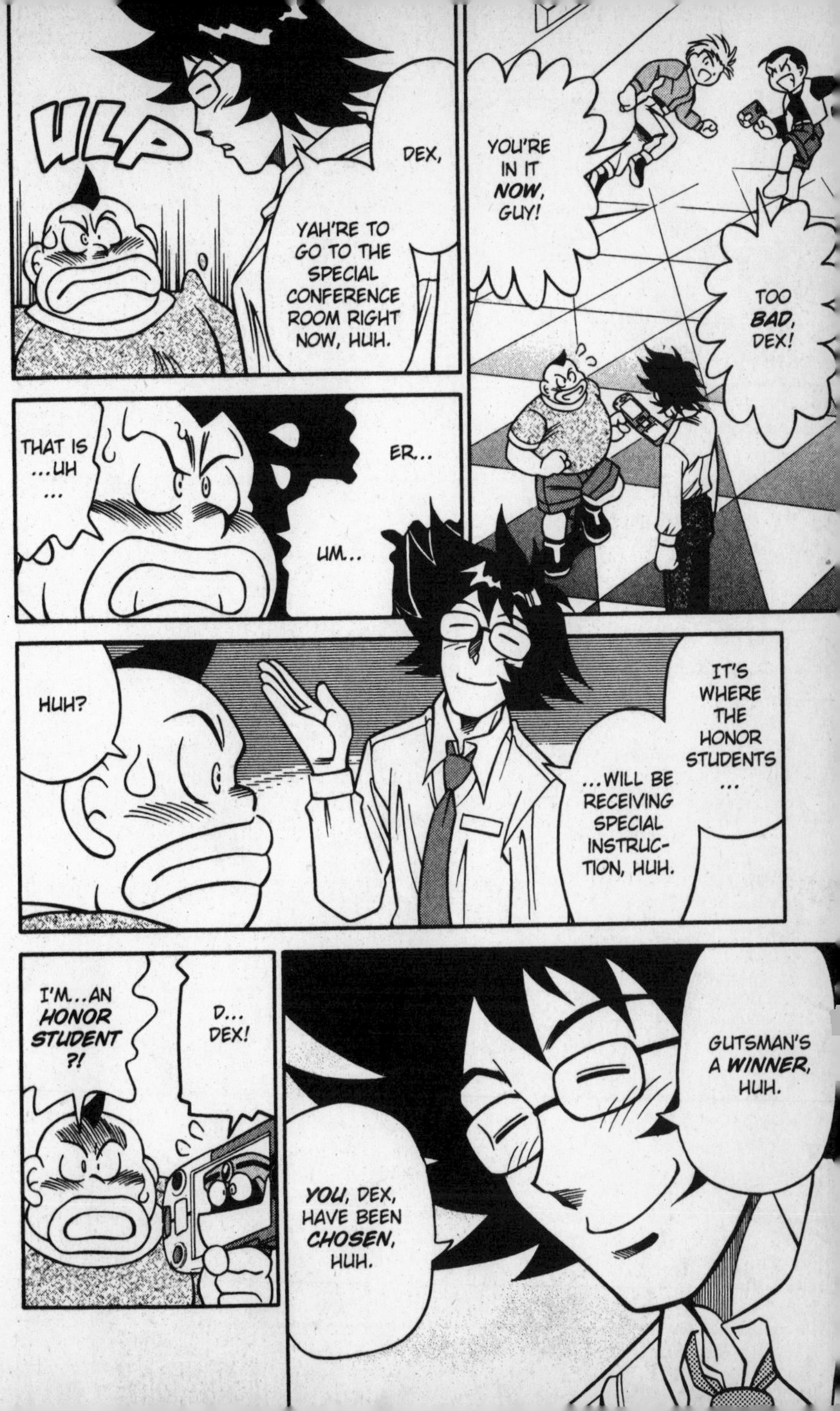
YOU'RE IN IT NOW, GUY!
TOO BAD, DEX!
DEX,
YAH'RE TO GO TO THE SPECIAL CONFERENCE ROOM RIGHT NOW, HUH.
ULP
ER...
UM...
THAT IS ...UH ...
IT'S WHERE THE HONOR STUDENTS ...
...WILL BE RECEIVING SPECIAL INSTRUC-TION, HUH.
HUH?
GUTSMAN'S A WINNER, HUH.
YOU, DEX, HAVE BEEN CHOSEN, HUH.
D... DEX!
I'M...AN HONOR STUDENT ?!

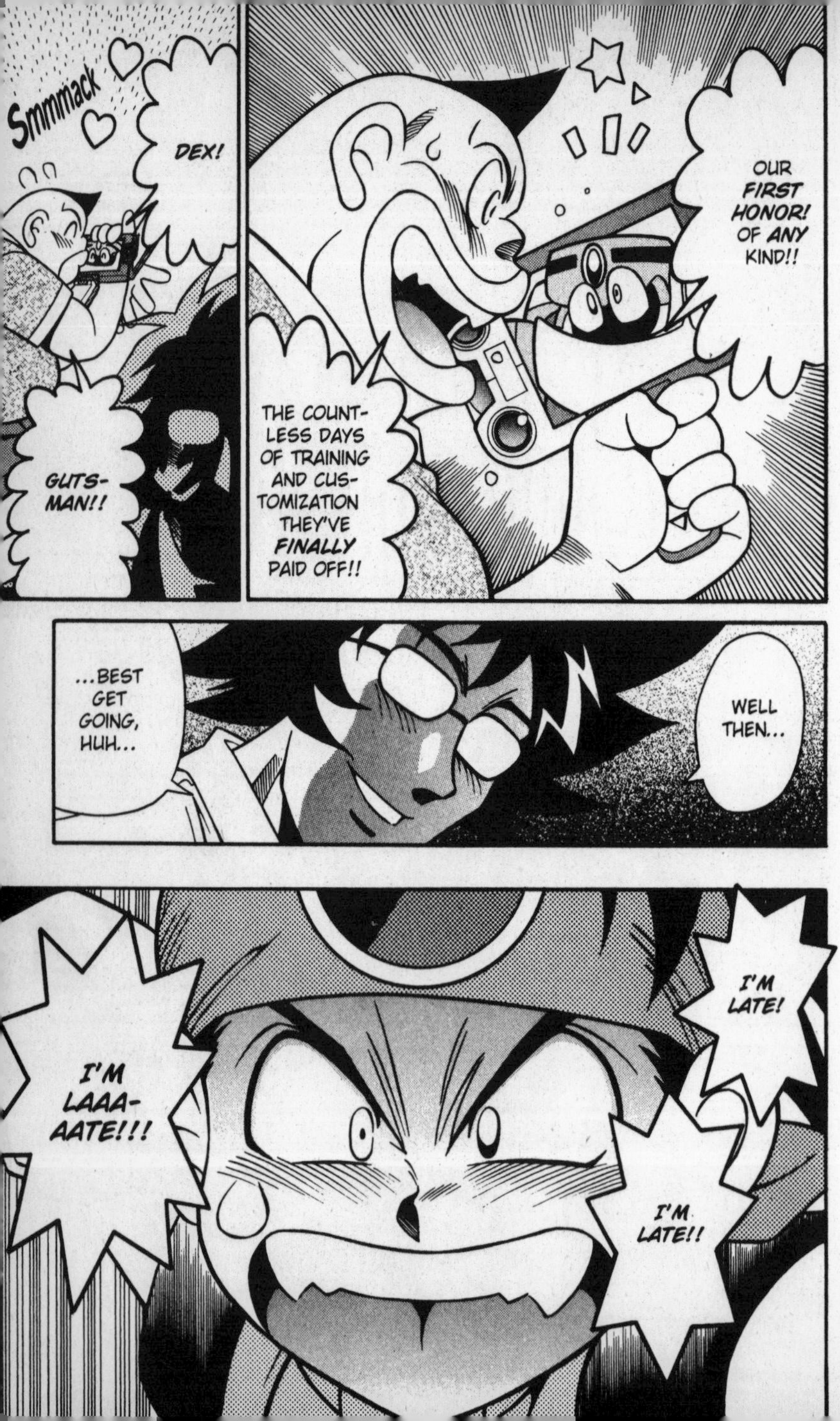
OUR FIRST HONOR! OF ANY KIND!!
THE COUNT-LESS DAYS OF TRAINING AND CUS-TOMIZATION THEY'VE FINALLY PAID OFF!!
Smmmack
DEX!
GUTS-MAN!!
WELL THEN...
...BEST GET GOING, HUH...
I'M LATE!
I'M LATE!!
I'M LAAA-AATE!!!

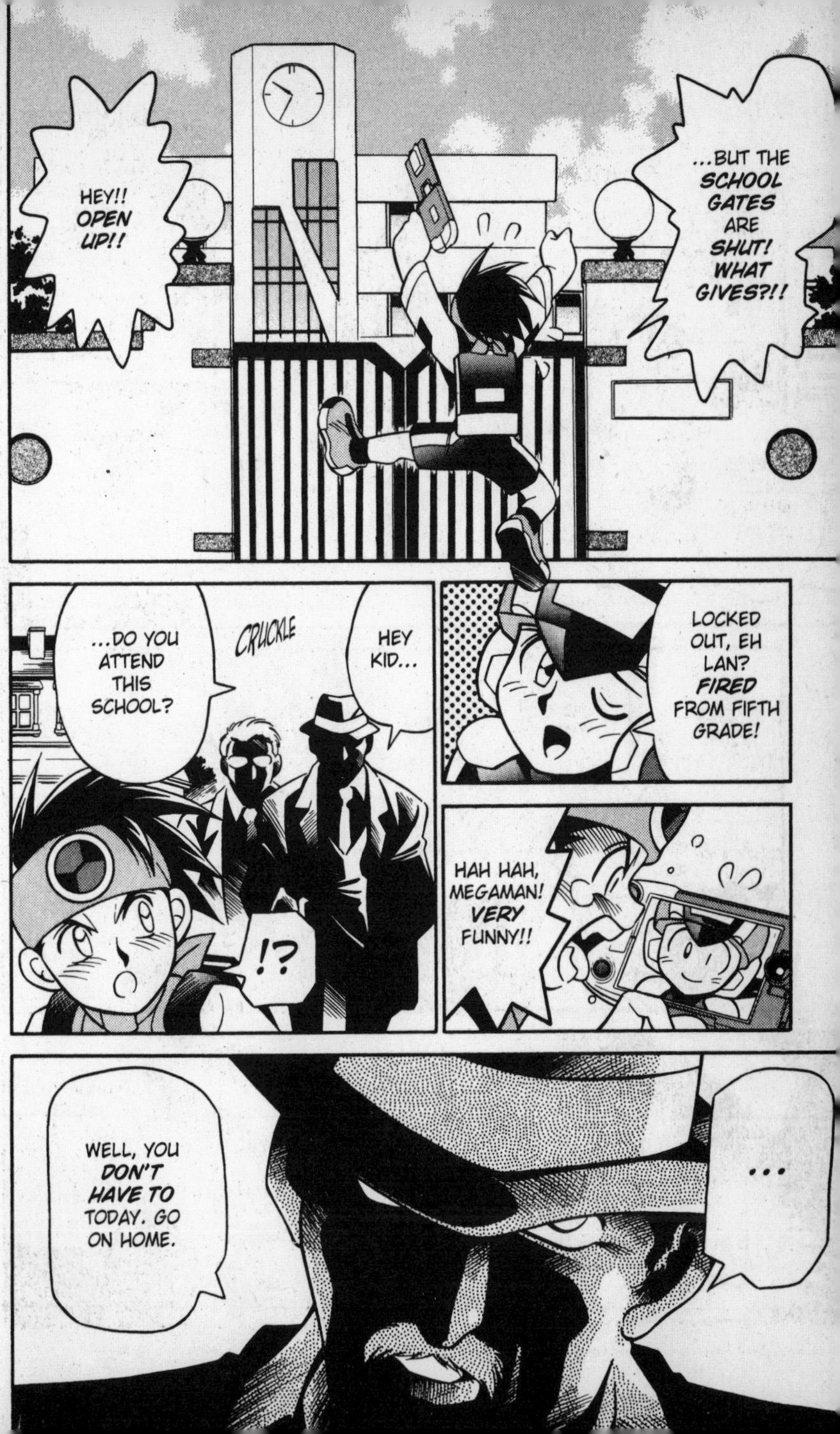
...BUT THE SCHOOL GATES ARE SHUT! WHAT GIVES?!!
HEY!! OPEN UP!!
LOCKED OUT, EH LAN? FIRED FROM FIFTH GRADE!
HAH HAH, MEGAMAN! VERY FUNNY!!
HEY KID...
CRUCKLE
...DO YOU ATTEND THIS SCHOOL?
!?
...
WELL, YOU DON'T HAVE TO TODAY. GO ON HOME.

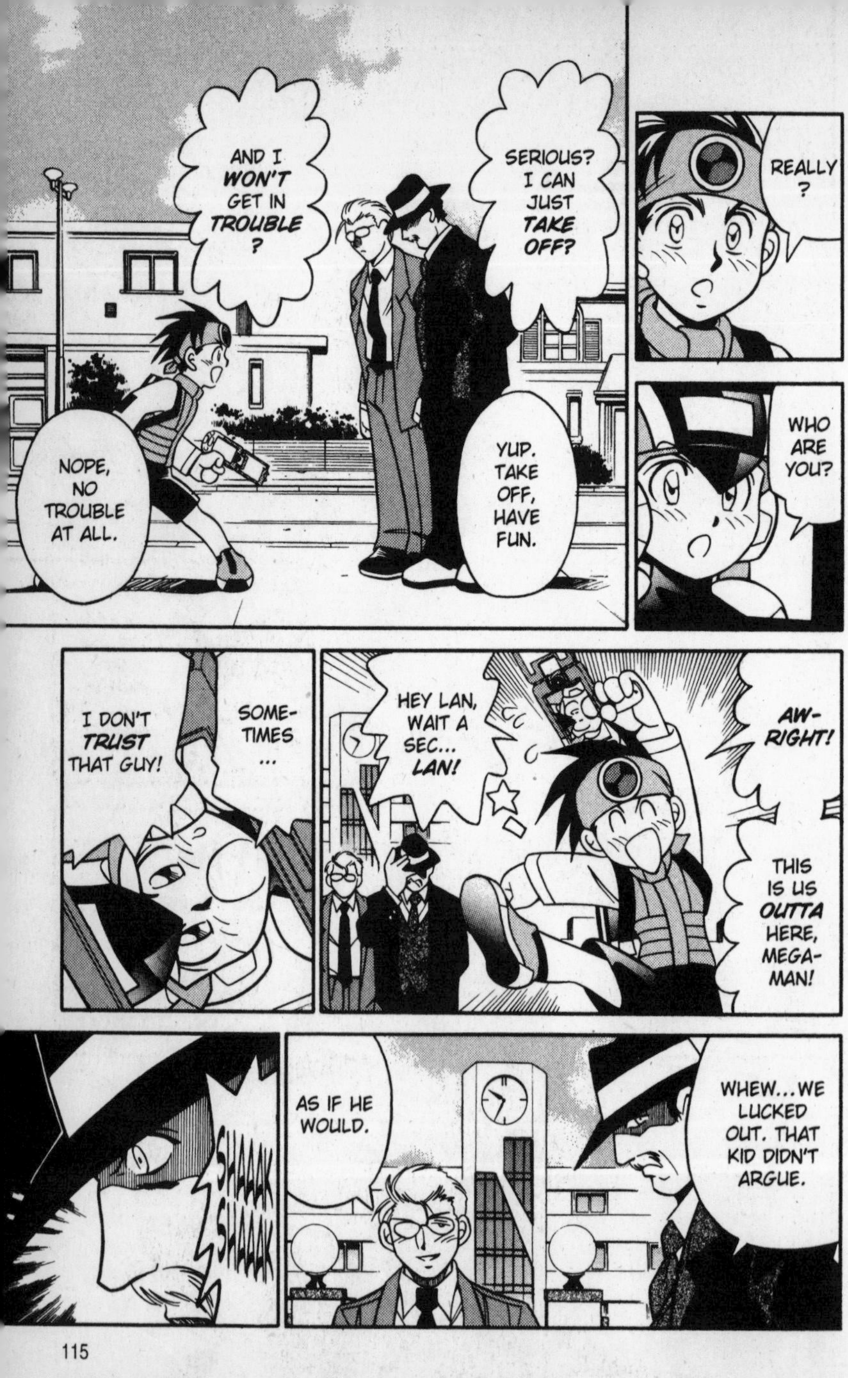
REALLY?
WHO ARE YOU?
SERIOUS? I CAN JUST **TAKE OFF?**
AND I **WON'T** GET IN **TROUBLE**?
YUP. TAKE OFF, HAVE FUN.
NOPE, NO TROUBLE AT ALL.
AW-RIGHT!
THIS IS US **OUTTA** HERE, MEGA-MAN!
HEY LAN, WAIT A SEC... **LAN!**
SOME-TIMES...
I DON'T **TRUST** THAT GUY!
WHEW...WE LUCKED OUT. THAT KID DIDN'T ARGUE.
AS IF HE WOULD.
SHAAAK SHAAAK

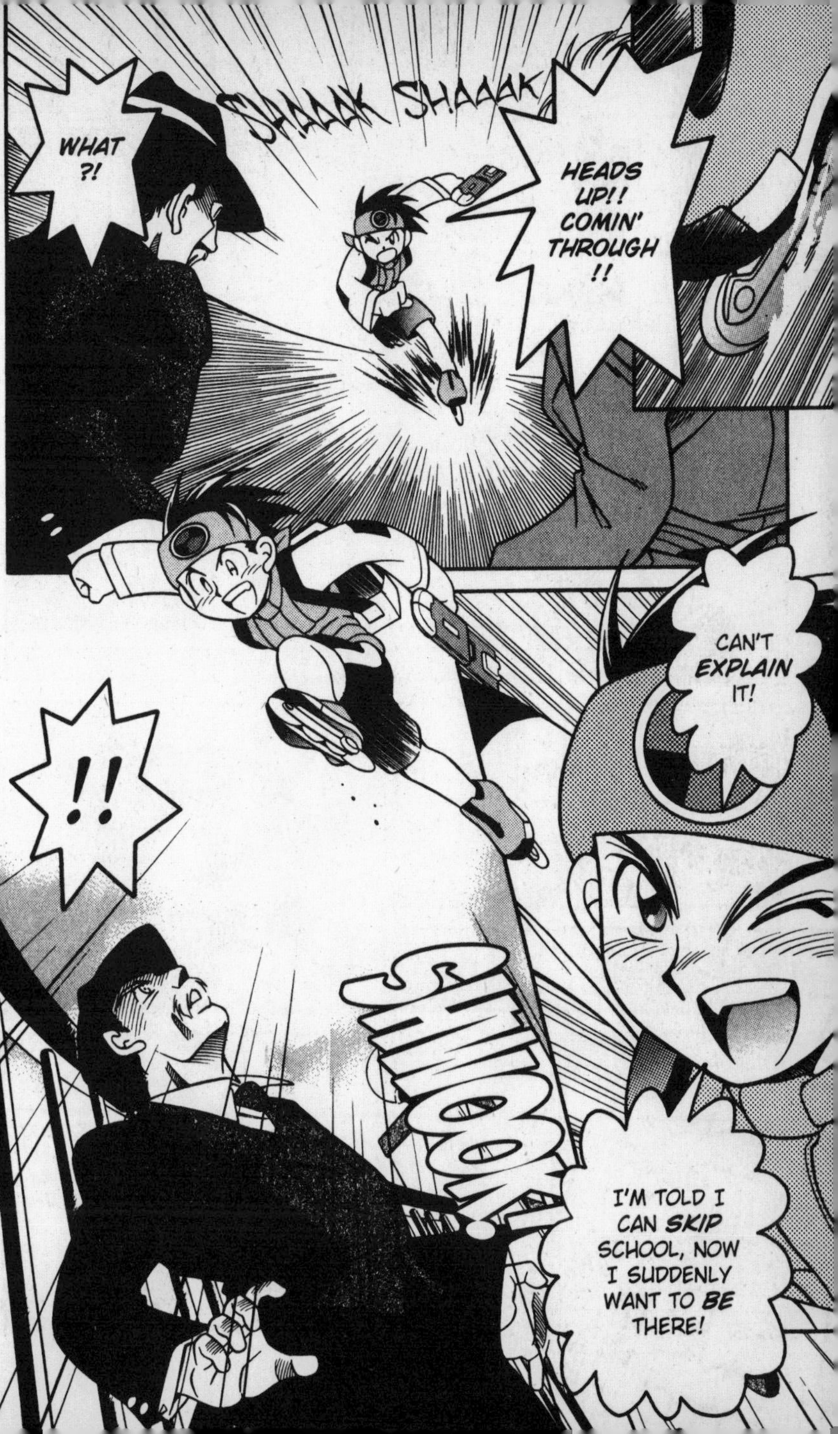
SHAAAK SHAAAK
HEADS UP!! COMIN' THROUGH!!
WHAT?!
CAN'T EXPLAIN IT!
I'M TOLD I CAN SKIP SCHOOL, NOW I SUDDENLY WANT TO BE THERE!
!!
SHWOOM!

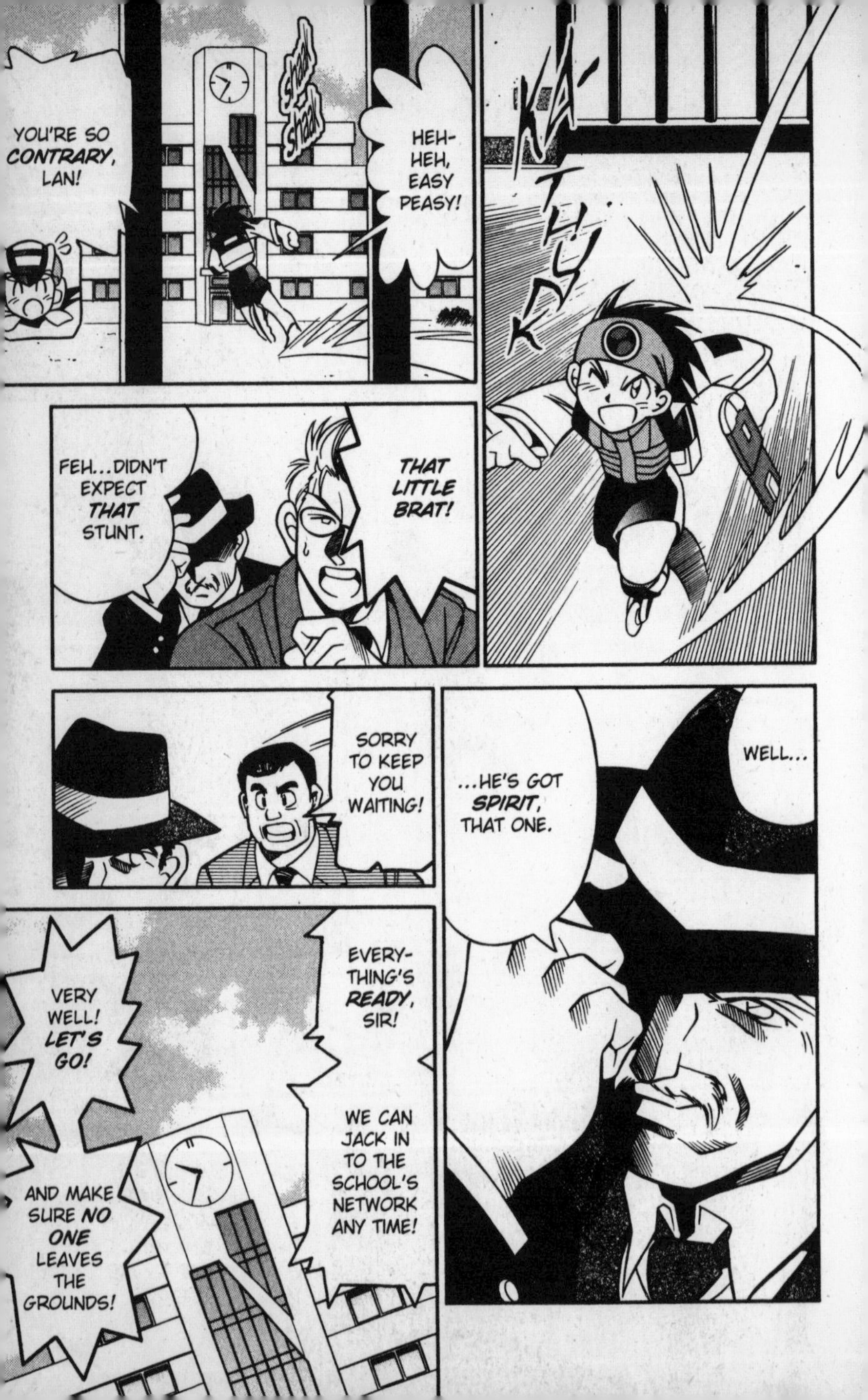
KA-THUNK
shaak shaak
HEH-HEH, EASY PEASY!
YOU'RE SO CONTRARY, LAN!
THAT LITTLE BRAT!
FEH...DIDN'T EXPECT THAT STUNT.
WELL...
...HE'S GOT SPIRIT, THAT ONE.
SORRY TO KEEP YOU WAITING!
EVERY-THING'S READY, SIR!
WE CAN JACK IN TO THE SCHOOL'S NETWORK ANY TIME!
VERY WELL! LET'S GO!
AND MAKE SURE NO ONE LEAVES THE GROUNDS!

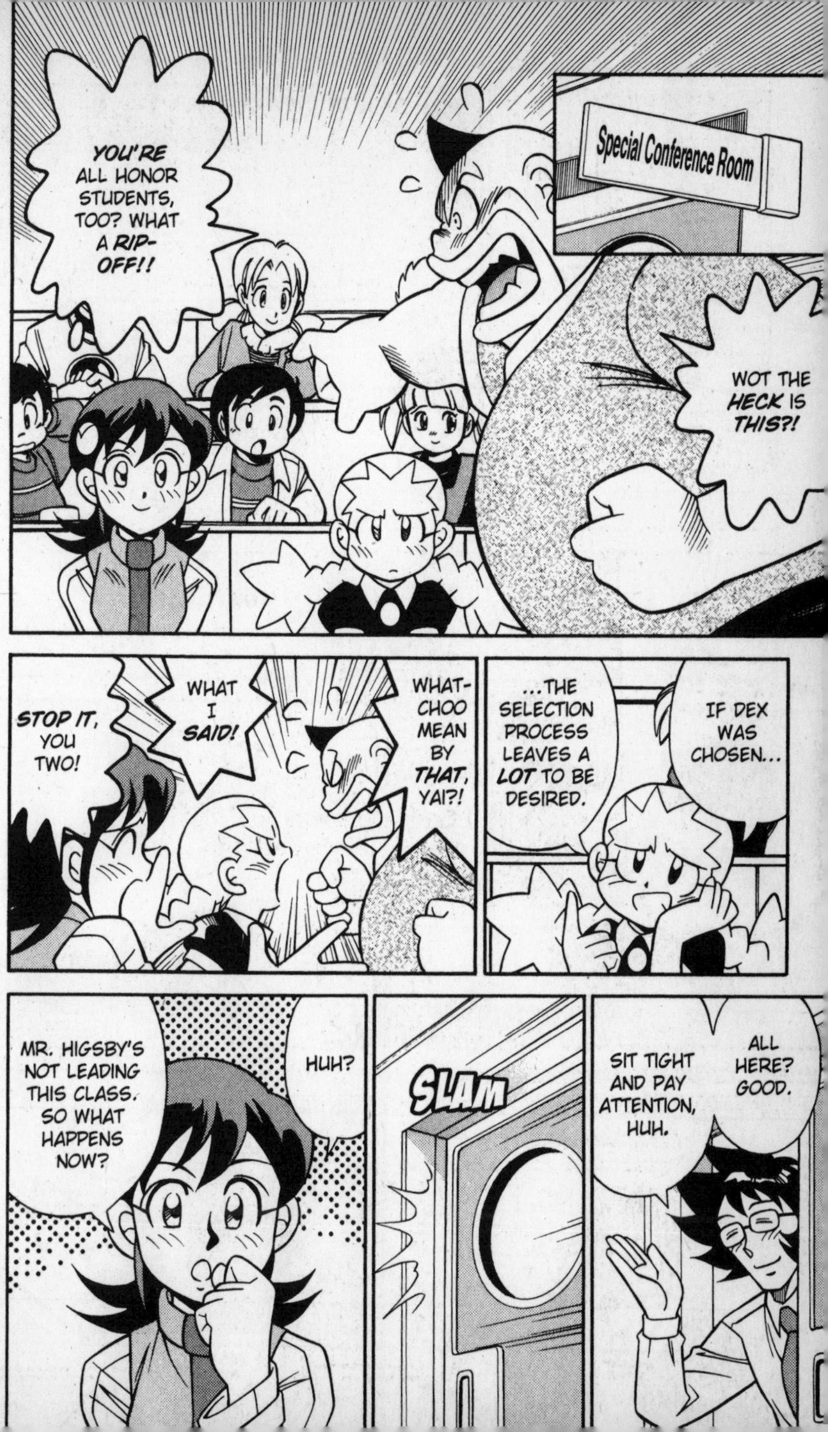
Special Conference Room
WOT THE HECK IS THIS?!
YOU'RE ALL HONOR STUDENTS, TOO? WHAT A RIP-OFF!!
IF DEX WAS CHOSEN...
...THE SELECTION PROCESS LEAVES A LOT TO BE DESIRED.
WHAT-CHOO MEAN BY THAT, YAI?!
WHAT I SAID!
STOP IT, YOU TWO!
ALL HERE? GOOD.
SIT TIGHT AND PAY ATTENTION, HUH.
SLAM
HUH?
MR. HIGSBY'S NOT LEADING THIS CLASS. SO WHAT HAPPENS NOW?

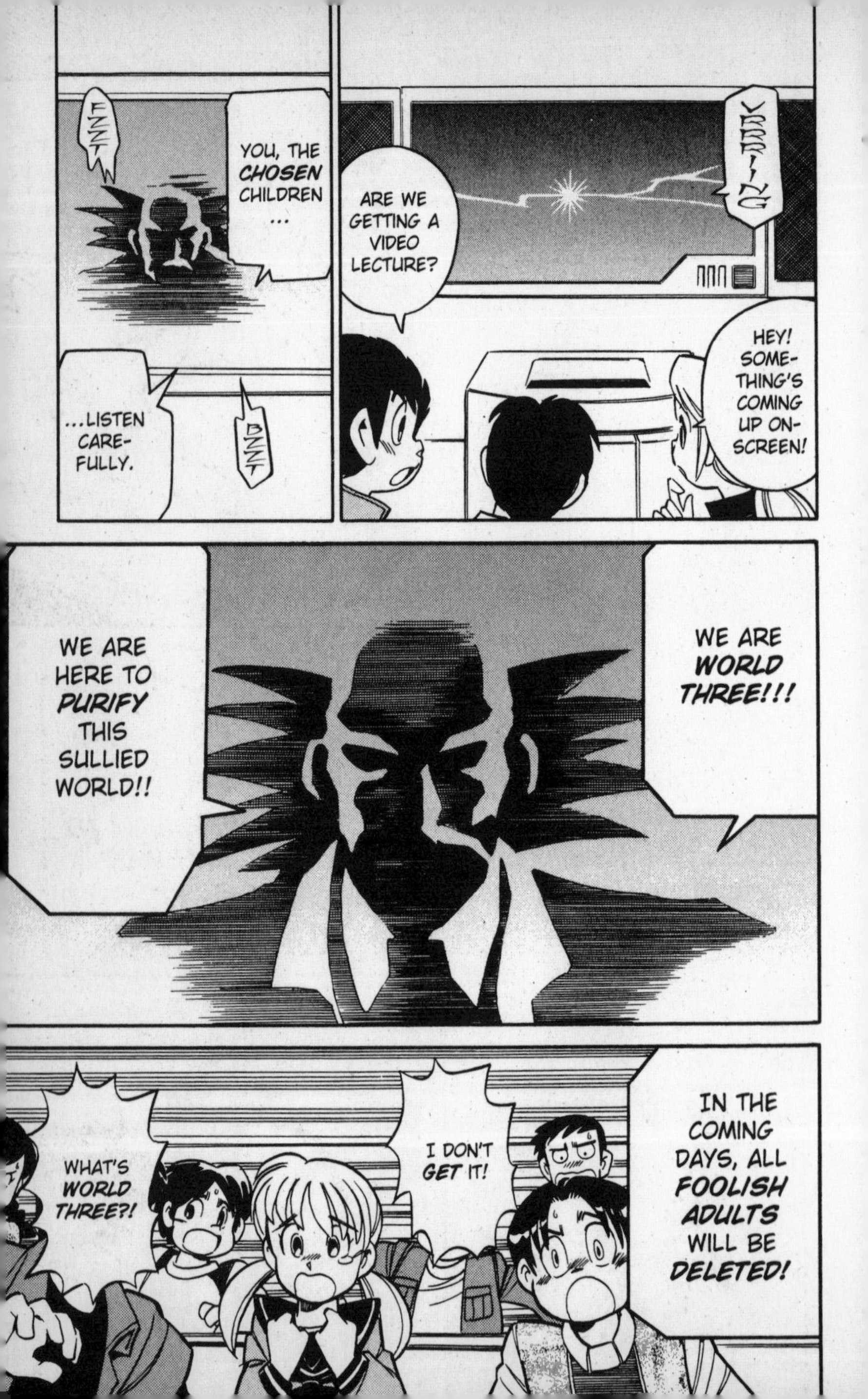

VRRRING
HEY! SOME-THING'S COMING UP ON-SCREEN!
ARE WE GETTING A VIDEO LECTURE?
FZZZT
YOU, THE CHOSEN CHILDREN ...
BZZZT
...LISTEN CARE-FULLY.
WE ARE WORLD THREE!!!
WE ARE HERE TO PURIFY THIS SULLIED WORLD!!
IN THE COMING DAYS, ALL FOOLISH ADULTS WILL BE DELETED!
I DON'T GET IT!
WHAT'S WORLD THREE?!

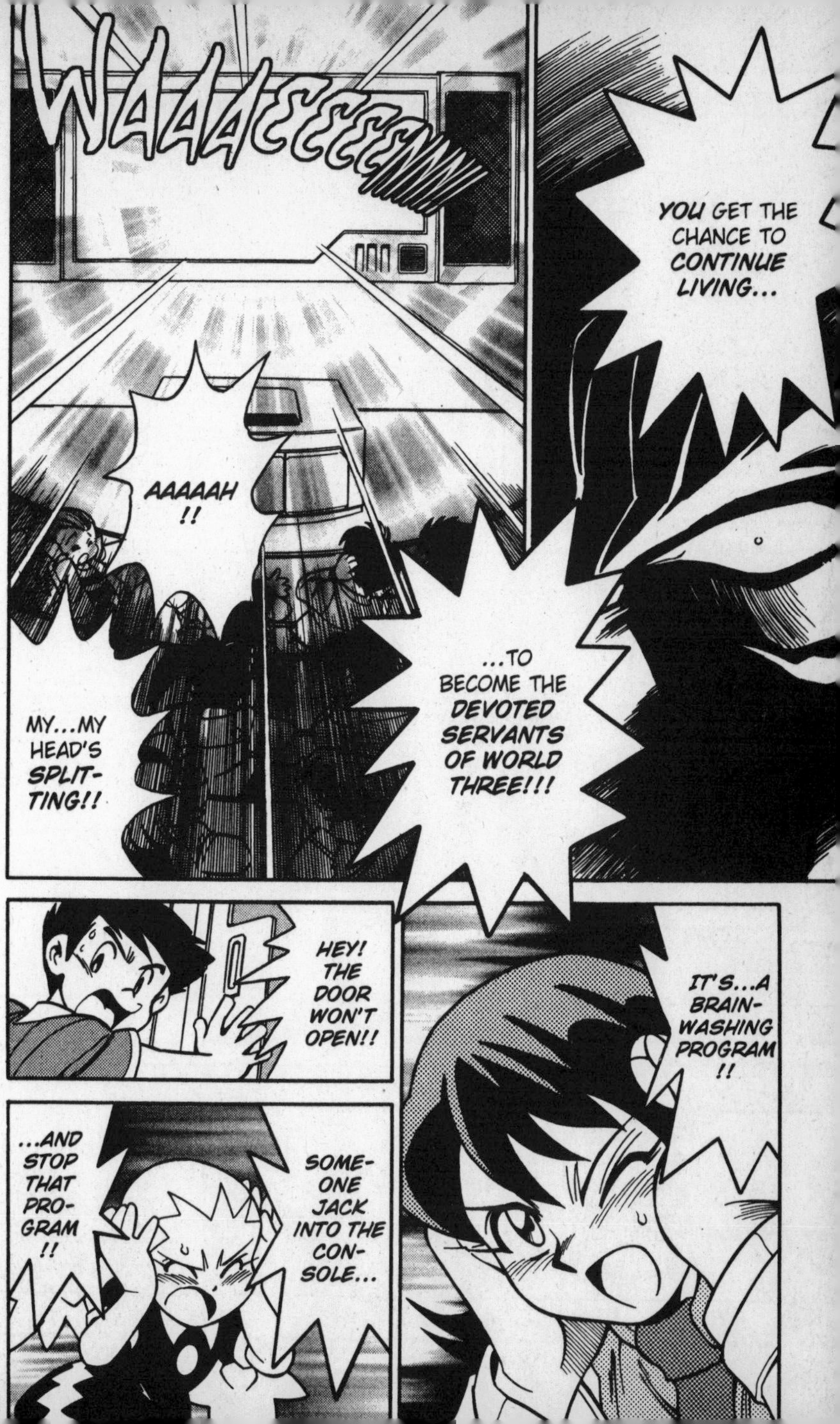
YOU GET THE CHANCE TO CONTINUE LIVING...
...TO BECOME THE DEVOTED SERVANTS OF WORLD THREE!!!
WAAAEEEEN
AAAAAH!!
MY...MY HEAD'S SPLIT-TING!!
IT'S...A BRAIN-WASHING PROGRAM!!
HEY! THE DOOR WON'T OPEN!!
SOME-ONE JACK INTO THE CON-SOLE...
...AND STOP THAT PRO-GRAM!!

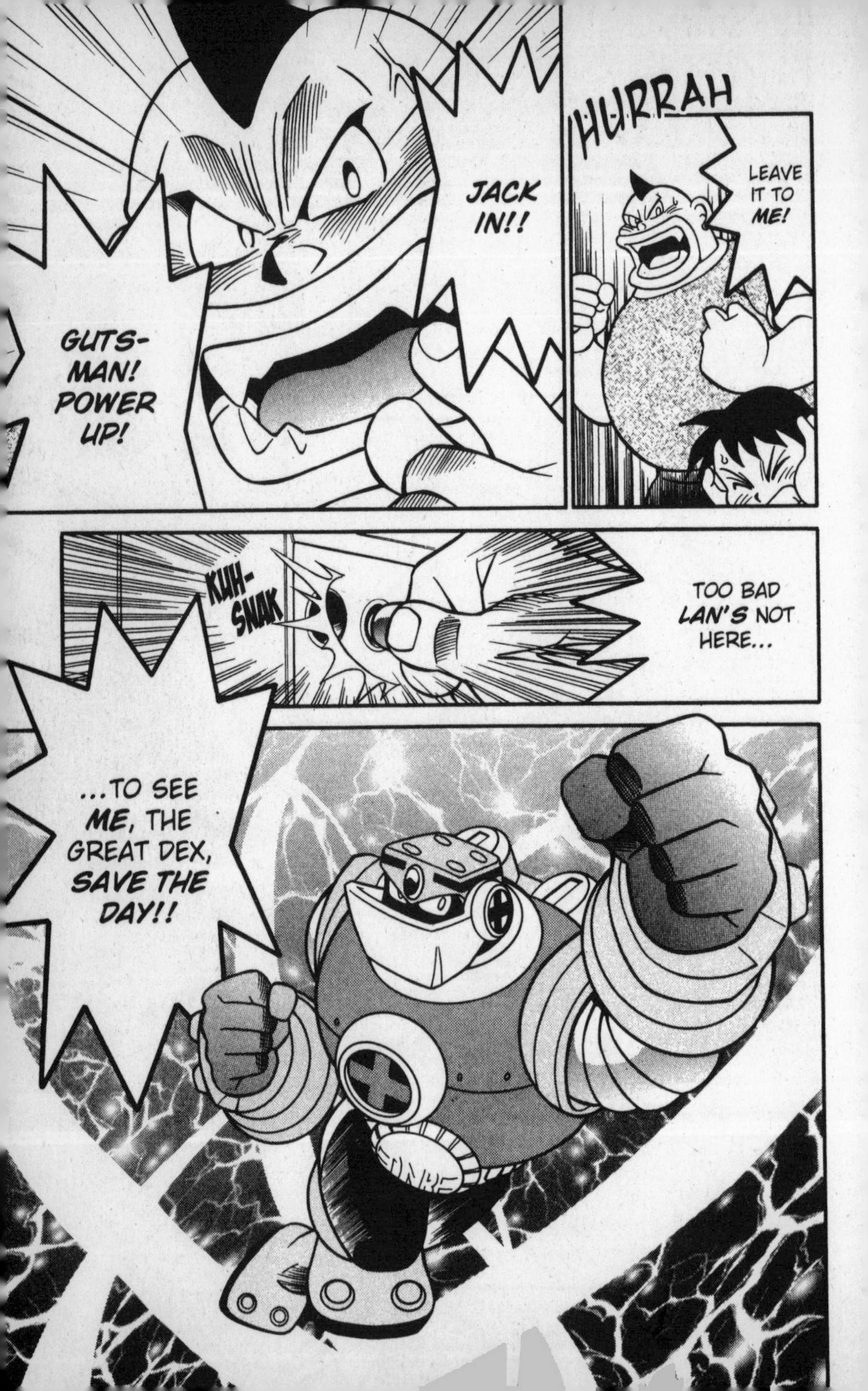
HURRAH
LEAVE IT TO ME!
JACK IN!!
GUTS-MAN! POWER UP!
TOO BAD LAN'S NOT HERE...
KUH-SNAK
...TO SEE ME, THE GREAT DEX, SAVE THE DAY!!

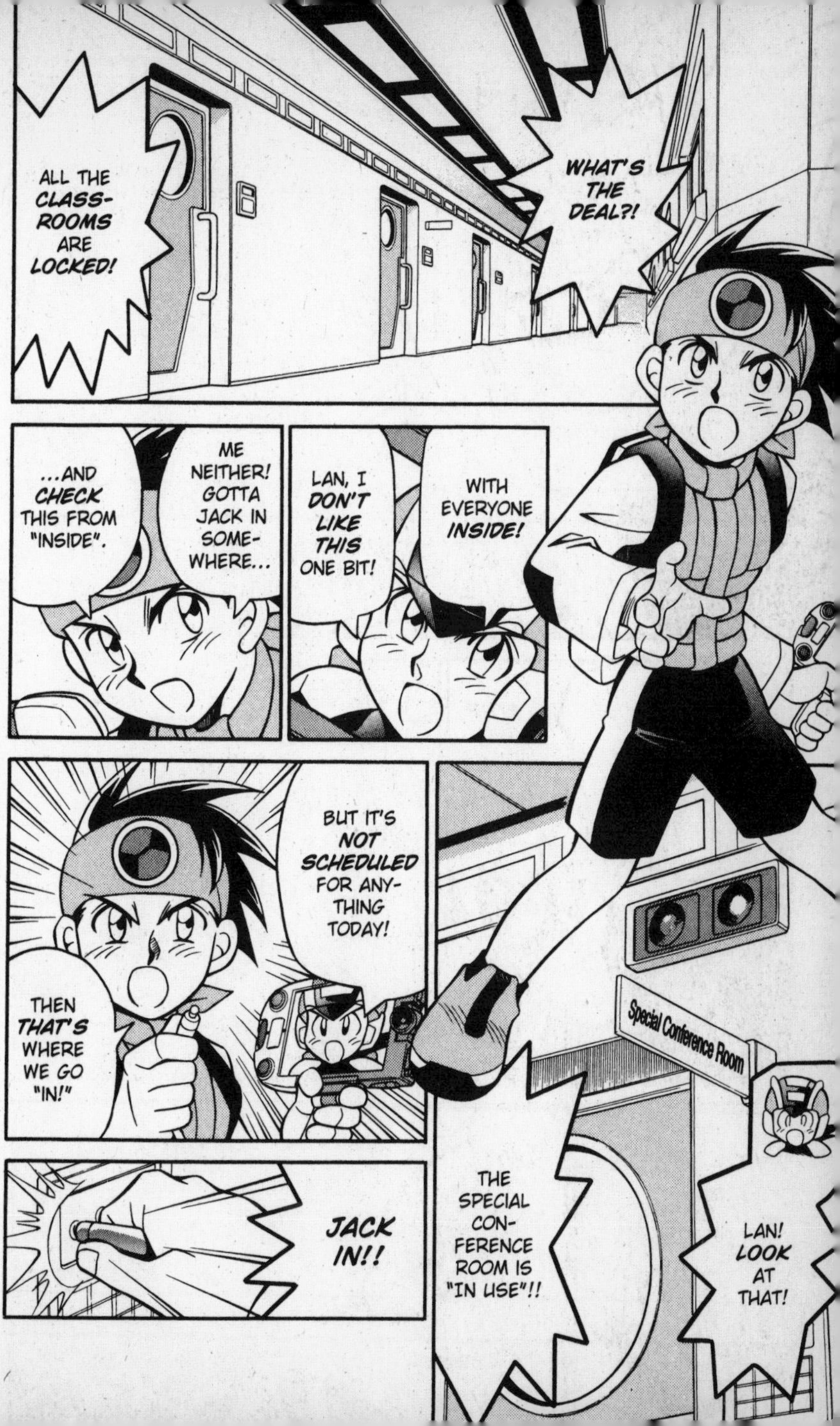
WHAT'S THE DEAL?!
ALL THE CLASSROOMS ARE LOCKED!
WITH EVERYONE INSIDE!
LAN, I DON'T LIKE THIS ONE BIT!
ME NEITHER! GOTTA JACK IN SOMEWHERE...
...AND CHECK THIS FROM "INSIDE".
LAN! LOOK AT THAT!
THE SPECIAL CONFERENCE ROOM IS "IN USE"!!
Special Conference Room
BUT IT'S NOT SCHEDULED FOR ANYTHING TODAY!
THEN THAT'S WHERE WE GO "IN!"
JACK IN!!

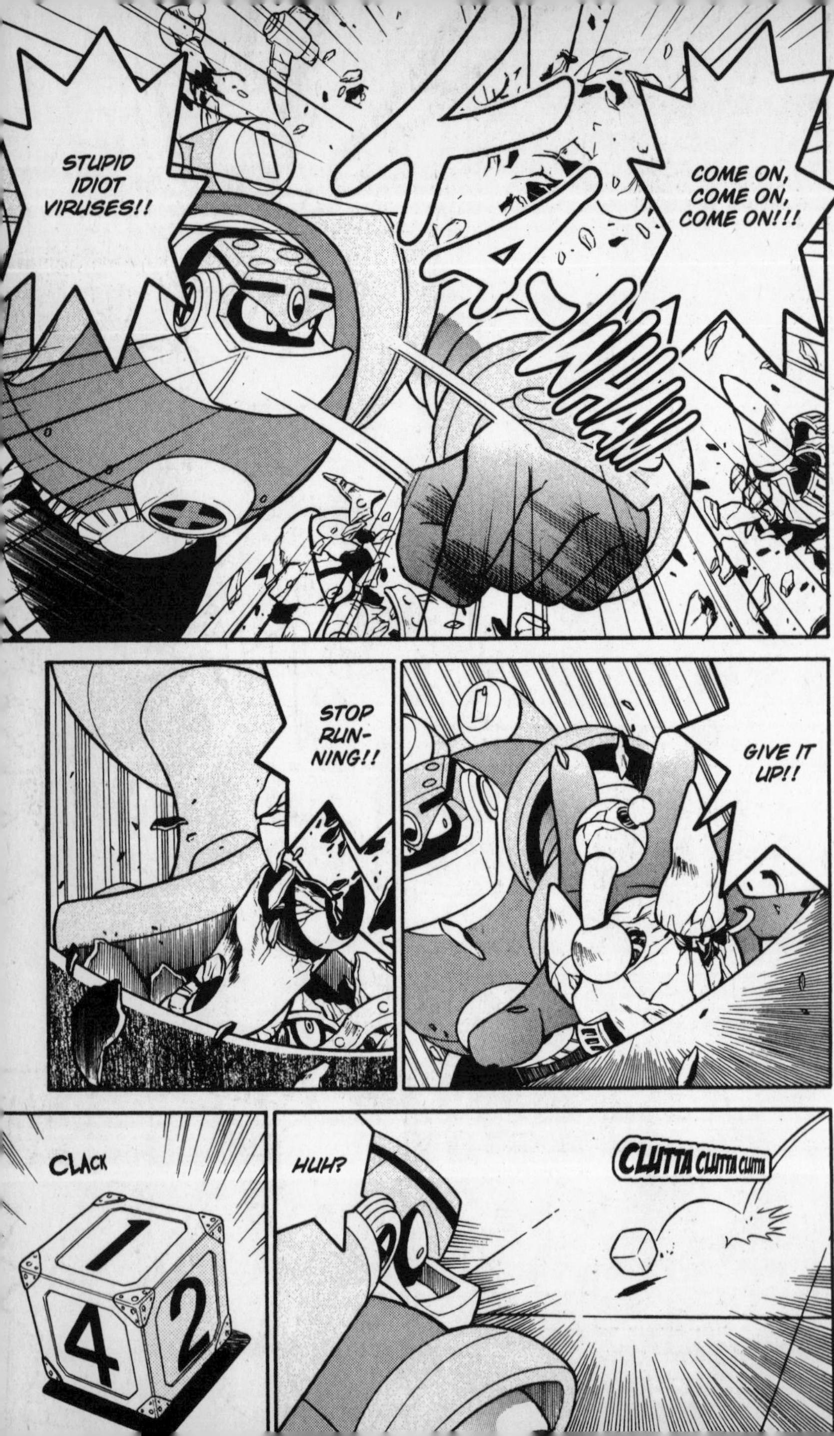
COME ON, COME ON, COME ON!!!
WHAM
STUPID IDIOT VIRUSES!!
GIVE IT UP!!
STOP RUN-NING!!
CLUTTA CLUTTA CLUTTA
HUH?
CLACK

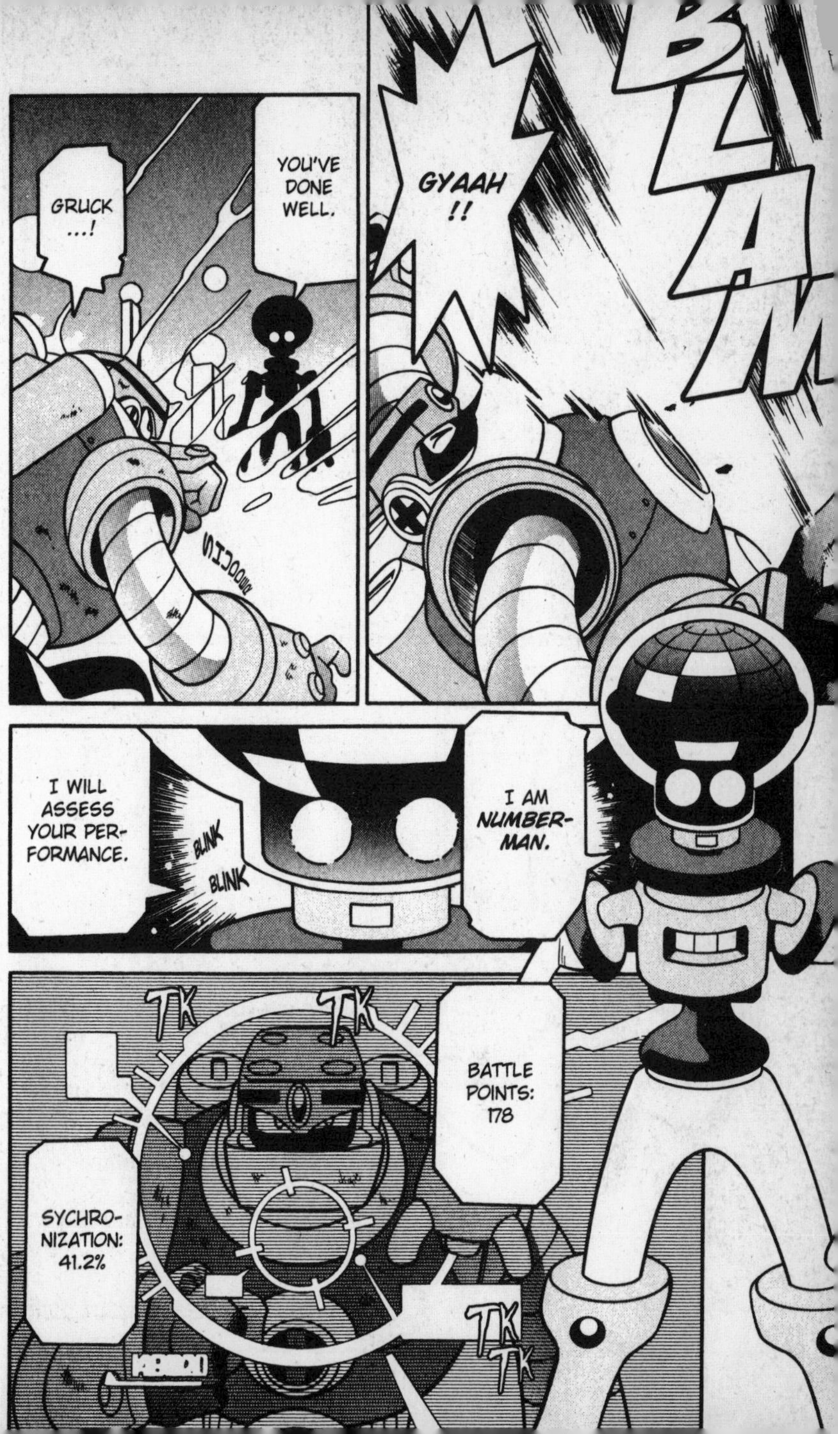
BLAM
GYAAH !!
YOU'VE DONE WELL.
GRUCK ...!
I AM NUMBER-MAN.
BLINK
BLINK
I WILL ASSESS YOUR PER-FORMANCE.
TK
TK
BATTLE POINTS: 178
SYCHRO-NIZATION: 41.2%
TK
TK

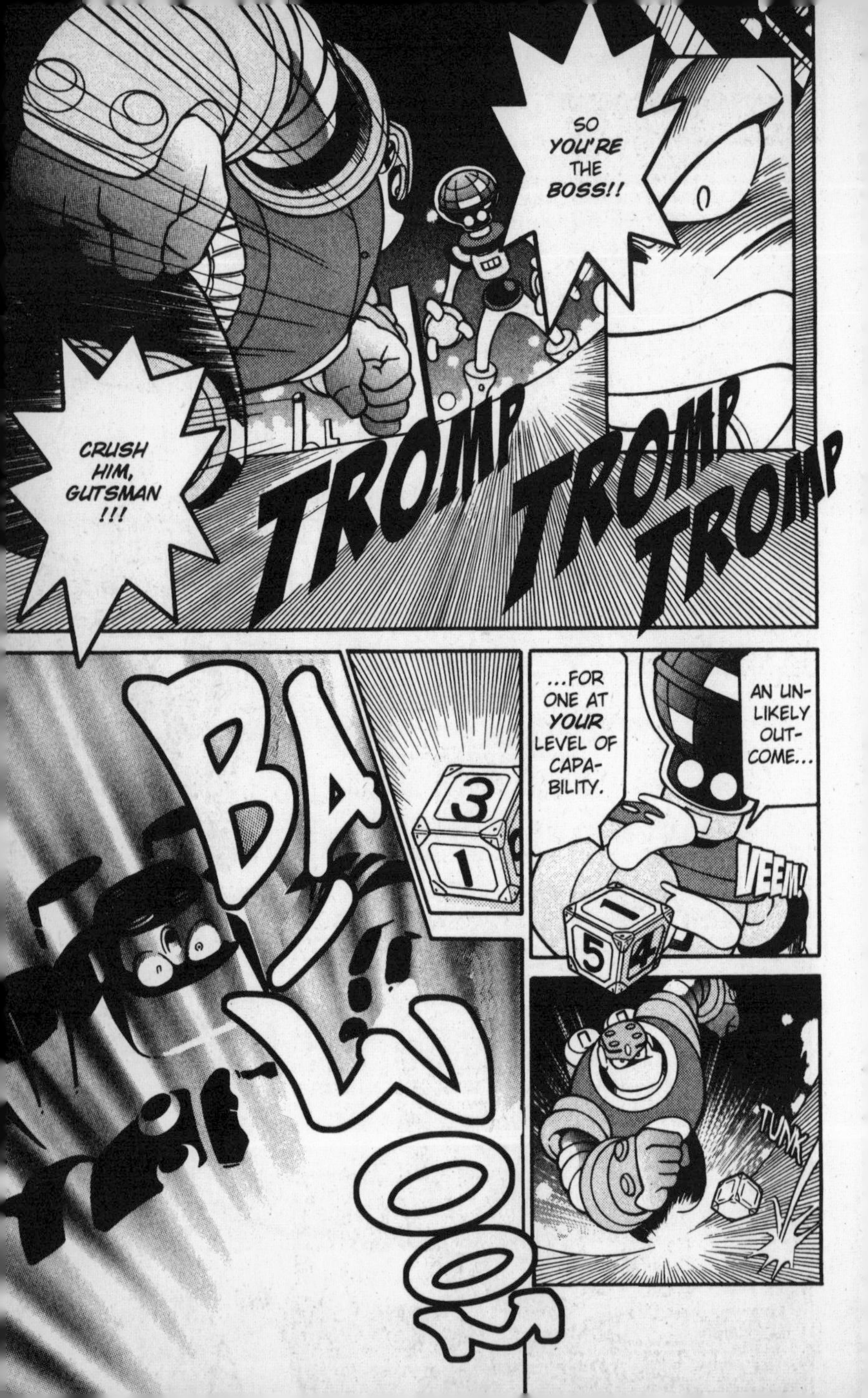
SO YOU'RE THE BOSS!!
TROMP TROMP TROMP
CRUSH HIM, GUTSMAN!!!
AN UN-LIKELY OUT-COME...
...FOR ONE AT YOUR LEVEL OF CAPA-BILITY.
VEEM!
TUNK
BAWOOO

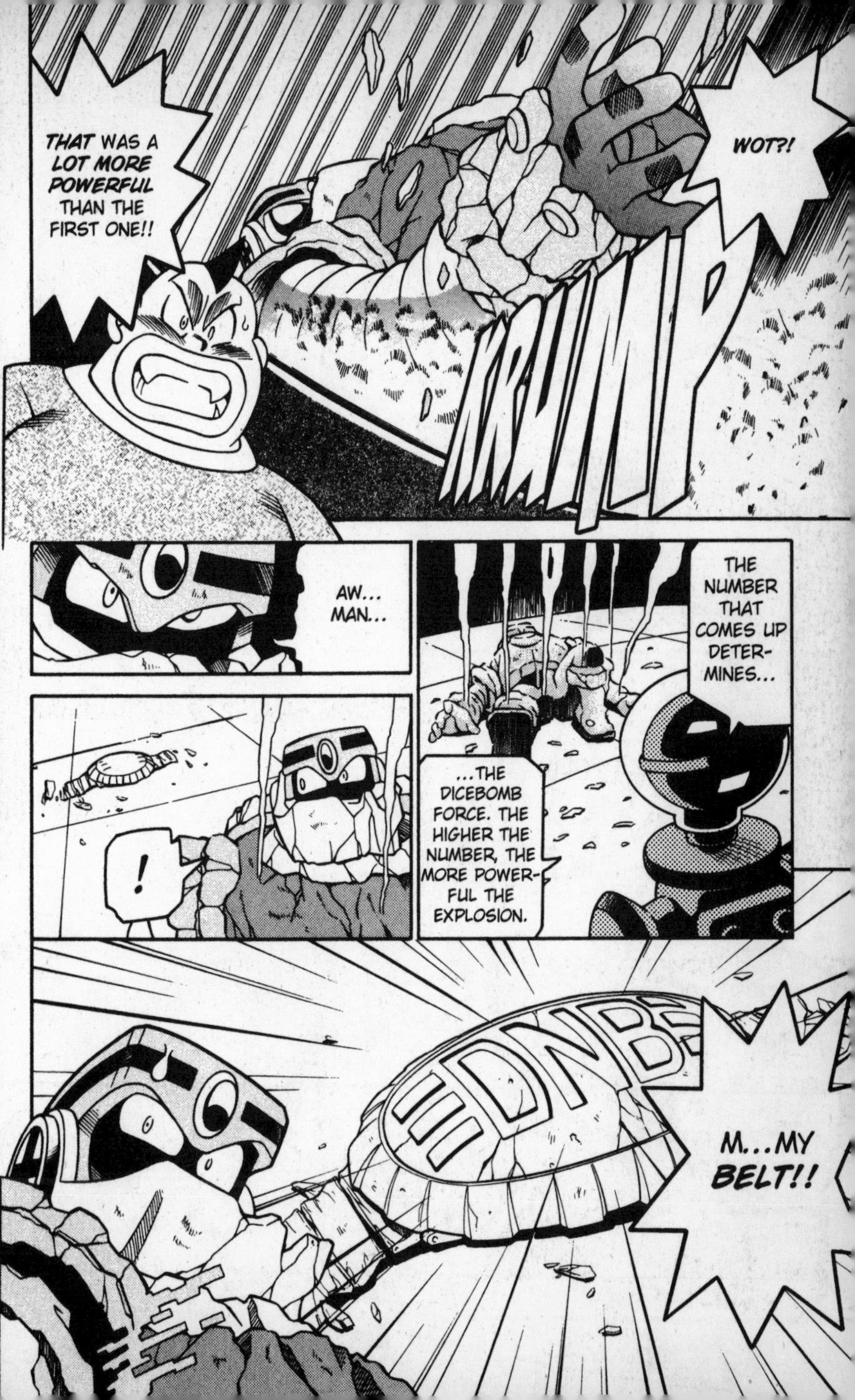
WOT?!
THAT WAS A LOT MORE POWERFUL THAN THE FIRST ONE!!
THE NUMBER THAT COMES UP DETER-MINES...
...THE DICEBOMB FORCE. THE HIGHER THE NUMBER, THE MORE POWER-FUL THE EXPLOSION.
AW... MAN...
!
M...MY BELT!!

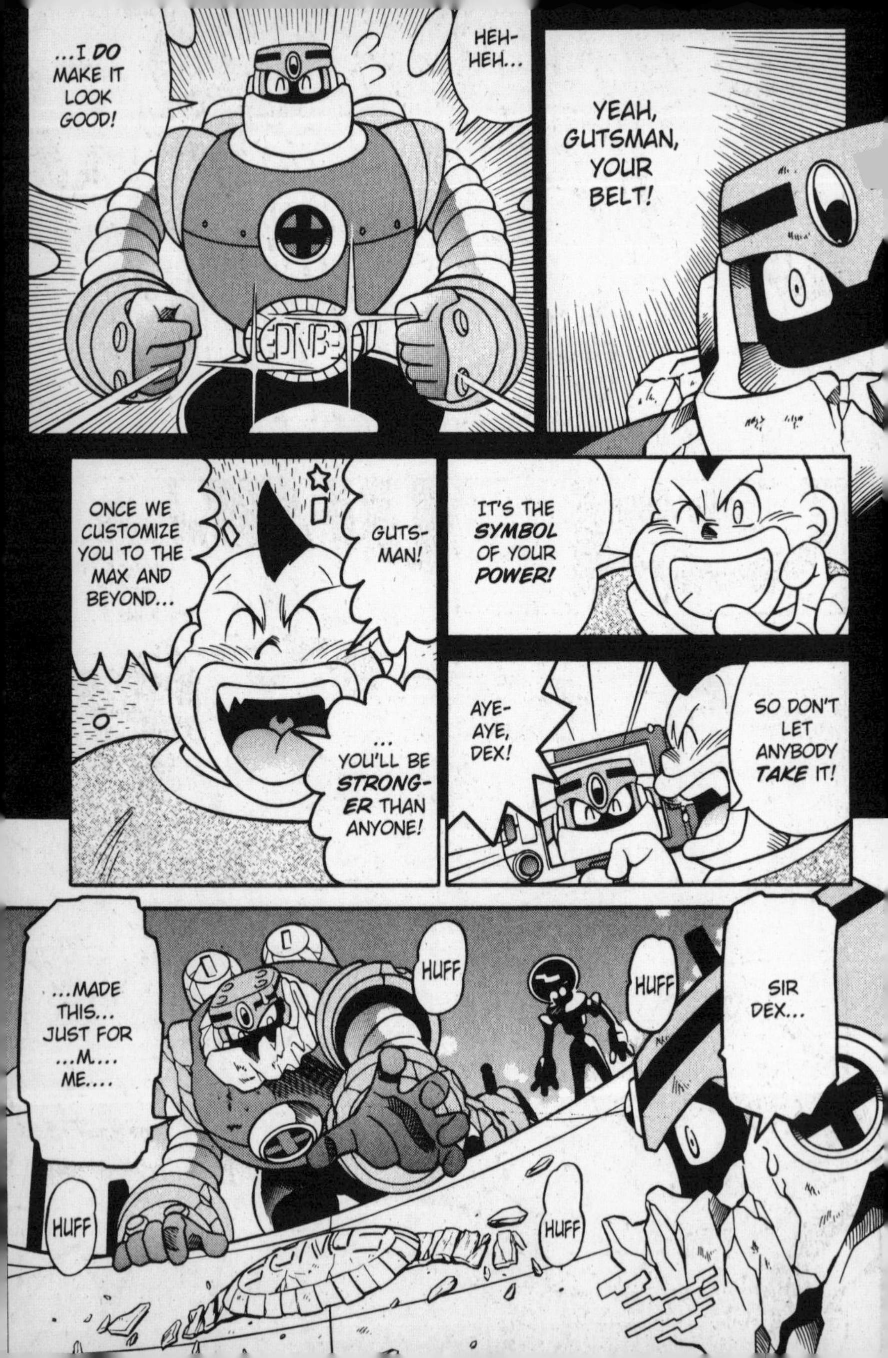
YEAH, GUTSMAN, YOUR BELT!
HEH-HEH...
...I DO MAKE IT LOOK GOOD!
IT'S THE SYMBOL OF YOUR POWER!
SO DON'T LET ANYBODY TAKE IT!
AYE-AYE, DEX!
GUTS-MAN!
ONCE WE CUSTOMIZE YOU TO THE MAX AND BEYOND...
...YOU'LL BE STRONGER THAN ANYONE!
SIR DEX...
HUFF
HUFF
HUFF
...MADE THIS... JUST FOR ...M... ME....
HUFF

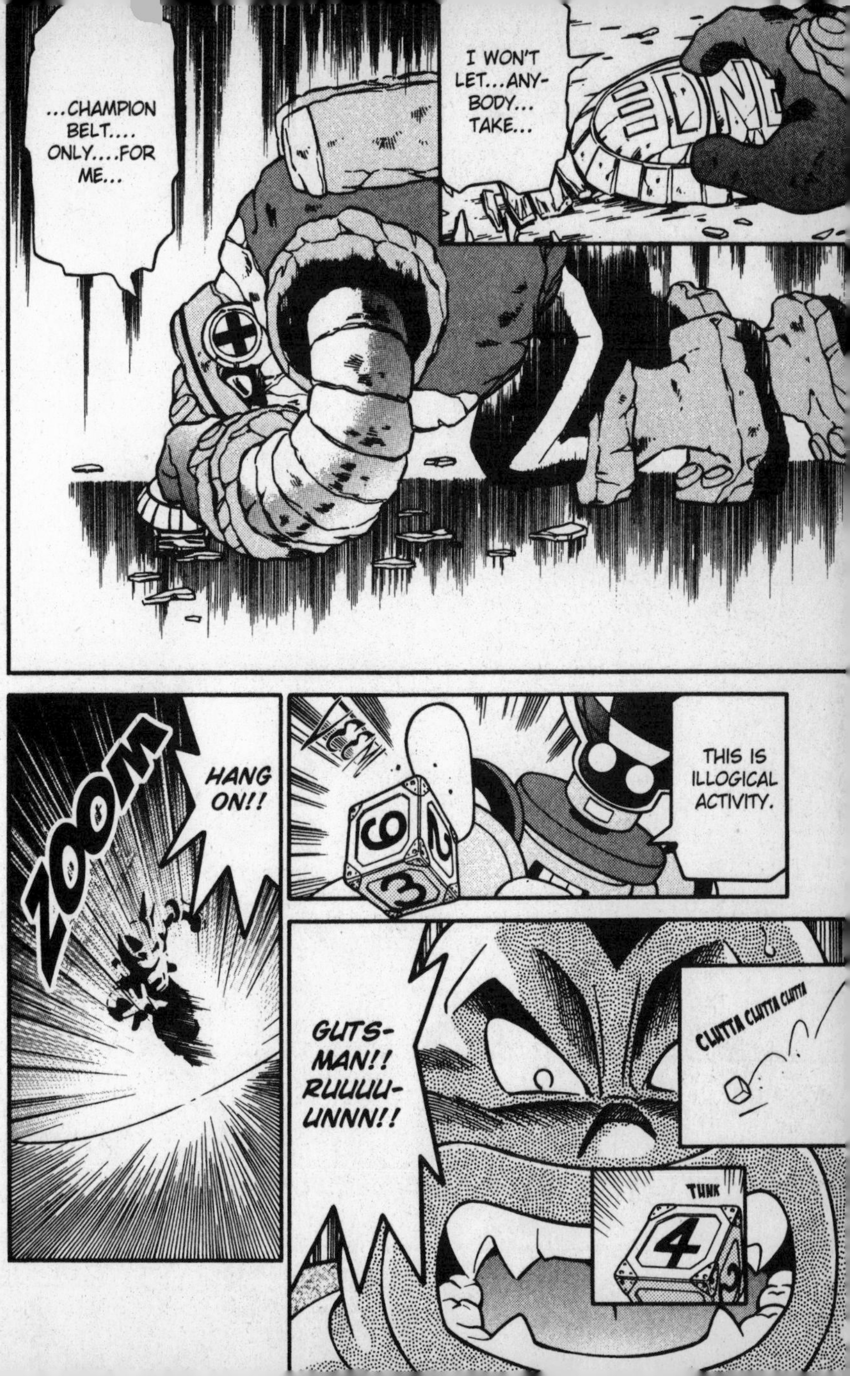

I WON'T LET...ANY-BODY... TAKE...
...CHAMPION BELT.... ONLY....FOR ME...
THIS IS ILLOGICAL ACTIVITY.
GUTS-MAN!! RUUUUU-UNNN!!
CLUTTA CLUTTA CLUTTA
TUNK
ZOOM
HANG ON!!

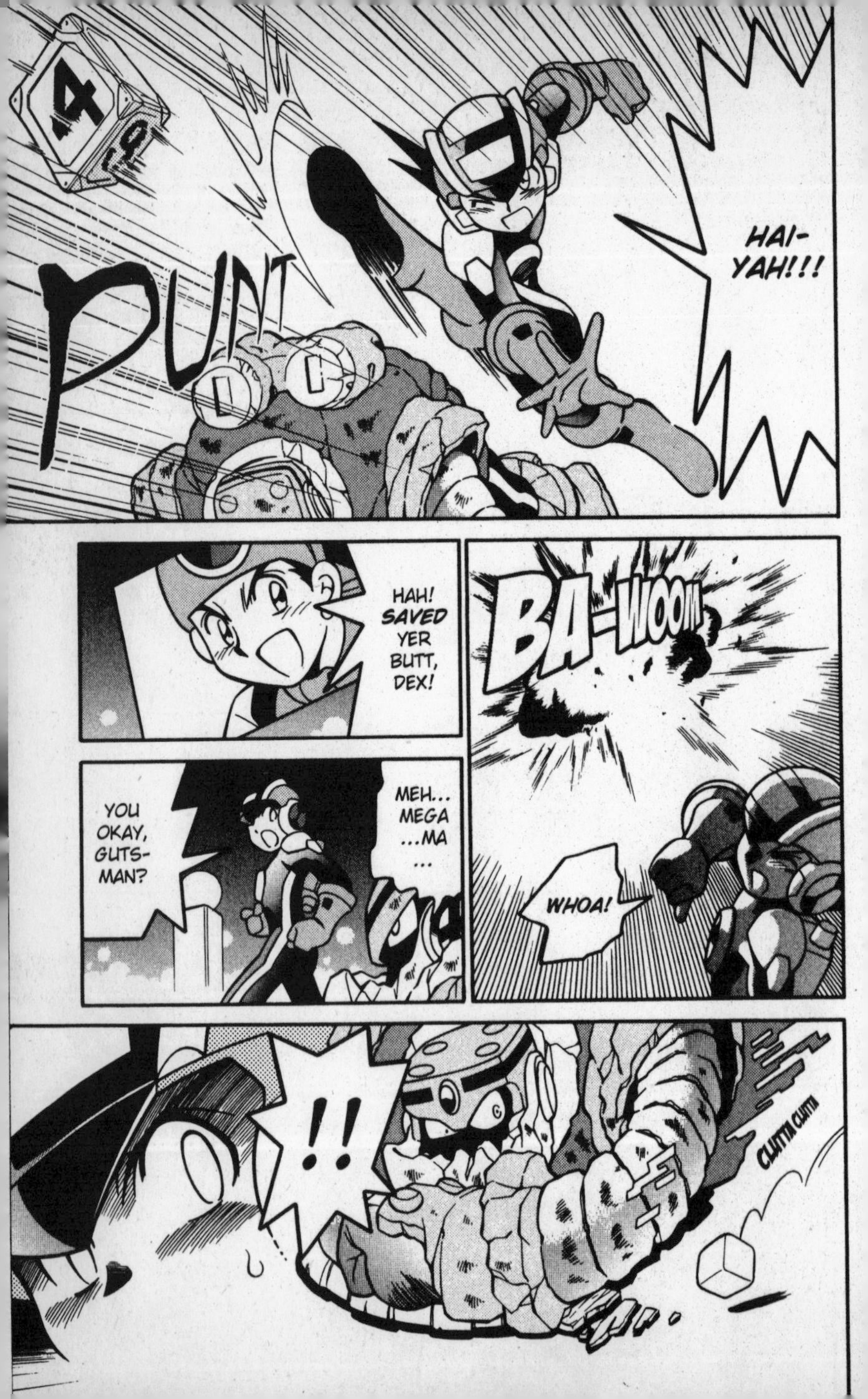
HAI-YAH!!!
PUNT
BA-WOOM
WHOA!
HAH! SAVED YER BUTT, DEX!
MEH... MEGA ...MA ...
YOU OKAY, GUTS-MAN?
CLUTTA CLUTTA
!!

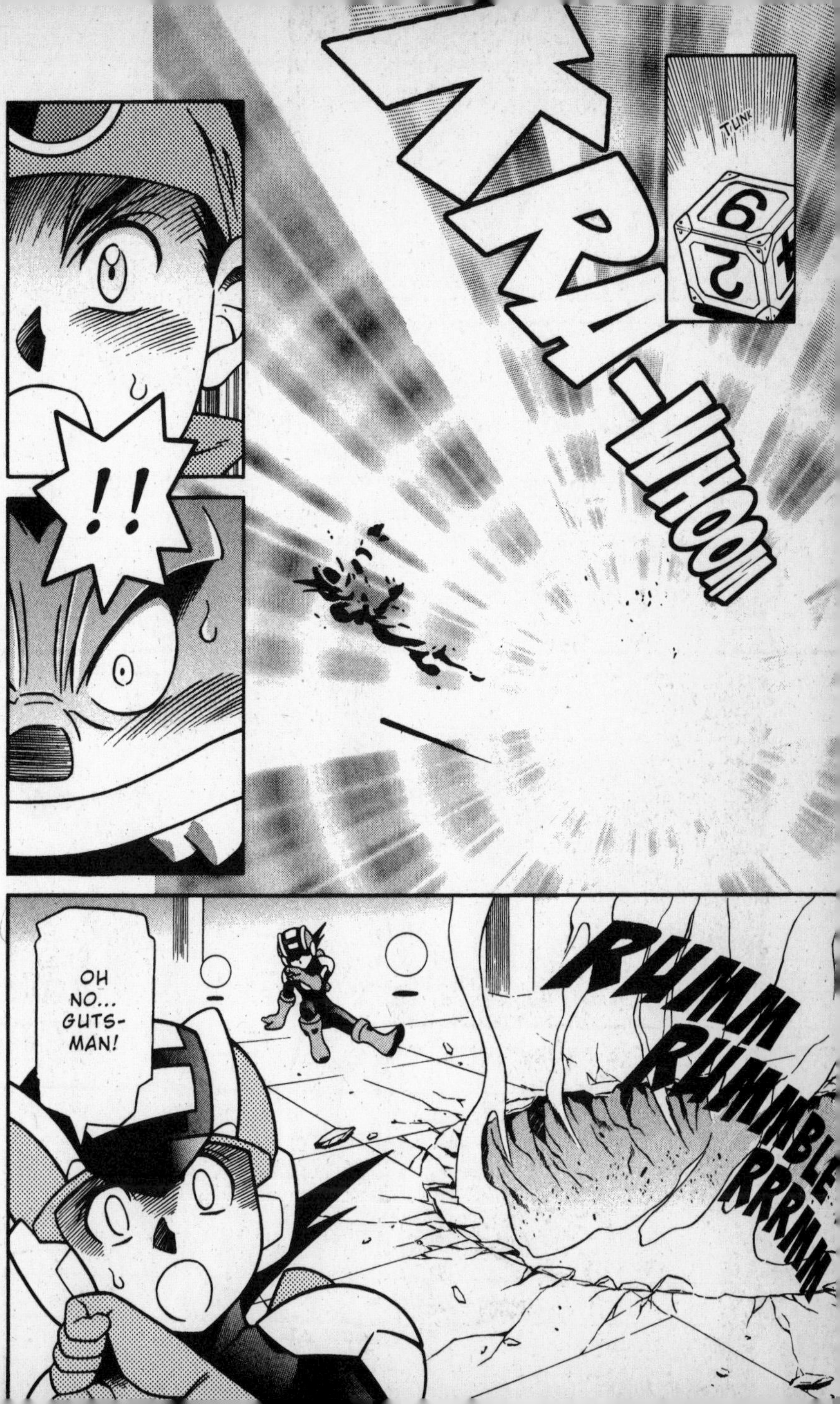
TUNK
KRA-WHOOM
!!
RUMM RUMMBLE RRRMM
OH NO... GUTS-MAN!

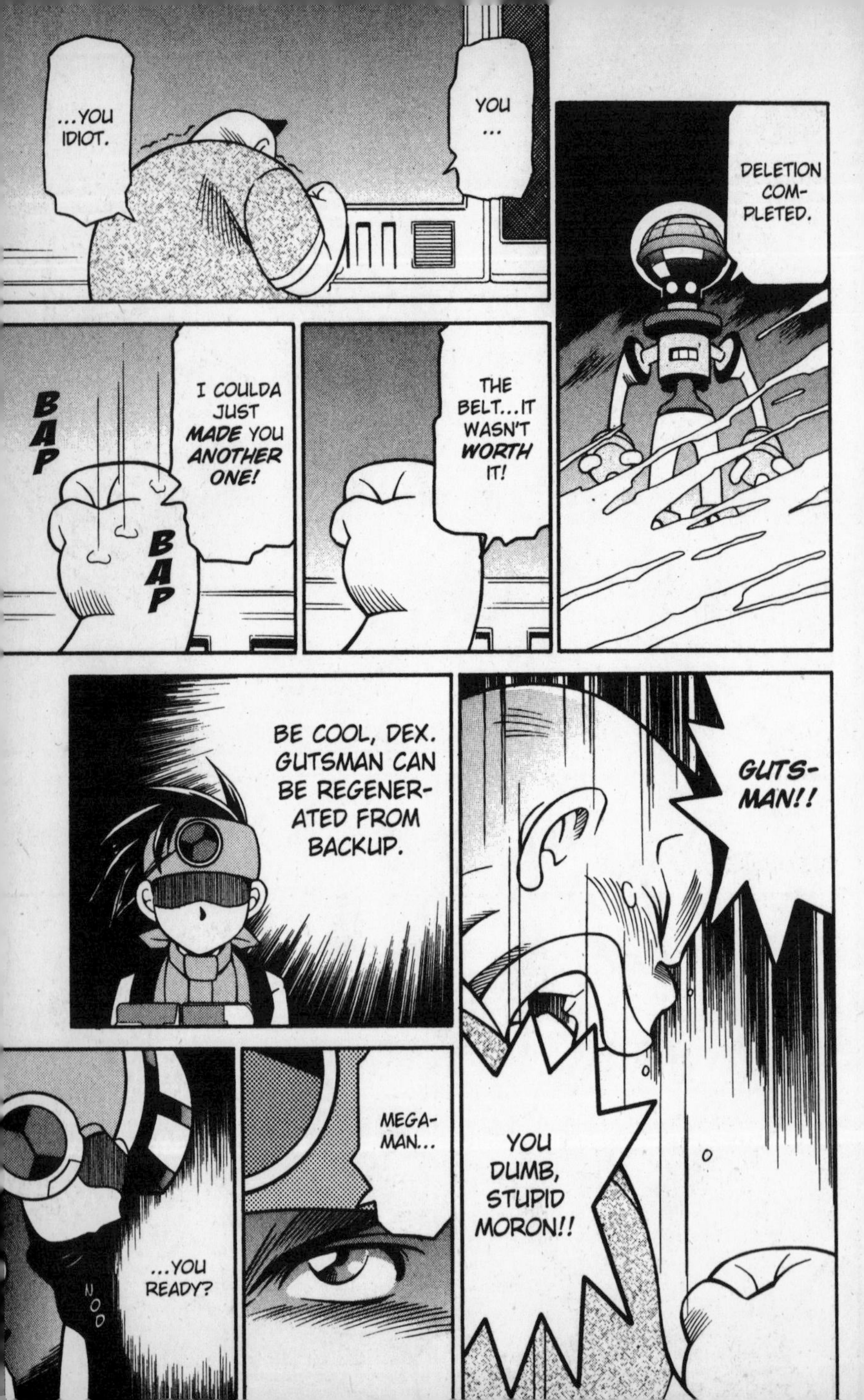
DELETION COM-PLETED.
YOU ...
...YOU IDIOT.
THE BELT...IT WASN'T WORTH IT!
I COULDA JUST MADE YOU ANOTHER ONE!
BAP
BAP
GUTS-MAN!!
YOU DUMB, STUPID MORON!!
BE COOL, DEX. GUTSMAN CAN BE REGENER-ATED FROM BACKUP.
MEGA-MAN...
...YOU READY?
NOO

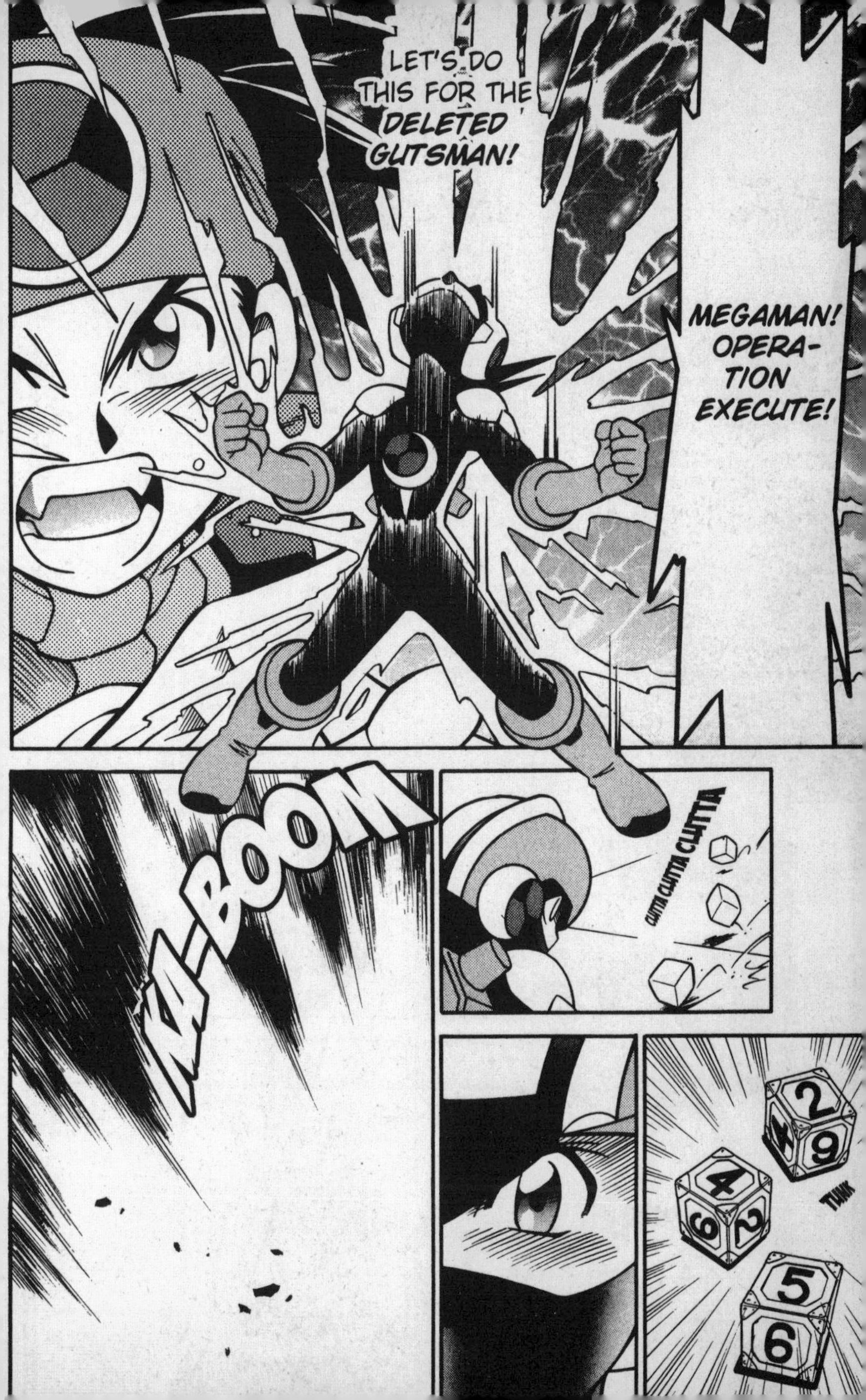
MEGAMAN! OPERATION EXECUTE!
LET'S DO THIS FOR THE DELETED GUTSMAN!
CLUTTA CLUTTA CLUTTA
TINK
BOOM

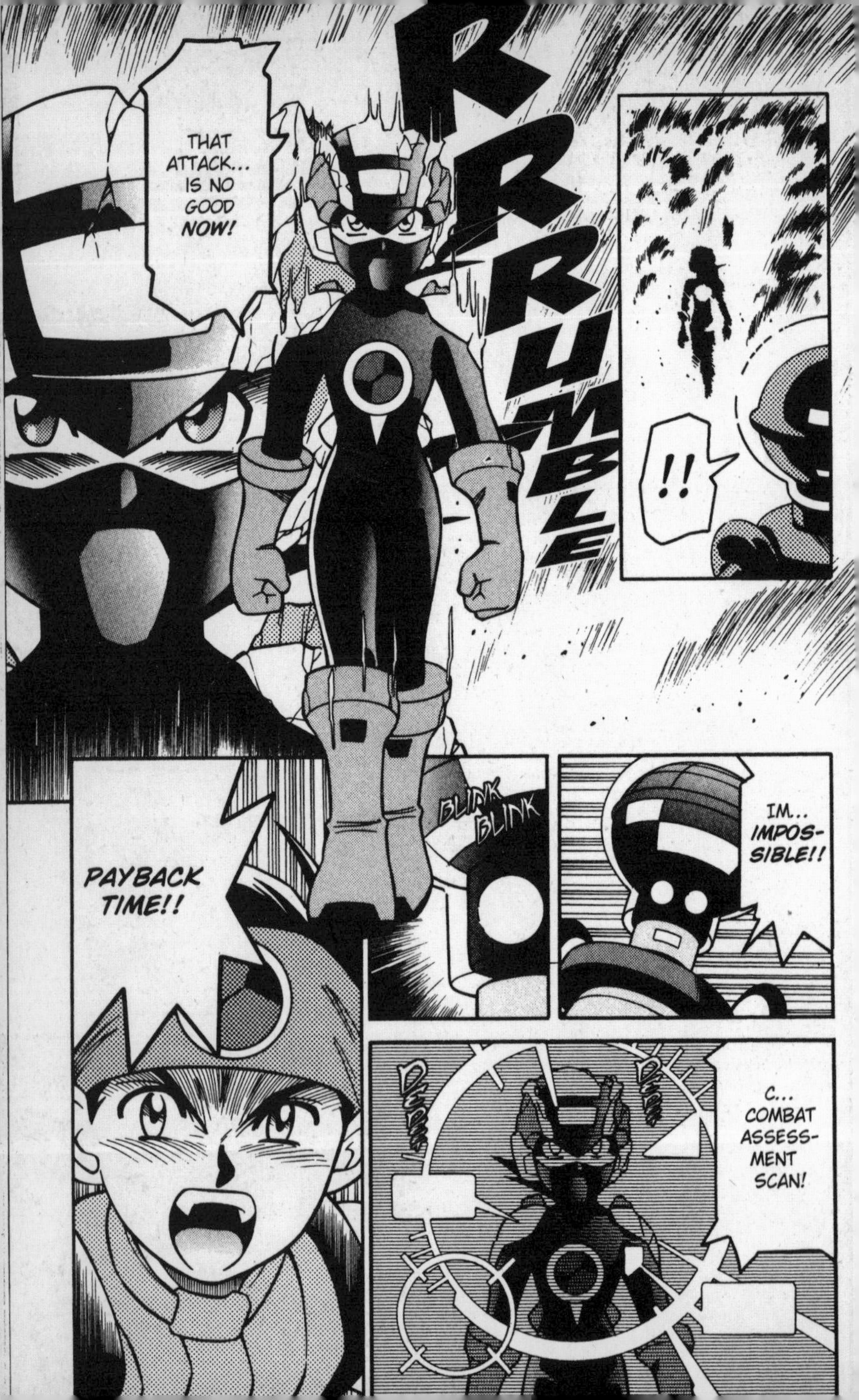
!!
RRUMBLE
THAT ATTACK... IS NO GOOD NOW!
IM.. IMPOSSIBLE!!
BLINK BLINK
C... COMBAT ASSESSMENT SCAN!
PAYBACK TIME!!

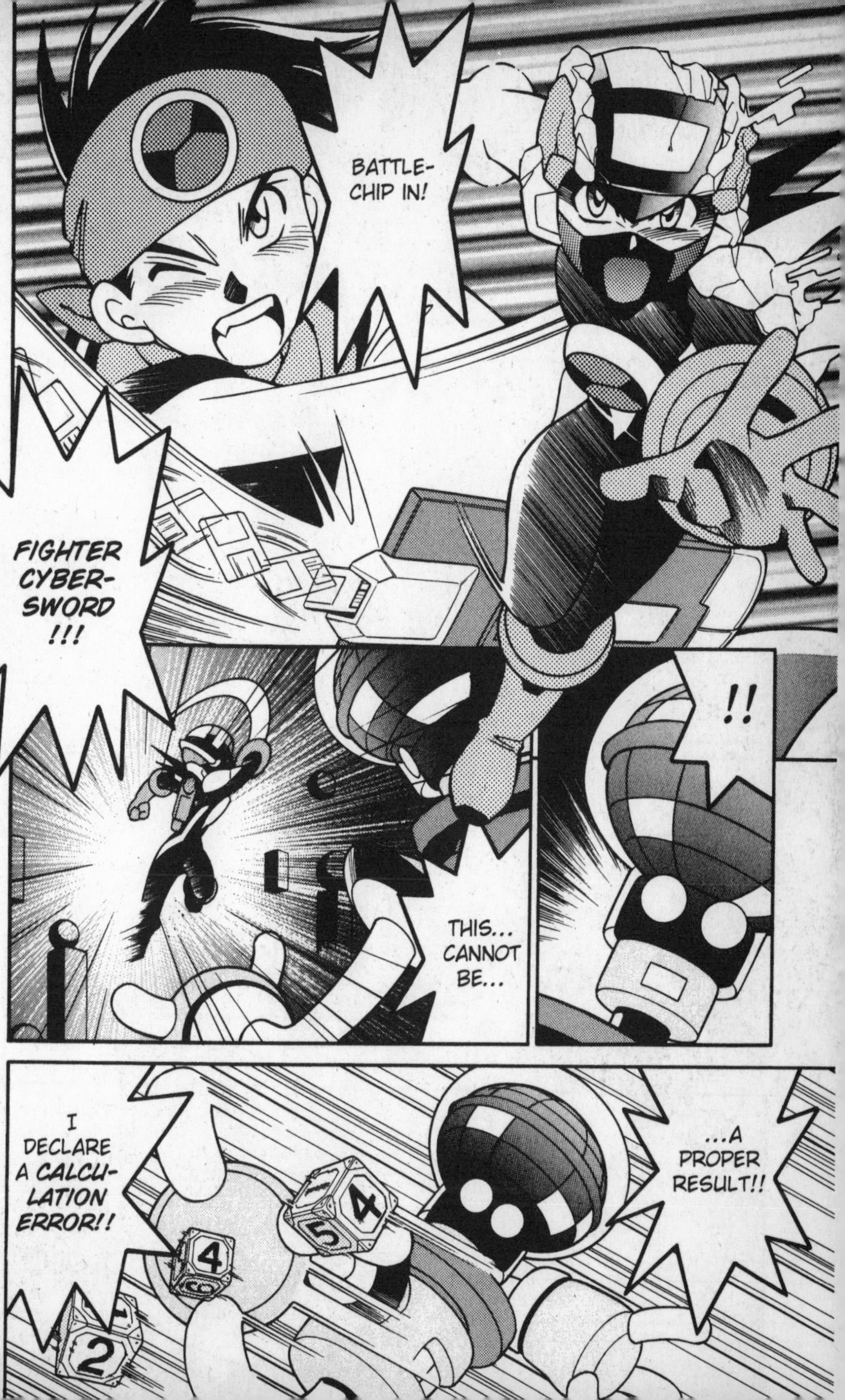
BATTLE-CHIP IN!
FIGHTER CYBER-SWORD !!!
!!
THIS... CANNOT BE...
...A PROPER RESULT!!
I DECLARE A CALCULATION ERROR!!

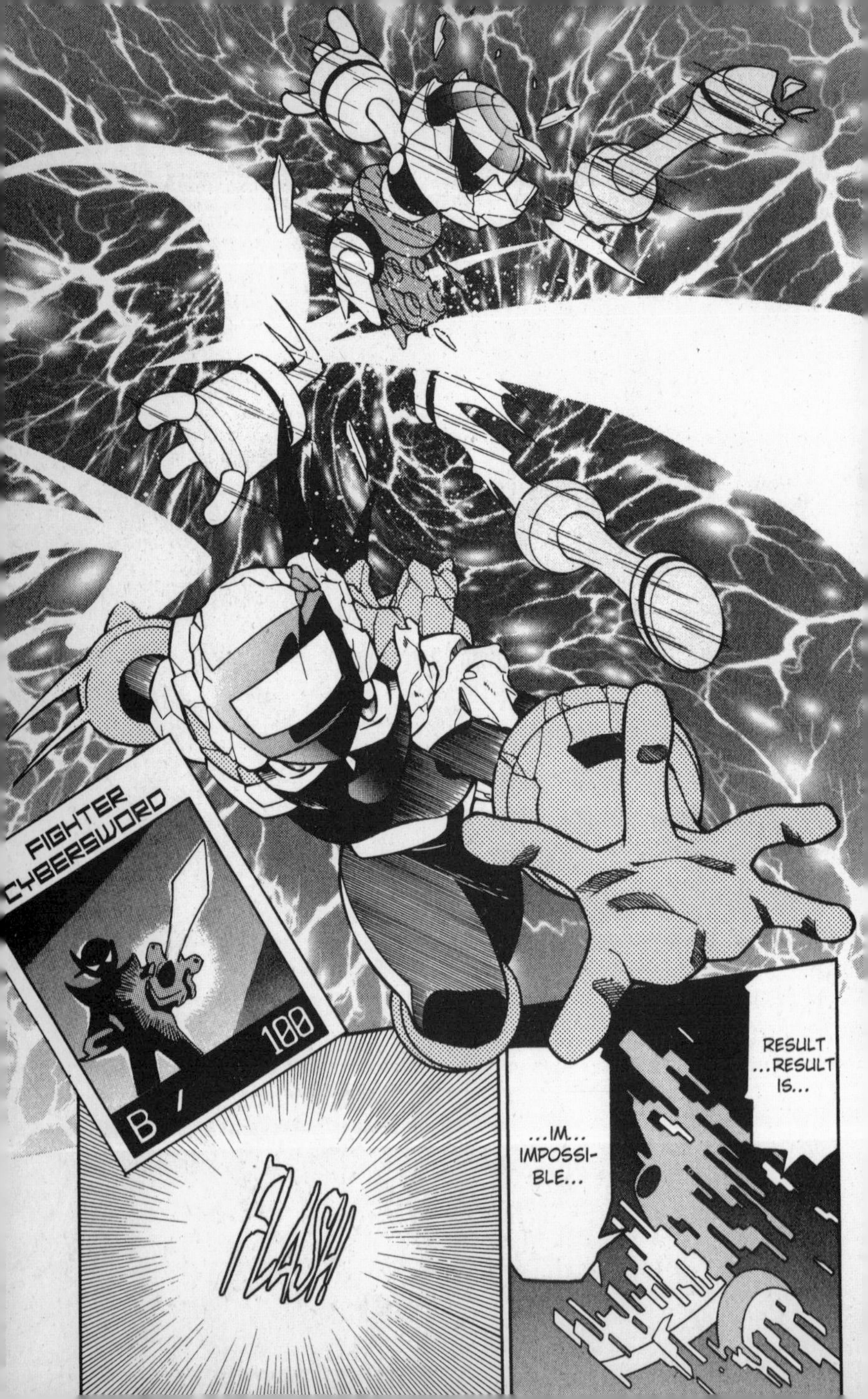
FIGHTER CYBERSWORD
100
B /
RESULT ...RESULT IS...
...IM... IMPOSSI-BLE...
FLASH!

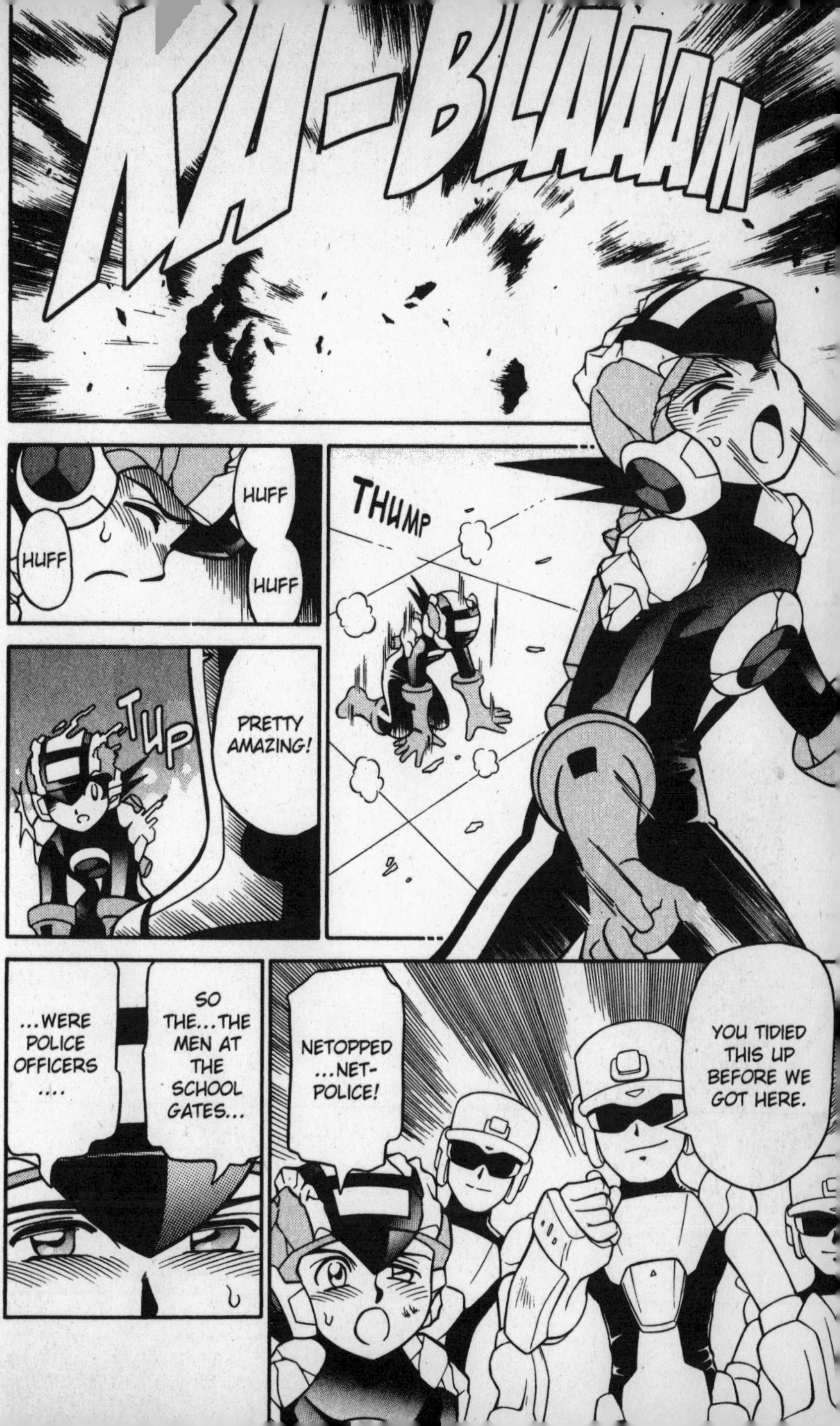
KA-BLAAAM
THUMP
HUFF
HUFF
HUFF
TUP
PRETTY AMAZING!
YOU TIDIED THIS UP BEFORE WE GOT HERE.
NETOPPED ...NET-POLICE!
SO THE...THE MEN AT THE SCHOOL GATES...
...WERE POLICE OFFICERS....

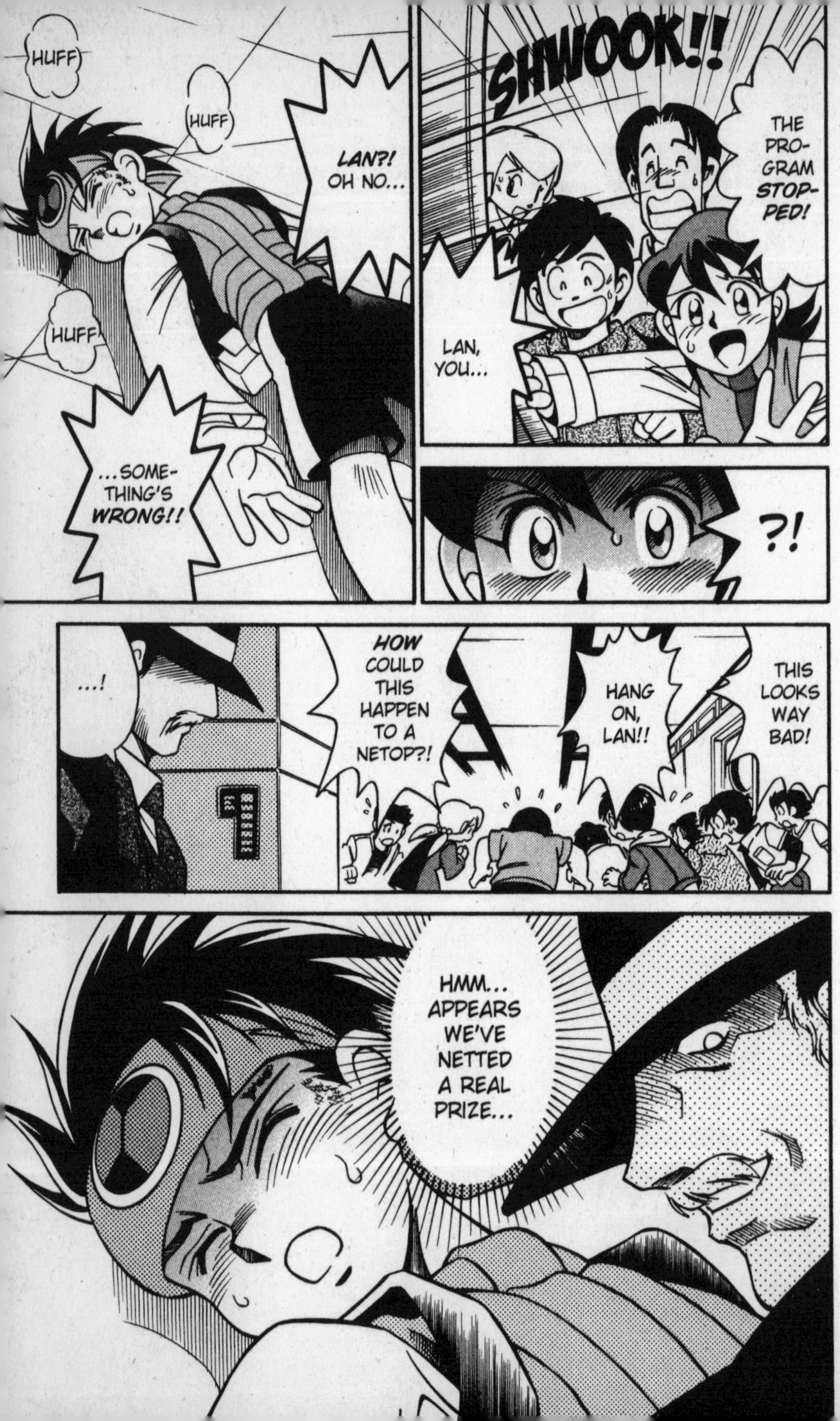
SHWOOK!!
THE PROGRAM STOPPED!
LAN, YOU...
?!
HUFF
HUFF
LAN?! OH NO...
HUFF
...SOMETHING'S WRONG!!
THIS LOOKS WAY BAD!
HANG ON, LAN!!
HOW COULD THIS HAPPEN TO A NETOP?!
...!
HMM... APPEARS WE'VE NETTED A REAL PRIZE...

CHAPTER 5:
FULLSYNCHRO UNLEASHED!!

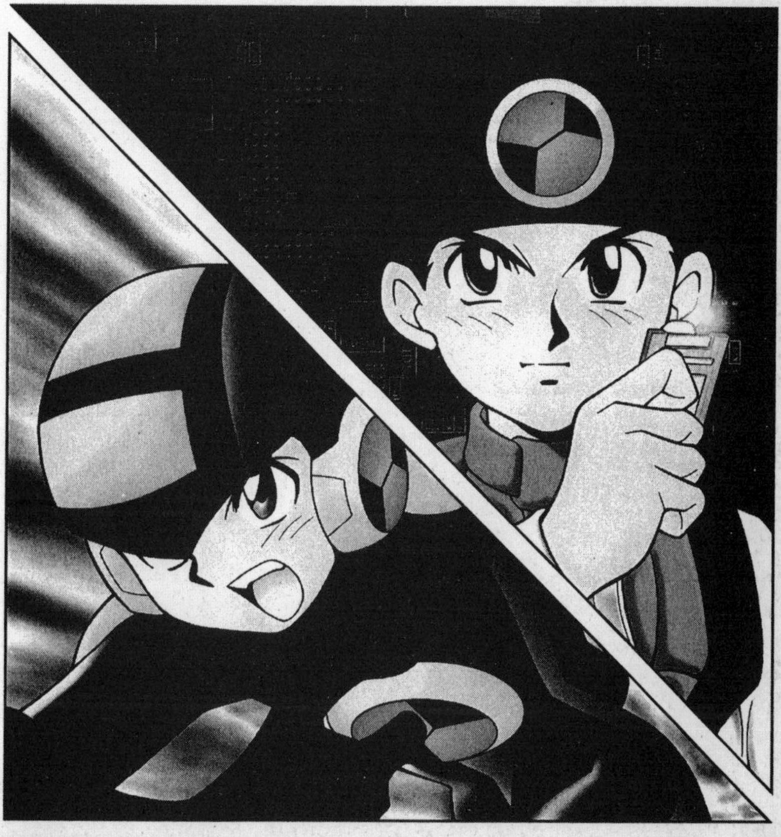

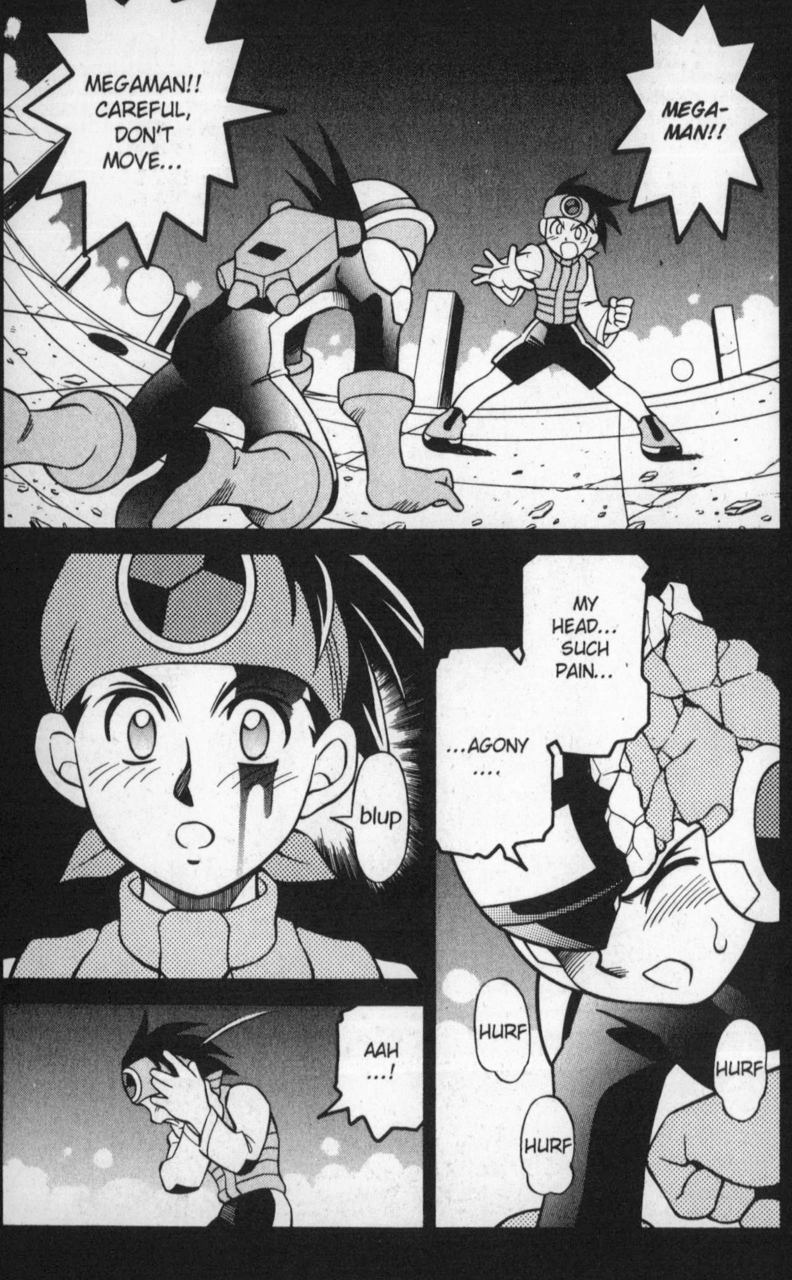
MEGA-MAN!!
MEGAMAN!! CAREFUL, DON'T MOVE...
MY HEAD... SUCH PAIN...
...AGONY ....
HURF
HURF
HURF
blup
AAH ...!

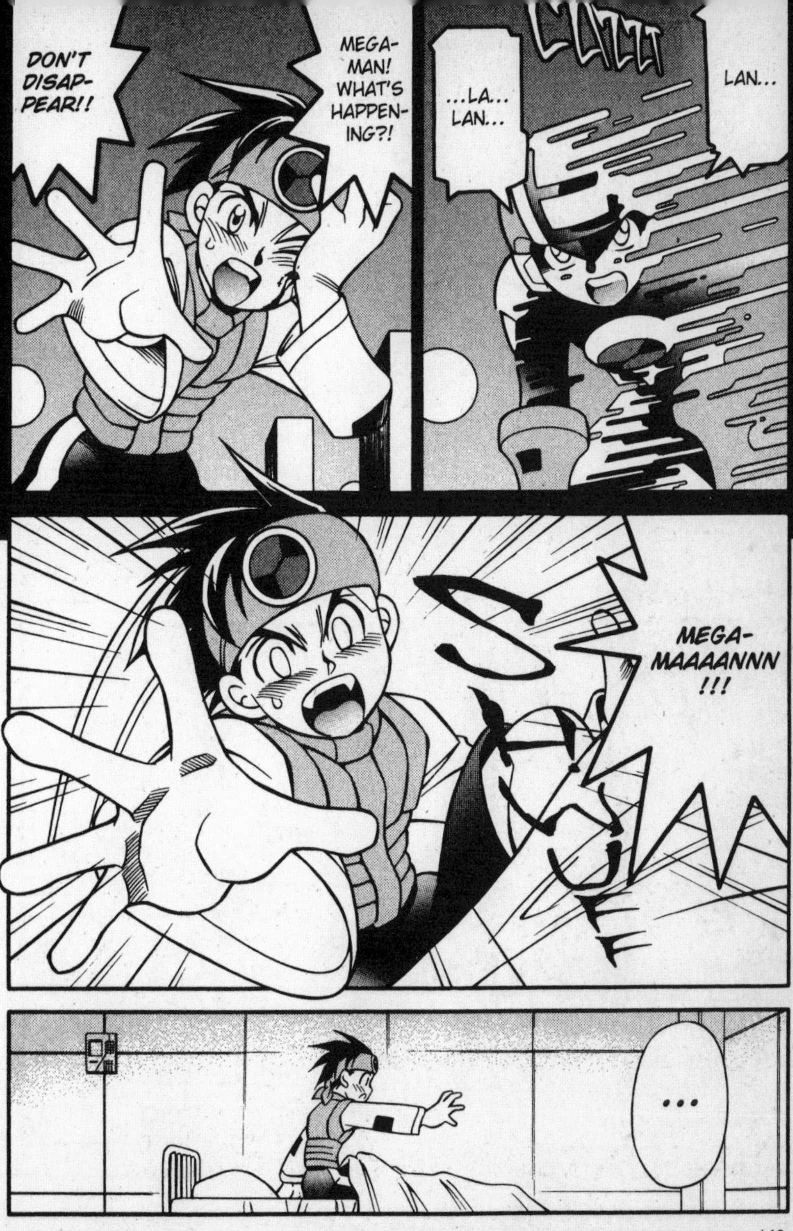
LAN...
...LA... LAN...
MEGA-MAN! WHAT'S HAPPEN-ING?!
DON'T DISAP-PEAR!!
MEGA-MAAAANNN!!!
...

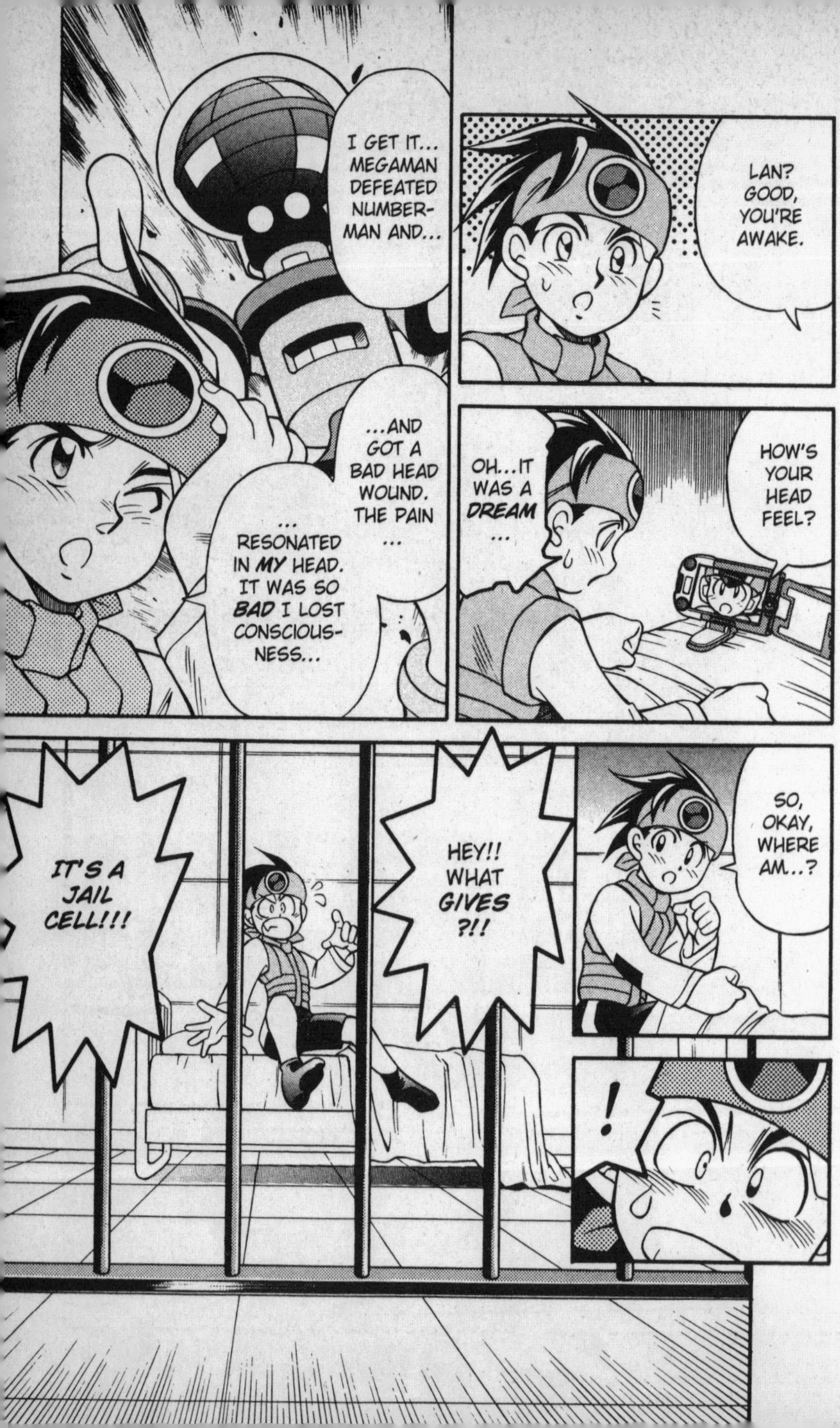
LAN? GOOD, YOU'RE AWAKE.
HOW'S YOUR HEAD FEEL?
OH...IT WAS A *DREAM*...
I GET IT... MEGAMAN DEFEATED NUMBER-MAN AND...
...AND GOT A BAD HEAD WOUND. THE PAIN...
...RESONATED IN *MY* HEAD. IT WAS SO *BAD* I LOST CONSCIOUS-NESS...
SO, OKAY, WHERE AM...?
!
HEY!! WHAT *GIVES* ?!!
IT'S A JAIL CELL!!!

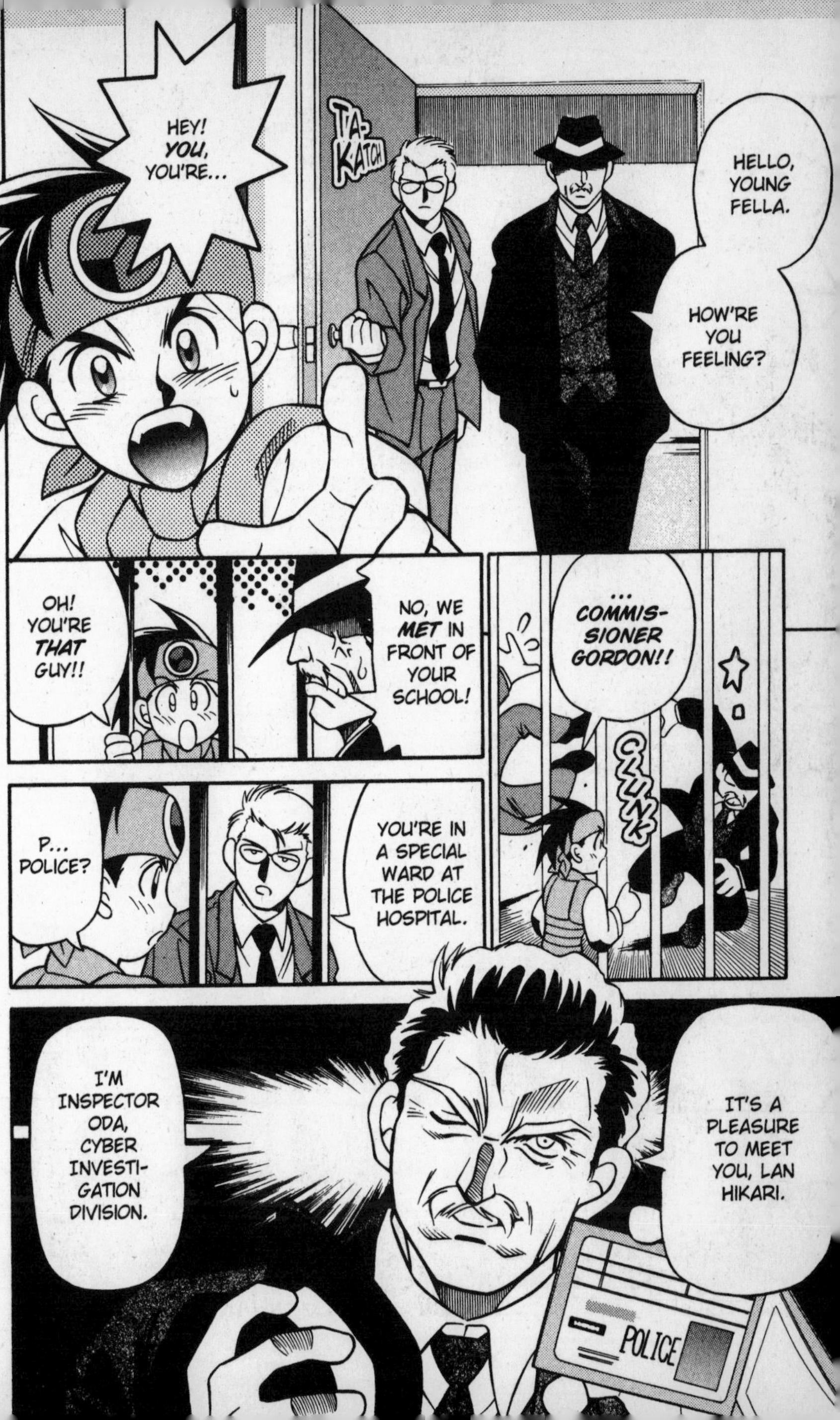
HELLO, YOUNG FELLA.
HOW'RE YOU FEELING?
TA-KATCH
HEY! ***YOU***, YOU'RE...
... ***COMMISSIONER GORDON!!***
CLUNK
NO, WE ***MET*** IN FRONT OF YOUR SCHOOL!
OH! YOU'RE ***THAT*** GUY!!
YOU'RE IN A SPECIAL WARD AT THE POLICE HOSPITAL.
P... POLICE?
IT'S A PLEASURE TO MEET YOU, LAN HIKARI.
I'M INSPECTOR ODA, CYBER INVESTIGATION DIVISION.
POLICE

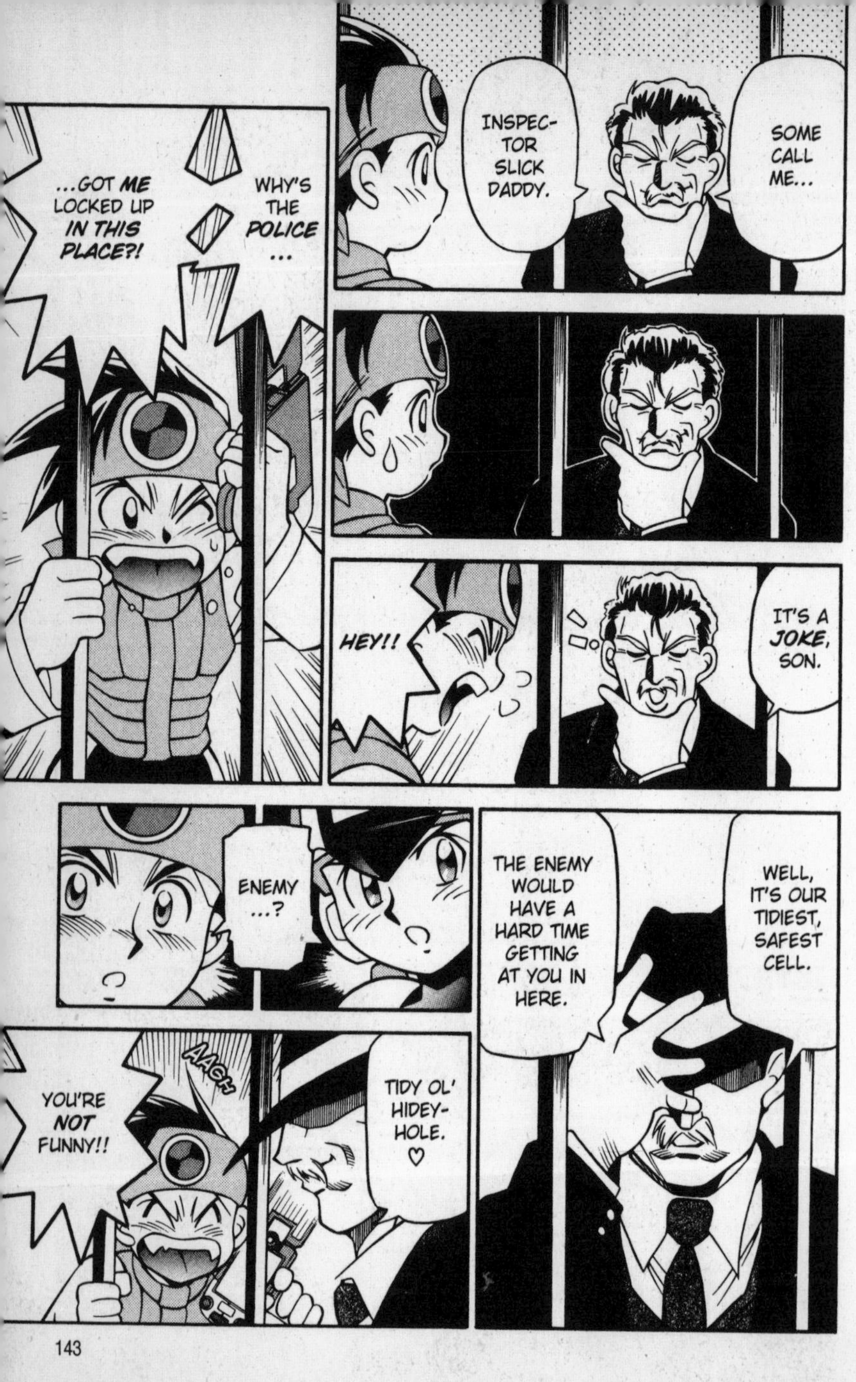
SOME CALL ME...
INSPECTOR SLICK DADDY.
IT'S A JOKE, SON.
HEY!!
WHY'S THE POLICE ...
...GOT ME LOCKED UP IN THIS PLACE?!
WELL, IT'S OUR TIDIEST, SAFEST CELL.
THE ENEMY WOULD HAVE A HARD TIME GETTING AT YOU IN HERE.
ENEMY ...?
TIDY OL' HIDEY-HOLE. ♥
AAGH
YOU'RE NOT FUNNY!!

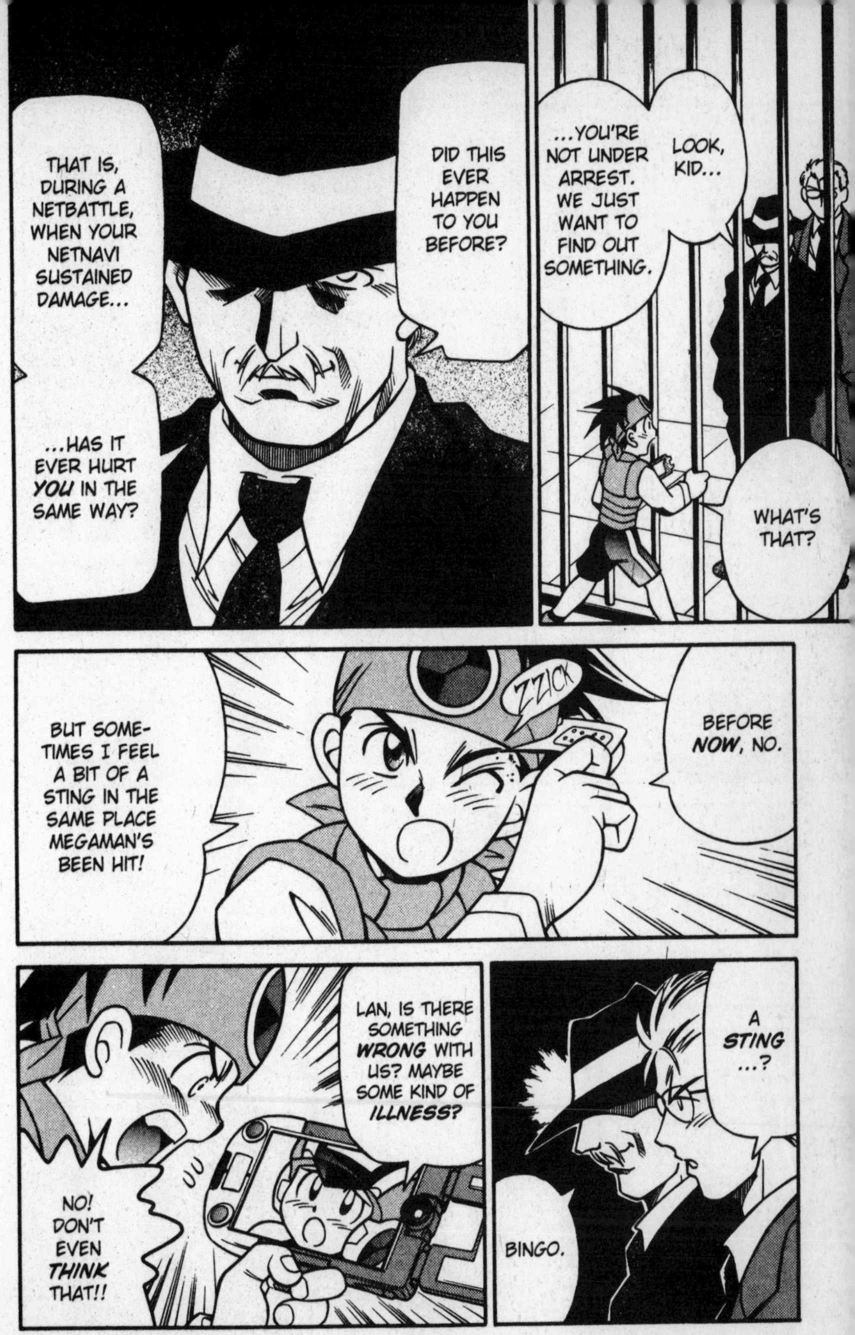
LOOK, KID...
...YOU'RE NOT UNDER ARREST. WE JUST WANT TO FIND OUT SOMETHING.
WHAT'S THAT?
DID THIS EVER HAPPEN TO YOU BEFORE?
THAT IS, DURING A NETBATTLE, WHEN YOUR NETNAVI SUSTAINED DAMAGE...
...HAS IT EVER HURT *YOU* IN THE SAME WAY?
Z'ZICK
BEFORE *NOW*, NO.
BUT SOME-TIMES I FEEL A BIT OF A STING IN THE SAME PLACE MEGAMAN'S BEEN HIT!
A *STING* ...?
BINGO.
LAN, IS THERE SOMETHING *WRONG* WITH US? MAYBE SOME KIND OF *ILLNESS?*
NO! DON'T EVEN *THINK* THAT!!

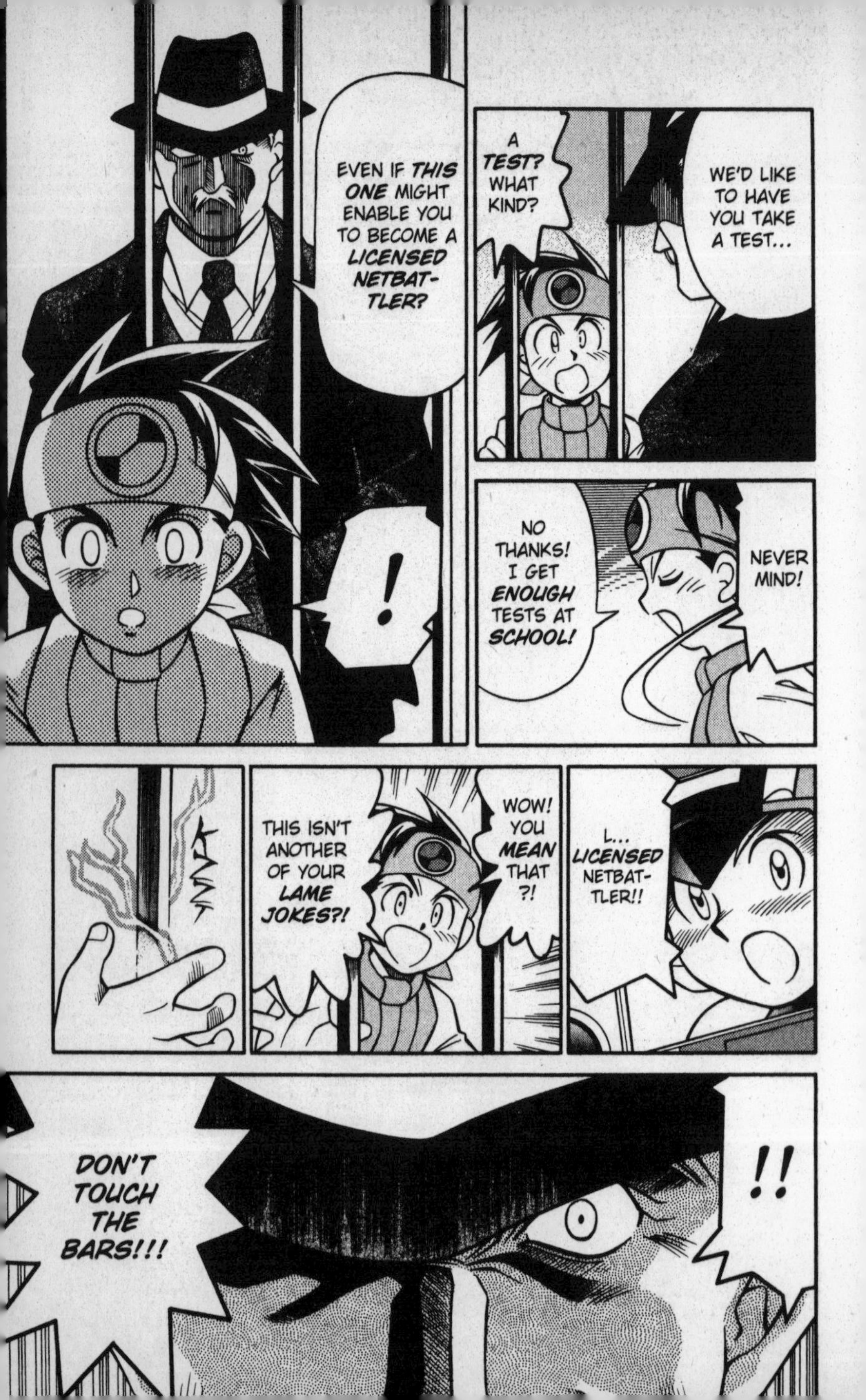
WE'D LIKE TO HAVE YOU TAKE A TEST...
A TEST? WHAT KIND?
NEVER MIND!
NO THANKS! I GET ENOUGH TESTS AT SCHOOL!
EVEN IF THIS ONE MIGHT ENABLE YOU TO BECOME A LICENSED NETBATTLER?
!
L... LICENSED NETBATTLER!!
WOW! YOU MEAN THAT?!
THIS ISN'T ANOTHER OF YOUR LAME JOKES?!
!!
DON'T TOUCH THE BARS!!!

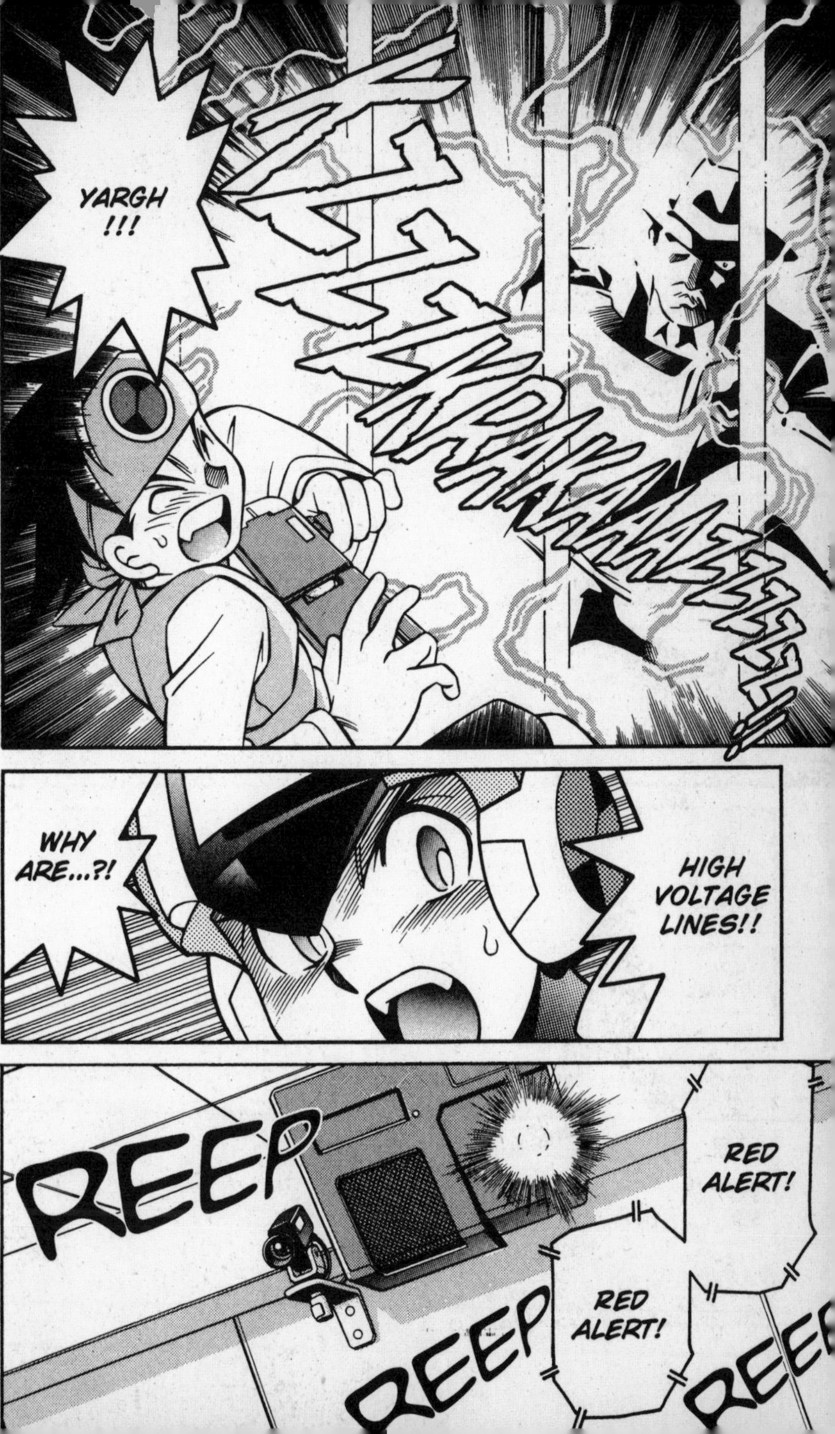
YARGH !!!
HIGH VOLTAGE LINES!!
WHY ARE...?!
RED ALERT!
REEP
RED ALERT!
REEP
REEP

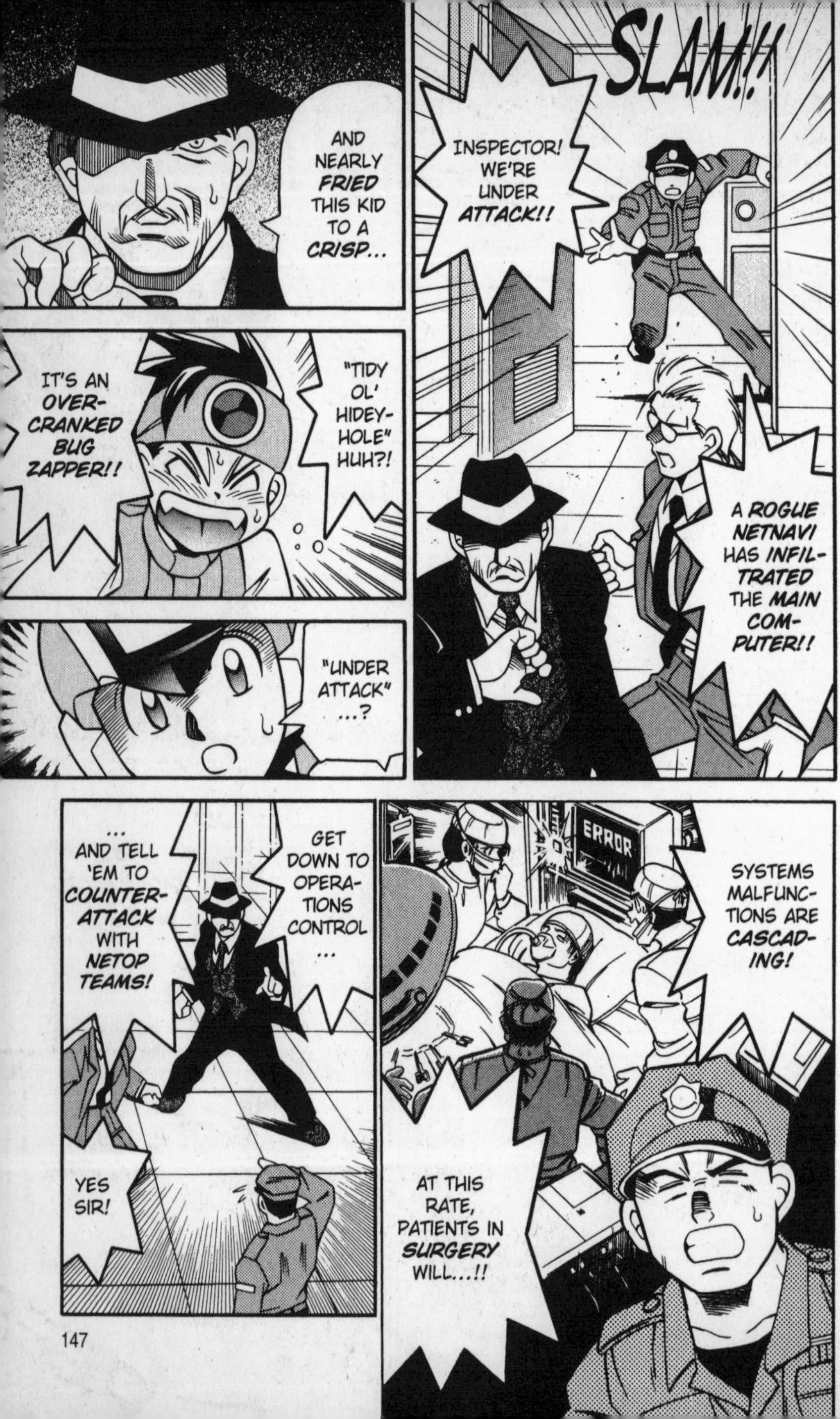
SLAM!!
INSPECTOR! WE'RE UNDER ATTACK!!
A ROGUE NETNAVI HAS INFILTRATED THE MAIN COMPUTER!!
AND NEARLY FRIED THIS KID TO A CRISP...
"TIDY OL' HIDEY-HOLE" HUH?!
IT'S AN OVER-CRANKED BUG ZAPPER!!
"UNDER ATTACK" ...?
ERROR
SYSTEMS MALFUNCTIONS ARE CASCADING!
AT THIS RATE, PATIENTS IN SURGERY WILL...!!
GET DOWN TO OPERATIONS CONTROL ...
... AND TELL 'EM TO COUNTER-ATTACK WITH NETOP TEAMS!
YES SIR!

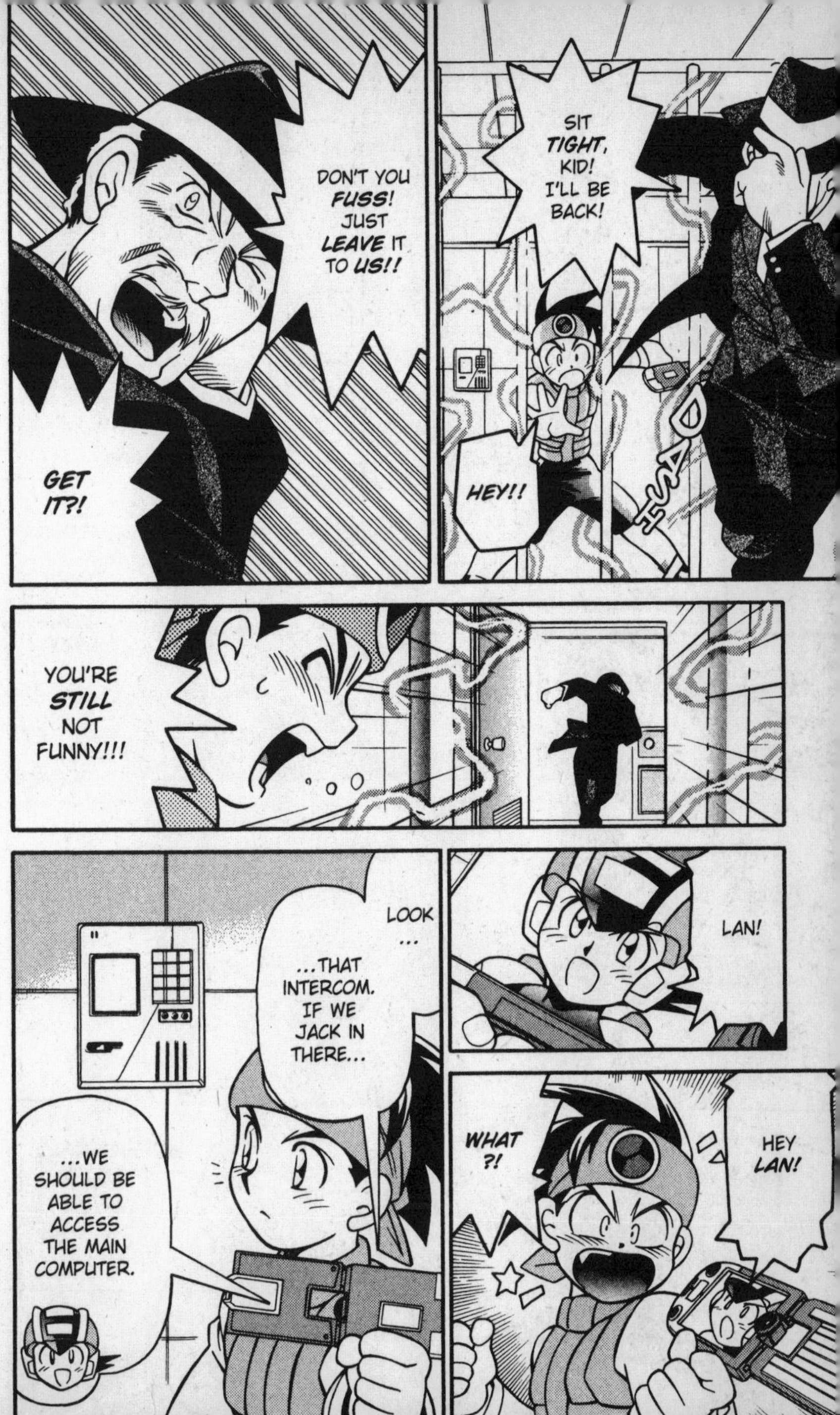
SIT TIGHT, KID! I'LL BE BACK!
HEY!!
DASH
DON'T YOU FUSS! JUST LEAVE IT TO US!!
GET IT?!
YOU'RE STILL NOT FUNNY!!!
LAN!
HEY LAN!
WHAT?!
LOOK...
...THAT INTERCOM. IF WE JACK IN THERE...
...WE SHOULD BE ABLE TO ACCESS THE MAIN COMPUTER.

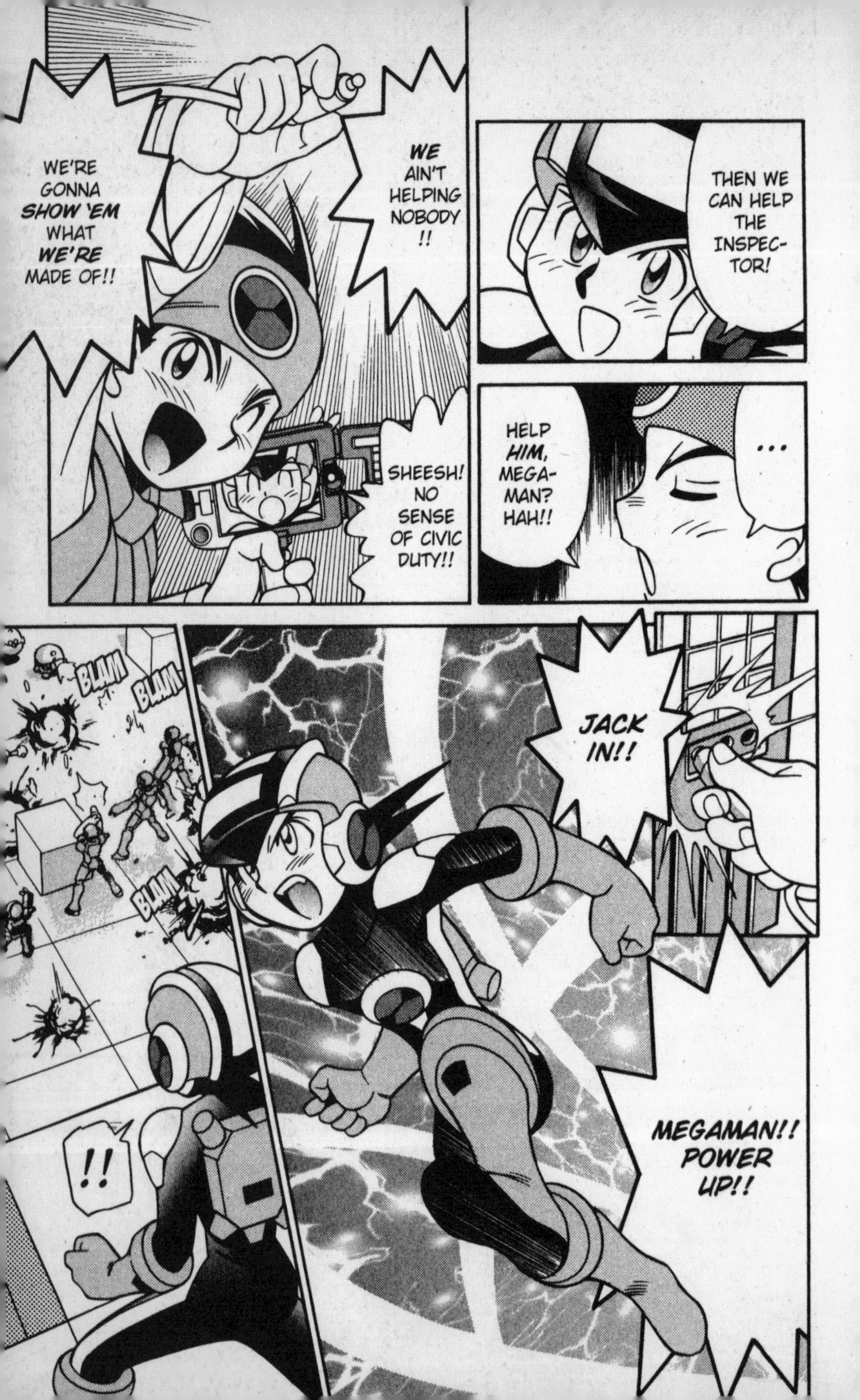
THEN WE CAN HELP THE INSPECTOR!
HELP HIM, MEGAMAN? HAH!!
...
WE AIN'T HELPING NOBODY!!
WE'RE GONNA SHOW 'EM WHAT WE'RE MADE OF!!
SHEESH! NO SENSE OF CIVIC DUTY!!
JACK IN!!
MEGAMAN!! POWER UP!!
BLAM
BLAM
BLAM
!!

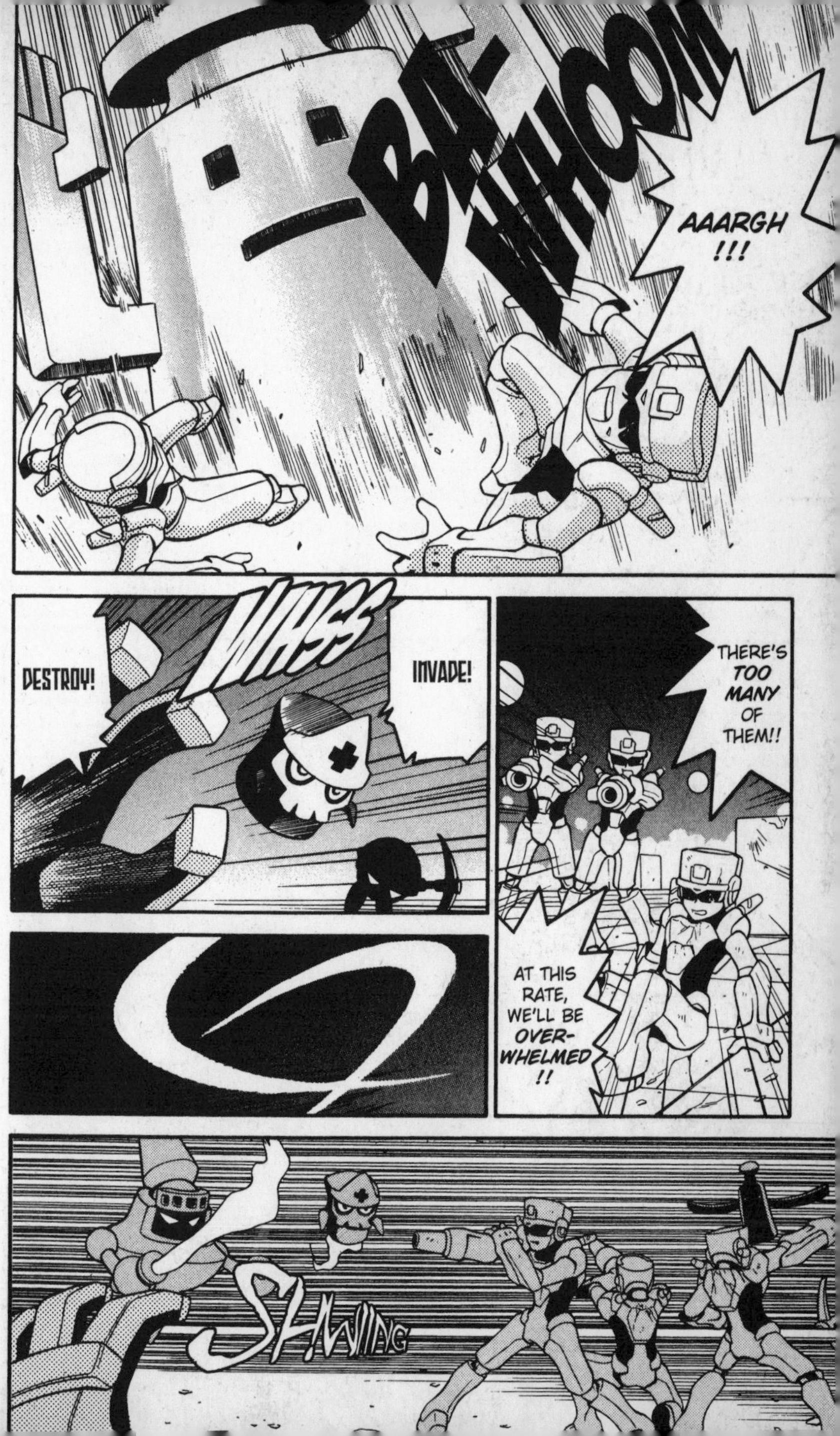
BA-WHOOM
AAARGH!!!
THERE'S TOO MANY OF THEM!!
AT THIS RATE, WE'LL BE OVER-WHELMED!!
WHSS
INVADE!
DESTROY!
SHWIING

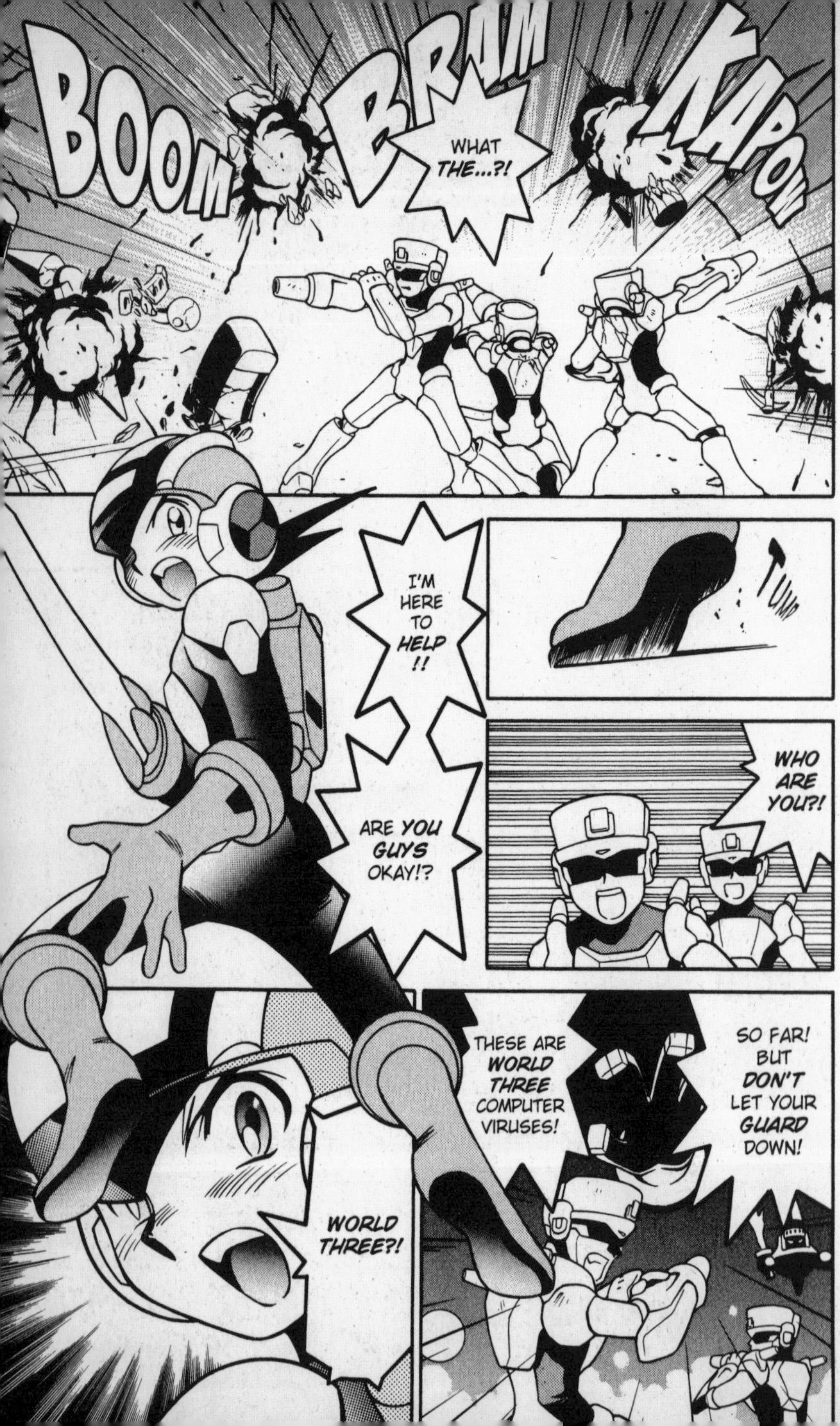
KAPOW
WHAT THE...?!
BRAM
BOOM
TUM
WHO ARE YOU?!
I'M HERE TO HELP!!
ARE YOU GUYS OKAY!?
SO FAR! BUT DON'T LET YOUR GUARD DOWN!
THESE ARE WORLD THREE COMPUTER VIRUSES!
WORLD THREE?!

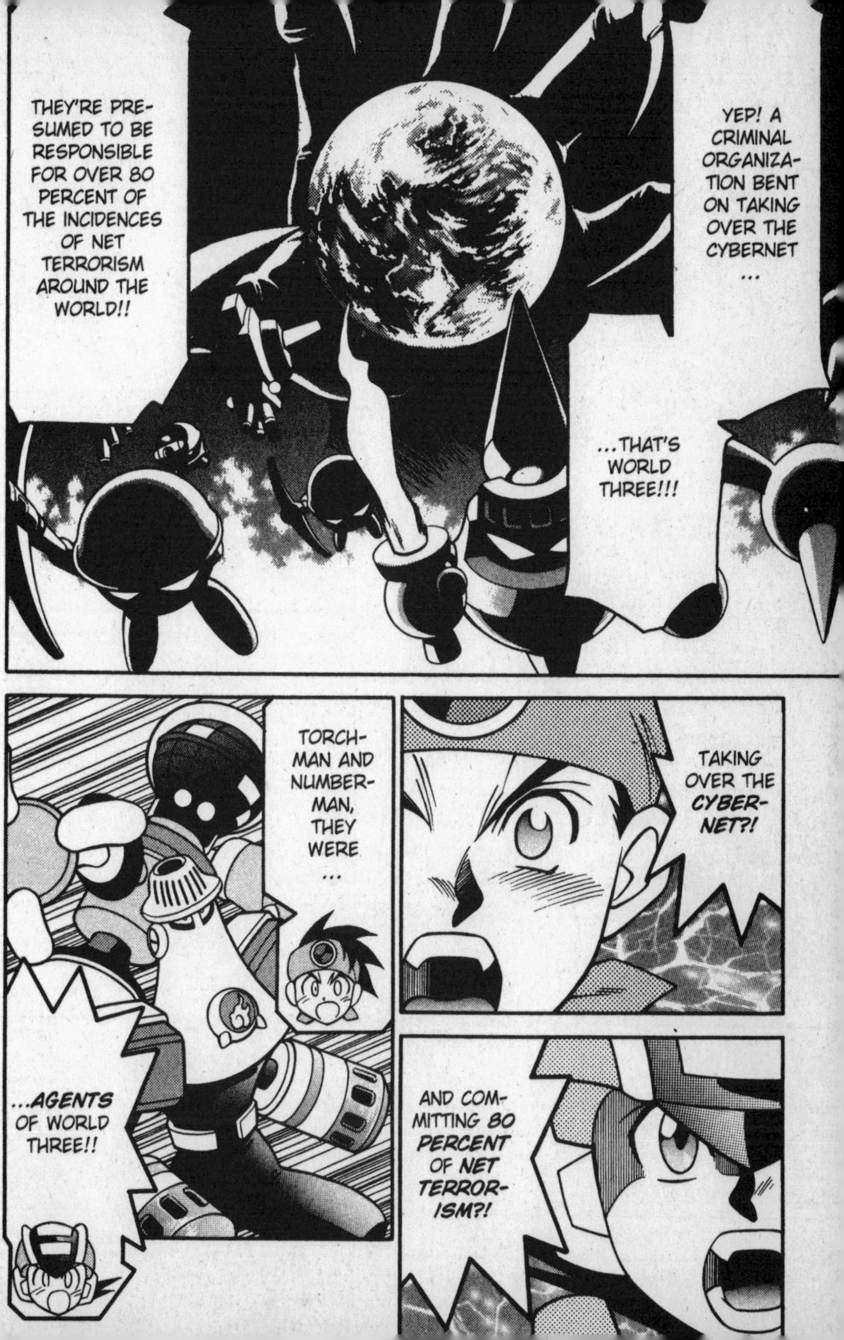
YEP! A CRIMINAL ORGANIZATION BENT ON TAKING OVER THE CYBERNET ...
...THAT'S WORLD THREE!!!
THEY'RE PRESUMED TO BE RESPONSIBLE FOR OVER 80 PERCENT OF THE INCIDENCES OF NET TERRORISM AROUND THE WORLD!!
TAKING OVER THE *CYBERNET*?!
AND COMMITTING 80 *PERCENT* OF *NET TERRORISM*?!
TORCHMAN AND NUMBERMAN, THEY WERE ...
...*AGENTS* OF WORLD THREE!!

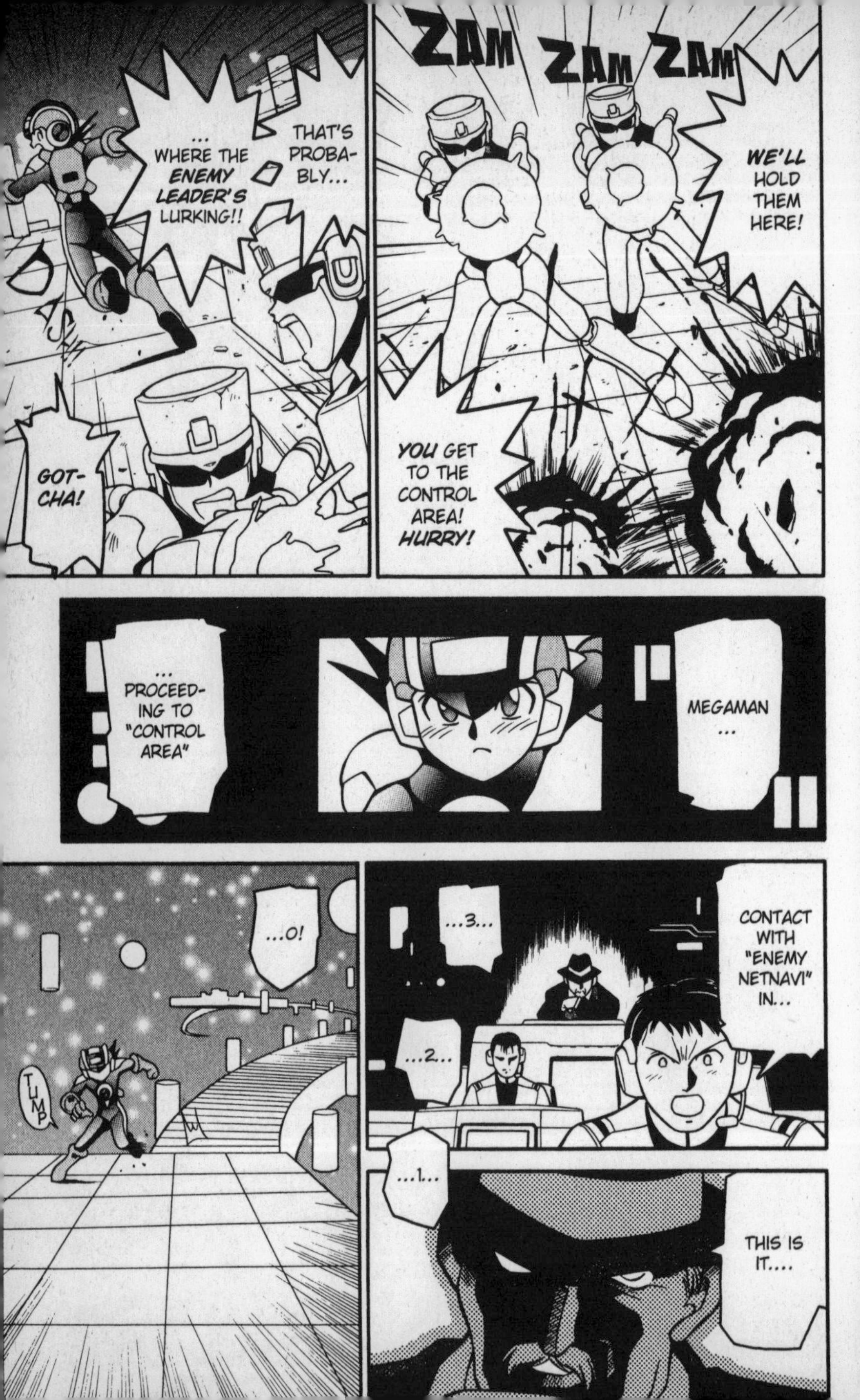
ZAM ZAM ZAM
WE'LL HOLD THEM HERE!
YOU GET TO THE CONTROL AREA! HURRY!
THAT'S PROBA-BLY...
... WHERE THE ENEMY LEADER'S LURKING!!
GOT-CHA!
MEGAMAN ...
... PROCEED-ING TO "CONTROL AREA"
CONTACT WITH "ENEMY NETNAVI" IN...
...3...
...2...
THIS IS IT....
...1...
...0!
TUMP

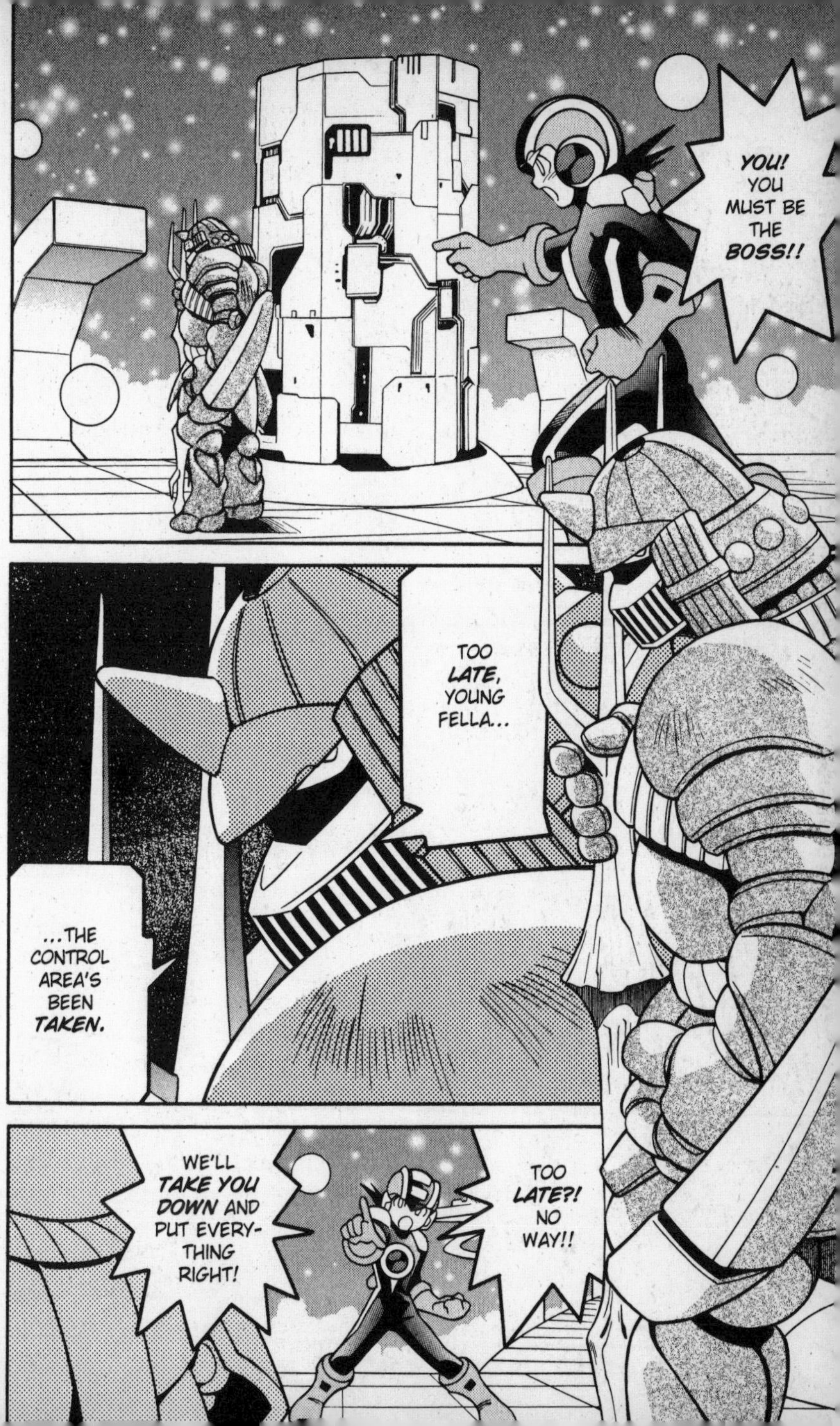
YOU! YOU MUST BE THE BOSS!!
TOO LATE, YOUNG FELLA...
...THE CONTROL AREA'S BEEN TAKEN.
TOO LATE?! NO WAY!!
WE'LL TAKE YOU DOWN AND PUT EVERY-THING RIGHT!

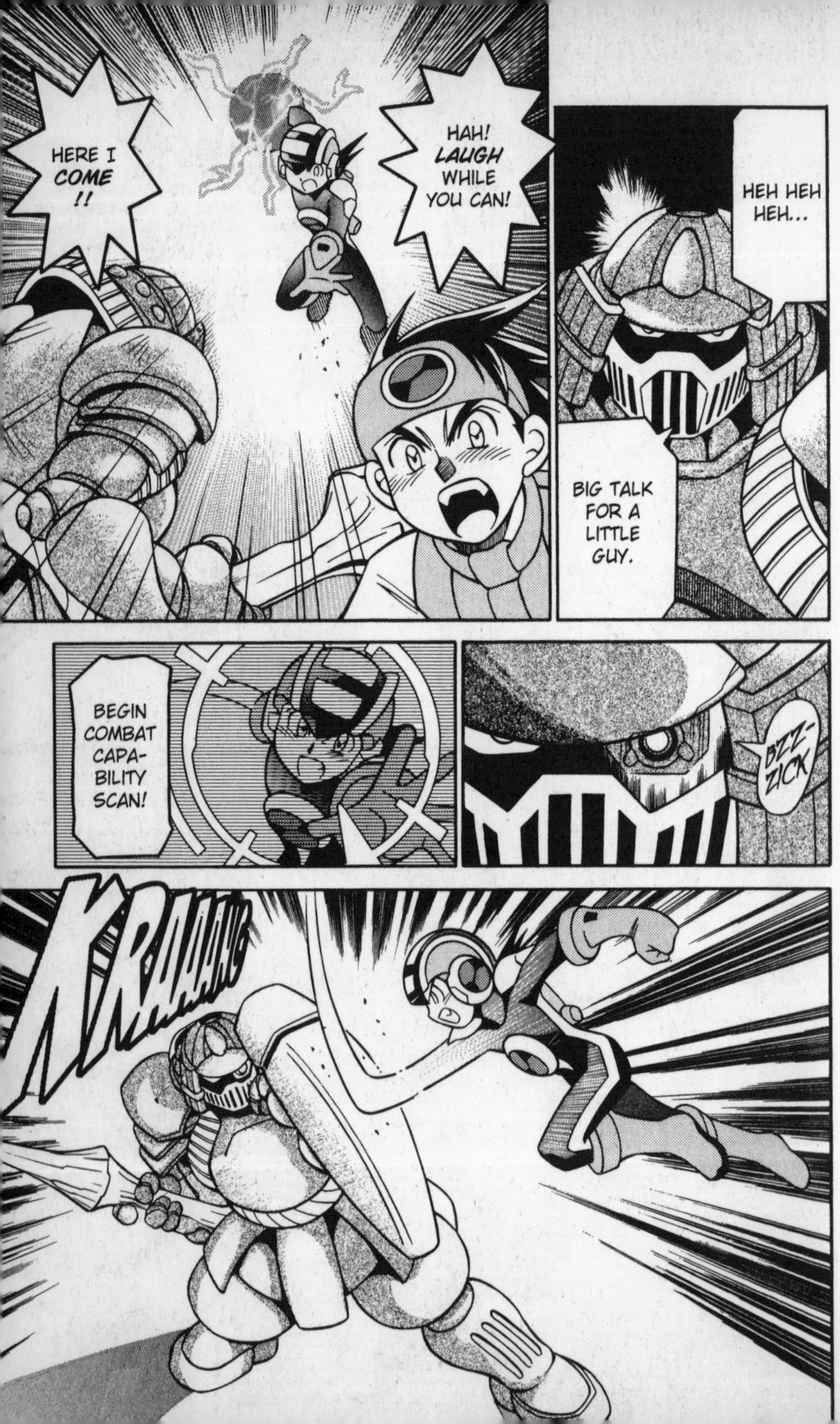
HEH HEH HEH...
BIG TALK FOR A LITTLE GUY.
HAH! *LAUGH* WHILE YOU CAN!
HERE I *COME* !!
BZZ-ZICK
BEGIN COMBAT CAPA-BILITY SCAN!

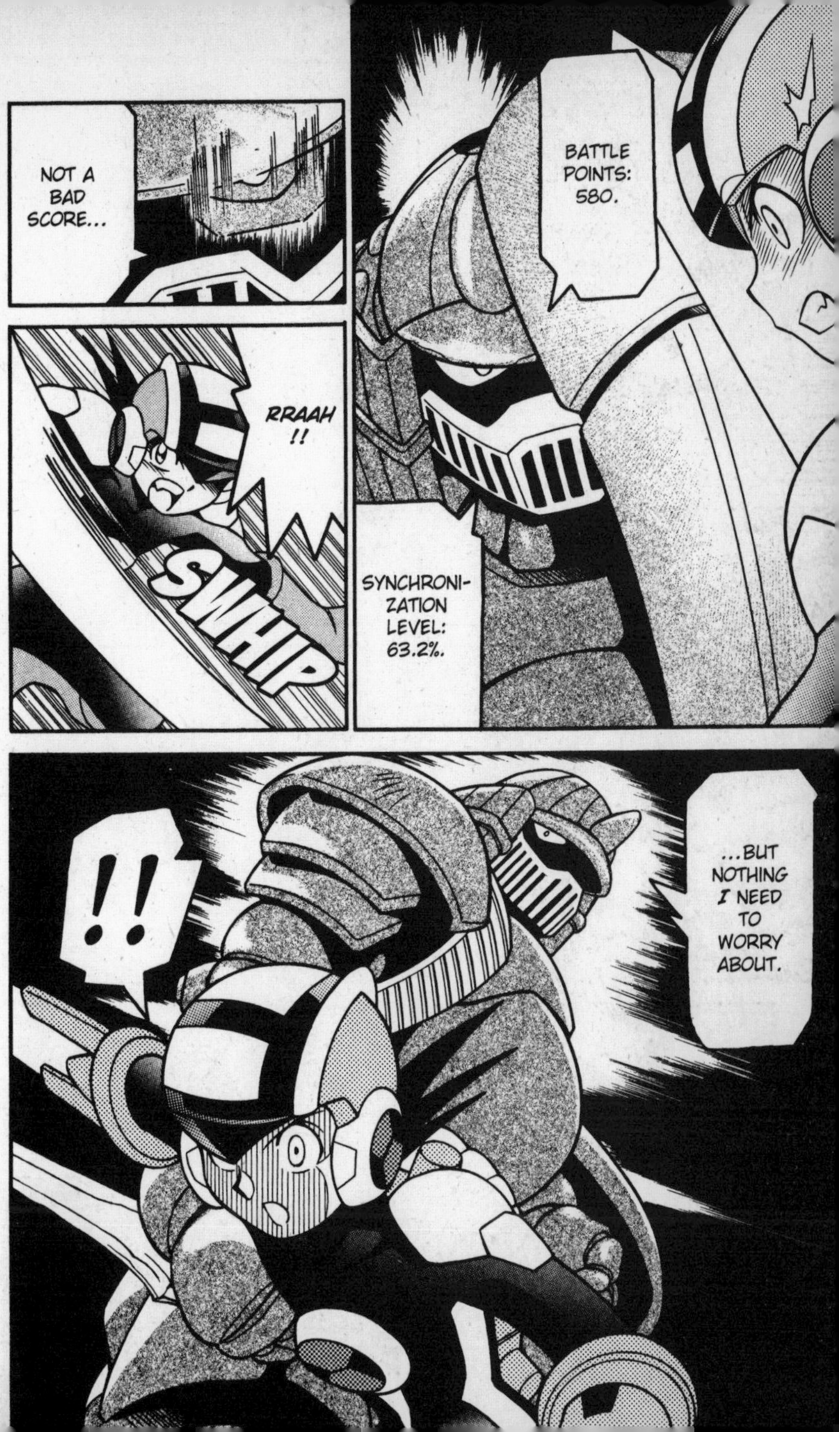
BATTLE POINTS: 580.
SYNCHRONIZATION LEVEL: 63.2%.
NOT A BAD SCORE...
RRAAH !!
SWHIP
...BUT NOTHING *I* NEED TO WORRY ABOUT.
!!

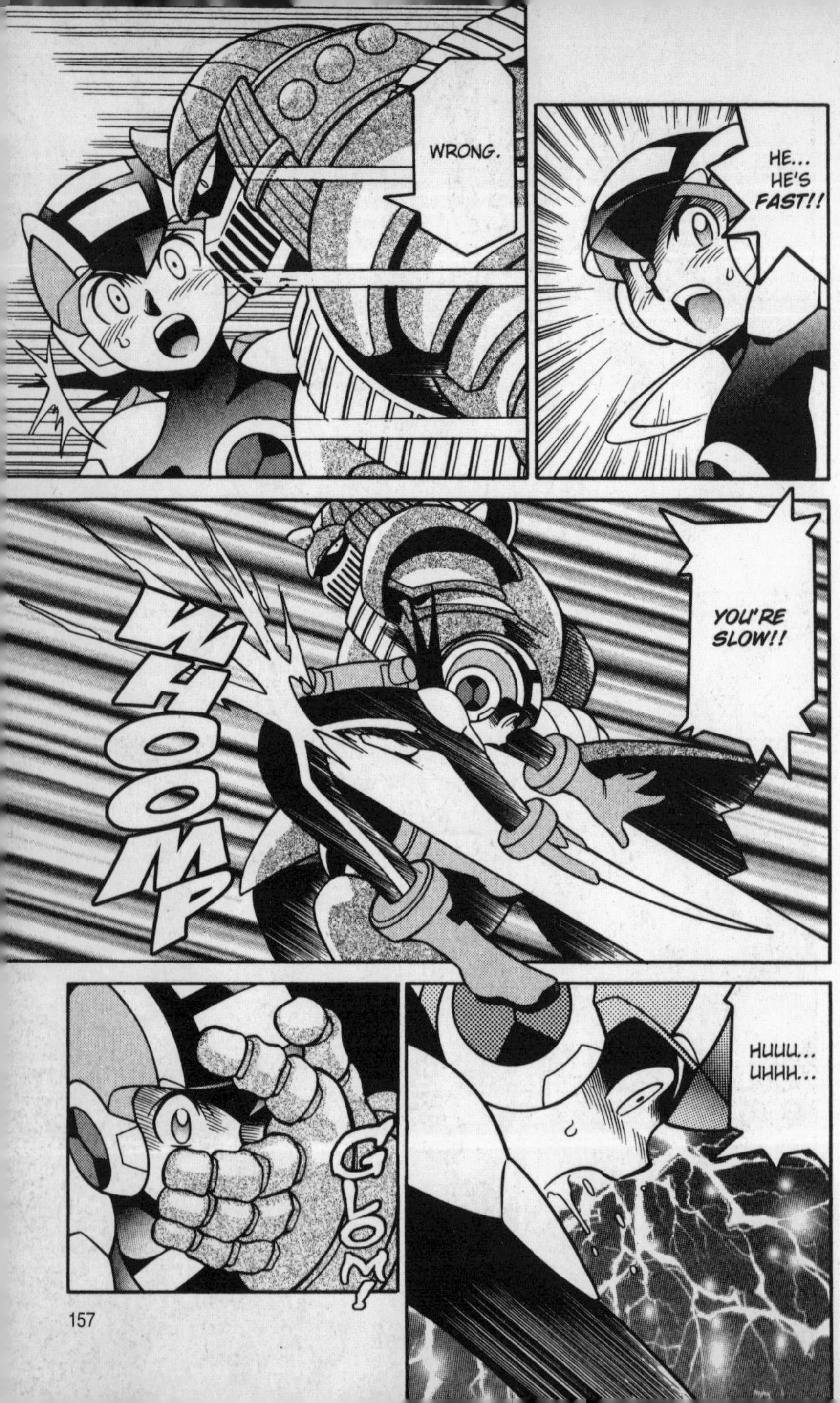
HE... HE'S FAST!!
WRONG.
YOU'RE SLOW!!
WHOOOMP
HUUU... UHHH...
GLOM!

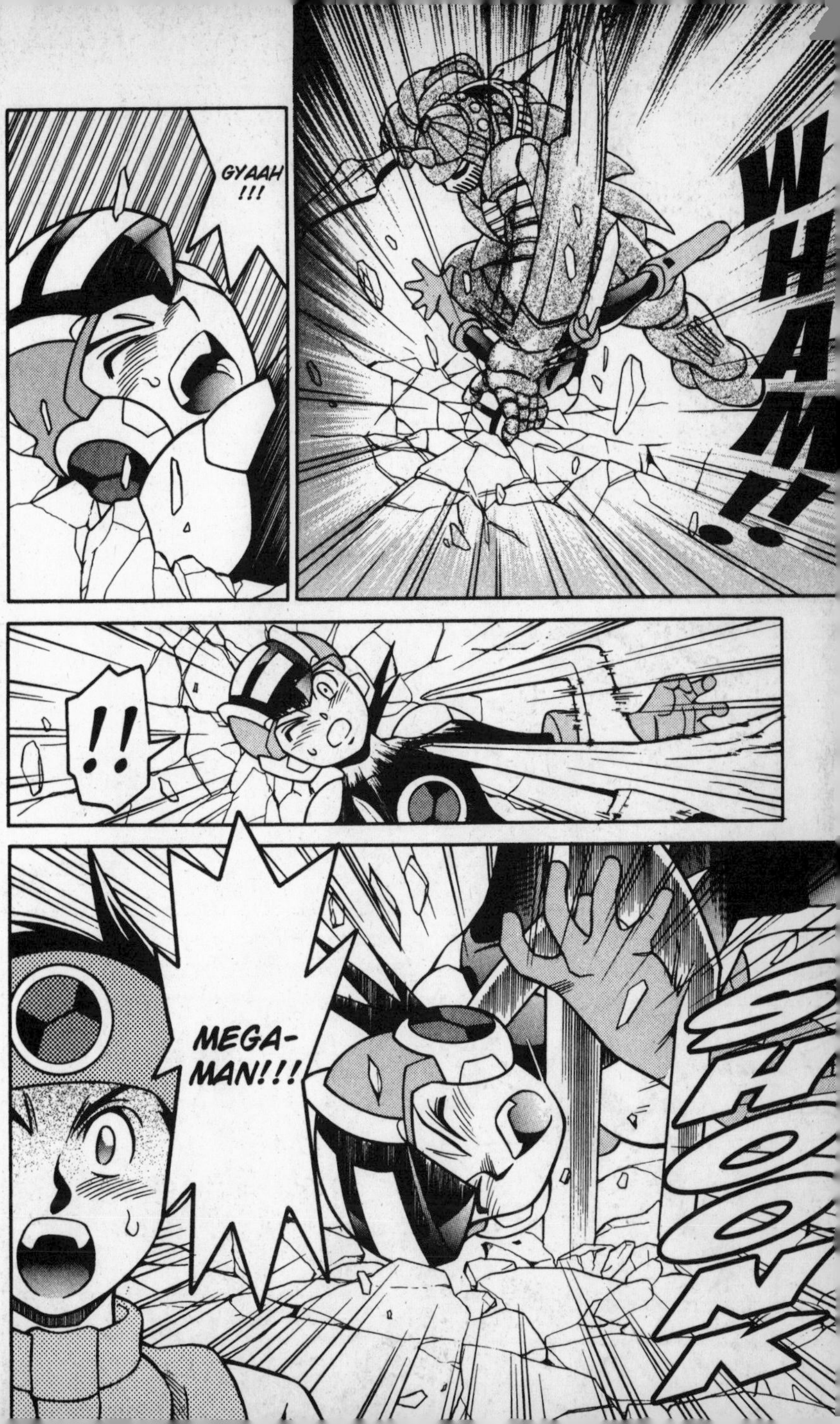
WHAM!!
GYAAH !!!
!!
MEGA-MAN!!!

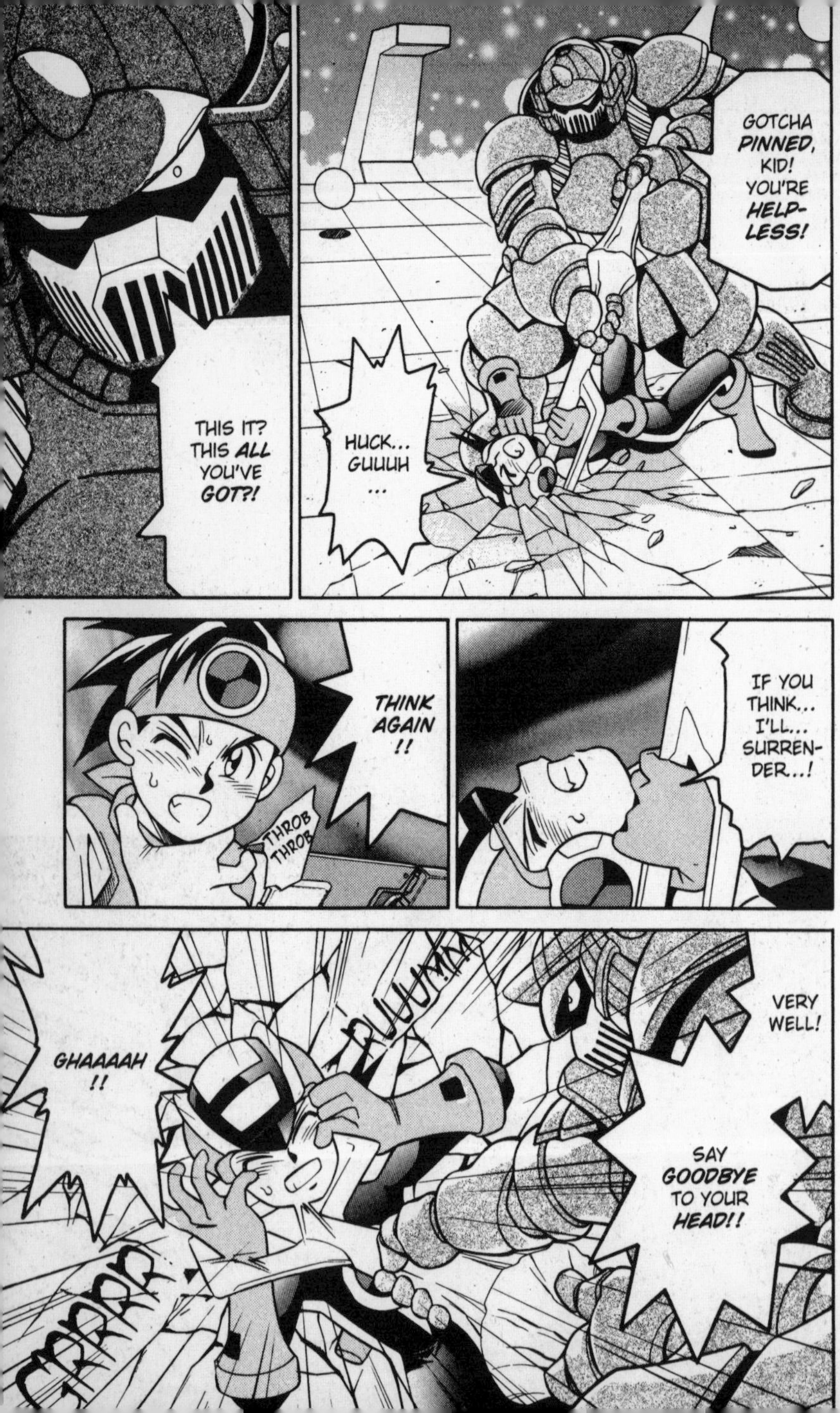
GOTCHA PINNED, KID! YOU'RE HELP-LESS!
HUCK... GUUUH ...
THIS IT? THIS ALL YOU'VE GOT?!
IF YOU THINK... I'LL... SURREN-DER...!
THINK AGAIN!!
THROB THROB
VERY WELL!
SAY GOODBYE TO YOUR HEAD!!
GHAAAAH!!

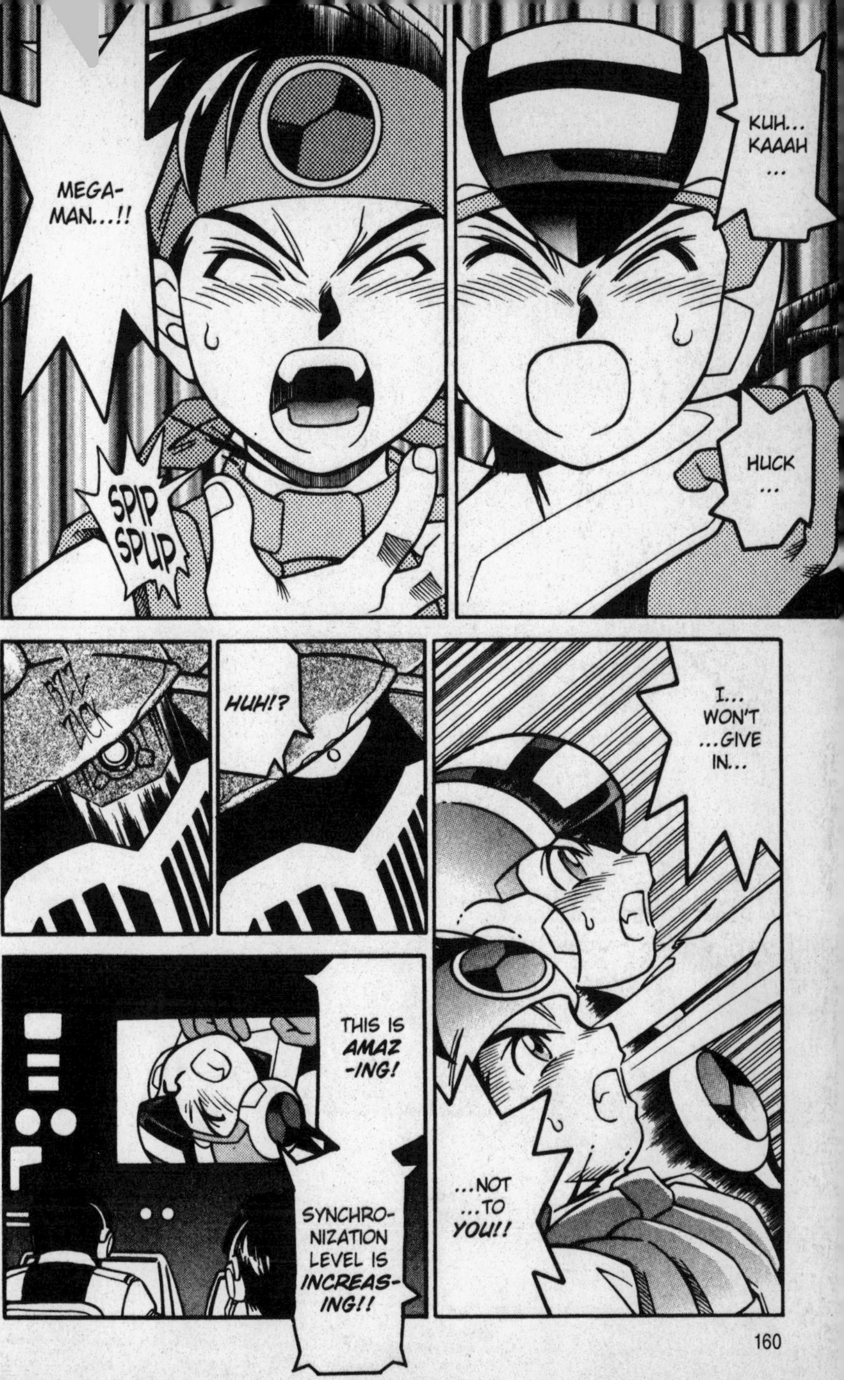
KUH... KAAAH ...
HUCK ...
MEGA-MAN...!!
SPIP SPUP
I... WON'T ...GIVE IN...
...NOT ...TO YOU!!
HUH!?
THIS IS AMAZ-ING!
SYNCHRO-NIZATION LEVEL IS INCREAS-ING!!

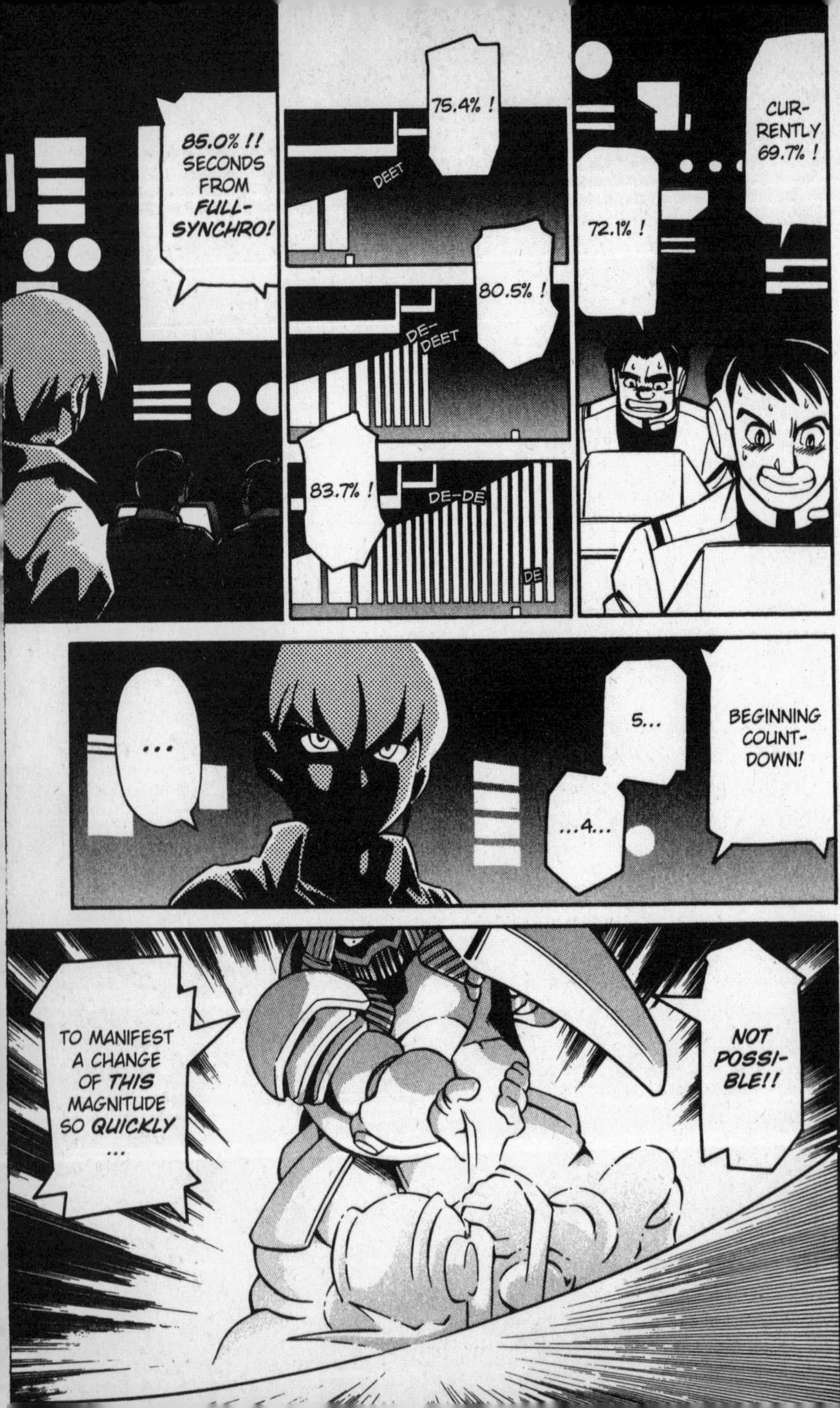
CURRENTLY 69.7%!
72.1%!
75.4%!
DEET
80.5%!
DE-DEET
83.7%!
DE-DE
DE
85.0%!! SECONDS FROM FULL-SYNCHRO!
BEGINNING COUNTDOWN!
5...
...4...
...
NOT POSSIBLE!!
TO MANIFEST A CHANGE OF THIS MAGNITUDE SO QUICKLY ...

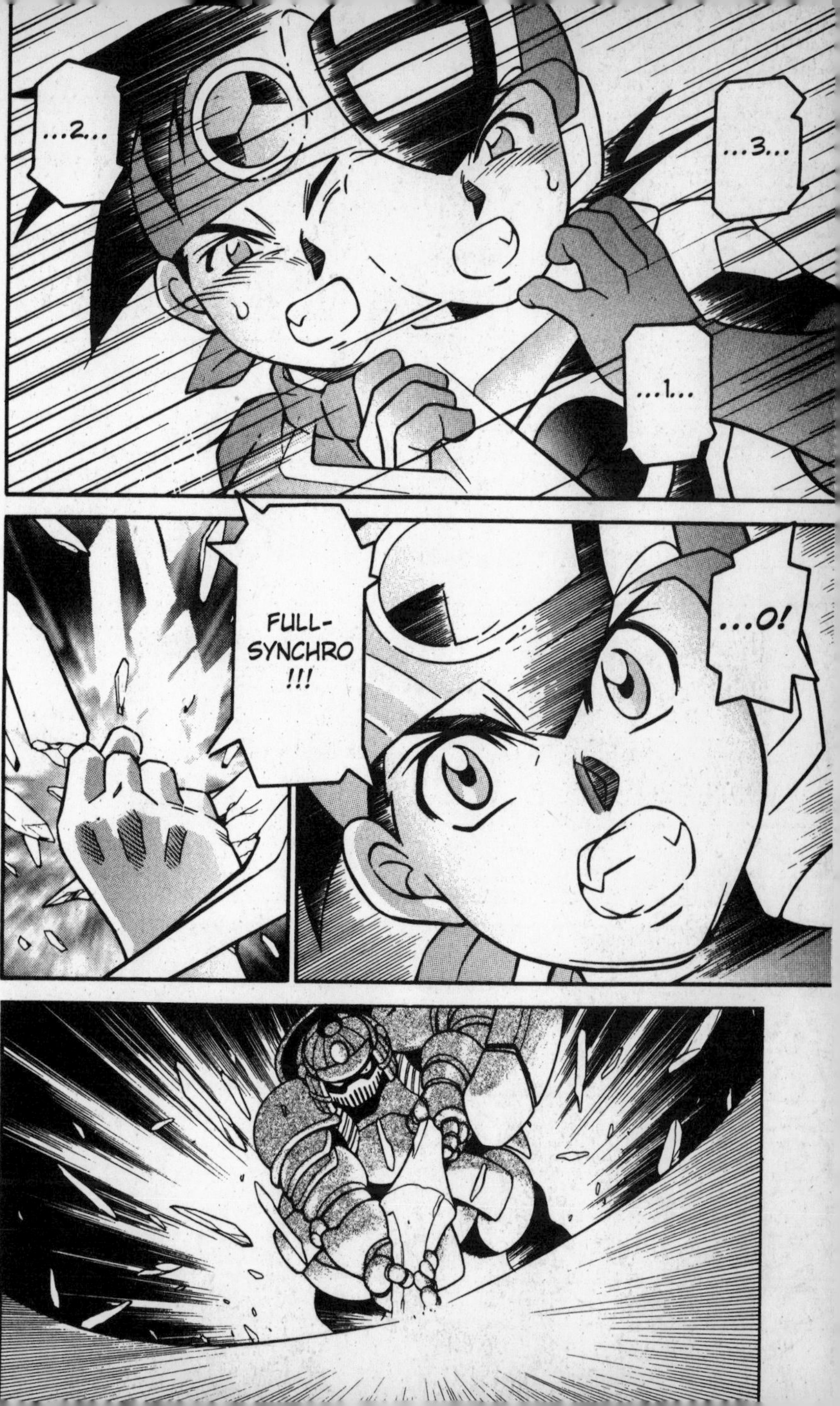
...3...
...2...
...1...
...0!
FULL-SYNCHRO!!!

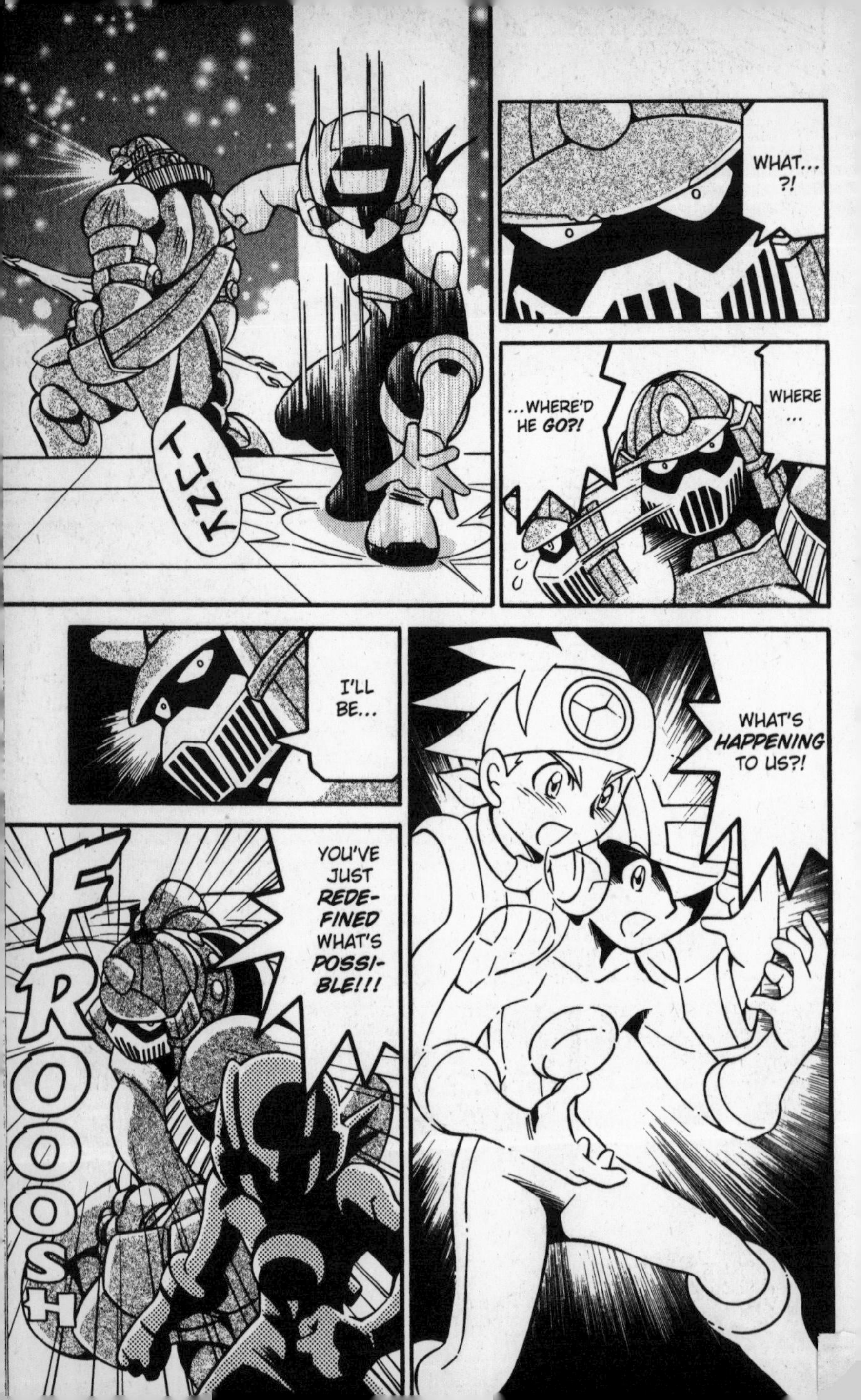
WHAT... ?!
WHERE ...
...WHERE'D HE GO?!
WHAT'S HAPPENING TO US?!
I'LL BE...
YOU'VE JUST REDEFINED WHAT'S POSSIBLE!!!
FROOOOOSH

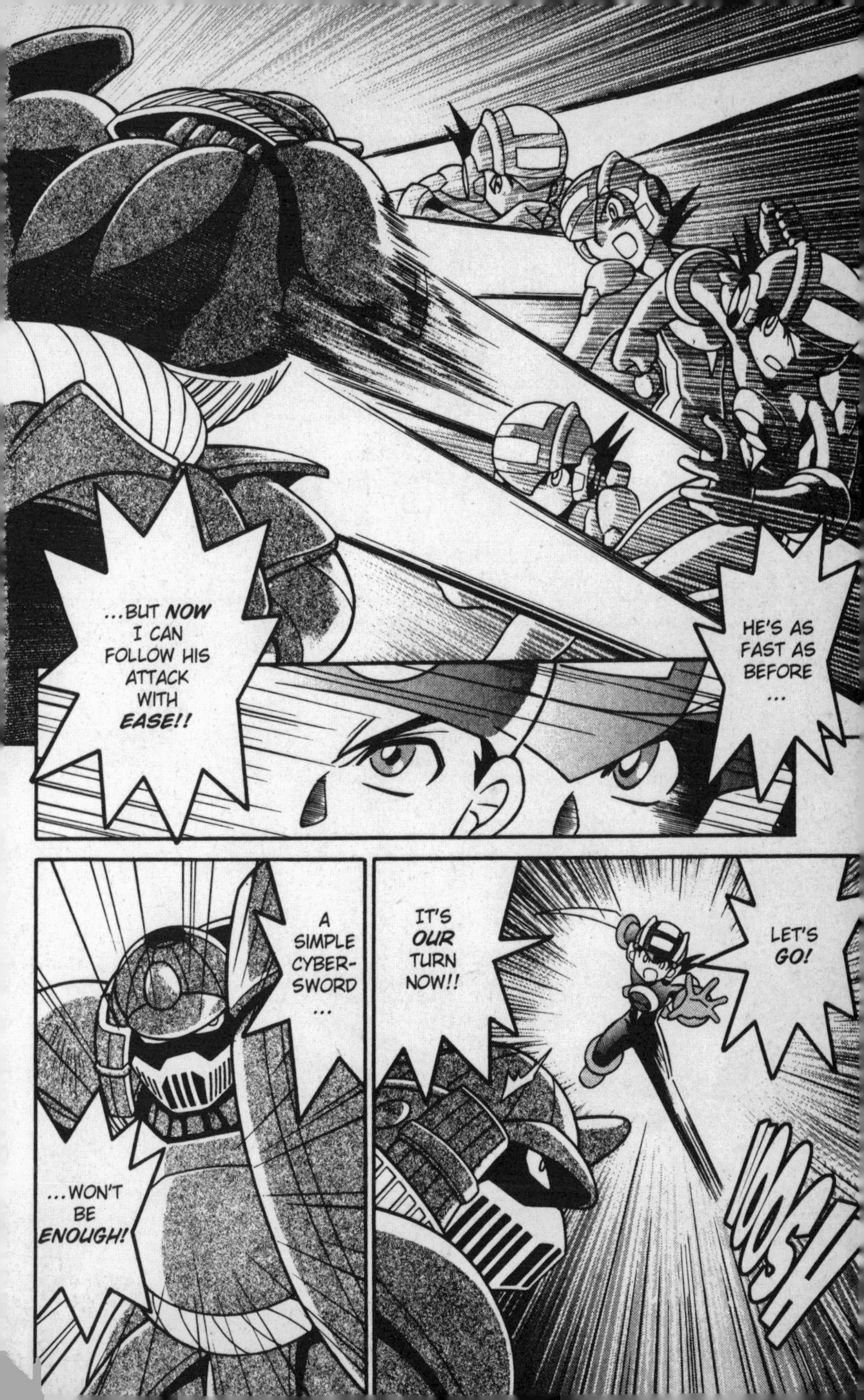
HE'S AS FAST AS BEFORE ...
...BUT NOW I CAN FOLLOW HIS ATTACK WITH EASE!!
LET'S GO!
IT'S OUR TURN NOW!!
WOOSH
A SIMPLE CYBER-SWORD ...
...WON'T BE ENOUGH!

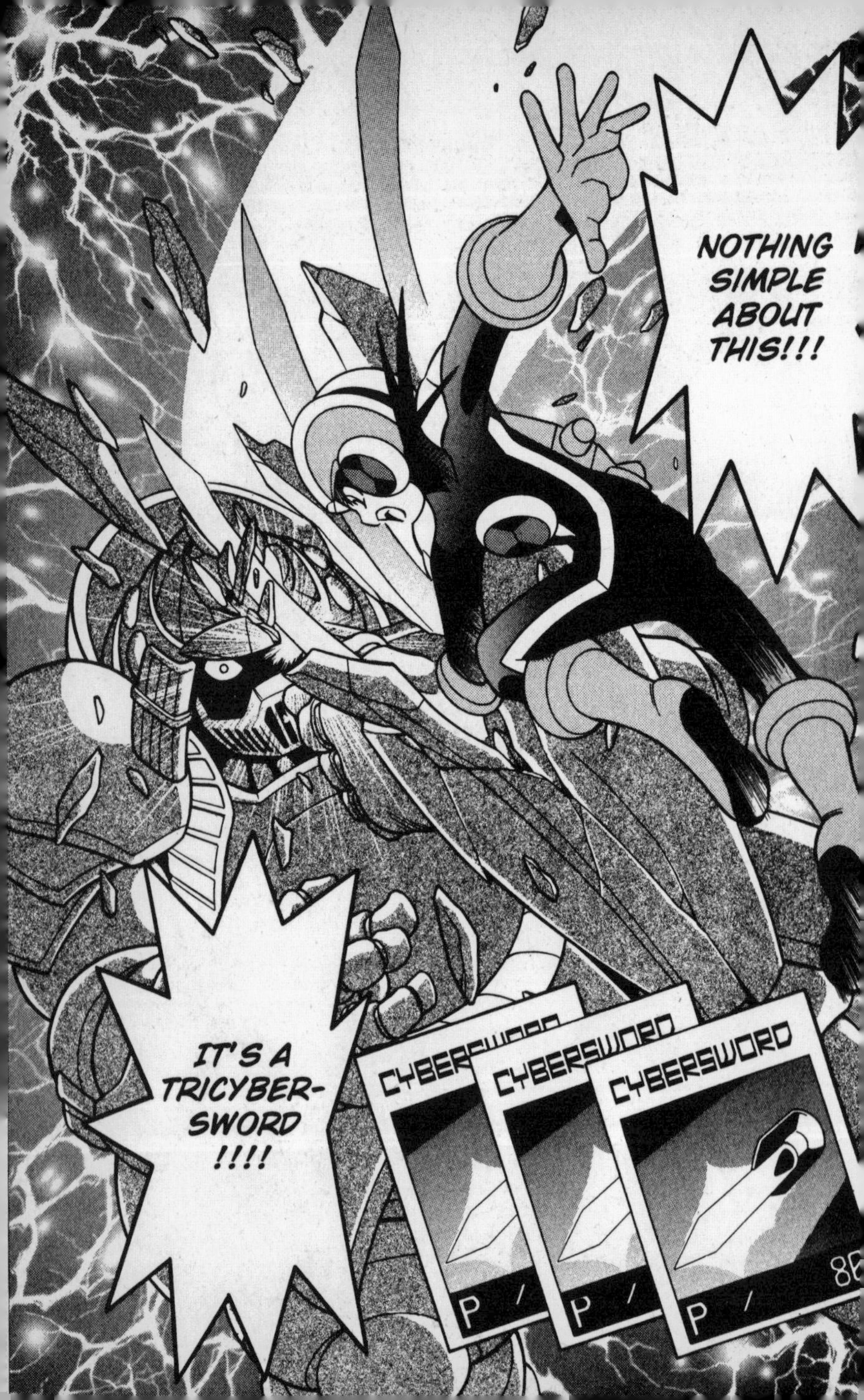
NOTHING SIMPLE ABOUT THIS!!!
IT'S A TRICYBER-SWORD!!!!
CYBERSWORD
CYBERSWORD
P
P
P

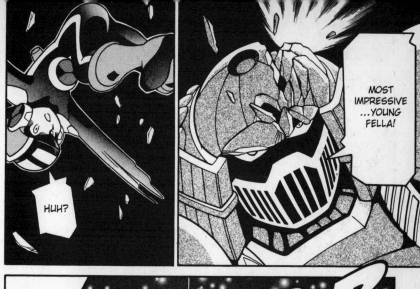

MOST IMPRESSIVE ...YOUNG FELLA!

HUH?

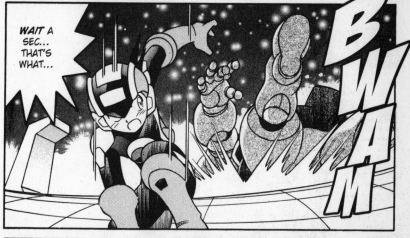

WAIT A SEC... THAT'S WHAT...

BWAM

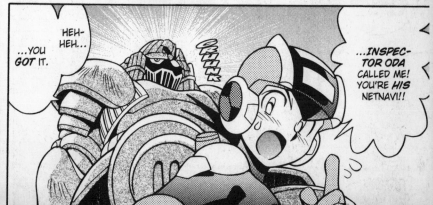

...YOU GOT IT.

HEH-HEH...

...INSPECTOR ODA CALLED ME! YOU'RE *HIS* NETNAVI!!

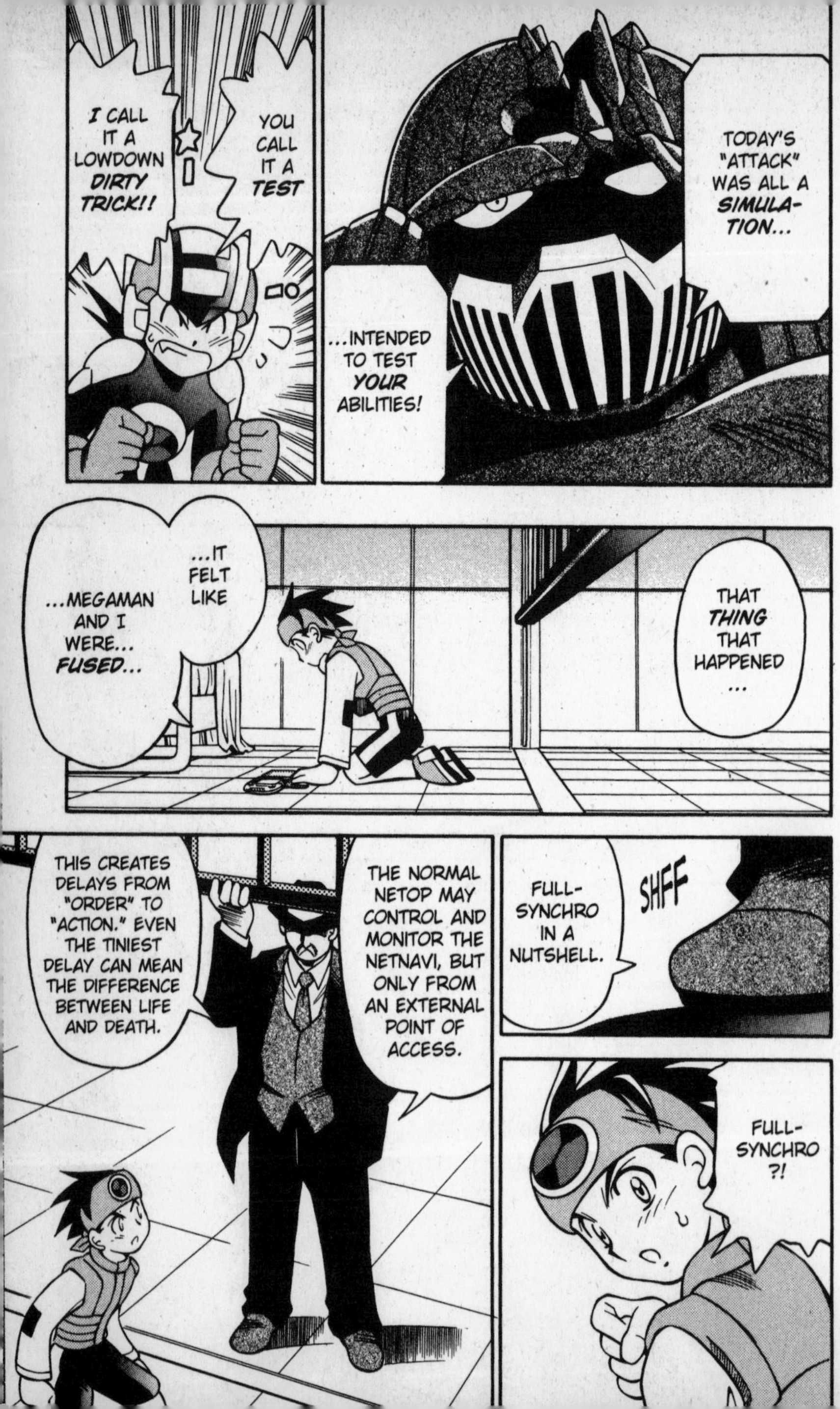
TODAY'S "ATTACK" WAS ALL A SIMULATION...
...INTENDED TO TEST YOUR ABILITIES!
YOU CALL IT A TEST
I CALL IT A LOWDOWN DIRTY TRICK!!
THAT THING THAT HAPPENED ...
...IT FELT LIKE
...MEGAMAN AND I WERE... FUSED...
SHFF
FULL-SYNCHRO IN A NUTSHELL.
FULL-SYNCHRO ?!
THE NORMAL NETOP MAY CONTROL AND MONITOR THE NETNAVI, BUT ONLY FROM AN EXTERNAL POINT OF ACCESS.
THIS CREATES DELAYS FROM "ORDER" TO "ACTION." EVEN THE TINIEST DELAY CAN MEAN THE DIFFERENCE BETWEEN LIFE AND DEATH.

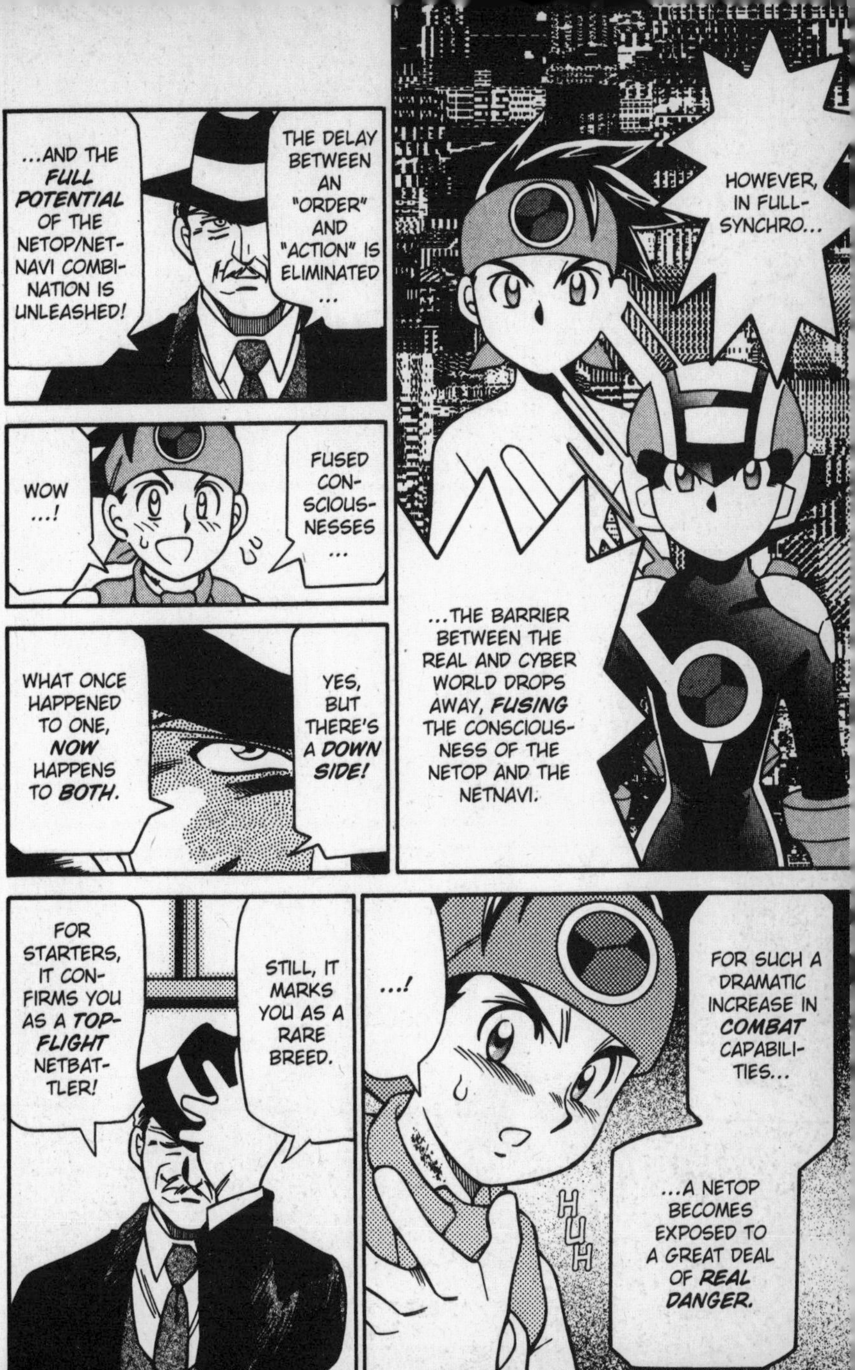
HOWEVER, IN FULL-SYNCHRO...
...THE BARRIER BETWEEN THE REAL AND CYBER WORLD DROPS AWAY, *FUSING* THE CONSCIOUSNESS OF THE NETOP AND THE NETNAVI.
THE DELAY BETWEEN AN "ORDER" AND "ACTION" IS ELIMINATED...
...AND THE *FULL POTENTIAL* OF THE NETOP/NET-NAVI COMBINATION IS UNLEASHED!
FUSED CONSCIOUSNESSES...
WOW...!
YES, BUT THERE'S A *DOWN SIDE!*
WHAT ONCE HAPPENED TO ONE, *NOW* HAPPENS TO *BOTH.*
FOR SUCH A DRAMATIC INCREASE IN *COMBAT* CAPABILITIES...
...A NETOP BECOMES EXPOSED TO A GREAT DEAL OF *REAL DANGER.*
HUH
...!
STILL, IT MARKS YOU AS A RARE BREED.
FOR STARTERS, IT CONFIRMS YOU AS A *TOP-FLIGHT* NETBATTLER!

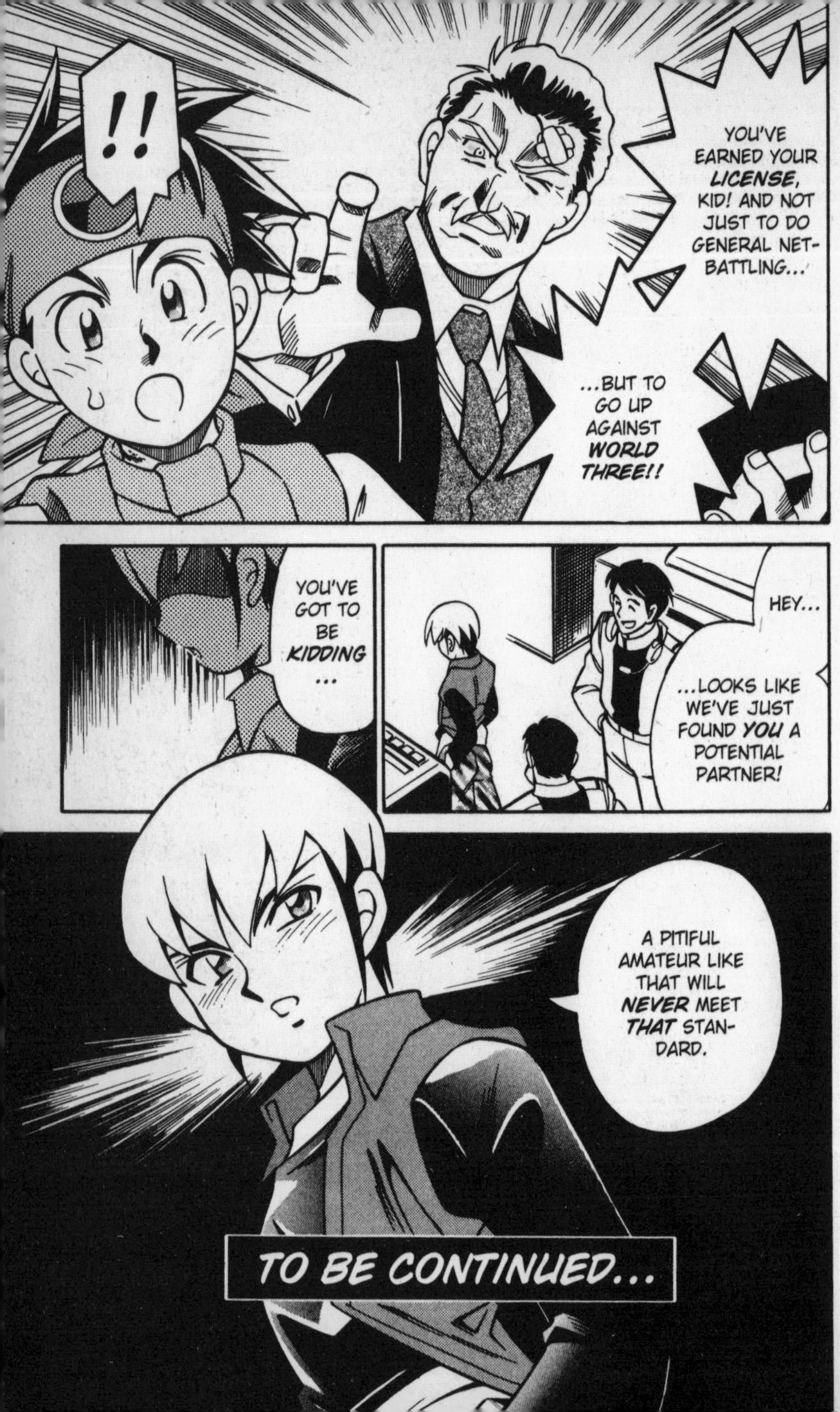
YOU'VE EARNED YOUR *LICENSE*, KID! AND NOT JUST TO DO GENERAL NET-BATTLING...
...BUT TO GO UP AGAINST *WORLD THREE!!*
!!
HEY...
...LOOKS LIKE WE'VE JUST FOUND *YOU* A POTENTIAL PARTNER!
YOU'VE GOT TO BE *KIDDING* ...
A PITIFUL AMATEUR LIKE THAT WILL *NEVER* MEET *THAT* STAN-DARD.
TO BE CONTINUED...

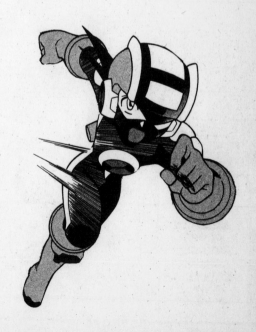

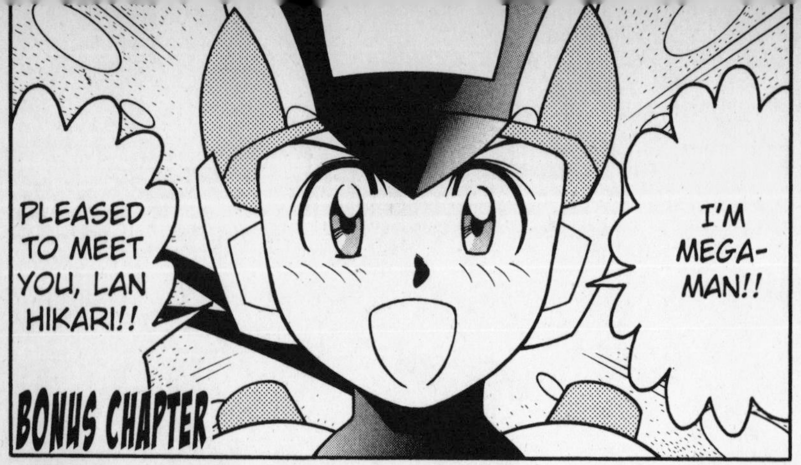
I'M MEGA-MAN!!
PLEASED TO MEET YOU, LAN HIKARI!!
BONUS CHAPTER

LAN AND MEGAMAN FIRST IMPRESSIONS

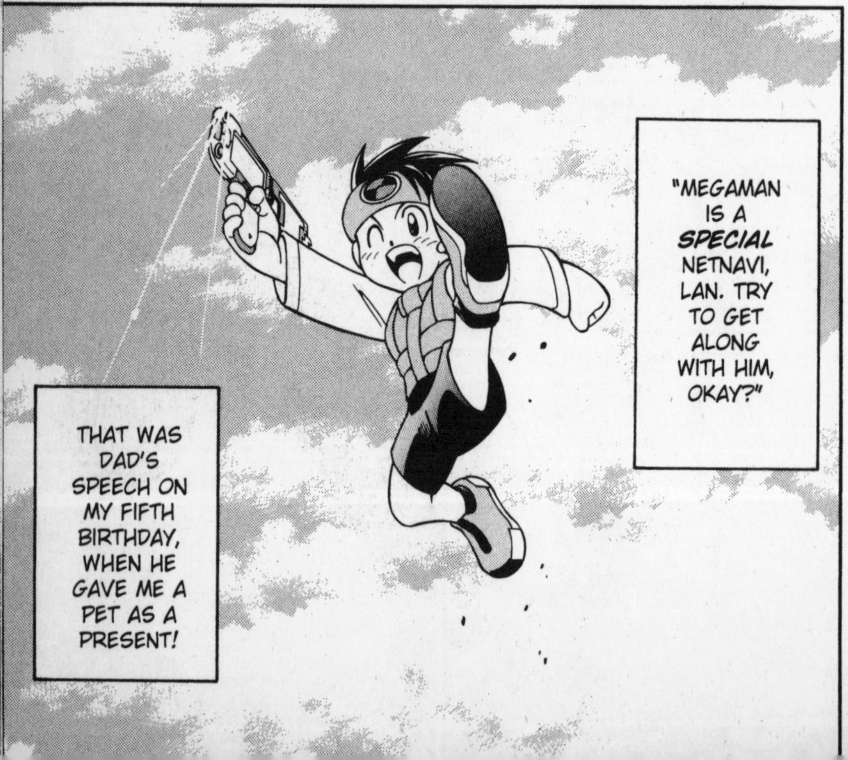
"MEGAMAN IS A *SPECIAL* NETNAVI, LAN. TRY TO GET ALONG WITH HIM, OKAY?"
THAT WAS DAD'S SPEECH ON MY FIFTH BIRTHDAY, WHEN HE GAVE ME A PET AS A PRESENT!

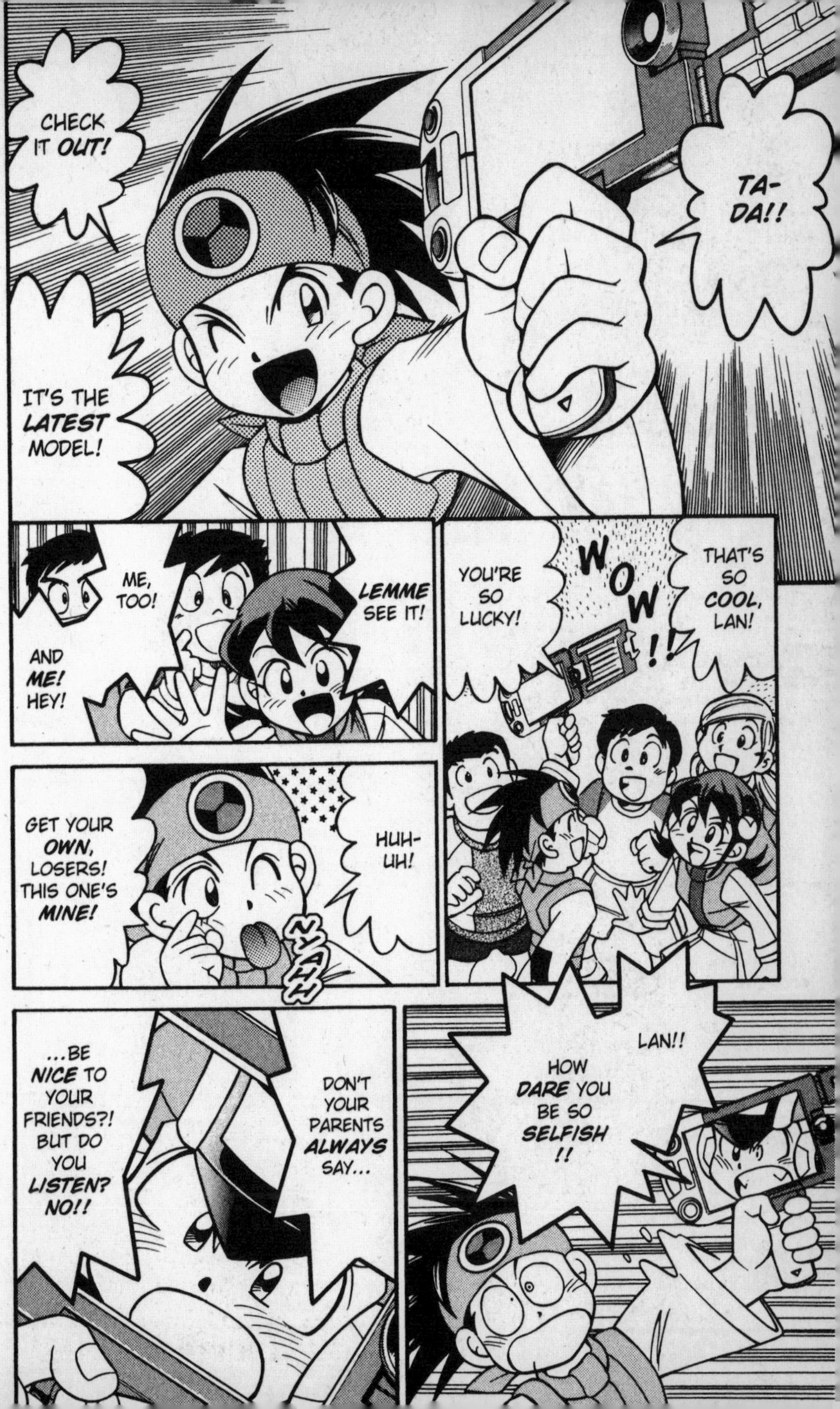
TA-DA!!
CHECK IT OUT!
HEY
IT'S THE LATEST MODEL!
THAT'S SO COOL, LAN!
WOW!!
YOU'RE SO LUCKY!
LEMME SEE IT!
ME, TOO!
AND ME! HEY!
HUH-UH!
GET YOUR OWN, LOSERS! THIS ONE'S MINE!
NYAHH
LAN!!
HOW DARE YOU BE SO SELFISH!!
DON'T YOUR PARENTS ALWAYS SAY...
...BE NICE TO YOUR FRIENDS?! BUT DO YOU LISTEN? NO!!

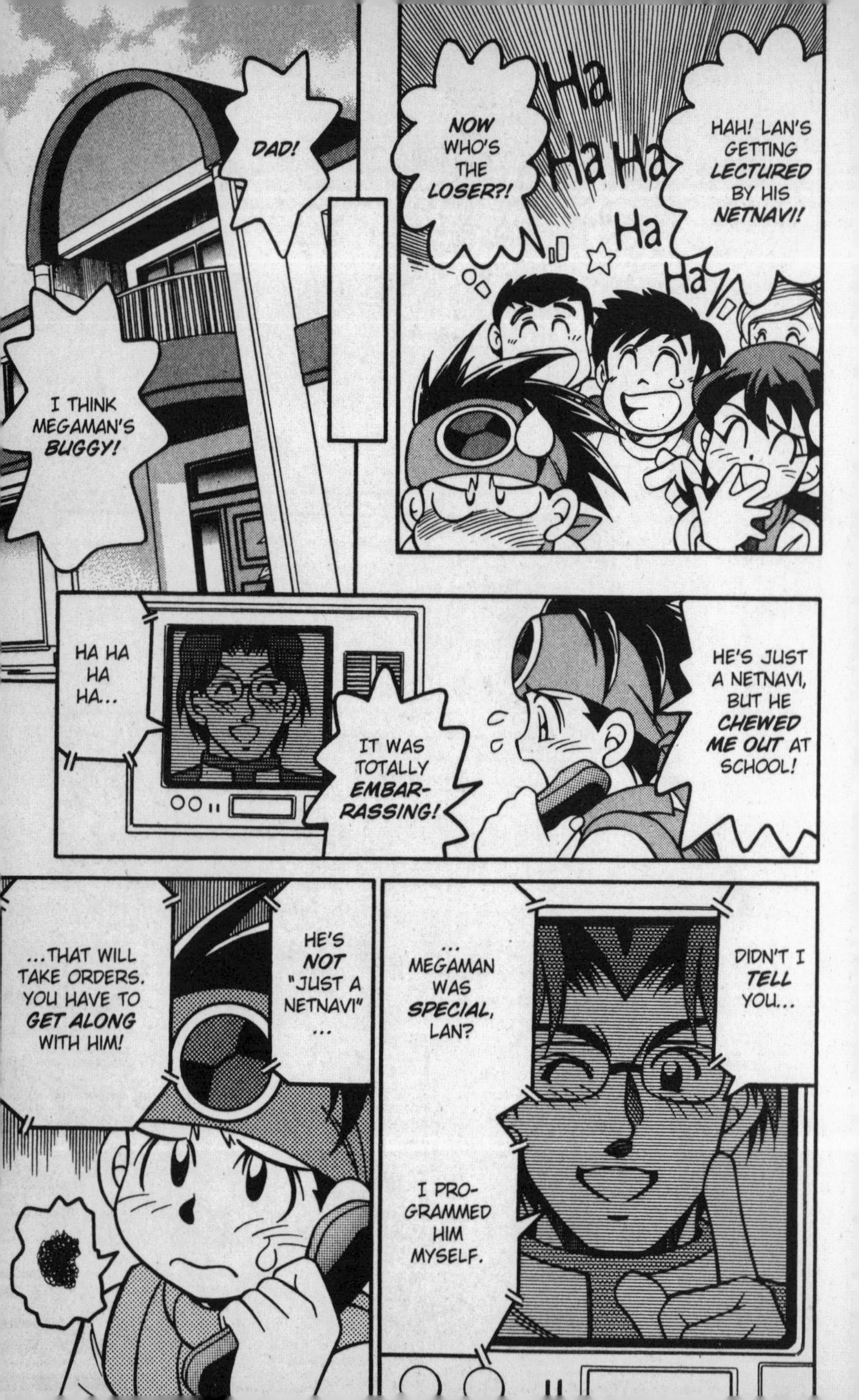
HAH! LAN'S GETTING LECTURED BY HIS NETNAVI!
Ha Ha Ha Ha Ha
NOW WHO'S THE LOSER?!
DAD!
I THINK MEGAMAN'S BUGGY!
HE'S JUST A NETNAVI, BUT HE CHEWED ME OUT AT SCHOOL!
IT WAS TOTALLY EMBAR-RASSING!
HA HA HA HA...
DIDN'T I TELL YOU...
... MEGAMAN WAS SPECIAL, LAN?
I PRO-GRAMMED HIM MYSELF.
HE'S NOT "JUST A NETNAVI" ...
...THAT WILL TAKE ORDERS. YOU HAVE TO GET ALONG WITH HIM!

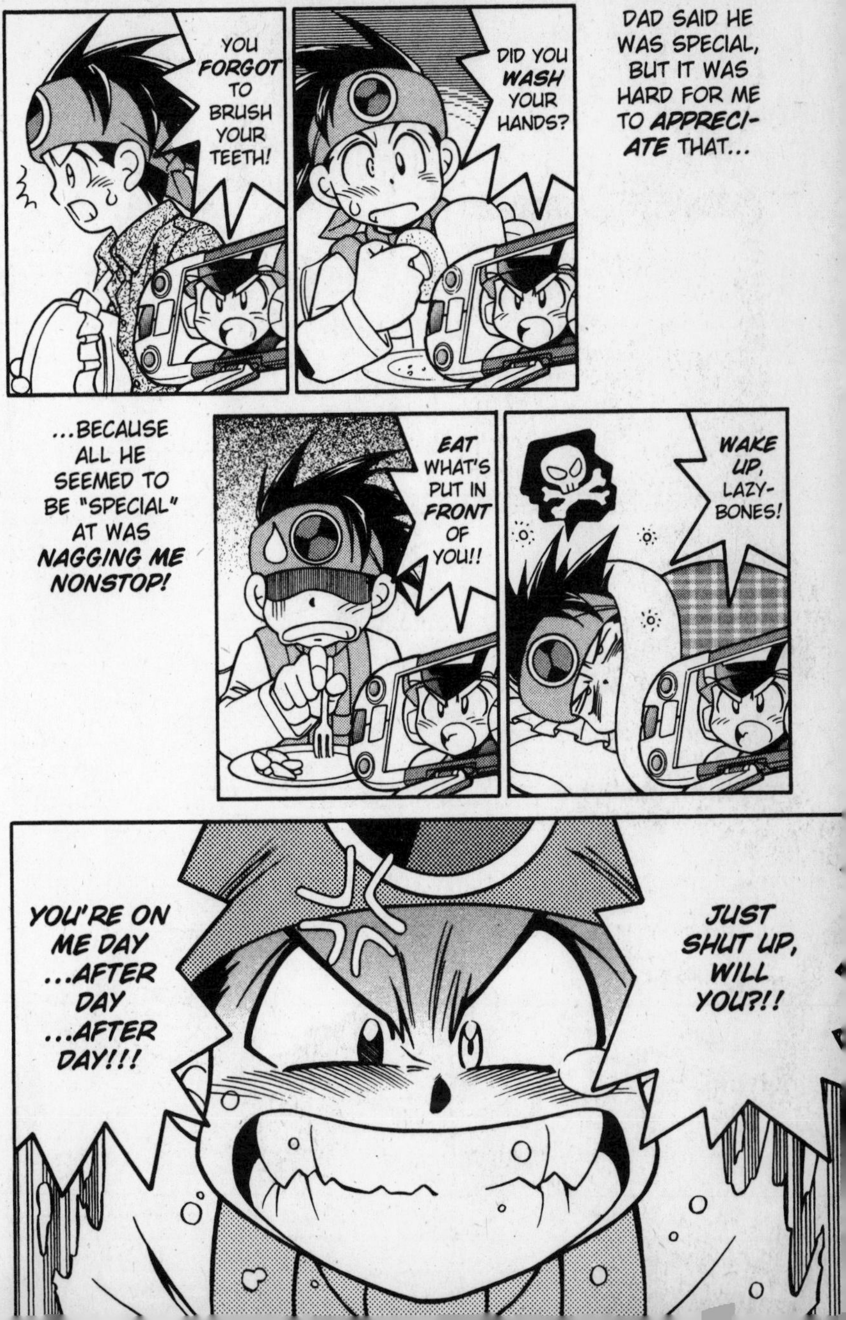
DAD SAID HE WAS SPECIAL, BUT IT WAS HARD FOR ME TO APPRECIATE THAT...
DID YOU WASH YOUR HANDS?
YOU FORGOT TO BRUSH YOUR TEETH!
WAKE UP, LAZY-BONES!
EAT WHAT'S PUT IN FRONT OF YOU!!
...BECAUSE ALL HE SEEMED TO BE "SPECIAL" AT WAS NAGGING ME NONSTOP!
JUST SHUT UP, WILL YOU?!!
YOU'RE ON ME DAY ...AFTER DAY ...AFTER DAY!!!

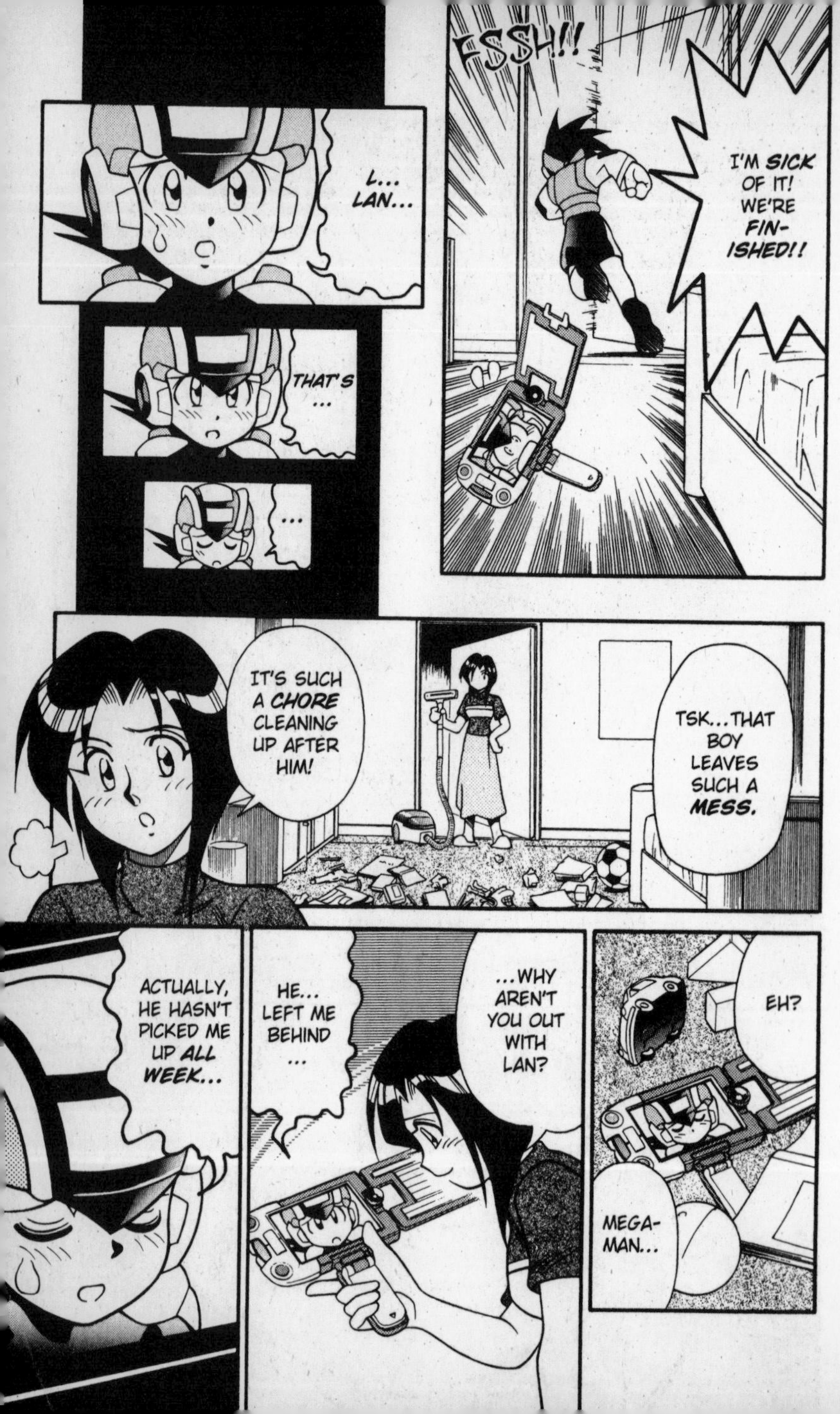
FSSH!!
I'M SICK OF IT! WE'RE FIN-ISHED!!
L... LAN...
THAT'S...
...
TSK...THAT BOY LEAVES SUCH A MESS.
IT'S SUCH A CHORE CLEANING UP AFTER HIM!
EH?
MEGA-MAN...
...WHY AREN'T YOU OUT WITH LAN?
HE... LEFT ME BEHIND...
ACTUALLY, HE HASN'T PICKED ME UP ALL WEEK...

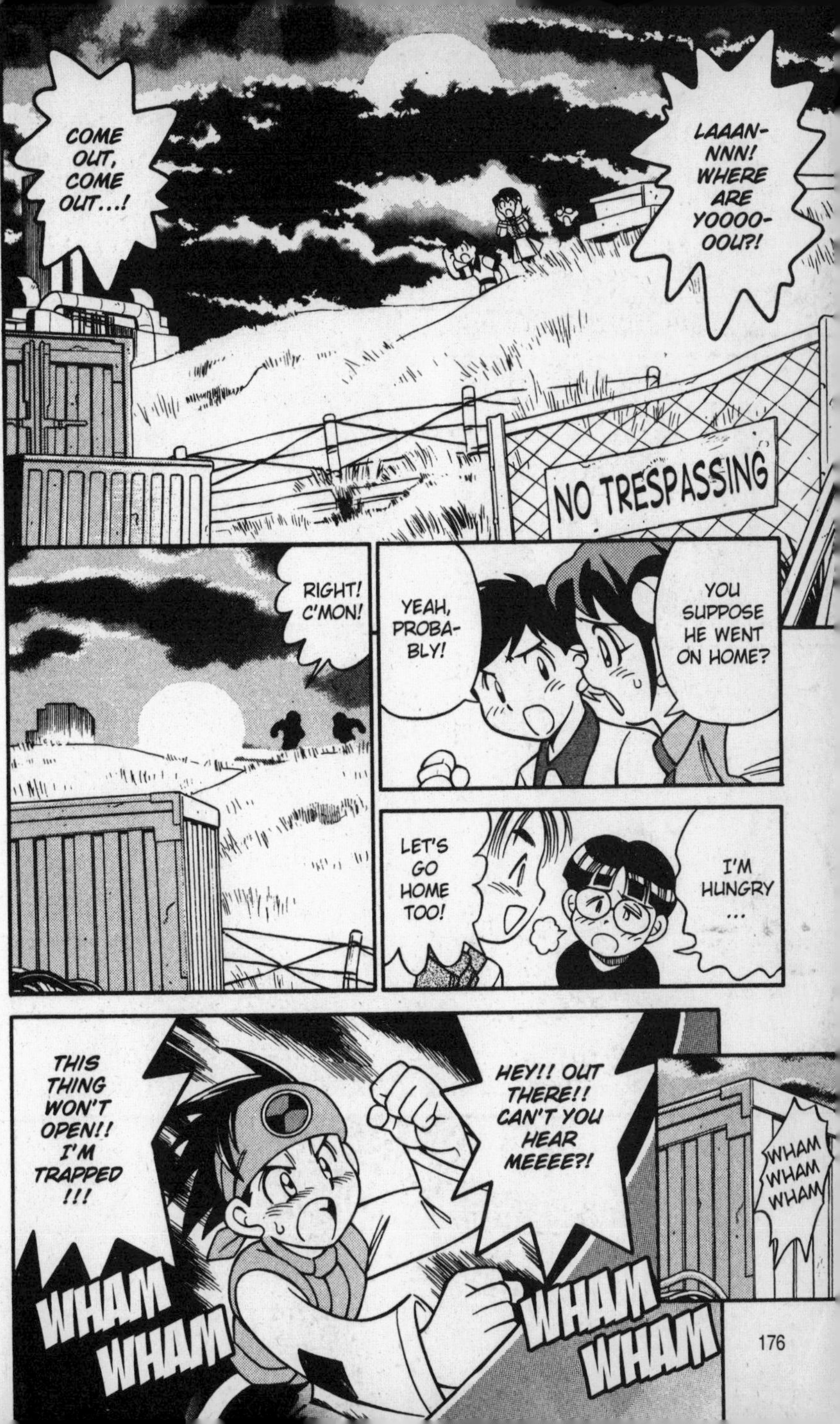
LAAANNNN! WHERE ARE YOOOOOOU?!
COME OUT, COME OUT...!
NO TRESPASSING
YOU SUPPOSE HE WENT ON HOME?
YEAH, PROBABLY!
I'M HUNGRY...
LET'S GO HOME TOO!
RIGHT! C'MON!
WHAM WHAM WHAM
HEY!! OUT THERE!! CAN'T YOU HEAR MEEEE?!
WHAM WHAM
THIS THING WON'T OPEN!! I'M TRAPPED!!!
WHAM WHAM

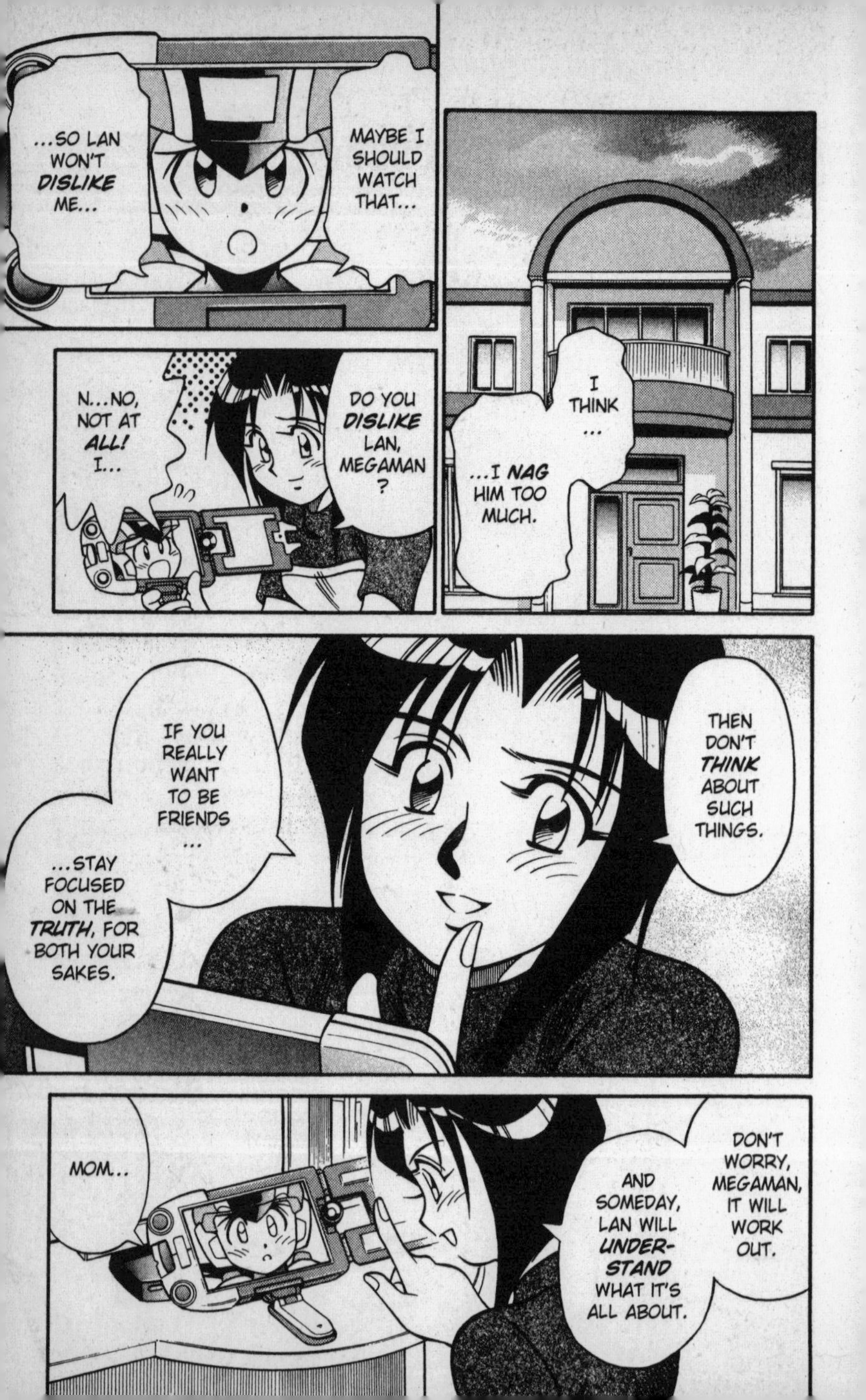
I THINK...
...I NAG HIM TOO MUCH.
MAYBE I SHOULD WATCH THAT...
...SO LAN WON'T DISLIKE ME...
DO YOU DISLIKE LAN, MEGAMAN?
N...NO, NOT AT ALL! I...
THEN DON'T THINK ABOUT SUCH THINGS.
IF YOU REALLY WANT TO BE FRIENDS...
...STAY FOCUSED ON THE TRUTH, FOR BOTH YOUR SAKES.
DON'T WORRY, MEGAMAN, IT WILL WORK OUT.
AND SOMEDAY, LAN WILL UNDER-STAND WHAT IT'S ALL ABOUT.
MOM...

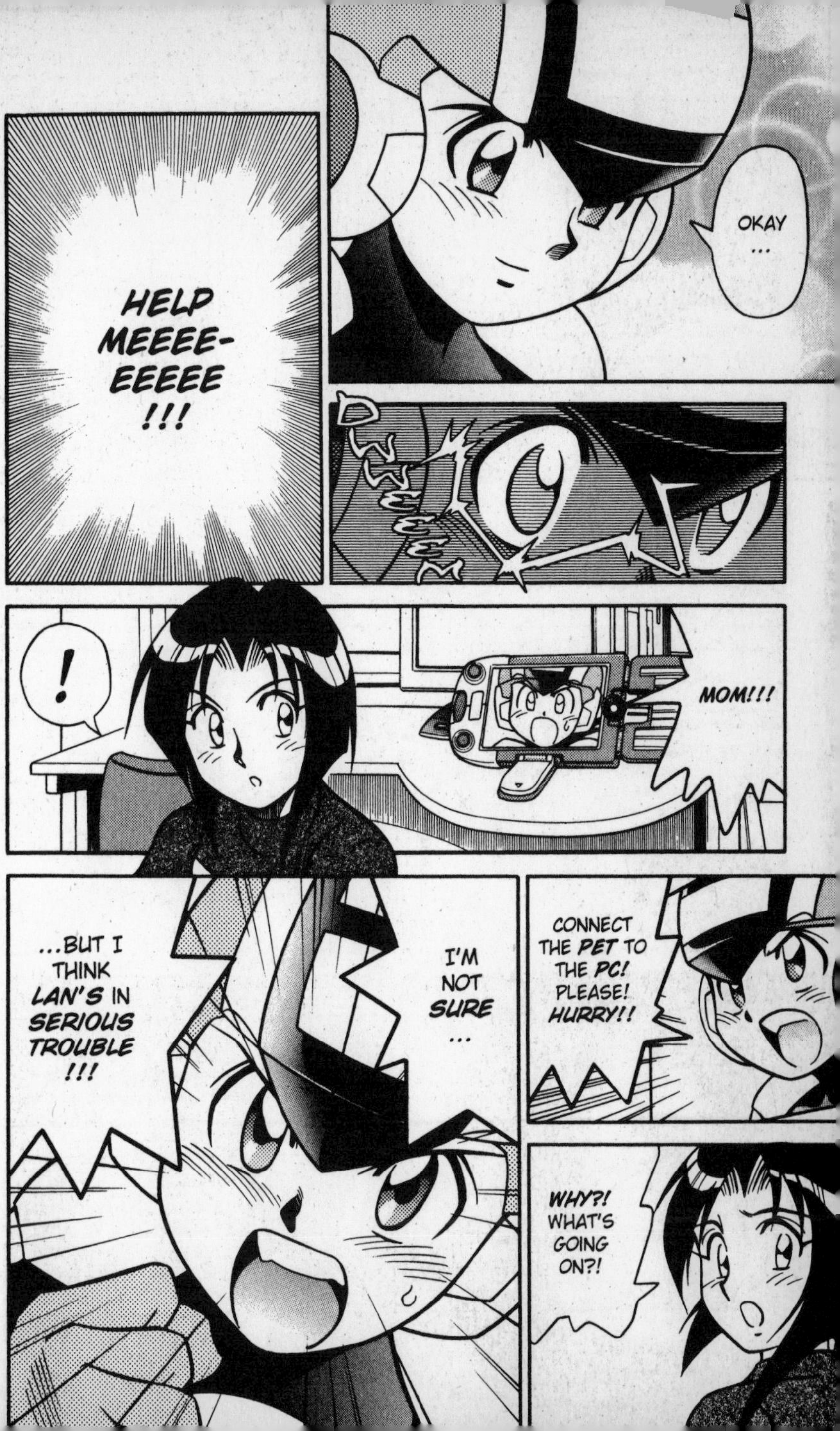
OKAY ...
DWEEEEM
HELP MEEEE-EEEEE !!!
MOM!!!
!
CONNECT THE PET TO THE PC! PLEASE! HURRY!!
WHY?! WHAT'S GOING ON?!
I'M NOT SURE ...
...BUT I THINK LAN'S IN SERIOUS TROUBLE !!!

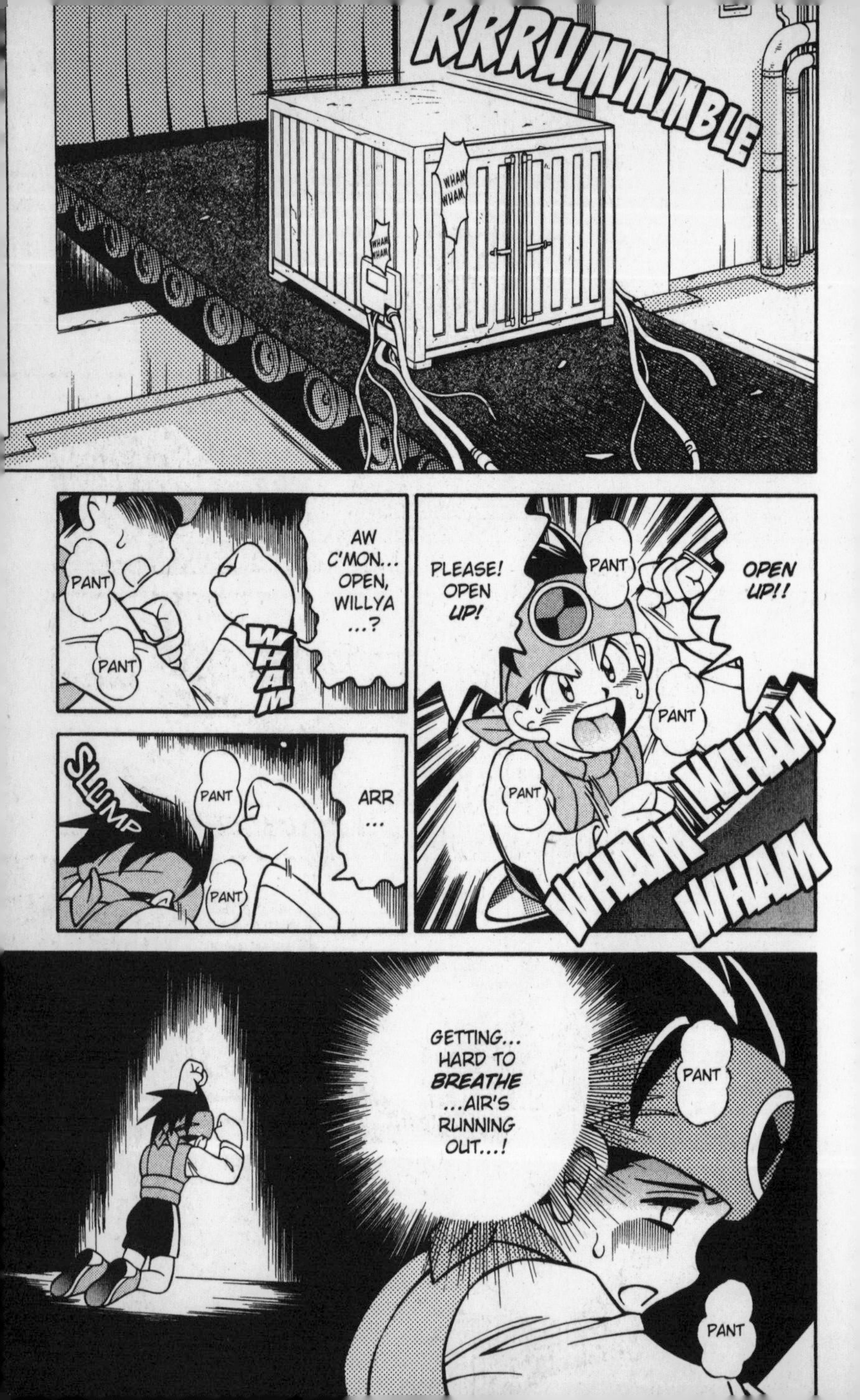
KRRUMMMBLE
WHAM WHAM
WHAM WHAM
OPEN UP!!
PANT
PLEASE! OPEN UP!
PANT
PANT
WHAM WHAM WHAM WHAM
AW C'MON... OPEN, WILLYA ...?
WHAM
PANT
PANT
ARR ...
PANT
SLUMP
PANT
PANT
GETTING... HARD TO BREATHE ...AIR'S RUNNING OUT...!
PANT

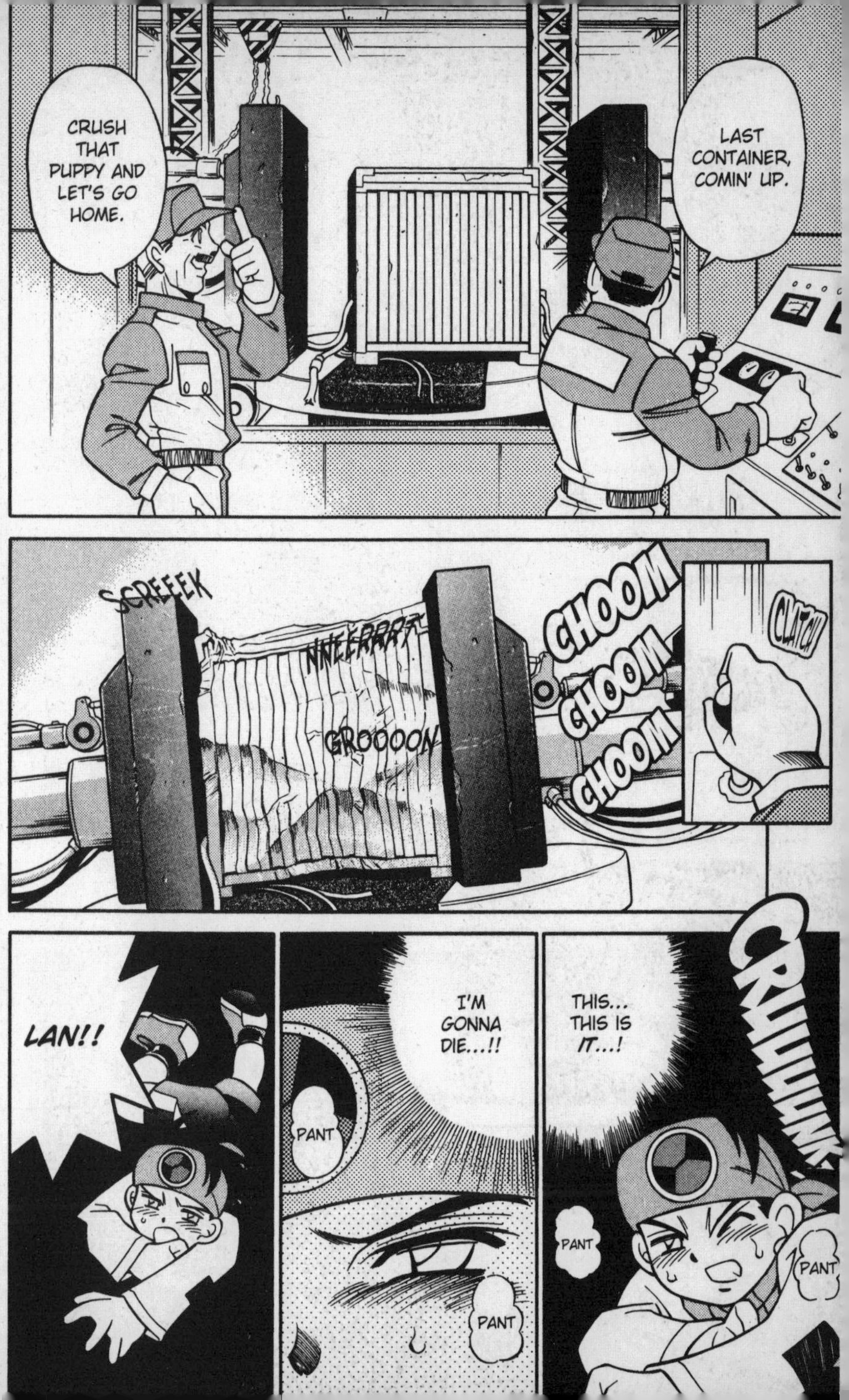
LAST CONTAINER, COMIN' UP.
CRUSH THAT PUPPY AND LET'S GO HOME.
CLATCH
CHOOM
CHOOM
CHOOM
SCREEEK
NNEERRRT
GROOOON
CRUUUNK
THIS... THIS IS *IT*...!
PANT
PANT
I'M GONNA DIE...!!
PANT
PANT
LAN!!

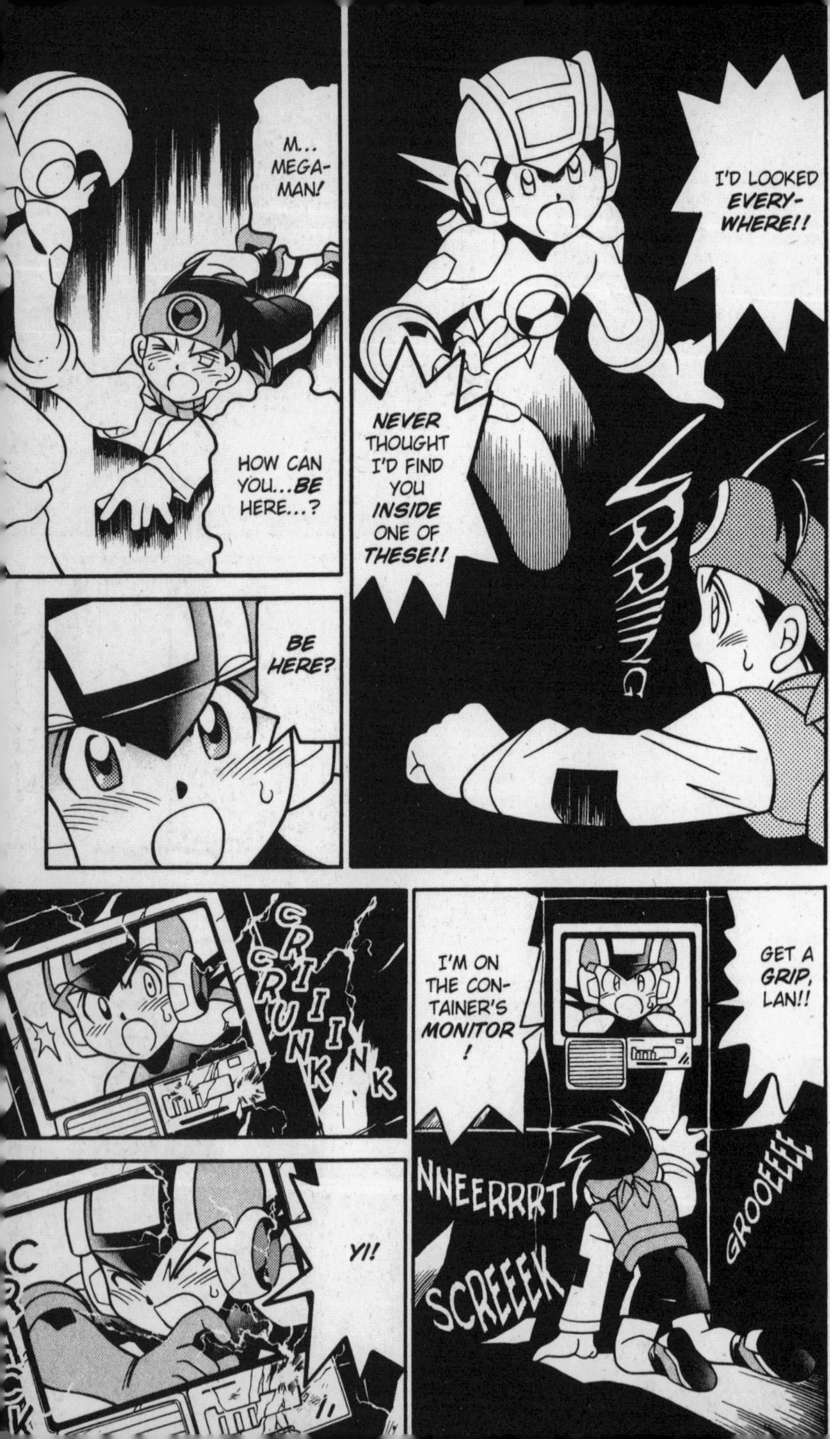
I'D LOOKED EVERY-WHERE!!
NEVER THOUGHT I'D FIND YOU INSIDE ONE OF THESE!!
VRRRING
M... MEGA-MAN!
HOW CAN YOU...BE HERE...?
BE HERE?
GET A GRIP, LAN!!
I'M ON THE CON-TAINER'S MONITOR!
GROOEEEE
NNEERRRT
SCREEEK
CRIIINK
CRUNK
YI!

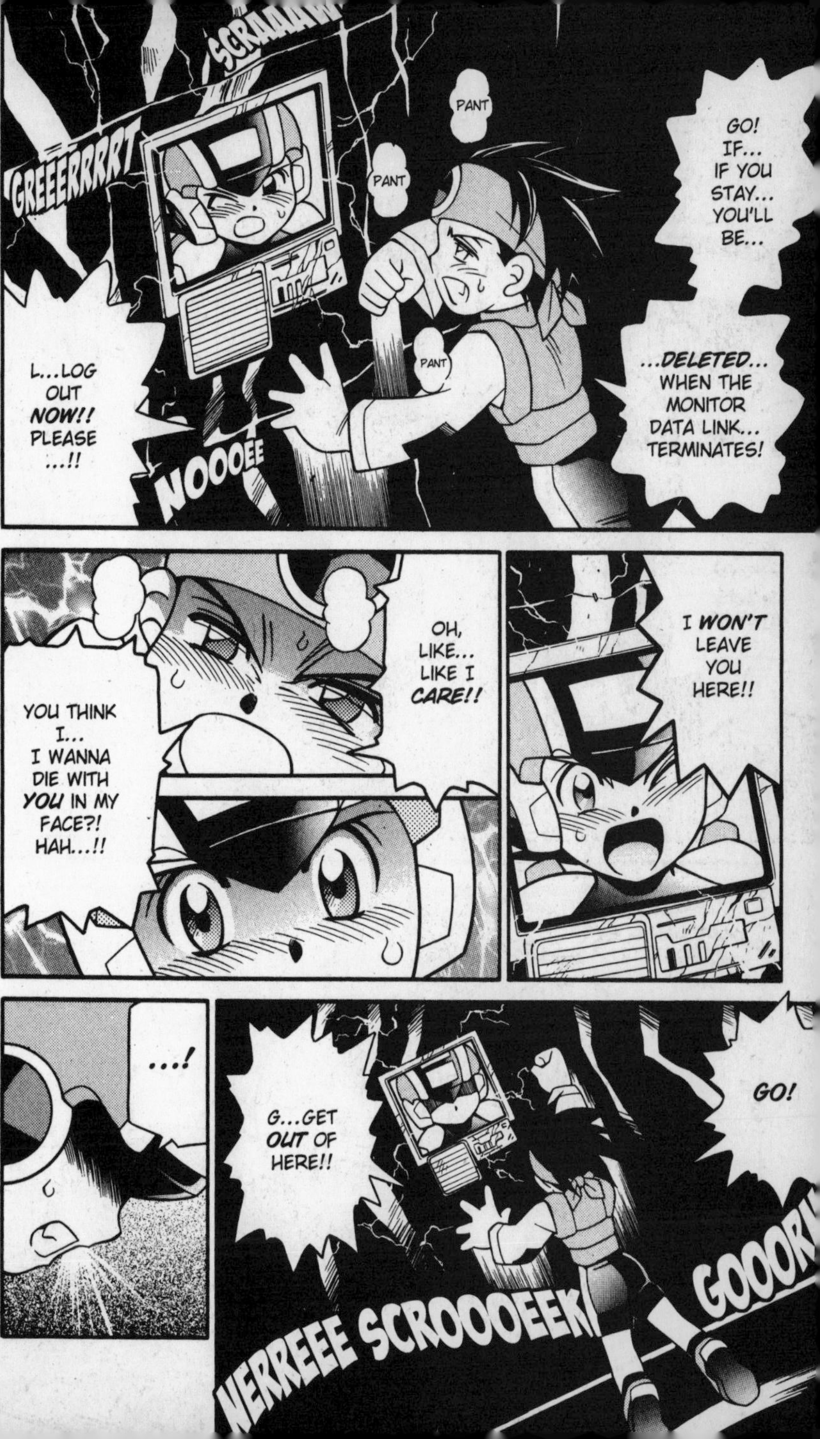
GO! IF... IF YOU STAY... YOU'LL BE...
SCRAAAW
PANT
GREEERRRRT
PANT
...DELETED... WHEN THE MONITOR DATA LINK... TERMINATES!
PANT
L...LOG OUT NOW!! PLEASE ...!!
NOOOEE
I WON'T LEAVE YOU HERE!!
OH, LIKE... LIKE I CARE!!
YOU THINK I... I WANNA DIE WITH YOU IN MY FACE?! HAH...!!
GO!
G...GET OUT OF HERE!!
GOOOR
NERREEE SCROOOEEK
...!

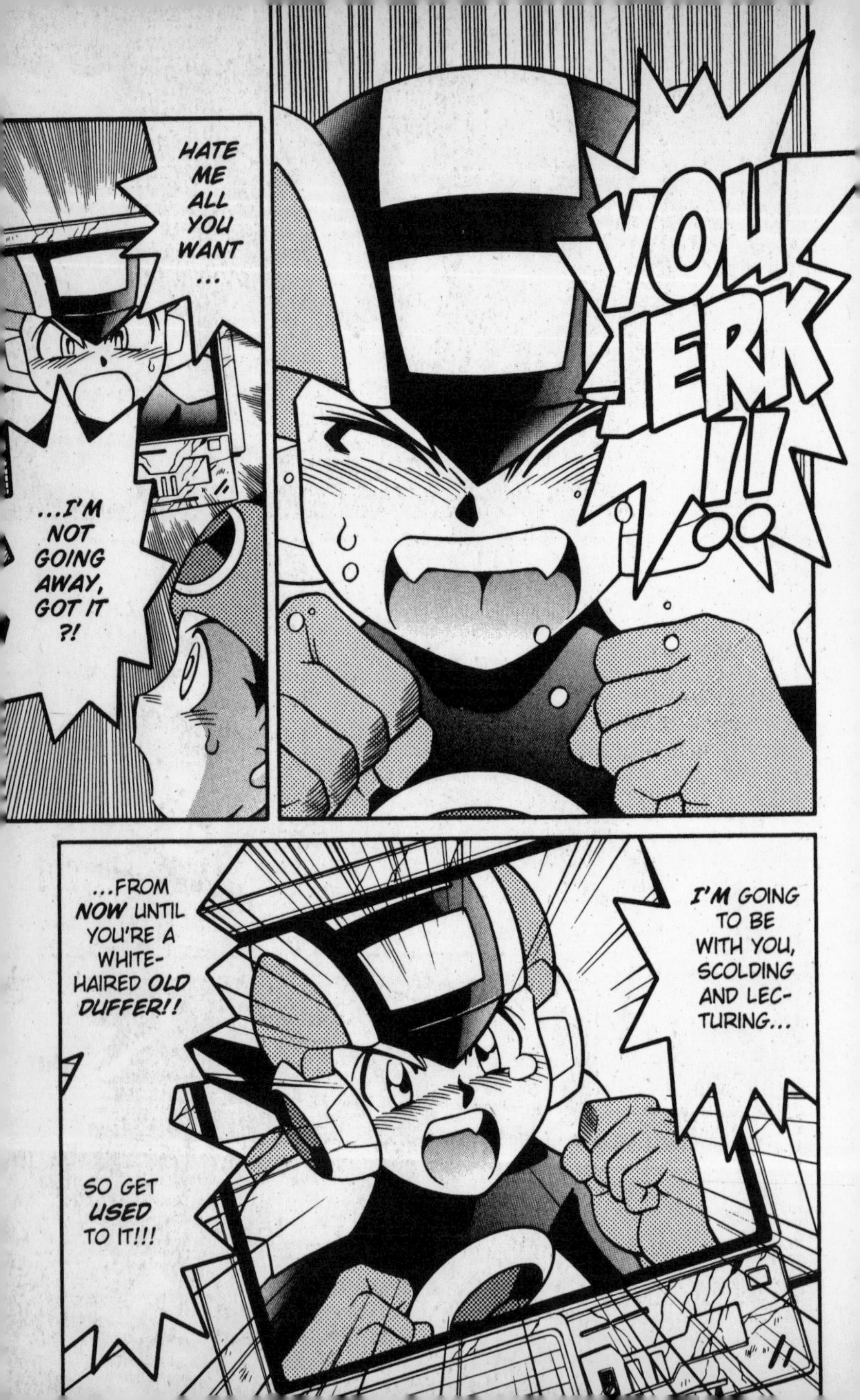
YOU JERK!!
HATE ME ALL YOU WANT...
...I'M NOT GOING AWAY, GOT IT?!
I'M GOING TO BE WITH YOU, SCOLDING AND LECTURING...
...FROM NOW UNTIL YOU'RE A WHITE-HAIRED OLD DUFFER!!
SO GET USED TO IT!!!

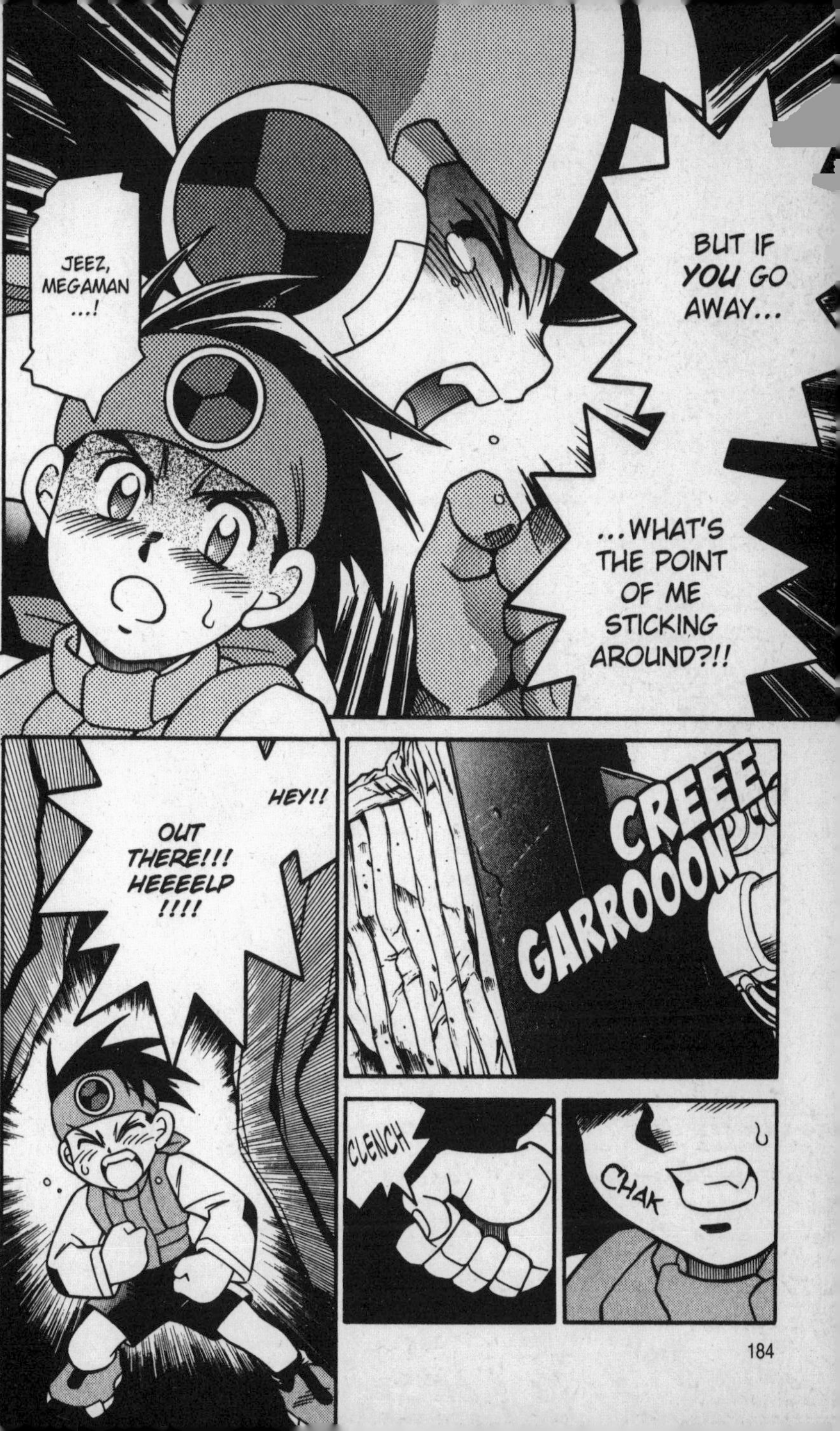
BUT IF *YOU* GO AWAY...
JEEZ, MEGAMAN ...!
...WHAT'S THE POINT OF ME STICKING AROUND?!!
CREEE GARROOON
CHAK
CLENCH
HEY!!
OUT THERE!!! HEEEELP !!!!

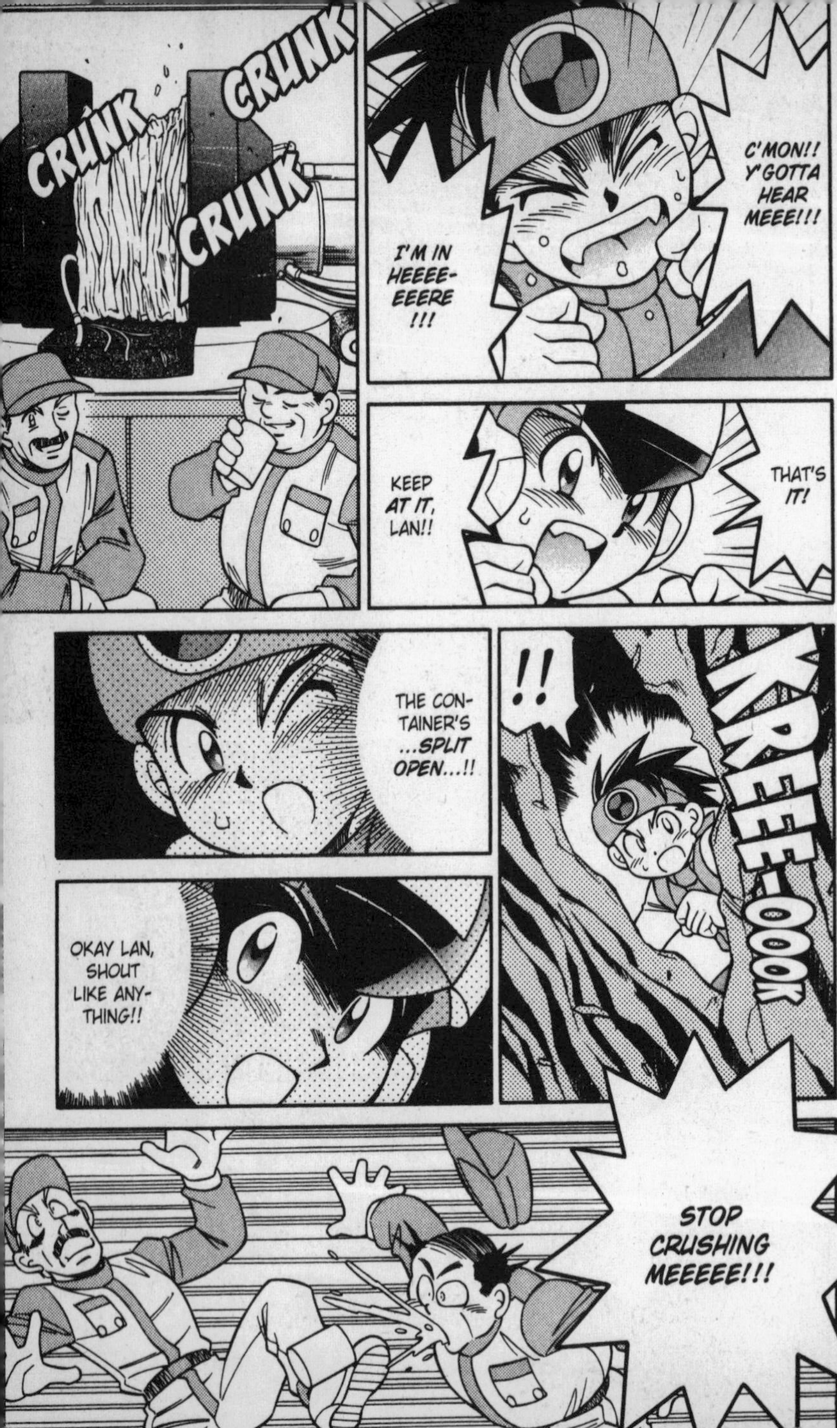
C'MON!! Y'GOTTA HEAR MEEE!!!
I'M IN HEEEE-EEERE !!!
THAT'S IT!
KEEP AT IT, LAN!!
CRUNK
CRUNK
CRUNK
!!
KREEEE-OOOK
THE CON-TAINER'S ...SPLIT OPEN...!!
OKAY LAN, SHOUT LIKE ANY-THING!!
STOP CRUSHING MEEEEE!!!

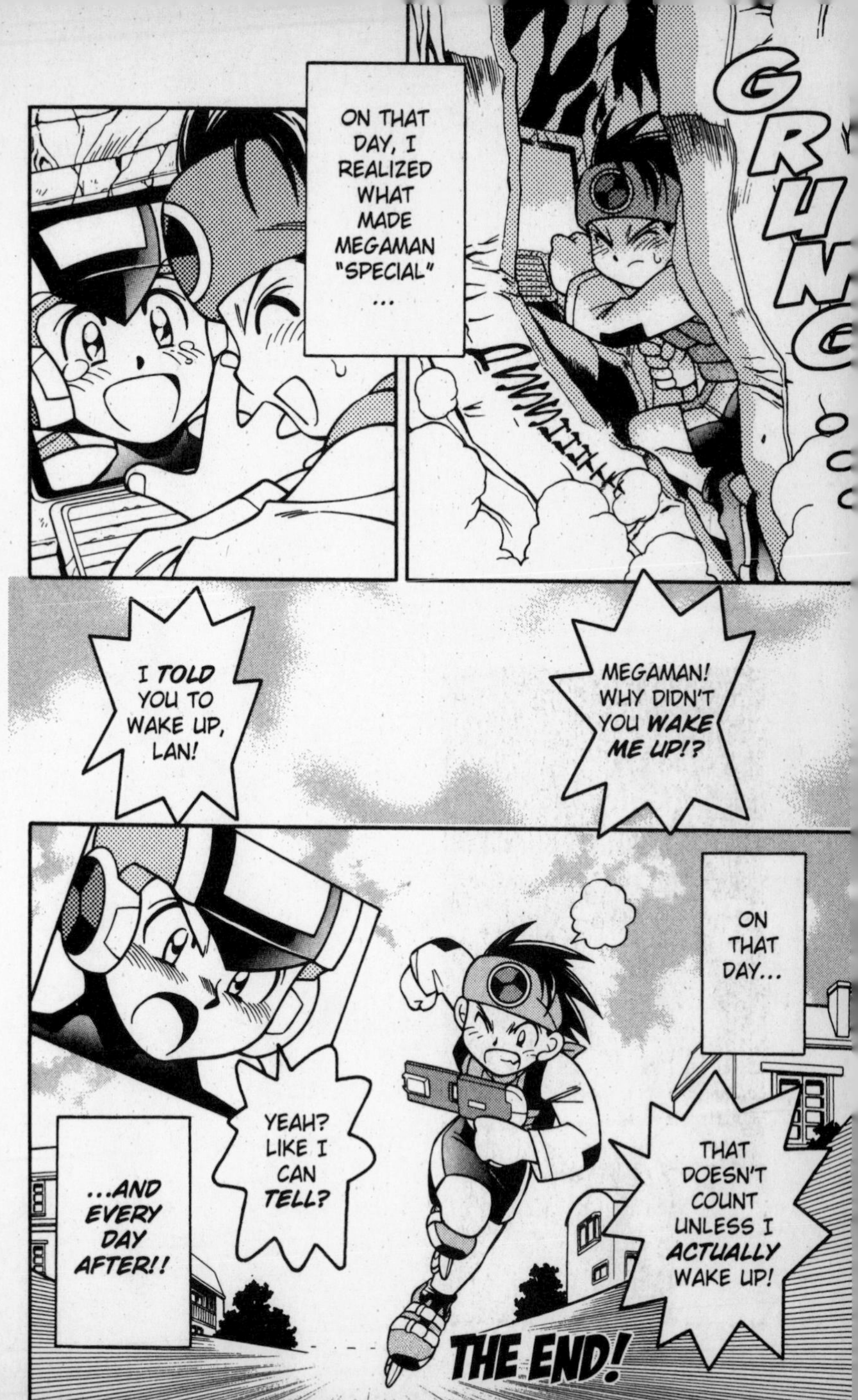
GRUNG
ON THAT DAY, I REALIZED WHAT MADE MEGAMAN "SPECIAL" ...
MEGAMAN! WHY DIDN'T YOU WAKE ME UP!?
I TOLD YOU TO WAKE UP, LAN!
ON THAT DAY...
THAT DOESN'T COUNT UNLESS I ACTUALLY WAKE UP!
YEAH? LIKE I CAN TELL?
...AND EVERY DAY AFTER!!
THE END!

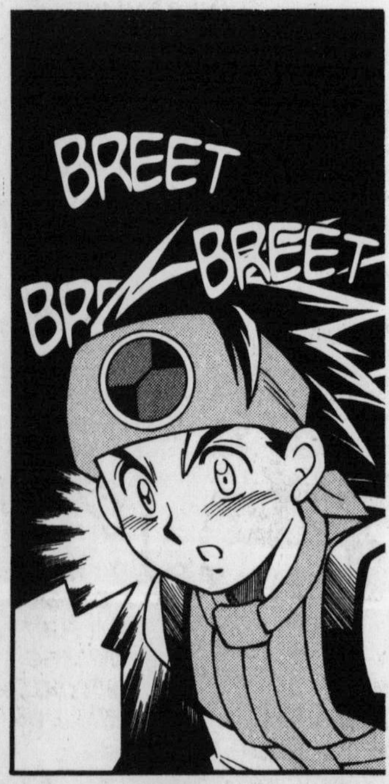
BREET
BREET
BR

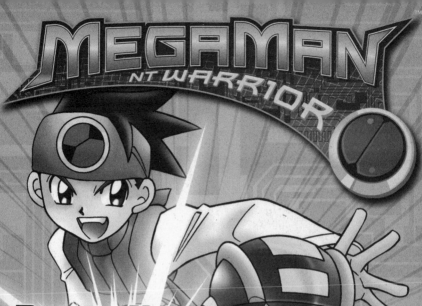

POWER UP YOUR COLLECTIONS!

In the year 200X, everyone is connected to the Cyber Network and the world is a virtual utopia. But computer hacking, viruses, and high-tech crime are on the rise, creating chaos in DenTech City. Can a kid named Lan and his NetNavi MegaMan stop the madness before it destroys the world?

Manga only $7.99!

DVD only $14.98!

Manga and anime now available —buy yours today at store.viz.com!

Prepare For Battle!

Tyson is a boy with a passion for Beyblades. His enemies are the militant Blade Sharks, who want to win at any cost! Can Tyson get the skills and training to beat them in a Beyblade battle?

From the JETIX anime series and the popular HASBRO toys — start your graphic novel collection today!

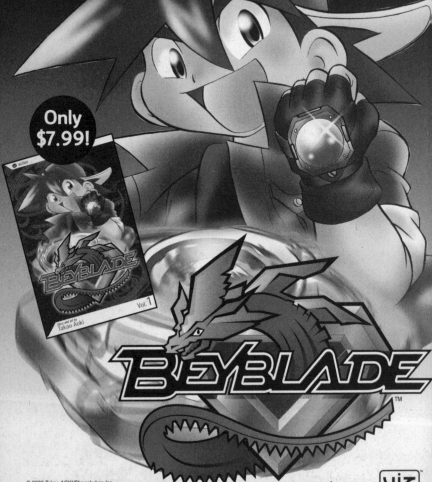

Only $7.99!

Vol. 1

Story and art by
Takao Aoki

BEYBLADE™

www.viz.com
store.viz.com

VIZ MEDIA

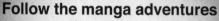
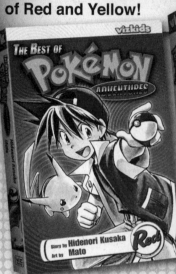
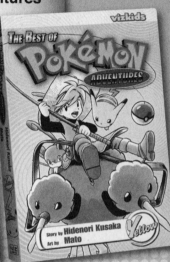
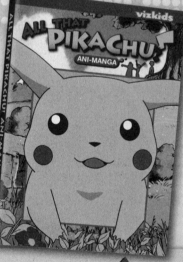

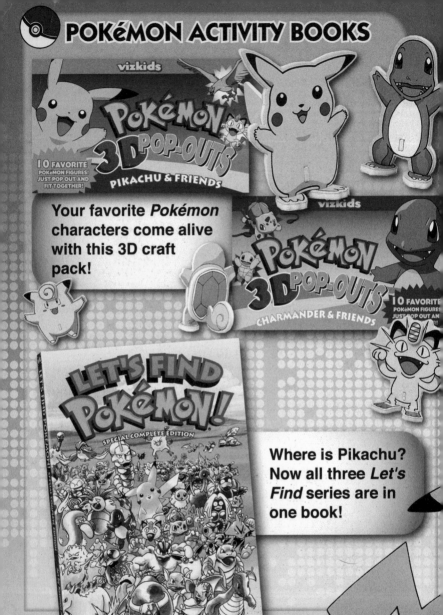

POKéMON ACTIVITY BOOKS

vizkids

Pokémon 3D POP-OUTS
PIKACHU & FRIENDS

10 FAVORITE POKéMON FIGURES! JUST POP OUT AND FIT TOGETHER!

Your favorite *Pokémon* characters come alive with this 3D craft pack!

vizkids

Pokémon 3D POP-OUTS
CHARMANDER & FRIENDS

10 FAVORITE POKéMON FIGURES! JUST POP OUT AN

LET'S FIND POKéMON!
SPECIAL COMPLETE EDITION

Where is Pikachu? Now all three *Let's Find* series are in one book!

LOVE MANGA?
LET US KNOW WHAT YOU THINK!

OUR MANGA SURVEY IS NOW AVAILABLE ONLINE. PLEASE VISIT: VIZ.COM/MANGASURVEY

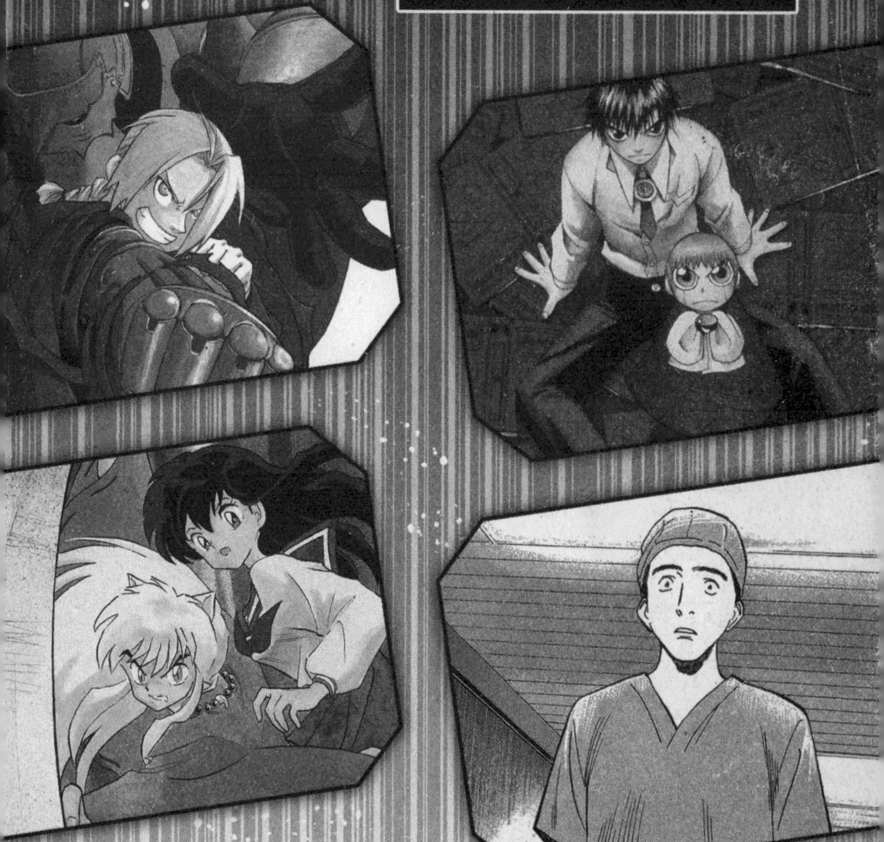

HELP US MAKE THE MANGA YOU LOVE BETTER!

viz media